ORIGINS OF CONTAINMENT

Origins of Containment

A PSYCHOLOGICAL EXPLANATION

By Deborah Welch Larson

PRINCETON UNIVERSITY PRESS
PRINCETON, NEW JERSEY

Published by Princeton University Press, 41 William Street,
Princeton, New Jersey 08540
In the United Kingdom: Princeton University Press, Guildford, Surrey

Library of Congress Cataloging in Publication Data will be
found on the last printed page of this book

ISBN 0-691-07691-X

Publication of this book has been aided by a grant from the
Whitney Darrow Fund of Princeton University Press

This book has been composed in Linotron Galliard

Clothbound editions of Princeton University Press books
are printed on acid-free paper, and binding materials are
chosen for strength and durability

Printed in the United States of America by Princeton University Press
Princeton, New Jersey

To David

CONTENTS

PREFACE   ix

ACKNOWLEDGMENTS   xiii

ABBREVIATIONS USED IN THE FOOTNOTES   xv

INTRODUCTION   3

ONE.   Social Psychological Theories of Attitude Change   24

TWO.   Taming the Bear   66

THREE.   Truman as World Leader   126

FOUR.   Keeping Agreements   150

FIVE.   Power Politics   213

SIX.   Drift and Indecision   250

SEVEN.   "This Terrible Decision"   302

CONCLUSIONS   324

SELECTED BIBLIOGRAPHY   357

INDEX   375

THE COLD WAR has been the commanding reality of international politics since World War II. Although a fragile U.S.-Soviet détente was patched together in 1955, 1959, 1963, and 1971-1972, the Cold War periodically reemerged, temporarily quiescent but not resolved. In part because of the Cold War's influence on nearly all international political phenomena—alliances, international organizations, aspirations of the third world—a vast body of scholarly literature on its origins has accumulated. Still, after a quarter of a century, there is no scholarly consensus on why the United States adopted Cold War policies in the postwar period.

This book analyzes the historical origins of the containment policy from a radically different perspective: cognitive social psychology. Since U.S.-Soviet conflict has been waged largely with words and symbols aimed at the "minds of men," it seems appropriate to focus on events in the human psyche—the development of the American Cold War belief system. Although it may be difficult for us to imagine today, during and immediately after the war the Soviet Union was widely perceived to be a valiant, benevolent, and trustworthy ally. Generalissimo Stalin was affectionately known as "Uncle Joe." This book uses various theories of attitude change in social psychology to explain why American policymakers' perceptions of the Soviet Union changed radically within a short period of time. The narrative centers on four men who were arguably the most influential in reorienting U.S. foreign policy from 1944 to 1947: W. Averell Harriman, Harry S Truman, James F. Byrnes, and Dean Acheson.

Reworking well-plowed historical ground with new concepts and ideas is risky but potentially productive. Conceptual tools and generalizations developed by practitioners in a different discipline—particularly the experimental laboratory—may not fit the disorder and noise of real-world foreign policy cables and memoranda. On the other hand, the use of psychological theories may sensitize the scholar to previously overlooked or discarded evidence, as well as imbue bits of information with new meaning by integrating them within a different unifying framework of understanding. Applied to the origins of the U.S. containment policy, cognitive social psychology has illuminated previously perplexing incongruities and inconsistencies in American policy, while casting doubt on some received wisdom.

Some political scientists and historians have argued that the Cold War was bound to occur once Germany was defeated, given the rise of two superpowers and the accompanying bipolar distribution of capabilities in the world. But the tragedy is that the United States and the Soviet Union could have defined their relationship altogether differently, even under the burden of ideological suspicion and the objective threat that each country's military power posed to the other. Further, had Henry A. Wallace or Franklin D. Roosevelt been president, the Cold War might not have occurred or assumed the bitter, intense ideological tone that it did. Had Dean Acheson been president, the United States would have launched the containment policy much sooner. In other words, though they confronted the same "objective" circumstances and received similar information and analyses of the world situation, the subjects of this study arrived at Cold War beliefs at different times, by separate paths.

Although President Harry S Truman is popularly known as the doughty World War I captain who told the Soviets just where to get off, he wavered and vacillated for nearly two years before he finally gave up trying to preserve world peace by cooperating with the Soviet Union. One reason why Truman was reluctant to relinquish the chance to develop a working partnership with Joseph Stalin was that he viewed the Russian dictator as another Boss Tom Pendergast, the machine politician who gave Truman his start in politics. Truman reasoned that Stalin, like any smart political boss, would at least have enough sense to go through the motions of holding elections in Eastern Europe for the benefit of American public opinion; the president knew from his personal experience with "ghost votes" in Jackson County that the machine in power—Soviet occupying forces—would determine the outcome. Truman also firmly believed that Stalin, like Boss Pendergast, could be trusted to keep his agreements—the ethical code of a machine politician.

Reputed to be a simple man of strong convictions, Truman had a Machiavellian streak. Truman believed in whatever the situation demanded, and he felt no discomfort at maintaining contradictory convictions simultaneously. Pragmatic politicians such as Truman and Byrnes create difficulties for cognitive dissonance theory, which builds on the proposition that people have an overwhelming drive to maintain consistency in their beliefs and opinions.

Ultimately, it was the need for decision that finally led Truman and other U.S. officials to change their image of the Soviet Union, not any positive act by the Soviets. In other words, the circumstances surrounding the Truman Doctrine speech forced Truman to reach cognitive closure, although the Soviets had initiated no aggressive or sub-versive actions against the West. President Truman did not adopt hard-line beliefs about the Soviet Union until several months after making the Truman Doctrine speech in March 1947. It has often been said that U.S. policymakers exaggerated the dangers of Soviet expansion into Western Europe because they viewed the conservative, cautious Stalin through the distorting prism of their image of Hitler. But although the experience of Munich was still fresh and vivid, U.S. leaders did not invoke the appeasement analogy or compare Stalin to Hitler.

So much solid research has gone into explaining the origins of the Cold War that one feels obliged to answer the question, why consider psychological factors at all? The introduction reviews Cold War historiography to show why existing intrepretations should be supplemented with systematic psychological analysis. Readers who are not historians, however, might find this analysis to be a digression from the overall argument, and their understanding of the rest of the book would not be impaired by avoiding it.

When using social psychological theories, one must avoid the temptation to find evidence of psychological bias where there is none, to distort the intentions and motives of historical characters in order to satisfy the requirements of a rigid theoretical scheme. To avoid falling into this well-known trap, I self-consciously tested alternative theories against archival evidence and tried to articulate the logic of causal inference so that other analysts can replicate or challenge my conclusions. Chapter One compares and contrasts different psychological theories of attitude change and provides a detailed description of how they were applied to documentary evidence. Those who have less interest in psychology than in understanding the development of American Cold War policies may wish to skip over this chapter and jump directly into the story.

Chapters Two through Seven trace U.S. policymakers' interpretation of Soviet actions from 1944 to 1947 and the impact of certain critical events on their beliefs and perceptions of the Soviet Union. Where applicable, I have drawn on psychological theories to explain why American leaders derived different conclusions about Soviet intentions and the prospects for U.S.-Soviet cooperation. But one must also consider the situational pressures and constraints under which these men were acting: insufficient time, a glut of raw information, inexperience in foreign policy, America's woeful lack of preparation for world leadership, and the absence of a clear-cut, historical policy.

American leaders confronted the ruins of world order, without the legacy of a balance-of-power tradition, amid the noise and spotlight of modern mass communications. Together, members of the Truman administration fashioned the Cold War consensus that continues to guide American foreign policy.

ACKNOWLEDGMENTS

AN INTERDISCIPLINARY STUDY such as this would not have been possible without the assistance of psychologists and historians as well as of political scientists.

Lee Ross of the Stanford Psychology Department furnished invaluable insights and suggestions at crucial points throughout the course of this study. Other social psychologists contributed to the research design. At an early stage of the project, Amos Tversky of Stanford University and Mark Snyder of the University of Minnesota made helpful criticisms of my research prospectus.

Barton Bernstein of the History Department at Stanford helped me devise an itinerary of the major depositories of archival material. In addition, he guided me through the baffling and sometimes frustrating maze of the National Archives. Ernest May of Harvard University read the entire manuscript and made very useful suggestions for its improvement from the standpoint of a diplomatic historian. In approaching the task of archival research, I benefited from discussions with other historians of the period, such as Martin Sherwin, University of California at Berkeley; Samuel Welles, Wilson International Center for Scholars; and Alonzo Hamby, Ohio University.

Michael Fry of the University of Southern California patiently tutored me on Cold War historiography. The departures from orthodox historiography found in the introduction are my fault, not his. His encouragement and confidence in the manuscript kept me going when the task of revision seemed insurmountable. In addition, the University of Southern California's VonKleinSmid Institute research fund allowed me to use the British archives at the London Public Record Office, and saved months of my time by financing the conversion of an IBM displaywriter disk format to an IBM PC diskette.

Robert Jervis of Columbia University wrote specific, detailed comments on several successive drafts of the entire, all-too-lengthy manuscript. His suggestions greatly improved my analysis of the historical evidence and the organization of the book. Needless to say, like other political psychologists, I have also relied on his pioneering theoretical work.

The chairman of my dissertation committee, Alexander George of Stanford University, was unfailingly tireless and generous in giving his wise counsel and incisive criticism from the germ of this study to its conclusion. I cannot count the many ideas I gained from my many stimulating discussions with him over the course of the project. Robert North also offered his expertise in designing the content analysis project.

A National Science Foundation Dissertation Research Grant made possible the extensive archival research and content analysis necessary to carry out this study. A grant from the Harry S Truman Library Institute financed my first visit to their extensive and valuable collection of historical materials. I would also like to express my appreciation to the International Security Studies Program of the Woodrow Wilson Center for Scholars for supporting me as a summer intern in 1979. I benefited from many informal discussions with the Wilson Center fellows, particularly Robert Donovan and Raymond Tanter. I would also like to thank the committee of the American Political Science Association's Helen Dwight Reid Memorial Award 1982-83, for displaying the confidence in the dissertation that sustained me through revisions.

Finally, I would like to thank my husband David. He did not type the manuscript, assist me with the archival research, or rewrite the drafts. But he did give me financial and emotional support throughout.

ABC   American-British Conversation Files of the Operations Division

CF   Confidential File

Clemson   Clemson University, Clemson, South Carolina

FO   Foreign Office

FDR: *His Personal Letters*   Elliot Roosevelt, ed. *F.D.R., His Personal Letters: 1928-1945.* 2 vols. New York: Duell, Sloan & Pearce, 1950.

FDRL   Franklin Delano Roosevelt Library, Hyde Park, New York

FR   U.S. Department of State. *Foreign Relations of the United States.* Annual volumes, 1944-1947. Washington, D.C.: Government Printing Office, 1965-1971.

FR: *Potsdam*   U.S. Department of State. *Foreign Relations of the United States: The Conference of Berlin (The Potsdam Conference), 1945.* 2 vols. Washington, D.C.: Government Printing Office, 1960.

FR: *Teheran*   U.S. Department of State. *Foreign Relations of the United States: The Conferences at Cairo and Teheran, 1943.* Washington, D.C.: Government Printing Office, 1961.

FR: *Quebec, 1944*   U.S. Department of State. *Foreign Relations of the United States: The Conference at Quebec.* Washington, D.C.: Government Printing Office, 1972.

FR: *Yalta*   U.S. Department of State. *Foreign Relations of the United States: The Conferences at Malta and Yalta, 1945.* Washington, D.C.: Government Printing Office, 1955.

GSHI, *DOPSR*   General Sikorski Historical Institute. *Documents on Polish-Soviet Relations, 1943-1945.* 2 vols. London: Heinemann, 1967.

HSTL   Harry S Truman Library, Independence, Missouri

LC   Library of Congress, Washington, D.C.

NA   National Archives, Washington, D.C.

Princeton   Princeton University Library, Princeton, New Jersey

PRO   Public Record Office, London

PSF   President's Secretary's File

RG   Record Group

Stalin's Correspondence   *Correspondence Between the Chairman of the Council of Ministers of the U.S.S.R. and the Presidents of the U.S.A.*

and the Prime Ministers of Great Britain During the Great Patriotic War of 1941-1945. 2 vols. Moscow: Foreign Language Publishing House, 1957.

SWNCC State-War-Navy Coordinating Committee

Truman Public Papers *Public Papers of the Presidents: Harry S Truman, 1945-1947*. Washington, D.C.: Government Printing Office, 1961-1963.

TS Top Secret

University of Virginia University of Virginia, Charlottesville, Virginia

WNRC Washington National Records Center, Suitland, Maryland

ORIGINS OF CONTAINMENT

THE COMPETITION and confrontation between the United States and the Soviet Union has given shape and impetus to international politics since World War II. Why did the United States adopt Cold War policies in the early postwar period? A coherent, rational answer to this question is important both for comprehending the present and designing policies to meet the future.

In 1944, Franklin D. Roosevelt assured the Foreign Policy Association that "the very fact that we are now at work on the organization of the peace proves that the great nations are committed to trust in each other." Roosevelt's "grand design" for the postwar order was premised on the collective enforcement of the peace by the great regional powers—the United States, Britain, the Soviet Union, and China. As part of these plans, Roosevelt firmly believed that the Soviet Union could be persuaded to assume the burdens and responsibilities of a great power for maintaining world order. For the most part, the American people and the bureaucracy shared FDR's optimism about the postwar world. In November 1944, a public opinion poll showed that 44 percent of the American people believed that Russia could be trusted to cooperate with the United States; 35 percent thought not; and 11 percent did not know. Though initially skeptical about the possibilities for enduring collaboration with a revolutionary regime, State Department officials also became infected with enthusiasm for FDR's vision. Nor did the Joint Chiefs of Staff cast a shadow over the appealing scenario by pointing out that the Soviet Union was the most likely candidate for America's postwar adversary. Anticipating no conflict with the Soviet Union or other European powers, the Joint Chiefs did not even consider locating permanent bases in Europe. Besides, FDR believed that the American people would not countenance continued responsibility for preserving peace and internal stability in Europe after the war. Similarly, State Department officials viewed the Northern Tier countries as a part of the British sphere of influence and pursued a policy of noninvolvement in the traditional British-Soviet rivalry in the region. When Harry S Truman assumed the presidency in April 1945, his public pledge to continue Roosevelt's policies issued from private conviction as well as political expediency.

Yet, in the Truman Doctrine speech of March 1947, President Truman initiated a radical innovation in American foreign policy.[1] Henceforth, the United States would contain further expansion of the burgeoning, battening Soviet Union. As Truman and other officials recognized, this heroic and unselfish endeavor would require American intervention in European political affairs. It would require replacing Great Britain as the dominant sea power in the Mediterranean. Harry Truman no longer believed that there was any point in trying to please the Soviets or get along with them. The American public agreed. The Soviet Union was the spearhead of totalitarianism, engaged in an attempt to subvert and destroy free nations.

Thus, within a short period of time, the American conception of the Soviet Union as a difficult but trustworthy ally was superseded by the image of a totalitarian state bent on unlimited expansion through subversion and conquest. Was the American acceptance of Cold War beliefs the cause, concomitant, or consequence of the adoption of the containment policy?

HISTORICAL INTERPRETATIONS OF AMERICAN COLD WAR POLICIES

In considering this question, among others, Cold War historiography has followed a familiar iterative cycle. Foreign policy officials present the administration's preferred interpretation of foreign policy events and crises in the form of official or "white paper"-style histories. Popular, impassioned, and often partisan contemporary attacks on the administration's foreign policy provoke a counter response from historians who defend the official interpretation, using a few archival sources. A subsequent, more scholarly and professional wave of revisionism sweeps in. And finally, after the passage of time an eclectic synthesis of different interpretations emerges.[2] The alternative historical interpretations reflect differing phases of scholarship, research bases, ideology, normative judgments about U.S. policy, causal factors, and environments. In addition, the competing historical explanations are based on different models of man—images of human behavior and decisionmaking.

Cold War historiography differs slightly from this pattern in that the first revisionist accounts appeared at the dawn of the Cold War,

---

[1] But see John Lewis Gaddis, "Was the Truman Doctrine a Real Turning Point?" *Foreign Affairs* 52 (January 1974): 386-402. Gaddis argues that it was the Korean War, not the Truman Doctrine, that marked the beginning of the U.S. commitment to contain communism everywhere.

[2] Warren F. Kimball, "The Cold War Warmed Over," *American Historical Review* 79 (1974): 1119-36.

before official histories could present a defense of the administration's foreign policy. From 1946 to 1950, disillusionment with the failure of the postwar world to live up to the grand ideals of the Atlantic Charter and the Four Freedoms sparked a revisionist response on the right wing of the ideological spectrum. Conservative critics such as Chester Wilmot, James Burnham, and W. H. Chamberlin reasoned that Soviet expansionism had been encouraged by American officials' wishful thinking, ignorance, and unreasoning desire to obtain Soviet cooperation in the postwar world. At each of the wartime conferences, so they said, U.S. officials handed over to Stalin territorial concessions unwarranted by the military balance of power or any objective need for Soviet military collaboration. Naive, idealistic, Roosevelt fought the war with Germany to an unconditional surrender without considering the political repercussions of allowing the Red Army to "liberate" Eastern and Central Europe. At the Yalta Conference in 1945, President Roosevelt eagerly appeased Stalin to win his personal trust and cooperation. He callowly betrayed the hopes of tens of millions of Eastern Europeans for freedom, and handed over German and Chinese territories to Stalin, violating the Atlantic Charter principle of self-determination. Truman and his advisers were duped and deceived by the Soviets at the Potsdam Conference. President Truman and Byrnes created fourteen million German refugees by turning over German territory to Poland, and failed to secure Stalin's adherence to the free elections promised in the Yalta Declaration on Liberated Europe. Throughout 1946, Truman and his advisers continued to vacillate and waver, responding to each instance of Soviet aggression without any overall design, because as politicians they were more concerned with winning the next election than with the long-term consequences of an unfavorable shift in the balance of forces.

Burnham, who later wrote a column for *National Review* under the title of "The Protracted Conflict," was an embittered ex-communist and former follower of Trotsky. He devoted the rest of his career to educating "liberals" about the menace of communism.[3] The conservative revisionists used memoirs of governmental participants, but of course drew their own conclusions about motive, intent, and consequence. For the right-wing revisionists, failed or misconceived policies must have been caused by character flaws of American leaders; this

---

[3] John P. Diggins, "Four Theories in Search of a Reality: James Burnham, Soviet Communism and the Cold War," *American Political Science Review* 70 (June 1976): 492-508.

premise reflected their implicit assumption that behavior can only be attributed to the actor's conscious intent and his personality traits.[4]

In the late 1940s, a time of trouble and increasing tension under the stress of the Czechoslovak coup, the Berlin blockade, and the fall of China, liberals began to question the official account of the origins of the Cold War, as presented in press conferences, speeches, and State Department pamphlets. British nuclear physicist P.M.S. Blackett reasoned that since Japan was already suing for peace in July 1945, and the American invasion of Kyushu was not scheduled until November 1945, Truman's decision to drop the bomb in August was prompted not by the official aim of saving American lives, but by the desire to end the war in the Pacific as quickly as possible, to preclude Soviet intervention and a struggle for postwar control of Japan. Thus, Blackett writes, "we conclude that the dropping of the atomic bombs was not so much the last military act of the second world war, as the first act of the cold diplomatic war with Russia now in progress."[5] Blackett attributes Truman's initiation of the Cold War to his desire to gain a decisive power advantage over the Soviet Union, which was a manifestation of the principles of *Machtpolitik*. In other words, Blackett assumes that Truman's decision to drop the atomic bomb was rationally calculated and indicative of the president's darker, Machiavellian motives. Later, to alleviate their guilt and remorse, American military and political officials rationalized that the use of the atomic bomb had been a normal act of state policy. If so, then the next "logical" conclusion was that the Soviets would, if they were able, also use the atomic bomb—against the United States.[6]

Another left-liberal revisionist scholar, D. F. Fleming, also argued that Truman had deliberately begun the Cold War, beginning with his famous tongue-lashing delivered to Soviet Foreign Minister Molotov on April 23, 1945. Truman, he said, began mulling over the containment policy as early as September 1945, when the Soviets refused to make concessions in Eastern Europe at the London Conference. He deliberately delayed introducing the new policy to the American public, however, until an opportune moment arose to spring the Truman Doctrine on a hostile Congress. Fleming attributes this funda-

---

[4] Chester Wilmot, *The Struggle for Europe* (London: Collins, 1952); W. H. Chamberlin, *America's Second Crusade* (Chicago: Henry Regnery, 1950; James Burnham, *Struggle for the World* (New York: John Day, 1947); Paul Seabury, "Cold War Origins," *Journal of Contemporary History* 3 (1968): 169-82.

[5] P.M.S. Blackett, *Fear, War, and the Bomb: Military and Political Consequences of Atomic Energy* (New York: McGraw-Hill, 1948), p. 139.

[6] Ibid., pp. 130-43.

mental shift in America's role to the president's personality. Truman reversed FDR's policy of Soviet-American cooperation because he was ignorant, parochial, pugnacious, and prone to rely on the advice of militaristic Cold Warrior Admiral Leahy.[7] In making inferences about Truman's motives, Fleming relied almost exclusively on contemporary journalists' critiques of Truman's foreign policy and the sometimes unreliable Truman *Memoirs*. In addition, Fleming uncritically used public statements by U.S. and Soviet officials as if they were undistorted reflections of individual beliefs and intentions. Because of the naiveté of his analysis and his injudicious use of source materials, Fleming's work is no longer cited, nor does it appear in most bibliographies of Cold War histories.

Realist scholars have contributed a more enduring strand of Cold War revisionism. As early as the 1940s, Hans J. Morgenthau and Walter Lippmann viewed the Cold War dispassionately as a great power struggle for hegemony. This is not to say that Realist analysts were not critical of what they perceived as the anomalies and fallacies of American policy. In 1947, for example, Lippmann argued that it was the presence of the Red Army in the heart of Europe which threatened western security, not the ideology of Karl Marx. Therefore, instead of trying to contain the ill-defined, amorphous threat of communism, United States policy should be directed toward removing the Red Army from Europe through a political settlement with the Soviet Union and restoration of the balance of power.

Writers such as Morgenthau, George Kennan, Norman Graebner, and Louis Halle subsequently developed a psychological explanation for what they perceived as the conceptual weakness of American foreign policy. Most Realists started with the arguable proposition that Stalin's ambitions bore more resemblance to those of Peter the Great than to the ideas of Trotsky. In other words, the principal danger to Western security was Russian imperialism, not world revolution. Nevertheless, the American people misperceived the East-West conflict as a struggle between good and evil, between differing systems of political morality, between two alternative ways of life. Why? According to Realist historians, the American people were shocked and disappointed by the failure of the postwar world to live up to the utopian expectations aroused by Roosevelt's rhetoric about the replacement of great power competition with cooperation, the Four Freedoms, and so on. In particular, the American people were outraged by Stalin's

[7] D. F. Fleming, *The Cold War and Its Origins, 1917-1960*, 2 vols. (Garden City, N.Y.: Doubleday, 1961), vol. 1.

refusal to hold free elections in Eastern Europe, in flagrant violation of agreements signed at the Yalta Conference. Nevertheless, the fate of Eastern Europe had been determined long before, when the U.S. government based its military policy on efficiency instead of political considerations, when American forces invaded the Continent through Western Europe instead of the Balkans. Unwilling to admit intellectual error or to acknowledge our naiveté and self-deception, the American people succumbed to the easy lure of viewing the Soviet Union as the source of evil. To rationalize our shame and humiliation at being duped once again, "Uncle Joe" was replaced in the popular mind by the "red devil," and the Soviet Union was used as a scapegoat for the postwar ills to which our political failures had given birth.

According to the Realist historians, the officials of the Truman administration were not so naive about the imperatives of power politics as to allow themselves to escape from unpleasant realities through moralistic thinking. But the administration cynically fanned the moralistic strain in American public opinion by depicting a modest request for an appropriation to provide aid to Greece and Turkey as part of a struggle between totalitarianism and democracy, between good and evil. They did this even though they knew that U.S. economic assistance was part of the American assumption of Britain's former responsibility for preventing Soviet penetration into the eastern Mediterranean and preserving the European balance of power. The Realists view American policymakers as rational, sober individuals with a valid understanding of the requirements of international power situation, who act contrary to U.S. national interests because they are swayed by social or domestic political pressures. Truman got his appropriation, but the American people were left with an unworkable, dangerous policy. The tragedy, according to Morgenthau, was that this misrepresentation of the containment policy to Congress was probably unnecessary. The Truman administration mistakenly identified a reactionary, Southern-dominated Senate with public opinion, and underestimated the public's native intelligence. They lost their chance to educate the American people and create support for a policy on the basis of real understanding.

Except for Kennan, who could draw on his own papers and memoranda, the Realists worked without the insights or ambiguities of archival sources. Nor were documents essential to their interpretation, which derived from recurring historical patterns in American foreign policy.[8]

---

[8] Walter Lippmann, *The Cold War* (New York: Harper & Bros., 1947); Hans J.

It was not until the mid-fifties that Herbert Feis and Joseph Jones published historical narratives reflecting policymakers' own interpretation of the events leading up to the development of the containment policy. Feis, clearly the "official" historian of the, Cold War, produced a solid recital of diplomatic negotiations based on privileged access to official archives and the private papers of Harry S Truman and Averell Harriman. Feis was a special consultant to three secretaries of war and economic adviser to Secretary of State Cordell Hull. Although Feis generally avoids interpretation or analysis, the careful reader may piece together the orthodox explanation for American Cold War policy: there was little that Roosevelt could have done to alter the shape of the postwar world, given Stalin's stubborn resolve to consume Eastern Europe for use as a buffer zone and base for further expansion of communism. The American people would not have approved the use of troops to push the Soviets back to their prewar frontiers. Between 1945 and 1947, wearying diplomatic stalemate, the fraying of the postwar accords, and Russian probes into Iran and Turkey finally awakened the American people to the totalitarian menace. Official historians accept the view of man as a seeker after reassuring consistency, trying to avoid unpleasant realities if possible, until the burden of evidence can no longer be sloughed off or ignored.[9]

But, official historians could not bank the flow of revisionism. William Appleman Williams stimulated a new strand of interpretation that articulated a more coherent theoretical interpretation of American foreign policy, and in support was able to draw on publiched documents and private papers as they became open.

Williams drew on Charles Beard for a general theory of economic causation. Although democratic socialism was his first ideological preference, Williams acknowledged that this vision was incompatible with the American people's long-standing infatuation with private property. Consequently, he looked to the past for an alternative model for a

---

Morgenthau, *In Defense of the National Interest* (New York: Knopf, 1951), pp. 76-78, 105-106, 108-12, 231-37; George F. Kennan, *Memoirs (1925-1950)* (Boston: Little, Brown, 1967; Bantam Books, 1969); Norman A. Graebner, *Cold War Diplomacy: American Foreign Policy, 1945-60* (Princeton: Van Nostrand, 1962); Louis J. Halle, *The Cold War as History* (New York: Harper & Row, 1967); Martin F. Herz, *Beginnings of the Cold War* (Bloomington: Indiana University Press, 1966).

[9] Herbert Feis, *Churchill, Roosevelt, Stalin: The War They Waged and the Peace They Sought* (Princeton: Princeton University Press, 1957); idem, *Between War and Peace: The Potsdam Conference* (Princeton: Princeton University Press, 1960); Joseph M. Jones, *The Fifteen Weeks (February 21-June 5, 1947)* (New York: Harcourt, Brace & World, 1955); Christopher Lasch, "The Cold War Revisited and Re-Visioned," *New York Times Magazine*, January 14, 1968, pp. 27ff.

more humane, equitable, and peaceful society. According to Williams, the American founding fathers were mercantilists. Enlightened gentry, they used state power to create a territorial and commercial empire not for selfish commercial interests, but for the good of the community as a whole. American mercantilists sought a favorable balance of trade through protectionism and promotion of exports. Their overriding concern was to prevent economic surpluses and unemployment that could endanger domestic stability and democracy. The only flaw in the American mercantilist strategy, as Williams perceives it, was their emphasis on economic expansion as a substitute for social reform. When the frontier appeared to be closed in the 1890s, American leaders redirected their energies from continental expansion to establishment of a commercial empire based on free trade. The new outlook was actualized in the war against Spain and Hay's Open Door Notes, which called on other nations to respect the principle of equal commercial opportunity in China. The open door policy embodied the strategy of creating as "informal empire" based on free trade. Ultimately, American leaders' drive for access and control over foreign markets and raw materials explains our participation in both world wars, the so-called containment policy, and continuing interventions abroad.

Williams simply denies that the American image of the Soviet Union softened or blurred, even while the two countries were cooperating to defeat Hitler: "There is little evidence to support the oft-asserted claim that Americans changed their basic attitude toward the Soviet Union during the war." From the moment he took office, President Truman resolved to exploit America's economic supremacy to establish the open door throughout the globe, even within the Soviet security zone in Eastern Europe. The Truman Doctrine in March 1947 was, he argued, merely the "ideological manifesto" of the traditional open door strategy, the political rationalization for America's program of acquiring new overseas markets and sources of raw materials.[10]

In the 1960s, the Vietnam War, race riots, and the War on Poverty led to a breakdown of the liberal consensus and a search for the origins of American imperialism and the absence of a domestic socialist tradition.[11] Williams' causal connection between intervention abroad and domestic conservativism at home was compelling for many young historians: Lloyd Gardner, Walter LaFeber, Gar Alperovitz, Robert J. Smith, Barton Bernstein, Thomas Paterson.

[10] William Appleman Williams, *The Tragedy of American Diplomacy*, 2nd ed., rev. and enl. (New York: Dell Publishing Co., Delta Book, 1972), pp. 229-30, 238-40, 243-44, 257-58, 269-70.

[11] Barton J. Bernstein and Allen J. Matusow, *Twentieth-Century American: Recent Interpretations* (New York: Harcourt, Brace & World, 1969), pp. 346-47.

William Appleman Williams is not, as some have charged, an economic determinist, for he accords an important causal role to ideas. Williams reasons that to explain foreign policy, one must reconstruct reality the way policymakers saw it at the time and interpret the prevailing circumstances through their world view. His sociological interpretation relies heavily on an evidentiary base of trade and unemployment statistics and economic policy statements by commercial and government leaders. In addition, Williams and his followers have used memoirs written at the height of domestic anticommunist hysteria by Truman, Byrnes, and others as "evidence" that U.S. policymakers distrusted the Soviets from the beginning. Several of Williams' followers go to great pains to point out that American Cold War policies did not simply spring from simple, crude economic motives; other important causal factors included an ideology that depicted world peace and prosperity as dependent on expanding trade, a desire to avoid the "mistakes" of the past, the illusion of American omnipotence, and Harry S Truman's pugnacious personality. As Lloyd Gardner observes, "what men think about the 'system' and what it needs to function well at a given time is often as important as its supposed determinants. Indeed, what men think about helps to determine the 'system.' "[12]

The tool by which Williams tries to analyze policymakers' perceptions is Mannheim's conception of *Weltanschauung* or ideology, defined as "definition of the world and how it works." Thus, Williams presents a cognitive explanation of American foreign policy. Williams emphasizes that because American leaders' world view distorted their perception of reality, one does not need to resort to the "psychology of the irrational" to explain their errors and miscalculations. Similarly, many social psychologists now reject the assumption running through experimental research as late as the 1950s and 1960s that human biases and errors necessarily can be traced to the intrusion of unconscious motives, drives, emotions, or ego-defenses. Instead, people are sometimes deceived by the simplifying and filtering operations of human cognitive processes, which put information into a manageable, usable format.

Williams also agrees with Mannheim's thesis that ideology is rooted in a particular social structure and milieu. But Williams does not adhere to the materialist conception of knowledge, whereby ideas are the superstructure of social relations of production. That ideas do not sim-

---

[12] Thomas G. Paterson, *Soviet-American Confrontation: Postwar Reconstruction and the Origins of the Cold War* (Baltimore: Johns Hopkins University Press, 1973), pp. 262-63; Lloyd C. Gardner, "Truman Era Foreign Policy: Recent Historical Trends," *The Truman Period as a Research Field: A Reappraisal, 1972*, ed. Richard S. Kirkendall (Columbia: University of Missouri Press, 1974), pp. 69-70.

ply reflect socioeconomic conditions is evidenced by the existence of many men who have undergone similar experiences yet have conflicting beliefs, and men who have contrasting backgrounds yet entertain similar opinions. Williams holds to the view now shared by most psychologists that individual beliefs are the residue of the interaction between a person's conceptual apparatus and the environment.[13]

Unlike many orthodox historians, open door revisionists have not been content with narration, but have sought explanation by postulating covering laws. They have tackled the difficult question of the relationship between ideals and interests, beliefs and action, ideology and strategic doctrine. Still, according to social science theory, there are several important deficiencies in their methodology. First, the concept of open door ideology or *Weltanschauung* is not defined or used systematically. Neither Williams nor his followers have synthesized the separate belief components of the ideology into a unified construct. Instead, elements of the ideology other than the concern for overseas expansion shift with individual and historical era. This makes the thesis difficult to test. Williams and his followers often use ideology as a catch-all to refer to beliefs, ideals, or conceptions that disguise reality, concealing from official policymakers their true interests in renouncing empire. It need not be pointed out that error and miscalculation reside in many sources other than ideology.

Second, Williams does not provide any rules or guidelines for inferring when a particular statement may be categorized as an example of the open door ideology. Without a priori criteria, there is a danger that the analyst will only see features of a discourse that seem to exemplify the ideology. Of course, there is always the risk of imposing the scholar's own ideological bias when trying to recapture from a collection of documents the perspective and beliefs of an individual from a different historical era. But the analyst should guard against the distorting effects of any conceptual apparatus by also considering alternative hypotheses. Several reviewers have criticized Williams and his students for ignoring evidence that American policymakers might have been motivated by balance of power concerns, security interests, or fear.[14]

Third, Williams argues that policymakers are rational and calculating in their efforts to obtain access for American products and investments overseas. He denies by implication the possibility that Truman and his

---

[13] William Appleman Williams, "Fire in the Ashes of Scientific History," *William and Mary Quarterly* 19 (April 1962): 275, 278.

[14] See Richard A. Melanson, "The Social and Political Thought of William Appleman Williams," *Western Political Quarterly* 31 (1978): 404.

advisers were simply "muddling through," responding as best they could to discrete events or diverse pressures without any overall strategy or consciousness of purpose. The assumption that policymakers consciously direct their actions to achieve larger goals is called into question by social psychological experiments showing that people frequently behave contrary to their professed beliefs; their convictions are often internally contradictory; and on many important issues they have no stable preconceived notions whatsoever.

Fourth, as presently defined, the open door ideology is indeterminate in its predictions. For example, from 1943 to 1947, prominent advocates of trade with Russia and the open door policy also favored accommodating the Soviets by providing them, for example, with a generous postwar loan or sharing American scientific information on atomic energy. These advocates of economic and scientific interchange with the Russians included Donald Nelson, Eric Johnston, Henry Stimson, and Henry Wallace.[15] Other enthusiasts for establishing a multilateral trading system include people whom Williams describes as categorically anti-Soviet: Averell Harriman, William Clayton, Harry Truman, and James Byrnes. Clearly, variables other than the open door ideology are needed to explain the shift in American perceptions and policies.

Other radical historians have applied a more orthodox, class-based, neomarxist analysis to American Cold War diplomacy.[16] For Kolko and Magdoff, United States political aims for the postwar world reflected the structural requirements of the capitalist system. Recognizing the need for assured access to foreign markets and raw materials, American leaders sought to create an international economic system that would allow businessmen to trade, operate, and profit without restriction anywhere in the world. Because American access to foreign sources of profits would be jeopardized by nationalist revolutions and communist subversion, the United States intervened throughout the globe against leftist movements and propped up conservative capitalist elites.[17]

[15] Williams, *Tragedy of American Diplomacy*, pp. 217-18, 245, 255; Arthur M. Schlesinger, Jr., "The Cold War Revisited," *New York Review of Books*, October 25, 1979, p. 46.

[16] For a Marxist historian's criticisms that Williams is an idealist who ignores the class struggle underlying imperialism, see Eugene D. Genovese, "William Appleman Williams on Marx and America," *Studies on the Left* 6 (1966): 70-86.

[17] Gabriel Kolko, *The Politics of War* (New York: Random House, 1968); Joyce and Gabriel Kolko, *The Limits of Power, 1945-1954* (New York: Harper & Row, 1972); Harry Magdoff, *The Age of Imperialism* (New York: Monthly Review Press, 1969).

Revisionist writing inevitably stimulated a countercurrent of traditional diplomatic history. Confirmationist historians—Charles Burton Marshall, Dexter Perkins, David Rees, Wilfred Knapp—though critical of some aspects of American diplomacy, generally upheld the official interpretation that the containment policy was a necessary response to Soviet expansionism.[18] In other words, the circumstances in which American leaders were placed gave them no choice but to respond as they did. From 1945 to 1947, the American people were in the grip of isolationism, enthusiasm for the United Nations, the desire for normalcy, and wishful thinking about the prospects for continuing Soviet-American collaboration. (Confirmationists share the official historians' image of man as driven by internal pressures to achieve cognitive consistency, and prone to rationalize or ignore unpleasant realities by reinterpreting the facts to support an established image or belief.) But gradually hope was lost and attitudes hardened in reaction to the steady, step-by-step advance of Soviet pressure outside the sphere occupied by the Red Army, such as the establishment of a Russian puppet government in Northern Iran, demands for bases on the Turkish Straits, and the outbreak of civil war in Greece.

Thus, confirmationists describe American policy as reactive to Soviet initiatives; they implicitly accept an image of man as tossed about and pulled by the force of outside stimuli, instead of acting of his own volition to achieve strategic goals. Yet, it is questionable whether the Soviet threat to American vital interests alone forced American policymakers to adopt Cold War policies. For, as will be argued below, alternative policies were possible. And in fact, when the Truman Doctrine was promulgated, the Soviets had withdrawn their troops from northern Iran, allowed the puppet state to collapse, made no further demands on Turkey after the United States issued a warning in August 1946, and were not responsible for the outbreak of civil war in Greece.

In the 1970s, an eclectic synthetic strand has emerged, which may be called reconciliationism. Best exemplified by scholars such as John Lewis Gaddis and George Herring, these historians have selected what they consider to be the most plausible hypotheses and interpretations immanent in a broad range of historical sources. While rejecting the all-encompassing theoretical framework of the mercantilists and neo-

[18] Charles Burton Marshall, *The Cold War: A Concise History* (New York: Franklin Watts, 1965); Dexter Perkins, *Diplomacy of a New Age* (Bloomington: Indiana University Press, 1967); David Rees, *The Age of Containment: The Cold War, 1945-1968* (London: St. Martin's Press, 1967); William H. McNeill, *America, Britain, and Russia: Their Co-operation and Conflict, 1941-1946* (London: Oxford University Press, 1953; reprint New York: Johnson, 1970).

marxists, reconciliationists accept some specific arguments and interpretations. Gaddis, for example, locates the origins of American Cold War policies within a sophisticated multicausal structure. In the conclusion, Gaddis rightly points to several factors—the bipolar distribution of power, the ideal of self-determination, domestic political constraints, misreading of the "lessons of history," fear of communism, the illusion of omnipotence fostered by American economic superiority and the atomic bomb—which influenced American policymakers. This balanced, objective synthesis of two decades of historical scholarship and wide-ranging archival sources is certainly an impressive achievement. Yet, missing from Gaddis' judicious account is any explicit causal connection between particular events or conditions and the Truman administration's desire to contain further Soviet expansion. In reading Gaddis' subtle and supple prose, we are never able to pinpoint exactly *why* American policymakers adopted a "tough" policy of refusing to make any more concessions to obtain Soviet cooperation.[19] It may be that implicit in the historical narrative are generalizations that guided Gaddis' structuring of the sequence of events leading up to the American adoption of the containment policy. But since we do not know what these generalizations are, there is no way to determine whether they are scientifically sound or internally consistent.

The interweaving of interpretations continues, as the release of government documents and private papers makes possible the writing of specialized monographs. Lynn Davis and A. W. DePorte, for example, have resurrected the Realist interpretation that American policymakers were naive idealists, who sought to carry out the principles of the Atlantic Charter in a world for which these Wilsonian ideals were at best ill-suited and at worst needlessly provocative to the Soviet Union. Confirmationist Lisle Rose has tried to defend policymakers from charges that they used the implied threat of the atomic monopoly to frighten the Soviets out of Eastern Europe. Some confirmationist historians have accused neomarxists and open door revisionists of sustaining an economic interpretation of American actions through distortion of documentary evidence and wrenching quotes out of context.[20]

[19] John Lewis Gaddis, *The United States and the Origins of the Cold War, 1941-1947* (New York: Columbia University Press, 1972). For a sustained critique of Gaddis' conclusions and underlying evidence, see Barton J. Bernstein, "Cold War Orthodoxy Restated," *Reviews in American History* (December 1973): 453-62; Robert D. Schulzinger, "Moderation in Pursuit of Truth Is No Virtue; Extremism in Defense of Moderation is a Vice," *American Quarterly* 27 (1975): 222-36.

[20] See, for example, Robert James Maddox, *The New Left and the Origins of the Cold*

In defense of the revisionists, other historians have argued that archival material is legitimately subject to differing interpretations depending on the historians' perspective.[21] According to an influential group in the philosophy of history, historical facts are *constructed* from documentary evidence by inferences based on historians' intuitive assumptions about human nature, knowledge about the culture of a particular era, and conceptual schemes. Competing historical explanations do not necessarily reflect some misguided scholar's misreading or deliberate distortion of the evidence to create a politically "usable" past; instead, they often stem from historians' implicit and largely unsystematic use of alternative theories about the past.[22] Consequently, conflicting interpretations cannot be evaluated by appealing to "facts," but by testing for the hypotheses and theoretical generalizations on which they are built.

The intuitive theories on which competing interpretations of American Cold War policies are constructed are often psychological. Underlying differing interpretations of the meaning of statements by U.S. officials are alternative naive conceptions of human decision processes, often resembling more formal empirical theories in psychology. For example, confirmationist historians argue that Truman and his advisers reluctantly changed their perception of the Soviets only when the weight of evidence of Soviet expansionist aims tipped the scales and became overwhelming. This thesis reflects the proposition, also found in consistency theories in social psychology, that people try to avoid unpleasant realities and evidence which contradicts cherished assumptions, and that their beliefs change only in response to an onslaught of inconsistent data. Open door revisionists work with the hypothesis that ideological beliefs blind individuals to reality, disguising their true interests and motives from themselves. There is a long tradition of research in psychology on the biasing effects of expectations, hopes, fears, and beliefs on our perception of the world. Realist historians, on the other hand, believe that foreign policymakers often recognize the requirements of achieving the national interest and the imperatives of preserving a balance of power, yet act contrary to their best judg-

War (Princeton: Princeton University Press, 1973); Oscar Handlin, "The Failure of the Historians," *Freedom at Issue*, September-October 1975, pp. 3-6.

[21] Kimball, "The Cold War Warmed Over"; Richard A. Melanson, "Revisionism Subdued? Robert James Maddox and the Origins of the Cold War," *Political Science Reviewer* 7 (1977): 229-71.

[22] See, for example, Murray G. Murphey, *Our Knowledge of the Historical Past* (New York: Bobbs-Merrill, 1973); and Cynthia Hay, "Historical Theory and Historical Confirmation," *History and Theory* 19 (1980): 39-57.

ment because of short-term political considerations. In psychological jargon, Realists are "situationists"; they assume that people often act contrary to their beliefs and attitudes because of social pressures.

If policymakers knew why they chose a particular action, we could simply use their contemporary explanations as reflected in documents to determine which historical interpretation best approximated the truth. But in fact, people often do not know the real causes of their own actions.[23] Or they may not wish to expose their motives to the harsh judgments of political rivals or muckraking historians. Thus, psychological generalizations about the way other people typically act in similar circumstances are a useful first step toward valid understanding.

If a major source of disagreement among different strands of Cold War historiography lies in the attribution of motives, beliefs, and rationality, then one can only infer that the next stage in resolving the controversy is to apply relevant social psychological research and theory to the primary evidence. It is easier to evaluate the merits of rival psychological hypotheses when tacit assumptions are made explicit. Further, social psychological hypotheses have the important advantage over intuitive theories of human behavior of having been subjected to tests in the laboratory under controlled conditions. Diplomatic historian Ernest May has criticized Cold War historiography for failing to draw on psychological theory and evidence in its examination of ideology and perception:

> Much writing about attitudes and perceptions had limited value because the authors did not pause to reflect enough on theoretical questions—e.g., the processes of attitude formation, the measurement of relative intensities of opinion, and the relationship between perceptions and behavior. Much writing about ideas and ideologies was marred by being too closely tied to simplistic theories of human behavior. Nevertheless, it is clear that the psychological aspects of international relations has become and will remain a major subject for scholarship.[24]

The use of social psychology to explain the origins of American Cold War policies can, however, be challenged on the grounds that policy-

[23] Richard E. Nisbett and Timothy DeCamp Wilson, "Telling More Than We Can Know: Verbal Reports on Mental Processes," *Psychological Review* 84 (May 1977): 231-59.

[24] Ernest R. May, "The Decline of Diplomatic History," in George Athan Billias and Gerald N. Grob, *American History: Retrospect and Prospect* (New York: Free Press, 1971), p. 421.

makers' actions are so narrowly constrained by the logic of the situation or domestic political pressures that a focus on individual cognitive processes adds no useful knowledge and indeed is a waste of time.

"LEVELS OF ANALYSIS" PROBLEM

All the historical interpretations provide a plausible account of the development of U.S.-Soviet conflict in the postwar period. But the explanations lack specificity and determinacy. None of these interpretations adequately explains why U.S.-Soviet relations assumed the form of an acutely conflictual "zero-sum" game, in which a "gain" in one part of the world was invariably perceived as a "loss" to U.S. security interests.

To construct a better explanation of the origins of American Cold War policies, the analyst must first choose a theory at an appropriate 'level of analysis'—international system, domestic political context, or individual policymaker. The choice is not a trivial matter of individual taste, because each "level" employs different variables, highlights different aspects of reality, and provides a different explanation.

From the perspective of the international system, the Cold War seems to have been inevitable. World War II destroyed what remained of the European state system. Only the United States and Russia emerged from the conflict as great powers, territorially enlarged, undefeated, political systems intact. The two countries were destined to view each other as enemies, since the security of each could only be threatened by the other. A Soviet-American condominium was impossible once Germany was defeated, because there was no longer a common threat against which to ally. The wrenching transition from one type of international system to another merely exacerbated the potential for conflict. The destruction of Germany left a power vacuum in the heart of Europe, which the Soviets were fated to fill. When the war ended, Soviet troops occupied not only the small states of Eastern Europe but parts of Austria and Germany as well. Western Europe lay prostrate, a tempting target for further Soviet expansion. In the Mediterranean, the decline of British power opened up the oil-rich Middle East to Soviet penetration. In Africa and Asia, the disintegration of prewar colonial empires was followed by the emergence of new states, objects of competition between the United States and the Soviet Union for military bases, raw materials, markets, outlets for investment. After some hesitation, the United States formed a coalition with other Western countries to create a new equilibrium of power. Through a process of action and reaction in the early Cold War period, the United States and the Soviet Union gradually created a stable bi-polar system.

But when one examines the historical sources, these certainties evap-orate. What seem to be inexorable social and historical forces appear, on closer examination, to be the result of unforeseen contingencies, personality factors, timing, chance, or an unusual confluence of causal factors. In *The Cold War as History*, Louis J. Halle begins by arguing that the Cold War was a "historical necessity," given the destruction of German power and the emergence of a vacuum on Russia's western frontier. Yet he later concedes that

> When we see what actually happens in operational terms, however, in terms of armies marching, statesmen negotiating, and people vot-ing, the whole situation appears to offer a range of possibilities in-compatible with the rigidity of physical laws. Accidents seem to play their part. The mistakes of individual statesmen are seen to be sig-nificant. The respiratory ailment that impaired Roosevelt's strength in the winter of 1944-45 has its effect. Unusual human weakness or unusual human virtue appears to alter what might otherwise have been the course of events. . . .
>
> We must beware of the absoluteness of the great abstractions represented by the metaphor of the power vacuum. We must as-sume a range of choice in the actual play of events.[25]

Apart from unanswerable questions of "historical inevitability," the systemic explanation is insufficiently specified and indeterminate. In the early postwar period, systemic theory predicts Soviet-American conflict, but does not discriminate between various forms that the ri-valry could have assumed. Within a bipolar structure of power, the United States and the Soviet Union could have defined their relation-ship in a variety of ways. For example, Roosevelt and Stalin could have signed a gentleman's agreement dividing the world into rival spheres of influence. Or, unable to agree on a solution to the "German problem," the United States and the Soviet Union might have engaged in destructive competition for the favors of a unified Germany. Con-versely, the United States might have reverted to isolation from the affairs of Europe, confining itself to the Pacific and the Western hem-isphere. In that event, because of the local power imbalance, Soviet dominance over Western Europe would not have been inconceivable. The United States and the Soviet Union could have adopted a "limited adversary" relationship—cooperating on some issues while competing

[25] Halle, *Cold War as History*, pp. 75-76.

on others. Or there could have been war. The distribution of power alone does not explain why U.S.-Soviet conflict took the form of a "zero-sum" game instead of one of these alternatives to the Cold War. The intensity of U.S.-Soviet conflict is inexplicable unless one considers the influence of the Cold War belief system.[26]

International systems theory describes the range of outcomes of interactions between states that is possible within a given system, but it cannot explain how particular states will react to the pressures and possibilities inherent within the structure of the system.[27] To increase the determinacy of the explanation, then, we must move to lower levels of analysis—the domestic political context and the individual policymaker.

Spheres of influence and U.S. isolation were precluded by the American public's aversion to power politics and newfound enchantment with Wilsonian internationalism in the aftermath of World War II. In addition, domestic political considerations played a major role in the Truman administration's deliberate cultivation of the Cold War image of the Soviet Union as an implacable adversary with whom there could be no negotiations or compromise. According to Thomas Trout, to obtain the legitimacy necessary for effective, consistent implementation of a foreign policy, the president must construct, present, and defend an image of the international system that is consistent with the action advocated. The Truman Doctrine speech depicted a global struggle between the forces of freedom and totalitarianism, creating an image that legitimized American Cold War policies.[28]

David Apter has provided a possible theoretical explanation for the effectiveness of ideological symbols used in the Truman Doctrine

[26] It is apropos to note that the author of the best systemic explanation of the Cold War, A. W. DePorte, observes that other historical outcomes were entirely possible. See *Europe between the Super-Powers: The Enduring Balance* (New Haven: Yale University Press, 1979), p. xii. According to Max Weber, the goal of social scientific inquiry is as follows: "We wish to understand on the one hand the relationships and the cultural significance of individual events . . . and on the other the causes of their being historically *so* and not *otherwise*." See Max Weber, *The Methodology of the Social Sciences*, ed. and trans. Edward Shils and Henry Finch (New York: Free Press, 1949), p. 72.

[27] Kenneth N. Waltz, *Theory of International Politics* (Reading, Mass.: Addison-Wesley Publishing Co., 1979), pp. 41-59.

[28] B. Thomas Trout, "Rhetoric Revisited: Political Legitimation and the Cold War," *International Studies Quarterly* 19 (September 1975): 251-84. For an analytical framework using Trout's concept of "policy legitimation," see Alexander L. George, "Domestic Constraints on Regime Change in U.S. Foreign Policy: The Need for Policy Legitimacy," in *Change in the International System*, ed. Ole R. Holsti, Randolph M. Siverson, and Alexander L. George (Boulder, Colo.: Westview Press, 1980), pp. 233-59.

speech in creating a public consensus behind what was to be an onerous policy of containing communist expansion. According to Apter,
the mythical elements of the ideology cement the solidarity of society
and buttress the moral authority of the rulers. An ideology also creates
a world image that contributes to the individual sense of identity.
These two functions act in conjunction with one another to legitimize
the authority of political elites.[29] In my study, following R. M. Christenson et al., ideology is defined as a belief system, held by a group,
that "explains and justifies a preferred political order for society, either
existing or proposed, and offers a strategy (processes, institutions, programs) for its attainment."[30] Not all belief systems qualify as ideologies, only those sets of beliefs that are consciously designed to guide
collective action. Ideology furnishes a link between general ideals and
more mundane, concrete actions; thus, it is extremely useful in mobi-
lizing members of a collectivity for concerted action for common
goals. But, as we shall see, ideology is less potent in motivating foreign
policy. The Cold War beliefs identified in this study are idiosyncratic,
limited to a historical context, and directly related to policy. Ideology
comprises the grand, overarching conceptual schemes that treat such
subjects as human nature, the individual's relationship to the state,
epistemology, equality, and the source of political authority.[31]

Trout's interpretation is consistent with standard historical accounts
which argue that President Truman felt he had no choice but to use
ideological rhetoric to "scare" Congress into supporting large-scale reconstruction aid to Europe.[32] Still, the requirements of policy legitimation cannot explain why U.S. policymakers internalized their own
rhetoric, why they accepted and acted on major premises of the Cold
War belief system. Further, an explanation based solely on domestic
political considerations sidesteps the crucial question of why U.S. lead-

[29] David E. Apter, "Introduction: Ideology and Discontent," in *Ideology and Discontent*, ed. David E. Apter (New York: Free Press, 1964), pp. 18-21.

[30] Reo M. Christenson et al., *Ideologies and Modern Politics*, 2nd ed. (New York:
Dodd, Mead, 1975), p. 6; M. Seliger, *Ideology and Politics* (New York: Free Press,
1976), pp. 14, 96-98, 120; Apter, "Ideology and Discontent," pp. 16-17; William E.
Connolly, *Political Science and Ideology* (New York: Atherton Press, 1967), pp. 2-3;
Willard A. Mullins, "On the Concept of Ideology in Political Science," *American Political
Science Review* 66 (June 1972): 498-510; Samuel H. Barnes, "Ideology and the Organ-
ization of Conflict: On the Relationship between Political Thought and Behavior," *Jour-
nal of Politics* 28 (August 1966): 513-30; Robert Lane, *Political Ideology* (New York:
Free Press, 1962), pp. 14-15.

[31] Roy C. Macridis, *Contemporary Political Ideologies: Movements and Regimes*, 2nd ed.
(Boston: Little, Brown and Co., 1983), pp. 2-13.

[32] See, for example, Jones, *Fifteen Weeks*.

ers decided to assume a leadership role in rebuilding the European economic system.

The "higher" levels of analysis—the international system and domestic political context—assume that U.S. policymakers' response to Soviet behavior was determined by the objective situation. But if individual policymakers interpreted the same external circumstances differently, then the analysis must incorporate individual-level variables to explain why the United States adopted Cold War policies.[33]

The actual latitude for individual decision available in the outcomes permitted by the bipolar structure of power in the international system is witnessed by the variety of solutions to the problem of managing U.S.-Soviet relations, reflecting differing interpretations of Soviet behavior, considered by U.S. policymakers. If U.S. Cold War policy were strictly determined by geopolitical position or domestic political pressure, one should not find opposing policy recommendations to meet the same objective circumstances.

It is a fundamental premise of cognitive psychology that individuals respond according to their interpretation of a stimulus, and that this interpretation does not necessarily agree with its "objective" properties. Cognitive psychologists view people as "information processors" whose behavior is largely determined by the way in which they select, code, store, and retrieve information from the environment. Consequently, a key to understanding individual variability lies in the study of cognitive processes. Still, to explain American Cold War policy entirely by individual policymakers' cognitive processes—ignoring objective U.S.-Soviet conflicts of interest or the imperatives to conflict inherent in the nature of the international system—would be patently reductionist.

What is the solution to this dilemma? This study presents a *multilevel* explanation of the origins of American Cold War policies, using variables on the level of the international system, domestic politics, and individual policymakers' cognitive processes. I did not attempt to integrate or synthesize the theories, but made complementary use of theoretical hypotheses at different levels of analysis to fill out and make more determinate the historical explanation. Although this approach lacks elegance and parsimony, the costs in economy are counterbalanced by the gain in explanatory power. Utilizing variables at a higher

---

[33] For a similar argument, see Robert Jervis, *Perception and Misperception in International Politics* (Princeton: Princeton University Press, 1976), pp. 18-21. Psychologist Walter Mischel applies the same reasoning to the task of determining the relative importance of situational vs. personality variables. See "Toward a Cognitive Social Learning Reconceptualization of Personality," *Psychological Review* 80 (1973): 252-83.

or lower level than the unit to be explained adds to the complexity of a research design; but, as Heinz Eulau argues, "the virtue of multi-level strategy is that it enriches the explantory power of analysis."[34]

Since international systemic, societal, or individual factors in isolation are themselves insufficient to explain the origins of American Cold War policies, we must examine their interaction. United States officials were complex, multifaceted human beings, with personality needs and political goals, trying to cope with a threatening international environment within constraints imposed by the nature of the U.S. political system. As psychologist William McGuire points out,

> While it is true that in science we seek the simplest possible explanation, we seek this simplicity within the restriction that it be the simplest explanation which is adequate for describing the empirical situation. . . . If we are seeking to describe a pretzel-shaped reality, we must be allowed to use pretzel-shaped hypotheses.[35]

It is in this way that we may approach the frustrating yet exciting, onerous yet irresistible task of understanding such important and consequential historical figures as Harry S Truman, James F. Byrnes, Dean Acheson, and Averell Harriman. Why did these men find it necessary to abandon all hope of a constructive, civilized relationship with the Soviet Union and embark on an altruistic if sometimes futile effort to preserve the balance of influence against the threat of Soviet gains throughout the world? The social psychological theories to be discussed furnish guideposts for our subsequent venture into the complexities of historical data.

[34] Heinz Eulau, "Multilevel Methods in Comparative Politics," *American Behavioral Scientist* 21 (September/October 1977): 47-48.

[35] William J. McGuire, "The Nature of Attitudes and Attitude Change," in *The Handbook of Social Psychology*, ed. Gardner Lindzey and Elliot Aronson, 2nd ed. (Reading, Mass.: 1969), 3:205.

CHAPTER ONE

Social Psychological Theories
of Attitude Change

RECENT developments in social psychology have increased its usefulness for explaining foreign policymaking. Social psychology has undergone a "cognitive revolution," in which investigators have adopted the
theories, hypotheses, and research techniques of cognitive psychology.
Psychologists in the subfields of cognitive balance and dissonance theories, persuasion research, social perception, and decisionmaking now
use information processing frameworks. The "cognitive revolution" in
psychology has been accompanied by an altered view of man as an
active agent who shapes his own behavior by constructing meaning
from the environment, rather than an S-R automaton buffeted about
by environmental stimuli. That psychologists of diverse training and
interests should converge on the importance of cognitive processes
suggests that the "cognitive revolution" is a genuinely progressive
"paradigm shift" reflecting a better scientific grasp of behavior, not
simply another example of intellectual faddism.

Social psychological theories of attitude change offer many hypotheses and concepts that help to explain why the American image
of the Soviet Union changed from benevolent ally to dangerous enemy—the origins of the Cold War belief system. Unlike previous explanations of foreign policymaking that have made use of cognitive
psychological concepts and hypotheses,[1] this study explicitly distinguishes and differentiates five major psychological theories. Instead of
picking and choosing from among available theories to formulate a
"cognitive processes" model, I have deliberately chosen to sharpen the
differences between alternative psychological approaches. Although
the theories often make similar predictions and are largely complementary in that they explain different attitude-change phenomena, the use
of alternative approaches has considerable heuristic value. Each theory

---

[1] See, for example, John D. Steinbruner, *The Cybernetic Theory of Decision: New Di-
mensions of Political Analysis* (Princeton: Princeton University Press, 1974); Janice Gross
Stein and Raymond Tanter, *Rational Decision-Making: Israel's Security Choices, 1967* (Columbus: Ohio State University Press, 1976); Jervis, *Perception and Misperception.*

suggests possible relationships and illuminates important explanatory variables that might otherwise be overlooked.

The use of competing social-psychological approaches may also provide a more valid explanation of foreign policymaking. Arguing that it is virtually impossible to prove a theory false through a "crucial" experiment, Lakatos and other philosophers of science have suggested that a more productive research strategy is to subject rival theories to empirical test.[2] Similarly, more than a decade ago, psychologist William McGuire observed that

> Our philosophy of science . . . has made it a principle of faith that a theory is "scientific" only to the extent that it is disprovable, that is, only when there is an empirical outcome which could disconfirm it. There seems to be a growing feeling among some of us that this formulation represents a slightly astigmatic view of the realities of scientific progress and that our science advances to the extent that our experiments are designed, not to confirm or disconfirm a hypothesis, but to confirm one hypothesis or an alternative one, each drawn from a well-formed theory.[3]

If this is true for psychology, armed with a battery of experimental techniques, how much more is it the case for political science, where it is impossible to control for extraneous factors to isolate a causal relationship? Since it is possible to find historical evidence for virtually any theoretical proposition, the foreign policy analyst must look for ways to check his or her subjectivity. The use of rival theories is one possible solution.

THE HOVLAND ATTITUDE CHANGE APPROACH

For over twenty years, the Yale program on attitude change, initiated by Carl Hovland, dominated social-psychological research.[4] Recently,

[2] Imre Lakatos, "Falsification and the Methodology of Scientific Research Programmes," in *Criticism and the Growth of Knowledge*, ed. Imre Lakatos and Alan Musgrave (Cambridge: Cambridge University Press, 1970).

[3] William J. McGuire, "The Nature of Attitudes and Attitude Change," in *The Handbook of Social Psychology*, ed. Gardner Lindzey and Elliot Aronson, 2nd ed. (Reading, Mass.: Addison-Wesley Publishing Co., 1969), 3:244-45, 265-66.

[4] The most influential statement of the concepts, assumptions, and hypotheses of this research tradition is Carl I. Hovland, Irving L. Janis, and Harold H. Kelley, *Communication and Persuasion* (New Haven: Yale University Press, 1953). For a review of more recent research on persuasion, see Alice H. Eagly and Samuel Himmelfarb, "Attitudes and Opinions," *Annual Review of Psychology* 29 (1978): 517-25. For a critical summary of representative research, see McGuire, "Nature of Attitudes and Attitude Change";

interest in this area has been rekindled as investigators have applied information processing concepts and hypotheses to traditional problems. The basic assumption of the Hovland approach is that attitudes change through learning a persuasive communication.

In this tradition, "attitude" is viewed as an affective reaction to a particular object or symbol. Attitudes are influenced by changing people's opinions on a particular subject.

According to the seminal theoretical statement of this approach,

> We assume that opinions, like other habits, will tend to persist unless the individual undergoes some new learning experiences. Exposure to a persuasive communication which successfully induces the individual to accept a new opinion constitutes a learning experience in which a new verbal habit is acquired.[5]

Thus, learning theory principles also apply to the process of attitude change.

A persuasive communication presents new information that may alter people's opinions, leading to a corresponding change in emotional orientation toward the attitude object. Whether people accept the implications of a message depends on the incentives offered in the communication. These incentives may be arguments or reasons supporting a conclusion, or anticipated rewards for adopting a new opinion. The recipient of the communication is assumed to be a rational individual trying to adjust his beliefs to accord more closely with reality. In learning new attitudes people are passive; they receive persuasive communications, absorb the arguments, and adjust their affective reaction to the attitude object.

The Hovland approach is not a well-developed formal theory, but a research program organized around Lasswell's question, *Who* said *what* to *whom* with *what effect*? That is to say, researchers have manipulated variables in source (expertise, trustworthiness, sex, race, attractiveness), message (discrepancy, order effects, fear appeals), and audience

---

Philip G. Zimbardo, Ebbe B. Ebbeson, and Christina Maslach, *Influencing Attitudes and Changing Behavior*, 2nd ed. (Reading, Mass.: Addison-Wesley Publishing Co., 1977); Chester A. Insko, *Theories of Attitude Change* (New York: Appleton-Century-Crofts, 1967); Charles A. Kiesler, Barry E. Collins, and Norman Miller, *Attitude Change: A Critical Analysis of Theoretical Approaches* (New York: John Wiley & Sons, 1967). For an application of this research tradition to the problem of changing mass opinion on foreign policy questions, see Irving L. Janis and M. Brewster Smith, "Effects of Education and Persuasion on National and International Images," in *International Behavior: A Social-Psychological Analysis*, ed. Herbert C. Kelman (New York: Holt, Rinehart and Winston, 1966).

[5] Hovland, Janis, and Kelley, *Communication and Persuasion*, p. 10.

(intelligence, self-esteem, cognitive complexity) to determine their effect on attitudes. The most important conclusion to emerge from several decades of research is that the relationship of these factors to attitude change is complex, contingent, and interactive. It is difficult to make any firm, unqualified generalizations about the variables that influence attitude change.[6]

Nevertheless, we can derive several working hypotheses for which there is substantial empirical evidence.[7] The influence of a message often depends on its source. For example, there will be greater opinion change if the communicator has high credibility than low. Credibility is expertise (factual knowledge) and trustworthiness (no ulterior motives). But contrary to the expectations of the Hovland group, high-credibility sources had no effect on the amount of the message that was learned. Indeed, people recalled more of the content of the communication when the source was neutral. This result is consistent with the notion that people are "lazy," and do not bother to learn the reasons underlying a conclusion if the source is highly credible or, conversely, unreliable. That the credibility of the communicator should influence acceptance of a message seems unexceptionable and entirely logical. But experiments have shown that various factors irrelevant to the evidentiary value of a message may influence perceived communicator credibility: race, social status, attractiveness, expertise unrelated to the issue.

Characteristics of the message affect its acceptability. The greater the discrepancy between the communicator's position and preexisting beliefs of the audience, the greater the amount of attitude change achieved, unless the difference is particularly extreme. When the message is antithetical, the individual will respond by derogating the communicator. For a highly credible source, however, the threshold at which the message is rejected will be at a higher level of discrepancy from the target's position.

An individual's personality affects his/her susceptibility to persuasive appeals. For example, people who have low self-esteem are more readily influenced. Some people are especially vulnerable to influence, altering their beliefs in response to each new appeal. Some of his aides and cabinet officials believed that Truman was easily swayed by per-

[6] James Jaccard, "Toward Theories of Persuasion and Belief Change," *Journal of Personality and Social Psychology* 40 (1981): 260.

[7] These propositions are taken from Zimbardo, Ebbeson, and Maslach, *Influencing Attitudes*, pp. 98-100; and McGuire, "Nature of Attitudes and Attitude Change," pp. 172-258.

suasive arguments, and that he adopted the position of the most recent visitor to the Oval Office.

The Hovland approach predicts that U.S. officials adopted Cold War attitudes toward the Soviet Union because they were presented with a more cogent analysis of Soviet behavior and a well-developed alternative policy. Cold War historians generally agree that George Kennan's "long telegram" of February 22, 1946, had a galvanizing effect on U.S. officials' attitudes toward the Soviet Union, providing the intellectual justification for the emerging containment policy.[8] According to this interpretation, Kennan's message gave U.S. policymakers a satisfying, useful analytical framework with which to explain Soviet foreign policy and a set of policy prescriptions to meet the Soviet threat. A member of the State Department recalls the reaction in Washington to Kennan's "long telegram": "There was a universal feeling that 'this was it,' this was the appreciation of the situation that had long been needed."[9] As one of eight foreign service officers selected for intensive training in Russian language and history in the twenties, before the program was discontinued due to budgetary reductions, George Kennan was certainly a credible communicator. Further, the gloomy but not alarmist description he painted of Soviet expansionist ambitions was at an intermediate level of discrepancy from the position of his State Department audience. Because of the Soviets' inexplicable recent behavior in Iran, Manchuria, and the United Nations, Washington officials had begun to question their previous optimism about the prospects for continued Soviet-American collaboration in the postwar world. Kennan himself acknowledged the importance of the timing of his appeal:

> Six months earlier this message would probably have been received in the Department of State with raised eyebrows and lips pursed in disapproval. Six months later, it would probably have sounded redundant, a sort of preaching to the convinced. . . . All this only goes to show that more important than the observable nature of external reality, when it comes to the determination of Washington's view of the world, is the subjective state of readiness on the part of Washington officialdom to recognize this or that feature of it.[10]

[8] See, for example, Gaddis, *Origins of the Cold War*, p. 304; Daniel Yergin, *Shattered Peace: The Origins of the Cold War and the National Security State* (Boston: Houghton-Mifflin Co., 1977), pp. 170-71; Hugh De Santis, *The Diplomacy of Silence: The American Foreign Service, the Soviet Union, and the Cold War, 1933-1947* (Chicago: University of Chicago Press, 1980), pp. 175-76.

[9] Halle, *Cold War as History*, p. 105.

[10] Kennan, *Memoirs*, p. 310.

Individual policymakers may differ in their acceptance of a persuasive policy recommendation because of factors unrelated to the quality of logic or evidence supporting the arguments—for example, the perceived credibility of the author, the discrepancy of the position advocated, or the self-esteem of the recipient. For instance, President Truman should have been among the first to adopt a hard-line view of the Soviets, because he was insecure about his intellectual qualifications for the presidency and easily persuaded by advisers. In contrast, other things being equal, one would expect Under Secretary of State Acheson to have been immune to abstract argumentation or vivid appeals that were not adequately supported by irrefutable evidence or his own personal experience. Complacent about his intellectual gifts and analytical discrimination—his enemies called it arrogance—Acheson was not readily convinced by inferior talents, particularly when they resorted to clichés or idealistic banalities.

COGNITIVE DISSONANCE THEORY

People do not always change their opinions in accord with persuasive communications. Cognitive dissonance theory provides one possible explanation of the imperviousness of preconceived opinions to rational disconfirmation. Unlike the Yale approach to attitude change, cognitive dissonance is stated as a formal theory from which "nonobvious" predictions can be deduced.

In his *Theory of Cognitive Dissonance*, Leon Festinger set forth the notion that inconsistencies within the cognitive system cause an uncomfortable state of tension that people are then motivated to reduce or eliminate.[11] The underlying assumption is that people's beliefs are highly interconnected and mutually coherent. When this harmony is disrupted by development of incompatible cognitions, a wave of cognitive or behavioral activity is stirred up until internal consistency is restored. The image of man is that of a harassed but amiable honest

[11] Leon Festinger, *A Theory of Cognitive Dissonance* (Stanford: Stanford University Press, 1957). This summary of cognitive dissonance theory is taken from Zimbardo, Ebbeson, and Maslach, *Influencing Attitudes*; Insko, *Theories of Attitude Change*; Kiesler, Collins, and Miller, *Attitude Change*; Elliot Aronson, "The Theory of Cognitive Dissonance: A Current Perspective," in *Cognitive Theories in Social Psychology*, ed. Leonard Berkowitz (New York: Academic Press, 1978), pp. 181-211; and William J. McGuire, "Attitudes and Opinions," *Annual Review of Psychology* 17 (1966): 475-514. For application of cognitive dissonance theory to international relations, see Jervis, *Perception and Misperception*, pp. 382-406.

broker striving to produce a compromise among conflicting elements with the least disturbance to the overall system.[12]

The basic units of the theory are "cognitive elements," defined as bits of information, opinions, or beliefs. Cognitive elements may be dissonant, consonant, or irrelevant to one another. Dissonance occurs when the opposite of one cognition follows from the other. For example, the cognitive element, "the Russians are untrustworthy," is dissonant with the knowledge that "the Russians are our allies against Germany." The inconsistency between two cognitive elements need not be logical for dissonance to arise. Dissonance may also result from psychological sources such as the violation of cultural mores or disconfirmation of expectancies based on past experience. This increases the generality of the theory, but also makes it difficult to predict when dissonance should occur, particularly outside the contrived conditions of an experiment.

The magnitude of dissonance experienced at any time is a function of the importance of the discrepant cognitions and the ratio of dissonant to consonant elements. For example, to the knowledge that the "Russians are our allies against Germany," we could add the idea that "alliances are based on common interests, not mutual trust," and dissonance would be somewhat alleviated.

According to Festinger, the existence of dissonance creates a negative drive state that will motivate the person to reduce or eliminate the inconsistency. The greater the dissonance, the greater the pressures for its reduction.

There are several possible ways of reducing dissonance: changing behavior associated with one of the dissonant cognitive elements; altering the psychological or physical environment; adding consistent cognitive elements to change the ratio of consonant to dissonant cognitions. In the real world, it is difficult to predict which mode of dissonance reduction a person will use in a given situation.

One type of situation in which attitude change is likely occurs when an individual is persuaded to behave contrary to his or her beliefs. Apparently, it is easier to alter one's private opinions than to deny actions witnessed by others. The term "forced compliance" refers to an experimental paradigm in which people are induced to behave against their private beliefs. For example, subjects may be asked to

[12] William J. McGuire, "Theory of the Structure of Human Thought," *Theories of Cognitive Consistency: A Sourcebook*, ed. Robert P. Abelson et al. (Chicago: Rand McNally and Co., 1968), pp. 140-62; idem, "The Development of Theory in Social Psychology," in *The Development of Social Psychology*, ed. Robin Gilmour and Steve Duck (London: Academic Press, 1980), p. 60.

argue publicly for a position opposed to their true attitudes on apolitical issue. According to the theory, such counterattitudinal behavior should produce considerable dissonance, which may be alleviated by changing one's private attitude so that it is more consistent with the position advocated publicly. In short, when people violate their preexisting beliefs, they may change their attitudes to rationalize their actions.

The amount of dissonance experienced in a forced-compliance situation is in *inverse* relation to the justification for complying. In other words, the more important the reasons for behaving contrary to one's convictions, the less dissonance is created. This means that when people are induced to engage in counterattitudinal behavior, a change in their beliefs is most probable when they perceive that their action was freely chosen and when there was insufficient external reward or punishment to force them to conform.[13]

In the classic experiment of this research area, subjects worked on an extremely boring task for an hour—putting spools on trays and turning pegs. After the hour was up, the subject was offered one dollar or twenty dollars if he would tell other prospective subjects that the experimental task had been interesting and fun. Dissonance theory predicts that subjects in the one dollar condition would experience great psychological discomfort, and would be likely to adopt more favorable attitudes toward the task, because the reward was not sufficient to justify lying. This was the case. In an "official survey," subjects actually rated the job as more enjoyable when they had been paid the smaller amount of money.[14]

Subsequent experiments have shown that people change their attitudes in "forced compliance" situations only when their actions result in undesired consequences—such as convincing an innocent individual to accept a lie, or having one's contrived arguments persuade authorities to change policy. Even when the feared consequences do not eventuate, however, subjects still adjust their beliefs to minimize dissonance.[15]

The Hovland approach works with the assumption that learning the verbal material contained in a persuasive communication leads to attitude change. But Festinger's cognitive dissonance theory argues that changes in internal beliefs and attitudes follow from *behavior* change. The two research programs differ in other, more subtle ways that affect

[13] Zimbardo, Ebbeson, and Maslach, *Influencing Attitudes*, p. 72.
[14] Leon Festinger and J. Merrill Carlsmith, "Cognitive Consequences of Forced Compliance," *Journal of Abnormal and Social Psychology* 58 (1959): 203-10.
[15] Eagly and Himmelfarb, "Attitudes and Opinions."

their usefulness for explaining foreign policymaking. The Hovlanders are more concerned with the dependent variable, "attitude change," and have been creative in searching out theoretical hypotheses that might explain it. In contrast, the Festingerians are more interested in the independent variable, "cognitive dissonance," and have sought out different situations to which the theoretical formulation could be applied. The Hovlanders try to control extraneous variables by deliberately incorporating them into the experimental design as moderator variables; the Festingerians try to eliminate extraneous factors by controlling for them in elaborately designed experimental situations. The Hovland approach results in complex interaction effects that are sometimes difficult to understand and interpret. The Festinger style leads to clear-cut experimental findings that are often difficult to duplicate in the real world because of the presence of confounding contextual variables.[16]

Cognitive dissonance theory postulates that U.S. policymakers adopted Cold War beliefs after being forced by situational pressures to act contrary to strongly held, consistent beliefs in favor of Soviet-American cooperation, without adequate justification and in spite of their fear of negative consequences. For attitude change to occur, however, U.S. policymakers must have felt that their decision to initiate a Cold War was voluntary. Otherwise, they could have reduced dissonance merely by denying their personal responsibility, or by blaming others for their actions.[17] This means that the situational or social pressures responsible for their conformity must have been subtle or illegitimate. Domestic political interests are not "supposed" to sway or bias foreign policy decisions—yet they do.

Thus, cognitive dissonance theory could account for evidence presented by Gaddis that Washington officials changed their estimate of Soviet foreign policy intentions in February 1946, a few months *after* the Truman administration had decided to adopt a "tougher" stance toward the Soviets in response to Republican criticism of the so-called "appeasement" policy.[18] American policymakers would have been reluctant to admit to themselves that, for illegitimate political motives, they had diminished the chances for Soviet-American cooperation and increased the risks of war. Accordingly, they would have been motivated to change their attitudes toward the Soviet Union, to make them more consistent with the public "hard-line" policy.

[16] McGuire, "Nature of Attitudes and Attitude Change," pp. 139-40.

[17] For a similar hypothesis, see Jervis, *Perception and Misperception*, pp. 401-402.

[18] Gaddis, *Origins of the Cold War*, pp. 289-304.

Cognitive dissonance theory would also lead us to expect individual policymakers to differ in the timing of their acceptance of Cold War beliefs. We may distinguish at least three ways in which individuals vary in their response to cognitive inconsistencies. First, people have differing thresholds of tolerance for inconsistency. Those individuals who are uncomfortable with uncertainty or complexity would be most likely to find discrepant cognitions unpleasant.[19] In addition, people who are not introspective and spend little time reflecting on their own beliefs are not bothered by gaping incongruities between their statements or thoughts from one moment to another. Truman and Byrnes were extroverted politicians who spent little time on self-reflection or developing a coherent worldview. Therefore, they would be immune to internal pressures to form a consistent image of the Soviet Union or bring their beliefs into line with their actions. On the other hand, Acheson was an intellectual who delighted in manipulating ideas, constructing an imposing edifice of argumentation. He had a remarkably complex, highly interconnected, and coherent system of beliefs about world politics. Thus, Under Secretary of State Acheson should have been among the first to adopt a logically consistent image of the Soviet Union compatible with the hard-line policies pursued by the Truman administration.

Second, what is inconsistent for one person may not be for another who has a different set of beliefs. As Robert Abelson commented, " 'What follows from what' can be elicited separately from different individuals, and the structure of these implications is not going to be perfectly identical for nuns, Red Guards, bookies, and nuclear scientists."[20] Thus, Washington officials may have had varying definitions of what was dissonant because they started out with differing sets of beliefs about Soviet aims and tactics.

Third, there is some evidence that people differ in their preferred method of reducing dissonance—for example, derogating the communicator of discrepant information, conforming to pressure to adopt another opinion, downgrading the importance of the issue, or searching for additional consistent cognitions.[21]

[19] David R. Shaffer and Clyde Hendrick, "Dogmatism and Tolerance for Ambiguity as Determinants of Differential Reactions to Cognitive Inconsistency," *Journal of Personality and Social Psychology* 29 (1974): 601-608.

[20] Robert P. Abelson, "Comment: Uncooperative Personality Variables," in *Theories of Cognitive Consistency*, ed. Abelson et al., p. 650.

[21] For hypotheses about individual differences in responses to cognitive dissonance, see Daryl J. Bem and David C. Funder, "Predicting More of the People More of the Time: Assessing the Personality of Situations," *Psychological Review* 85 (November

Cognitive dissonance theory also posits that without external pressures forcing them to assume an anti-Soviet stance, U.S. policymakers would have tried to maintain their benevolent image of the Soviet Union, even when they were confronted with disconfirming evidence. Thus, for example, the theory would lead us to expect American leaders to downgrade or dismiss the significance of information concerning the Soviets' suppression of democratic freedoms and installation of police-state regimes in Eastern Europe.

ATTRIBUTION THEORY

From the mid-1950s to the mid-1960s, the dominant theoretical school in social psychology viewed man as a "consistency seeker," driven to avoid the discomfort caused by cognitive contradictions. But no one principle of human cognitive or motivational processes adequately describes or explains thought and behavior in all situations. People are capable of tolerating great inconsistency in their beliefs and actions. They are not aware of glaring contradictions in their opinions, are not greatly concerned about possible incongruities, and spend little time or attention trying to achieve the elusive goal of a coherent belief system. Even at the height of consistency theory's popularity, in the "Bible" of that paradigm, several skeptics expressed doubt that the drive for cognitive consistency was entirely ubiquitous or influential in shaping most people's behavior.[22]

Even as social psychologists assumed that the drive for cognitive balance determined our interaction with reality, political scientists in studies of voting and mass belief systems demonstrated the appalling lack of ideological structure in the average person's political opinions.[23]

During the seventies, social psychologists gradually drifted away from motivational models to information-processing approaches in

1978): 495; also, Elliot Aronson, "Dissonance Theory: Progress and Problems," in *Theories of Cognitive Consistency*, ed. Abelson et al., p. 23; and articles in Section IVB, ibid.

[22] See articles by Daniel Katz, Leonard Berkowitz, Jerome Singer, and Jonathan Freedman in *Theories of Cognitive Consistency*, ed. Abelson et al.

[23] Michael Billig, *Ideology and Social Psychology: Extremism, Moderation and Contradiction* (Oxford: Basil Blackwell, 1982), p. 150; Philip E. Converse, "The Nature of Belief Systems in Mass Publics," in *Ideology and Discontent*, ed. David Apter (New York: Free Press, 1964), pp. 206-61; Daniel Katz, "Consistency for What? The Functional Approach," in *Theories of Cognitive Consistency*, ed. Abelson et al., p. 179; Herbert McClosky, "Consensus and Ideology in American Politics," *American Political Science Review* 58 (June 1964): 361-82.

what has been called a "paradigm shift." In attribution theory, there are no internal pressures to achieve cognitive consistency, no motivational constructs of any kind. From this perspective, people are "naive scientists" or problem solvers, not "rationalizers" or "ego-defenders." Like social psychologists, they are interested in understanding human interaction. People are engaged in a quest for meaning, not cognitive harmony; for validity, not consistency. Thus, attribution theory portrays the person as relatively open-minded in the search for truth, untrammeled by the need to maintain a favorable self-image or preserve a favored belief.[24]

Attribution theory is concerned with people's attempts to explain the events of everyday life, draw inferences about the unchanging properties of their social milieu, and make predictions about the behavior of other people. Specifically, attribution theorists seek to discover the principles of "naive epistemology," the rules and procedures laymen use in gathering and interpreting data, as opposed to those associated with the model of scientific epistemology. How do people know what is real and, more important, how do they know that they know?

This suggests that the concepts and hypotheses of attribution theory might be useful for understanding foreign policymaking: because it is impossible for policymakers to satisfy the requirements of the scientific model in their attempts to explain and interpret international events, they must resort to principles of "naive epistemology" in making judgments about other states.[25]

There are several competing models of the attribution process, differing in their description of the cognitive processes, information used, and outcome.[26] Thus, attribution theory is a general rubric used to tie together many different research studies that share certain basic assumptions. Specifically, all the models assume that people try to for-

[24] Shelley E. Taylor, "The Interface of Cognitive and Social Psychology," in *Cognition, Social Behavior, and the Environment*, ed. John H. Harvey (Hillsdale, N.J.: Lawrence Erlbaum, 1980); McGuire, "The Development of Theory in Social Psychology," p. 62; Billig, *Ideology and Social Psychology*, pp. 172-73.

[25] Jervis was among the first to develop the implications of attribution theory for the study of foreign policymaking. See *Perception and Misperception*, pp. 32-43. A Norwegian political scientist, Daniel Heradstveit, has used some hypotheses from attribution theory to analyze the Arab-Israeli conflict. See *The Arab-Israeli Conflict: Psychological Obstacles to Peace* (Oslo: Universitetsforlaget, 1979).

[26] For a discussion of the important theoretical models of Heider, Kelley, and Jones-Davis, see David J. Schneider, Albert H. Hastorf, and Phoebe C. Ellsworth, *Person Perception*, 2nd ed. (Reading, Mass.: Addison-Wesley Publishing Co., 1970), pp. 46-73.

mulate causal explanations of behavior, and this interpretation shapes their reaction.

Harold Kelley has proposed the most influential model of attribution processes. Kelley originally posited that in formulating causal explanations, "the effect is attributed to that condition which is present when the effect is present and which is absent when the effect is absent."[27] In other words, an effect is attributed to the cause with which it covaries.

Kelley also theorized that people make use of three types of information in formulating causal explanations: "distinctiveness," the degree to which the effect occurs primarily in the presence of one potential cause instead of another; "consistency," the extent to which an effect is observed whenever a potential cause is present; and "consensus," the degree to which other people respond in the same way whenever the causal candidate is present. In using this information on covariation to identify the true cause of someone's actions, the individual follows procedures analogous to those employed by a trained social scientist in "analysis of variance"[28] or those outlined by J. S. Mill in his method of differences. Several experiments have shown that people *do* substantially follow statistical rules of inference in interpreting evidence concerning various patterns of covariation to formulate causal explanations.[29]

Further developing the metaphor of the "naive scientist," Nisbett and Ross assess people's judgments against scientific rules of inference, arguing that many of the everyday problems facing the layperson are analogous to those confronted by scientists. For example, the naive scientist must describe accurately an individual *datum* (an object or event), characterize a *sample* of data, generalize to the *population of objects or events*, assess the magnitude of *covariation* between events, formulate *causal explanations*, *predict* future events, and *test theories*.[30]

[27] Harold H. Kelley, "Attribution Theory in Social Psychology," in *Nebraska Symposium on Motivation* (Lincoln: University of Nebraska Press, 1967), p. 194.

[28] Ibid.

[29] See, for example, Leslie Ann McArthur, "The How and What of Why: Some Determinants and Consequences of Causal Attribution," *Journal of Personality and Social Psychology* 22 (1972): 171-93; Bruce R. Orvis, John D. Cunningham, and Harold H. Kelley, "A Closer Examination of Causal Inference: The Rules of Consensus, Distinctiveness, and Consistency Information," *Journal of Personality and Social Psychology* 32 (1975): 605-16; Bernard Weiner et al., "Perceiving the Causes of Success and Failure," in *Attribution: Perceiving the Causes of Behavior*, ed. Edward E. Jones et al. (Morristown, N.J.: General Learning Press, 1972).

[30] Richard E. Nisbett and Lee Ross, *Human Inference: Strategies and Shortcomings in Social Judgment* (Englewood Cliffs, N.J.: Prentice-Hall, 1980), pp. 8-9.

Although people do not always use evidence according to scientific canons of inquiry, this does not prove that human cognitive capacities are innately flawed or inadequate. Instead, Nisbett and Ross argue that errors arise from ignorance of or failure to apply formal statistical rules of inference as well as overuse of certain intuitive "shortcuts." They compare their own work on attribution biases to research by cognitive psychologists on visual illusions:

> Perception researchers have shown that in spite of, and largely because of, people's exquisite perceptual capacities, they are subject to certain perceptual illusions. No serious scientist, however, is led by such demonstrations to conclude that the perceptual system under study is inherently faulty. Similarly, we conclude from our own research that we are observing not an inherently faulty cognitive apparatus, but rather, one that manifests certain explicable flaws.[31]

Attribution theory assumes that many attitudes or beliefs have their origins in people's efforts to understand the behavior of others. Thus, the theory would suggest that American officials adopted new beliefs about the Soviet Union as a result of their attempts to explicate enigmatic Soviet actions. Social psychologists have found evidence for several generalizations about the principles underlying the average individual's common, everyday explanations that seem also to apply to the process by which the Cold War belief system was formed.

Most attribution theorists classify the reasons given for people's actions into two categories: dispositional and situational. Dispositional causes refer to enduring characteristics of the individual such as personality traits, ability, character, motives, and so on. Situational causes identify transient features of the context that influence people to behave in a certain way. Social psychologists have found that although actors attribute their own behavior to situational requirements, observers attribute the same behavior to the actors' dispositional characteristics.[32]

The divergent perceptions of actors and observers exemplify the tendency for people to attribute causality to whatever captures their attention or is salient.[33] Thus, the actor's attention is normally directed

[31] Ibid., p. 14.

[32] Edward E. Jones and Richard E. Nisbett, "The Actor and the Observer: Divergent Perceptions of the Causes of Behavior," in *Attribution: Perceiving the Causes of Behavior*, ed. Edward E. Jones et al., pp. 79-94; for a review of relevant research, see Edward E. Jones, "How Do People Perceive the Causes of Behavior?" *American Scientist* 64 (May-June 1976): 300-305.

[33] Shelley E. Taylor and Susan T. Fiske, "Point of View and Perceptions of Causality,"

to his environment and the situational cues to which he must respond; he literally cannot see himself. When asked to account for his own behavior, the actor will naturally report that he was reacting to some feature of his surroundings. In contrast, the observer's attention is focused on the actor, who stands out against the static background. Consequently, the observer is inclined to infer that the actor's behavior is intentional and represents his personality.

Similarly, policymakers tend to infer that the actions of their own state were compelled by circumstances, even while they attribute the behavior of other states to the fundamental "character" of the nation or its leaders. Applied to the problem of explaining the change in U.S. foreign policymakers' orientation toward the Soviet Union, attribution theory would suggest that Washington officials were too willing to impute ideological, expansionist motives to Soviet actions that could just as plausibly reflect security calculations similar to those that prompted analogous policies pursued by the United States. In the early postwar period, for example, some State Department officials regarded Soviet attempts to establish an exclusive sphere of influence in Eastern Europe as evidence that the Soviets had unlimited expansionist ambitions. At the same time, these officials insisted that the area covered by the Monroe Doctrine remain out of reach of the new U.N. Security Council. As Hans Morgenthau observed, the Monroe Doctrine is the "most comprehensive, unilateral proclamation of a sphere of influence in modern times."[34]

Consistent with experimental evidence that people attribute effects to whatever happens to catch their attention, researchers have also found that vivid information has a disproportionate impact on people's judgments and explanations. Vivid information is: emotionally involving, concrete, and based on personal experience or firsthand knowledge.[35]

Journal of Personality and Social Psychology 32 (1975): 439-45; Shelley E. Taylor and Susan T. Fiske, "Salience, Attention, and Attribution: Top of the Head Phenomena," in *Advances in Experimental Social Psychology*, ed. Leonard Berkowitz (New York: Academic Press, 1978), 11:249-88; Michael D. Storms, "Videotape and the Attribution Process: Reversing Actors' and Observers' Point of View," *Journal of Personality and Social Psychology* 27 (1973): 165-75.

[34] Hans J. Morgenthau, in *The Origins of the Cold War*, ed. Lloyd Gardner, Arthur Schlesinger, Jr., and Hans J. Morgenthau (Waltham, Mass.: Ginn and Co., 1970), p. 86.

[35] Nisbett and Ross, *Human Inference*, pp. 43-51. In his useful discussion on how decisionmakers learn from history, Jervis argues cogently that firsthand experience is a powerful determinant of the images that national leaders maintain of other states. See *Perception and Misperception*, pp. 239-40.

Concrete, firsthand information has greater influence on foreign policy judgments than more abstract theoretical material. It is well known that U.S. leaders often give undue importance to impressions acquired in transient, artificial "personal" encounters with other leaders at summit conferences and state visits. For example, FDR's optimism about the chances for U.S.-Soviet cooperation was based, in part, on the images impressed in his mind during his face-to-face talks with Stalin at the Teheran Conference. Similarly, *New York Times* columnist C. L. Sulzberger inferred from his conversations with the president that "Truman used Potsdam as a symbol of all relations with Russia because this was his own personal experience of Russian methods." Diplomatic historian Hugh De Santis found that foreign service officers stationed in Eastern Europe, confronted with day-to-day evidence of Soviet brutalities and suppression of individual liberties, altered their optimistic image of Soviet postwar intentions sooner than State Department officials insulated in Washington.[36]

Even secondhand material that is anecdotal or contains vivid descriptions will have a greater effect on policymakers' judgments than more abstract analyses. One would expect the degree of confidence placed in a generalization to have some tenuous relationship to the number of cases on which it is based. But because concrete anecdotal information is more striking, many established foreign policy beliefs are derived from one or two memorable cases.

Perhaps the least vivid, most uninvolving information is that to be derived from the *nonoccurrence* of potential events or an actor's *nonresponse*. As the preceding discussion suggests, this kind of evidence is particularly apt to be ignored or underutilized when people make inferences or formulate explanations.[37] People have difficulty making appropriate use of negative information when formulating concepts or making generalizations.

It seems highly probable that policymakers do not adequately con-

[36] Samuel I. Rosenman, ed., *The Public Papers and Addresses of Franklin D. Roosevelt* (New York: Harper & Bros., 1950), 12:138; Sumner Welles, *Where Are We Heading?* (New York: Harper & Bros., 1946), p. 36; Robert E. Sherwood, *Roosevelt and Hopkins: An Intimate History*, rev. ed. (New York: Harper & Bros., 1948), pp. 798-99; C. L. Sulzberger, *A Long Row of Candles: Memoirs and Diaries, 1934-1953* (New York: Macmillan, 1969), p. 364; Hugh De Santis, "Conflicting Images of the USSR: American Career Diplomats and the Balkans, 1944-1946," *Political Science Quarterly* 94 (Fall 1979): 475-94.

[37] Lee Ross, "The Intuitive Psychologist and His Shortcomings: Distortions in the Attribution Process," in *Advances in Experimental Social Psychology*, ed. Leonard Berkowitz (New York: Academic Press, 1977), 10:173-220; Nisbett and Ross, *Human Inference*, pp. 48-49; Jervis, *Perception and Misperception*, p. 235.

sider the information conveyed by the *nonoccurrence* of a foreign policy event. For example, diplomatic historian Ernest May perceptively points out that Truman and his advisers might not have concluded that Soviet expansion into Eastern Europe was comparable to Hitler's policies, had they taken into consideration those actions which the Soviets did not take. In Finland, Soviet authorities did not object to the existence of a noncommunist regime that provided assurances of nonhostility toward the Soviet Union. In Hungary, Soviet occupation authorities did not interfere with elections that produced an over-whelmingly noncommunist parliament and cabinet. Hungary did not become a full-fledged Soviet satellite until 1947—*after* the announcement of the Truman Doctrine. In Czechoslovakia, the Russians did not suppress a coalition government in which communists were not the dominant faction. May concludes:

> Yet Truman and his advisers apparently paid little attention to oc-currences in Finland, Hungary, or Czechoslovakia. Instead, they took Soviet actions in Poland, Rumania, and Bulgaria to be indic-ative of what the Soviet government intended to do everywhere else.[38]

Attribution theory gives a description of the process of attitude change that contrasts with that of the Hovland approach or cognitive dissonance theory. According to the Hovland research tradition, atti-tudes change when people learn and accept new information. From the perspective of attribution theory, people actively seek out infor-mation and formulate causal explanations, and do not passively adopt the arguments of a persuasive communication. New attitudes are formed based on the person's own diagnosis of the causes of an event, not internalization of somebody else's conclusions.

Attribution theory does not challenge the cognitive dissonance proposition that people often maintain consistent belief structures at the cost of ignoring or misinterpreting relevant evidence. Since they do not try to erect a grand theory deduced from a few underlying premises, attribution theorists accept the idea that ostensibly compet-itive cognitive theories may actually be complementary; that is, instead of arguing that human thought strives for "balance" or "hierarchical organization" or "consistency," attribution theorists are willing to ad-mit that various formulations of human cognitive responses may val-idly describe the way people think and interpret information at differ-ent times.[39]

[38] Ernest R. May, *"Lessons" of the Past: The Use and Misuse of History in American Foreign Policy* (London: Oxford University Press, 1973), pp. 44-45.

[39] Billig, *Ideology and Social Psychology*, pp. 170-71.

In particular, attribution theory concedes that the "naive scientist" often preserves intuitive theories beyond the point at which the weight of available evidence would seem to dictate their rejection or at least modification. Yet, that people interpret incoming information in a biased fashion does not prove that they have a *drive* or compelling need for consistent beliefs. Human biases usually can be traced to "cold" cognitive processes, not the intrusion of "hot" motives. A long tradition of research in cognitive and social psychology has demonstrated that people tend to adjust and twist incoming information to fit their beliefs, regardless of whether the sensory data has any affective significance.[40]

According to Nisbett and Ross, people frequently maintain their opinions even when confronted with incontrovertible data not because they are emotionally committed to particular values, but because they have succumbed to common errors in handling information. For example, people generally try to *confirm* their hypotheses by searching for consistent evidence; they do not act according to the scientific rule that the most efficient way to establish the validity of a proposition is to try to falsify it. Subjects asked to test the hypothesis that a particular individual is an extrovert will ask questions designed to elicit examples of sociable behavior; those informed that a person is a likely introvert, will draw out evidence of that individual's shy and retiring nature. Further, many prophecies are self-fulfilling. A statesman convinced that another state is implacably hostile and aggressive may, by building up defensive armaments, provoke the feared reaction from the adversary. Finally, it is simpler and requires less mental effort to assume that one's fundamental beliefs are correct: no one could accomplish the simple job of living if each hypothesis had to be tested anew.[41]

Attribution theory would lead us to expect that American officials' inferences about the source of Soviet behavior were the most important cause of their changed beliefs. American foreign policymakers leaped to the conclusion that the establishment of a Soviet sphere in Eastern Europe was proof that the Stalin regime was establishing a springboard for further infiltration into Western Europe. In addition, attribution research would suggest that U.S. officials also inferred that Soviet demands for bases on the Turkish Straits in August 1946 re-

[40] Nisbett and Ross, *Human Inference*, pp. 12, 228-48. Jervis provides an incisive critical discussion of psychological research which has attempted to demonstrate the impact of desire, fears, and other affects on perceptions. See *Perception and Misperception*, pp. 117-202, 356-381.

[41] Nisbett and Ross, *Human Inference*, pp. 179-92; Mark Snyder and William Swann, "Hypothesis-Testing Processes in Social Interaction," *Journal of Personality and Social Psychology* 36 (1978): 1202-12.

flected Stalin's long-term designs on the eastern Mediterranean; yet, American leaders would ignore the double standard implicit in their request for bases in Iceland and the Pacific.

At the same time, U.S. policymakers should have overlooked possible information about Soviet motives conveyed by nonevents—for example, Stalin's failure to eliminate free elections and establish a police-state regime in Hungary, Czechoslovakia or Finland; the Soviets' withdrawal of their troops from Iran; or the Soviets' sudden quiescence on the Straits issue once the United States made its position known.

Finally, Harry Truman's attitude toward the Soviet Union should have been indelibly marked by his personal experience during the negotiations and informal social encounters with Stalin at the Potsdam Conference in August 1945. Similarly, one would expect Averell Harriman and those State Department officials who were stationed in Moscow or in an Eastern European post to adopt beliefs reflecting their treatment by the Russians or the difficulties they encountered in getting Russian diplomats to agree to the American position.

SELF-PERCEPTION THEORY

Whereas attribution theory explains how people infer the motives and personality characteristics of others, self-perception theory is about how they know their *own* attitudes and beliefs.

According to Daryl Bem's self-perception theory, individuals come to "know" their attitudes, emotions, and other internal states, in part by observing their own behavior and the context in which they are acting. Whenever internal cues or feelings are ambiguous and difficult to label, the person is no better off than an outside observer, who must also rely on external evidence to make some judgment about that individual's private beliefs or emotions. Deprived of any access to their cognitive processes, people trying to figure out their attitudes on a particular subject will often use their actions as a guide to their inner states. This is particularly apt to be the case when they cannot think of a plausible external cause for them to behave as they do: "Gee, I must like whole-wheat bread. Nobody forces me to eat it every day for lunch."[42]

Bem argued that this self-inference of attitudes, not any desire to reduce cognitive dissonance, caused people to change their beliefs

[42] Daryl J. Bem, "Self-Perception Theory," in *Advances in Experimental Social Psychology*, ed. Leonard Berkowitz (New York: Academic Press, 1972), 6:1-61.

when they took personal responsibility for behaving contrary to their true convictions. For example, in the classic Festinger and Carlsmith experiment discussed previously, subjects paid twenty dollars for telling other students that a boring task was interesting and enjoyable need not conclude that they really liked the experiment; the money was sufficient to justify their lying. Subjects paid only one dollar, however, were in a different position. They found it difficult to view their behavior as externally directed, because the reward was so paltry. Therefore subjects concluded, "I just told someone that the experiment was interesting. I guess I must have liked it after all." In sum, subjects did not rationalize actions of which they were ashamed, but tried to reason what their attitudes must have been for them to behave as they did.[43]

As this suggests, self-perception theory radically revises the traditional concept of attitude. Daryl Bem challenges the idea that people have enduring attitudes that guide behavior. Instead, behavior leads to the development of attitudes by providing evidence of what we *really* believe. When presented with an opinion questionnaire, people construct their attitudes "off the top of the head" by recalling instances of their previous behavior, what they might have said in the past, or by copying their responses from other people. An attitude is not a predisposition to behave in a certain way, but a judgment constructed to answer the question, "What is your attitude?"

Numerous experiments have shown that people often do rely on extraneous external cues in inferring their attitudes, instead of consulting their internal feelings.[44] For example, Salancik and Conway affected students' judgments of their attitudes toward religion by subtly influencing what actions they recalled. The experimenters accomplished what would seem to be a difficult feat through using a simple linguistic manipulation. Salancik and Conway inserted the adverbs "on occasion" or "frequently" into statements of religious or antireligious

[43] Daryl J. Bem, "Self-Perception Theory," in *Cognitive Theories in Social Psychology: Papers from Advances in Experimental Social Psychology*, ed. Leonard Berkowitz (New York: Academic Press, 1978), pp. 226-27.

[44] See, for example, Richard J. Bandler, George R. Madaras, and Daryl J. Bem, "Self-observation as a Source of Pain Perception," *Journal of Personality and Social Psychology* 9 (1968): 201-209; Lee Ross, Judith Rodin, and Philip G. Zimbardo, "Toward an Attribution Therapy: the Reduction of Fear through Induced Cognitive-Emotional Arousal," *Journal of Personality and Social Psychology* 12 (1969): 279-88; Michael D. Storms and Richard E. Nisbett, "Insomnia and the Attribution Process," *Journal of Personality and Social Psychology* 16 (1970): 319-28; Stuart Valins, "Cognitive Effects of False Heart-rate Feedback," *Journal of Personality and Social Psychology* 4 (1966): 400-408.

behavior. They reasoned that people would be more likely to endorse sentences containing the words "on occasion" than "frequently." Half the students were induced to remember past actions that would suggest that they were religious. For example, these subjects were asked whether they had on occasion attended church or synagogue, on occasion refused to step on ants, on occasion refused to read books by atheist authors. The other half of the subjects were reminded of their lack of piety by asking whether they could endorse the same statements, qualified by the word frequently. When Salancik and Conway later asked the subjects to indicate how religious they were, students who had been tricked into remembering their religious actions reported more favorable attitudes toward religion than those who had been influenced to recall irreligious behavior.[45]

Not only do people frequently invent their attitudes at a moment's notice, but they often cannot even recall their previous position. Goethals and Reckman achieved a marvelous demonstration of this effect. Small groups of high-school students discussed school busing to achieve racial integration, an issue selected out of an opinion questionnaire they had filled out one to two weeks previously. A confederate was armed with persuasive arguments in favor of a position contrary to the consensus of the group, and his task was to change their attitudes using logic and facts. He was remarkably successful in altering the opinions of the group members. Immediately after the discussion, the subjects were tested on their new attitudes. After this form was collected, the experimenter gave them a second questionnaire including eight items from the original pretest. He explained that he was testing the accuracy of survey data, and asked them to duplicate their original positions as closely as possible. The experimenter emphasized that he would be checking on the accuracy of their recall by comparing their answers to the pretest. Control subjects remembered their previous attitudes clearly. In contrast, experimental subjects thought that their previous attitudes were consistent with their current beliefs. The original antibusing subjects recalled themselves to be more in favor of busing than they actually were, whereas those who had been in favor of busing actually thought that they had been opposed! Further, the high-school students behaved as if they were genuinely unaware that their attitudes had changed. When asked on the opinion questionnaire

---

[45] Gerald R. Salancik and Mary Conway, "Attitude Inferences from Salient and Relevant Cognitive Content about Behavior," *Journal of Personality and Social Psychology* 32 (1975): 829-40. See also J. R. Salancik, "Inference of One's Attitude from Behavior Recalled under Linguistically Manipulated Cognitive Sets," *Journal of Experimental Social Psychology* 10 (1974): 415-27.

what effect the discussion had on their attitudes, most reported that it had broadened their awareness of the issues or provided support for their original position. No student admitted that the discussion had any influence on his or her beliefs. Even more surprising, during debriefing, subjects continued to deny that anyone in the group had influenced them to change their attitudes, and some even asked to see the pretest.[46]

This is not to suggest that people are always in the position of an outside observer "looking in" when asked to describe their beliefs. People have some awareness of internal states such as pain, effort, fear, or sexual attraction. They know what a particular stimulus means to them personally, and the chain of associations it evokes. They also have knowledge of their past behavior in similar situations. Consequently, people do not always use their superficial behavior or other external information as evidence for their beliefs and attitudes. When pain or fear is sufficiently strong, the person will ignore physiological feedback or behavior which would imply that he feels differently.[47] For issues on which an individual has well-defined or strongly felt beliefs, he will not need external prompting to deduce his true sentiments.[48]

If beliefs are the epiphenomena of behavior, does that mean that a person's attitudes, thoughts, or opinions are readily separable from a scientific explanation of his actions? Do we need to waste any time on trying to infer an individual's inner states when situational variables give a much more parsimonious and efficient interpretation? Self-perception research has also demonstrated that once people are convinced that they acted on the basis of their beliefs, they are more likely to let their convictions guide their behavior in the future. Experimental research on the "foot-in-the-door" phenomenon illustrates how self-perception influences behavior as well as attitudes.

In a pioneering study, two experimenters went door to door and asked housewives to sign a petition urging their senators to support

[46] George R. Goethals and Richard F. Reckman, "The Perception of Consistency in Attitudes," *Journal of Experimental Social Psychology* 9 (1973): 491-501. For similar results, see Daryl J. Bem and H. Keith McConnell, "Testing the Self-Perception Explanation of Dissonance Phenomena: On the Salience of Premanipulation Attitudes," *Journal of Personality and Social Psychology* 14 (1970): 23-31; and D. R. Wixon and James D. Laird, "Awareness and Attitude Change in the Forced-Compliance Paradigm: The Importance of When," *Journal of Personality and Social Psychology* 34 (1976): 376-84.

[47] Bem, "Self-Perception Theory," in *Advances in Experimental Social Psychology*, 6:50-54; Schneider, Hastorf, and Ellsworth, *Person Perception*, p. 98.

[48] Shelly Chaiken and Mark Baldwin, "Affective-Cognitive Consistency and the Effect of Salient Behavioral Information on the Self-Perception of Attitudes," *Journal of Personality and Social Psychology* 41 (1981): 1-12.

legislation on safe driving. Most of the people contacted agreed to this modest request. Two weeks later, a different experimenter returned to each house and asked each homemaker if she would agree to place a large, ugly billboard promoting auto safety in her front yard. Another group of subjects who had not been approached previously was also presented with this unusual request. As any successful insurance salesman could predict, there was a substantial foot-in-the-door effect. Housewives who had agreed to the small request were much more likely to comply with the larger, more effortful favor several weeks later. The experimenters reasoned that the housewives had altered their self-image through participation in the experiment. Once they had agreed to sign the petition in favor of a good cause, the homemakers began to see themselves as concerned citizens, as political activists, as the kind of people who act on their beliefs, not shirk them. This new image shaped their response in an entirely different situation, when they were asked to put their opinions to a more onerous test.[49]

Although both attribution and self-perception theories depict the person as a reasonable problem-solver, there are important differences in the model of human nature at the center of each formulation. Both theories stress the individual's "need to know" and naive epistemology, but self-perception research assumes that people are passive and only rarely generate an explanation spontaneously for their own actions. The individual in self-perception theory is not at all introspective or concerned with discerning the reasons for his or her own actions. In contrast, the subject of attribution theory is actively engaged in testing hypotheses and forming theories about social relations and other people. In attribution theory, people do not take any statement about another person's dislikes or likes at face value; they attempt to infer intuitively the cause of the other's preferences.

The archrival of self-perception theory, of course, is cognitive dissonance. Both theories argue that attitude change follows from changes in behavior. But they make different assumptions about the mediating cognitive processes. Festinger argues that people change their attitudes because dissonance creates an unpleasant state of tension; Bem portrays the self-inference of attitudes as a "cool" cognitive process. Dissonance theorists contend that people try to *rationalize* their behavior; self-perception theorists counter that people construct attitudes as a means of *explaining* their own actions. One theory as-

[49] Jonathan L. Freedman and Scott C. Fraser, "Compliance without Pressure: The Foot-in-the-Door Technique," *Journal of Personality and Social Psychology* 4 (1966): 195-202; Seymour W. Uranowitz, "Helping and Self-Attributions: A Field Experiment," *Journal of Personality and Social Psychology* 31 (1975): 852-54.

sumes a need for a favorable self-image; the other a need for meaning.[50] In addition, whereas cognitive dissonance theory adopts the traditional view that attitudes are learned predispositions, self-perception theory regards attitudes as epiphenomena invented "off the top of the head," using whatever information happens to be available and obvious at the time. From the perspective of self-perception theory, the individual has no stable or well-defined beliefs.

Various attempts at constructing a "crucial" experiment capable of distinguishing between the two theories have failed to settle the controversy. Despite their different explanations of the process of attitude change, the predictions made by cognitive dissonance theory and self-perception theory are often identical. According to Bem and McConnell,

> It seems unlikely that a "crucial" experiment for discriminating between the two theories will ever be executed. At this juncture, each theory appears capable of claiming some territory not claimed by the other, and one's choice of theory in areas of overlap is diminishing to a matter of loyalty or aesthetics.[51]

One area not claimed by cognitive dissonance theory is attitude change brought about when a person's behavior is generally consistent with his or her previous attitude but more radical than one would predict, given the original belief. In one study, subjects were asked to argue against air pollution in front of strangers on a nearby street corner. Some subjects then heard a confederate remark, "I'll proselytize for auto safety because it is important to me" (belief-relevant condition) while others were told "I'll do it because this is a worthwhile experiment" (belief-irrelevant condition). Those subjects who were cued that their attitudes were responsible for their actions shifted to a more extreme position. These subjects would not have gone out on their own and preached to passers-by, regardless of how opposed they were to air pollution. But being induced to make a commitment led to a strengthening and polarization of their original beliefs.[52] In sum,

[50] McGuire, "The Development of Theory in Social Psychology," pp. 62-63.

[51] Bem and McConnell, "Testing the Self-Perception Explanation of Dissonance Phenomena," p. 30. Anthony Greenwald argues that because cognitive dissonance and self-perception theories lack accepted operational definitions relating theoretical concepts to research procedures, neither theory is falsifiable, and hence a "crucial test" is not possible. See "On the Inconclusivess of 'Curcial' Cognitive Tests of Dissonance versus Self-Perception Theories," in *Journal of Experimental Social Psychology* 11 (1975): 490-99.

[52] Charles A. Kiesler, Richard E. Nisbett, and Mark P. Zanna, "On Inferring One's Belief from One's Behavior," *Journal of Personality and Social Psychology* 11 (1969): 321-

whereas cognitive dissonance theory predicts attitude change only when an individual is persuaded to behave contrary to his beliefs, self-perception theory suggests that belief-consistent actions may also lead to a strengthening and reinforcement of attitudes when a person is forced to adopt a more extreme position than the original convictions would warrant.

Fazio et al. played the role of peacemaker and suggested that both theories are correct within their respective areas of application.[53] That is to say, they proposed that self-perception processes are found whenever a person's behavior is in line with but more extreme than his preferred position—that is, within his latitude of acceptance. On the other hand, dissonance theory explains attitude change that occurs when a person chooses to act contrary to his attitudes, without adequate justification. There is indirect experimental evidence that behaving opposite to their convictions makes people feel uncomfortable and upset when they cannot excuse their actions by blaming some external cause.[54]

Even more important for our purposes here, Fazio et al. suggest that self-perception theory is most likely to apply when a person's attitude is not yet fully crystallized or formed. They reason that people are more likely to infer their beliefs from their actions when they are tolerant of a broad range of opinions on an issue. Before an attitude is molded, the individual is likely to endorse any of a broad range of positions on an opinion questionnaire. On the other hand, once a person has taken a firm position on an issue, the range of acceptable

---

27; Michael S. Pallak and Randall R. Kleinhesselink, "Polarization of Attitudes: Belief Inference from Consonant Behavior," *Personality and Social Psychological Bulletin* 2 (1976): 55-62.

[53] Russell H. Fazio, Mark P. Zanna, and Joel Cooper, "Dissonance and Self-perception: An Integrative View of Each Theory's Proper Domain of Application," *Journal of Experimental Social Psychology* 13 (1977): 464-79. For a critique of the theoretical derivations of Fazio et al. and their experimental data, see David L. Ronis and Anthony G. Greenwald, "Dissonance Theory Revised Again: Comment on the Paper by Fazio, Zanna, and Cooper," *Journal of Experimental Social Psychology* 15 (1979): 62-69. Fazio, Zanna, and Cooper defend their formulation of dissonance and self-perception theories and research procedures in "On the Relationship of Data to Theory: A Reply to Ronis and Greenwald," *Journal of Experimental Social Psychology* 15 (1979): 70-76.

[54] Mark P. Zanna and Joel Cooper, "Dissonance and the Pill: An Attribution Approach to Studying the Arousal Properties of Dissonance," *Journal of Personality and Social Psychology* 29 (1974): 703-709; Charles A. Kiesler and Michael S. Pallak, "Arousal Properties of Dissonance Manipulations," *Psychological Bulletin* 83 (1976): 1014-25; E. Tory Higgins, Frederick Rhodewalt, and Mark P. Zanna, 'Dissonance Motivation: Its Nature, Persistence, and Reinstatement," *Journal of Experimental Social Psychology* 15 (1979): 16-34.

alternatives is correspondingly narrowed. Such a person would be likely to suffer cognitive dissonance if forced to adopt a position within his latitude of rejection, which would not be difficult given the rigidity of his beliefs. Fazio et al. conclude that "while self-perception seems applicable to the early stages of attitude development, dissonance theory may be most relevant to later stages when an individual is more certain of his feelings toward an attitude object."[55]

Applied to the origins of American Cold War policies, self-perception theory predicts that U.S. leaders accepted major premises of the Cold War belief system after the pressure of external events led them to adopt an anti-Soviet policy. Further, American leaders had not reached any firm conclusions about Soviet motivations before circumstances required them to adopt a clear-cut policy. Soviet behavior was ambiguous and volatile, and the cost of error could be the next generation's chances for an enduring peace. Self-perception theory predicts that Washington officials did not pursue a consistent policy to achieve well-defined ends, but responded to each Soviet overture, rebuff, or violation on its own merits, using the pattern of information available at the time. It was action that forced American leaders to reach cognitive closure, to resolve any remaining doubts about Soviet motives or the wisdom of alternative policies.

Self-perception and cognitive dissonance theories may be complementary in another way: they may apply to different people. People who are not aware of or sensitive to feelings or motives, including their own, would be more likely to be influenced by external cues in inferring their attitudes or beliefs. Extroverted persons who lack insight into their own motives and goals would also be prone to use their actions as a basis for judging their own opinions. Finally, people who lack an integrated, coherent belief structure would readily change their attitudes in response to events, since their cognitions lack any "anchor" in previous experience or related assumptions.[56]

Astute politicians such as Harry Truman and Jimmy Byrnes fit the profile of the type of individual most prone to self-inference of attitudes. Their career success depended on successfully molding their political opinions and personality to the expectations of voters and influential people. An elected politician generally has little time to acquire expertise on more than one or two issues; foreign policy questions typically win few votes at home. Consequently, the foreign policy po-

[55] Fazio, Zanna, and Cooper, "Dissonance and Self-Perception," p. 477.
[56] Bem and Funder, "Predicting More of the People More of the Time," pp. 485-501.

sitions of politicians fluctuate with the political winds and the shifting advice of staff members. Self-perception theory would lead us to expect Truman and Byrnes to be fickle in their stated opinions and attitudes toward the Soviet Union, and to shift policy abruptly with each change in advisers.

SCHEMA THEORY

Attribution theory treats only the rational, deliberative side of human beings. But in performing everyday mental tasks, people are not solely oriented toward accuracy. Sometimes they seek the reassurance and solidity found in familiar experience and consistent information. In addition, people often resort to shortcuts, ways of making inferences and judgments with minimum expenditure of thought and energy.

Research in cognitive psychology has demonstrated that human beings frequently make important decisions and judgments on the basis of sparse information, haphazardly combined. People simply do not have the time or capacity to follow more elaborate, systematic, or thorough decisionmaking procedures. Human cognitive capacities are finite; rationality is "bounded." Cognitive psychologists have found evidence for a long list of cognitive limitations, ranging from difficulties in assessing covariation and inability to integrate information, to biases in estimating probability. These errors represent "mental economics." Since human intellectual capabilities are limited, people must have some means of simplifying and sorting out the vast quantity of information impinging on them.[57]

Schema theory presents an image of the person as "categorizer" and "labeler," overwhelmed by sensations and information, trying to sort out what is important by developing a set of categories into which experiences can be conveniently classified.[58]

Evidence is beginning to accumulate that people do not always follow the quasi-scientific rules and procedures postulated by attribution theory when making inferences about their social milieu. Instead, they make "snap judgments" about other people on the basis of appearance,

---

[57] See, for example, Robyn M. Dawes, "Shallow Psychology," in *Cognition and Social Behavior*, ed. John S. Carroll and John W. Payne (Hillsdale, N.J.: Lawrence Erlbaum Associates, 1976); Paul Slovic, Baruch Fischhoff and Sarah Lichtenstein, "Behavioral Decision Theory," in *Annual Review of Psychology* 28 (1977): 1-39; Baruch Fischhoff, "Attribution Theory and Judgment under Uncertainty," in *New Directions in Attribution Research*, ed. John H. Harvey, William J. Ickes, and Robert F. Kidd (Hillsdale, N.J.: Lawrence Erlbaum Associates, 1976) 1:419-50.

[58] McGuire, "The Development of Theory in Social Psychology," p. 61.

context, or certain "tell-tale" actions.[59] It is not necessary to observe an individual behaving in a variety of situations or to estimate the causal weight of social norms. We all make such judgments about others quickly, automatically, and with little deliberation.

Psychological research on cognitive schemas explains how people make use of "diagnostic" information to form judgments about objects, people, and situations. Because people are limited in what information they can process, they must resort to stored knowledge or *cognitive schemas* to make some sense of the world around them. Researchers from three areas in psychology have converged on schemas as a central explanatory concept: cognitive psychologists studying concept formation and memory; artificial intelligence scholars and cognitive scientists trying to create machines capable of producing and comprehending language; and social psychologists studying "mindless" and routinized social interactions.

A schema is a generic concept stored in memory, referring to objects, situations, events, or people. It is a collection of knowledge related to a concept, not a dictionary definition; a schema describes what is usually the case, not necessarily true. Thus, the schema for bird includes variables for color, size, beak shape, and nesting patterns. As stored in memory, a schema has default values for all these variables, providing a prototype against which specific examples can be compared. The prototypical bird for most people is a robin; the typical fruit, an apple or orange.[60] A schema differs from an attitude because it has no affective significance or evaluative component; schemas are purely cognitive.[61]

Cognitive schemas serve important functions in memory and perception. First, schemas allow us to select what is important out of the flux of experience. The individual cannot possibly attend to all the information impinging on him. Schemas include hypotheses about the

[59] Schneider, Hastorf, and Ellsworth, *Person Perception*.

[60] Eleanor Rosch, "On the Internal Structure of Perceptual and Semantic Categories," in *Cognitive Development and the Acquisition of Language*, ed. Timothy E. Moore (New York: Academic Press, 1973); idem, "Cognitive Representations of Semantic Categories," *Journal of Experimental Psychology: General* 104 (1975): 192-233; idem, "Classification of Real-World Objects: Origin and Representations in Cognition," in *Thinking*, ed. P. N. Johnson-Laird and P. C. Wason (New York: Cambridge University Press, 1977).

[61] Shelley E. Taylor and Jennifer Crocker, "Schematic Bases of Social Information Processing," in *Social Cognition: The Ontario Symposium*, ed. E. Tory Higgins, C. Peter Herman, and Mark P. Zanna (Hillsdale, N.J.: Lawrence Erlbaum Associates, 1981), p. 125.

way the world works; these provide guidelines and selection criteria for processing information quickly and efficiently.

Second, a schema is an economical means of storing memories of objects and events. The individual stores a partial copy of a schema, not the full stimulus configuration. This facilitates recall because a simple, nonredundant memory structure is less susceptible to decay over time.

Third, schemas enable a person to go beyond the information given and make inferences about an object or situation. For example, if someone tells us that he went to a restaurant, the general knowledge contained in the restaurant schema would allow us to infer that he was presented with a menu, gave his order to the waiter or waitress, was presented with a check, and paid for the meal before leaving.

Fourth, schemas enable a person to envision and carry out a sequence of actions to achieve a particular goal. For example, a schema for making coffee includes a temporally ordered series of steps such as filling the coffeepot with water, putting coffee in the filter, turning on the coffeemaker switch, and so on. These event schemas may also include much more complex and long-term behavior sequences, such as the skills and achievements necessary to achieve a career promotion within five years.[62]

The organization of memory into schemas or prototypes has important implications for human understanding. Comprehension is a "matching" process. To understand the world, a person attempts to "match" what he is experiencing to past incidents stored in memory; in other words, he searches until he has found a schema that summarizes and categorizes one or more similar stimulus configurations in the past. This "matching" process requires analogical reasoning, since every stimulus configuration has unique features.[63]

[62] Terry Winograd, "A Framework for Understanding Discourse," in *Cognitive Processes in Comprehension*, ed. Marcel Adam Just and Patricia A. Carpenter (Hillsdale, N.J.: Lawrence Erlbaum Associates, 1977); David E. Rumelhart and Andrew Ortony, "The Representation of Knowledge in Memory," in *Schooling and the Acquisition of Knowledge*, ed. Richard C. Anders, Rand J. Spiro, and William Montague (Hillsdale, N.J.: Lawrence Erlbaum Associates, 1977); Nancy Cantor and Walter Mischel, "Traits as Prototypes: Effects on Recognition Memory," *Journal of Personality and Social Psychology* 35 (1977): 38-48; Daniel G. Bobrow and Donald A. Norman, "Some Principles of Memory Schemata," in *Representation and Understanding: Studies in Cognitive Science*, ed. Daniel G. Bobrow and Allan Collins (New York: Academic Press, 1975); Taylor and Crocker, "Schematic Bases of Social Information Processing," pp. 90-93, 112.

[63] Winograd, "A Framework for Understanding Discourse"; Andrew Ortony, Ralph E. Reynolds, and Judith A. Arter, "Metaphor: Theoretical and Empirical Research," *Psychological Bulletin* 135 (September 1978): 919-43; Bobrow and Norman, "Some

The attempt to fit ongoing experience into a priori patterns may introduce biases and distortion into our understanding of the world. Psychologists use the term "assimilation" to refer to the adaptation of incoming information to fit a preconceived schema. Vivid and memorable examples of this phenomenon can be found in the history of representational art. Thus, a sixteenth-century Dutch artist, trying to capture the unusual sight of a whale beached on the shore, painted a creature with ears and a head resembling a wild boar; the artist lacked a schema for whale. The comic situations that result from people's use of the wrong schema have fascinated playwrights for centuries. The "mistaken identity" device has been a much-used plot hinge from William Shakespeare's *Twelfth Night* to the more recent movie *La Cage Aux Folles*.[64]

Errors in memory retrieval may occur when use of a schema in conjuring up a past situation leads people to "remember" events or details that never occurred.[65] Truman's "missing ultimatum" in the Iranian crisis of March 1946 provides a good illustration of a schema-based memory intrusion. The Iranian crisis was precipitated by the Soviets' refusal to withdraw their troops from northern Iran, as they had agreed to do by treaty. Secretary of State Byrnes sent two diplomatic notes protesting the illegal retention of Russian troops in Iran. The Soviet government did not bother to reply to either note. On April 15, the Soviets announced that they would be withdrawing their troops within six weeks, and that an Iranian-Soviet oil company would be established, with majority Soviet ownership. Byrnes commented privately that the Soviets' withdrawal was the payoff for an Iranian oil concession. Several years later in both his memoirs and a press conference, Truman claimed to have sent an ultimatum to the Soviets demanding that they pull out of Iran. As an influential State Department expert on Iran, George Allen, later commented, Truman's memory "played him false." There was no ultimatum. The information within Truman's memory was assimilated to, and made consistent with, the

---

Principles of Memory Schemata"; Rumelhart and Ortony, "Representation of Knowledge," p. 120; Schneider, Hastorf, and Ellsworth, *Person Perception*, pp. 251, 267.

[64] E. H. Gombrich, *Art and Illusion* (Princeton: Princeton University Press, 1969); Winograd, "A Framework for Understanding Discourse"; Bobrow and Norman, "Some Principles of Memory Schemata," p. 145; Taylor and Crocker, "Schematic Bases of Social Information Processing," pp. 115-17. For a discussion of policymakers' propensity to assimilate even ambiguous information to their preexisting beliefs, see Jervis, *Perception and Misperception*, pp. 117-202.

[65] Taylor and Crocker, "Schematic Bases of Social Information Processing," pp. 104-105; Rumelhart and Ortony, "Representation of Knowledge," p. 117; Cantor and Mischel, "Traits as Prototypes."

cognitive schema he had derived from the incident: "getting tough" had contained Soviet aggression.[66]

Three types of schemas are relevant for explaining foreign policy-makers' perceptions of the world and their interpretation of ongoing events: scripts, metaphors, and personae.

Robert Abelson has formulated a theory of cognitive scripts that promises to have wide applicability in explaining social behavior.[67] A cognitive script is a stereotyped sequence of events characterizing a well-known situation. A script is composed of a chain of captioned scenes telling a story, and is roughly analogous to a cartoon strip. A simple form of script might consist of one scene setting up the situation (such as communists attack free-world nation) joined to another illustrating the outcome (United States intervenes to prevent communist takeover).

From this starting point, Abelson distinguishes two kinds of cognitive scripts. The most basic form of script is an *episodic* one, consisting of a sequence of events describing a single experience. For example, a policymaker may have stored in memory a "Munich" script, in which appeasement of Hitler is seen as leading to World War II.

After having undergone several similar experiences, the individual may generalize from the common features to form one *categorical* script. Thus, a policymaker may abstract from the concrete details of Munich and other seemingly similar incidents to form a more general categorical script: "appeasement only encourages aggressors to make more extreme demands."

According to Abelson, scripts mediate social behavior in two ways: the individual selects a particular script as the best representation of the situation; and he decides to take a participant role in the script. Similarly, scripts mediate foreign policy judgments by providing policymakers with a diagnosis of the background and underlying causes of emerging situations, and an indication of what actions must be taken to achieve national objectives. Scriptal processing is automatic, routine; it requires little or no conscious thought or planning. Foreign

---

[66] Paterson, *Soviet-American Confrontation*, pp. 179-82; Stettinius Calendar Notes, March 14, 1946, Edward R. Stettinius, Jr. Papers, University of Virginia.

[67] Robert P. Abelson, "Script Processing in Attitude Formation and Decision-making," in *Cognition and Social Behavior*, ed. Carroll and Payne, pp. 33-45; Roger C. Schank and Robert P. Abelson, *Scripts, Plans, Goals and Understanding: An Inquiry into Human Knowledge Structures* (Hillsdale, N.J.: Lawrence Erlbaum Associates, 1977). There are important parallels between Abelson's script theory and Jervis's discussion of how decisionmakers learn from history. See *Perception and Misperception*, pp. 217-82.

policymakers simply react as they have responded to similar situations in the past.

The second type of schema relevant to foreign policymaking is the "metaphor." Psychologists are rediscovering the importance of "metaphor" in human understanding. As discussed above, to understand the social milieu, a person tries to match what he is experiencing to a preconceived schema describing analogous situations in the past. When no schema adequately accounts for the incoming information, the individual's memory system selects the schema that best represents the situation. Sometimes the resemblance is only metaphorical. Still, a metaphor may help to make the unfamiliar intelligible and understandable. In science, metaphors or "models" have played a seminal role in scientific discoveries by enabling scientists to visualize and form hypotheses about the unknown. The use of the metaphor of a computer for the human mind, for example, has made modern cognitive psychology possible.[68]

The role played by metaphors in foreign policymaking is still unexplored. Nevertheless, governmental officials frequently invoke metaphors in public and private to describe and interpret events in international politics. Truman, for example, used metaphors from poker to analyze Soviet-American relations and make decisions on diplomatic strategy.

Nisbett and Ross have identified a third type of schema that often influences judgments about others—the "persona." Personae are cognitive structures representing the personality characteristics and typical behaviors of certain "stock characters." Most people have well-developed images of particular stereotypical characters—Archie Bunker, the Jewish mother, the hippie, "Flo" the truck-stop waitress, and so on. Personae may be highly idiosyncratic, the product of personal experience (Dr. Szell, the sadistic dentist) or shared within a culture (Shakespeare's Falstaff). When evoked, a persona influences judgments and expectations formed about the referent individual. Often people make inferences about the personality characteristics of casual acquaintances on the basis of their superficial resemblance to a persona.[69]

Similar thought processes may influence a policymaker's perception

[68] Rumelhart and Ortony, "Representation of Knowledge"; Bobrow and Norman, "Some Principles of Memory Schemata"; Robert J. Sternberg, *Intelligence, Information Processing and Analogical Reasoning: The Componential Analysis of Human Abilities* (Hillsdale, N.J.: Lawrence Erlbaum Associates, 1977); Richard Boyd, "Metaphor and Theory Change: What Is 'Metaphor' a Metaphor for?" in *Metaphor and Thought*, ed. Andrew Ortony (Cambridge: Cambridge University Press, 1979), p. 360.

[69] Nisbett and Ross, *Human Inference*, p. 35.

of a foreign leader. For example, Stalin reminded Truman of Boss Pendergast, his mentor in Jackson County politics. Since Stalin evoked the Pendergast persona, Truman assumed that the Russian dictator had at least one personality characteristic in common with the Missouri machine politician: he could be trusted to keep his word.[70]

In contrast to the Hovland approach, schema theory does not depict people as inert learners of the arguments and evidence presented in persuasive communications. Instead, information is made consistent with what the receiver already knows; the cognitive structure that the individual constructs, codes, and stores in memory may contain either less or more information than was actually presented in a message.[71]

Schema theory also presents a description of the way people process information that is dissimilar to that of attribution theory. Research on cognitive schemas indicates that people do not bother to estimate covariation, weigh the relative influence of potential causes, and formulate causal explanations. Instead, people understand and structure their milieu quickly and economically by reasoning analogically.

Applied to the origins of the Cold War, schema theory suggests that beliefs about the Soviet Union changed because American policymakers adopted new schemas. Washington officials did not try to generalize based on Soviet actions in many situations, consider the possible constraints placed by geographical location and domestic regime on Stalin's freedom of action, and formulate a logical interpretation of Soviet actions; they used facile metaphors and analogies. Schema theory would lead us to expect that a foreign policymaker's application of a favored analogy was not the product of a considered judgment about the degree of similarity between the objects, events, or people compared. Instead, one might predict that the metaphor was strained, the historical events only superficially parallel, the persona a stereotype.

Little is known about the conditions under which a schema is evoked. But one determinant of whether a particular schema will be applied is its cognitive "availability," or accessibility in the human mind. Events that are more recent, memorable, or easily imagined,

---

[70] Alfred Steinberg, *The Man from Missouri: The Life and Times of Harry S Truman* (New York: G. P. Putnam's Sons, 1962), p. 255; Ayers diary, August 7, 1945, Eben A. Ayers Papers, HSTL; Daniels interview, August 30, 1949, Jonathan Daniels Papers, HSTL.

[71] John D. Bransford, John R. Barclay, and J. Franks, "Sentence Memory: A Constructive versus Interpretive Approach," *Cognitive Psychology* 3 (1972): 193-209; Carl H. Frederickson, "Effects of Context-Induced Processing Operations on Semantic Information Acquired from Discourse," *Cognitive Psychology* 9 (1975): 139-66.

have greater cognitive availability.[72] Consequently, one would expect policymakers to be predisposed to perceive those aspects of a situation that superficially resemble recent, salient historical events, evoking episodic scripts.

Schema theory, then, suggests that U.S. policymakers' perceptions of the Soviet Union were unduly influenced by their efforts to apply the "lessons of history" to current problems. Diplomatic historian Ernest May argues that the containment policy cannot be explained without considering the "lessons" policymakers drew from the events of the thirties.[73] They believed that World War II had been made inevitable by the failure of the Western democracies to resist Hitler soon enough. Troubled by Soviet totalitarianism, U.S. officials were predisposed to see Soviet repression in Poland, Rumania, and Bulgaria as analogous to the Nazi invasion of Czechoslovakia and Austria. Other historians of the Cold War have agreed with May that the "Munich analogy" played an important role in the Truman administration's decision to contain the Soviet Union.[74] Had the "Munich script" been less salient to Washington officials, they would have realized that the Soviet Union's industrial and military capacity had been almost totally devastated by the Nazi onslaught and that the Soviets were incapable of starting World War III; they might also have understood the Soviet regime's almost paranoiac insistence on the guaranteed security of a buffer zone in Eastern Europe.

APPLYING SOCIAL PSYCHOLOGY TO HISTORY

Although anyone reasonably informed about American foreign policymaking can readily summon up illustrations of cognitive biases, working these theories into a valid historical explanation of a single case is considerably more complex. As stressed earlier, to account for the development of American Cold War policies, one must adopt a multilevel approach, considering factors such as the structure of the

[72] Amos Tversky and Daniel Kahneman, "Availability: A Heuristic for Judging Frequency and Probability," *Cognitive Psychology* 5 (1973): 207-32; Nisbett and Ross, *Human Inference*, pp. 36-37. Similarly, Jervis has presented evidence that foreign policymakers are most apt to "learn" from recent, major events such as a revolution or the last war. See *Perception and Misperception*, pp. 262-71.

[73] May, *"Lessons" of the Past*, pp. 19-51.

[74] Gaddis, *Origins of the Cold War*, p. 134; Paterson, *Soviet-American Confrontation*; idem, *On Every Front: The Making of the Cold War* (New York: W. W. Norton & Co., 1979), pp. 74-75; Bruce R. Kuniholm, *The Origins of the Cold War in the Near East: Great Power Conflict and Diplomacy in Iran, Turkey and Greece* (Princeton: Princeton University Press, 1980), pp. xix-xx.

international system after World War II and domestic politics within the United States, as well as individual policymakers' cognitive processes.

Once the United States and Soviet Union faced each other across the corpse of Europe, some form of rivalry or conflict was almost inevitable. But the emerging bipolar structure did not in itself preclude alternative forms that Soviet-American competition could have assumed—a romantic triangle for the favors of a united Germany, U.S. isolation from European political affairs, a limited adversary relationship, a gentleman's agreement dividing Europe into spheres of influence, or war.

Similarly, domestic public opinion constrained President Roosevelt from concluding an explicit spheres-of-influence agreement with Stalin and allowed him to establish an active internationalist course for the United States. But it is impossible to explain why American Cold War policies were conducted as if the competition with the Soviets were a zero-sum game unless one considers the influence of the Cold War belief system.

Once we move to the question of how Cold War attitudes were formed, we enter the disciplinary realm of social psychology. The lack of consensus about Soviet motives within the U.S. government and the range of interpretations American officials offered suggests that the cognitive processes of influential individuals helped determine which alternative relationship was finally chosen.

Social psychological theories are useful for explaining how American leaders interpreted, analyzed, and utilized information about Soviet actions. In addition, through use of psychological concepts and hypotheses, we can understand why foreign policymakers formulated and accepted the new premises about Soviet behavior contained in the Cold War belief system. To explain why the United States reoriented its policy from cooperation to containment of the Soviet Union, however, we must add causal factors from the international system and the domestic political environment. Thus theoretical hypotheses from the different levels of analysis are used complementarily to provide a more determinant, specified explanation of the adoption of American Cold War policies.

It is not my intention here to explain the origins of the "Cold War." Instead, I have chosen to focus on one-half of the strategic interaction between the United States and the Soviet Union—the "black box" on the American side.

I am not testing the validity of the alternative psychological theories; the psychological literature on which I have drawn has already been demonstrated through experiments. In an ex post facto case study such as this, it is impossible to control for extraneous factors that might affect a hypothesized relationship. Experimental controls can be imposed only in the laboratory. In short, this analysis of the origins of American Cold War policy is what Harry Eckstein and others have called a "disciplined-configurative" case study—that is, the explanation of a case that mobilizes existing theories. The type of explanation is "nomological" in Hempel's sense: the investigator tries to show that a given event could have been predicted with a high degree of probability by applying certain general laws to specified antecedent conditions.[75] A "disciplined-configurative" case study is theoretical only to the extent that existing theories are applicable to the problem which is to be explained. Further, the results of the case study cannot disprove or prove the validity of the theory.

Nevertheless, one can determine which theory best fits the evidence in this context. Therefore, I have tried to deduce from each theory what circumstances we could expect would lead American policymakers to adopt new attitudes toward the Soviet Union in the early postwar period, and which officials would be most likely to alter their beliefs first. In this way, we can determine which psychological theory best explains the formation of the Cold War belief system. In addition, applying psychological theories to a real-world context for which they were not designed and where extraneous factors cannot be controlled should provide some indication of whether social psychological hypotheses can be imported to explain foreign policymaking.

This book focuses on changes in the beliefs of four men who were particularly influential in shaping the redirection of American foreign policy from cooperation with the Soviet Union to containment from 1944 to 1947—Averell Harriman, Harry S Truman, James F. Byrnes, and Dean Acheson. Why choose these four men for intensive investigation? Suddenly catapulted into the presidency in the midst of war, Truman initially had to rely heavily on Roosevelt's advisers to provide the continuity in American foreign policy on which wartime allied relationships rested. And Harriman was most influential in interpreting FDR's foreign policy for Truman. Truman himself was conscious of his limited knowledge of foreign affairs, and did not hesitate to accept the advice of men who he recognized had greater expertise.

[75] Harry Eckstein, "Case Study and Theory in Political Science," in *Handbook of Political Science*, ed. Fred I. Greenstein and Nelson W. Polsby (Reading, Mass.: Addison-Wesley Publishing Co., 1975) 7:79-138; Sidney Verba, "Some Dilemmas in Comparative Research," *World Politics* 20 (1967): 111-27; Carl G. Hempel, *Aspects of Scientific Explanation and Other Essays in the Philosophy of Science* (New York: Free Press, 1965).

However, Truman insisted that his advisers keep him informed, and he reserved the final decision for himself. As secretary of state, James Byrnes insisted on maintaining an ostentatious and exaggerated independence from bureaucratic constraints. He presided over the postwar treatymaking that determined the shape of the postwar order. While Byrnes was away at various conferences, Dean Acheson was in control of the day-to-day operations of the State Department, which placed him in a strong position to influence U.S. policy. As Acheson himself observed, "one fact is clear to anyone with experience in government: the springs of policy bubble up, they do not trickle down."[76]

Historical documents were used as a basis for reconstructing what these men believed about Soviet aims and methods, the sources of Soviet policy, the relative utility of alternative ways of dealing with the Soviets, and the requirements of world order. To determine when and to what degree each man changed his beliefs about the Soviet Union, I applied qualitative content analysis techniques to the documentary evidence from the period 1944-1947.

Whenever possible, private or intragovernmental documents were used to infer beliefs. In public speeches, the source's communication goals and strategy intervene, affecting his choice of language and interfering with the analyst's efforts to discover his "true" beliefs, attitudes, or opinions. Therefore, one must use contextual clues to infer what purpose the subject was pursuing through language in that situation, and discount his words accordingly. In other words, one must consider *who* said *what* to *whom* and under *what circumstances* as a means of inferring *what goal* the speaker was trying to achieve.[77]

Ideally, only statements made by policymakers *at the time* should be used as a basis for inferring their beliefs. Experimental psychological research has demonstrated that people are unaware of the distorting effects exerted by "hindsight" on their thinking, and they are unable to reconstruct their state of mind before an event's occurrence.[78] Mem-

---

[76] Dean Acheson, *Present at the Creation: My Years in the State Department* (New York: W. W. Norton & Co., 1969), p. 266.

[77] Another way of compensating for the shortcomings of public statements as an index of beliefs is to use documentary evidence from as many different contexts as possible. If the individual was consistent in public and private in his statements about the Soviet Union, then they were probably an expression of his true convictions. If he was inconsistent, however, then the analyst must allow for the possibility that the subject was manipulating language to achieve extraneous ends.

[78] Baruch Fischhoff, "Hindsight ≠ Foresight: The Effect of Outcome Knowledge on Judgment under Uncertainty," *Journal of Experimental Psychology: Human Perception and Performance* 1 (1975): 288-99; Baruch Fischhoff and Ruth Beyth, " 'I Knew It Would Happen:' Remembered Probabilities of Once Future Things," *Organizational Behavior and Human Performance* 13 (1975): 1-16.

oirs and interviews are apt to exaggerate the logic and coherence of decisionmaking processes. What self-respecting policymaker would admit that he was influenced by a metaphor or the physical resemblance of a foreign leader to an old friend?[79] Reliance on retrospective sources does not allow the analyst to determine whether the reasons that policymakers give for decisions are rationalizations, as both cognitive dissonance and self-perception theory would suggest.

As Holsti points out, for documentary sources there is often the problem of determining authorship.[80] For example, cables to overseas embassies are usually drafted by lower-level State Department officials, then dispatched under the signature of the secretary of state. Policy memoranda frequently go through several drafts by committee before being sent to the president under the imprimatur of the secretary of state. Reliance solely on the published documents collected in the State Department's *Foreign Relations* series would not allow the analyst to infer whether the words of a memo were actually written by the nominal author. But the copies of the documents stored in the National Archives contain the hand-written initials of the author and, in addition, often have marginal notations. Therefore, in this study, whenever the authorship of a document was in doubt, I examined the original copy at the National Archives before using it as a basis for inferring someone's beliefs.

The use of historical documents to infer beliefs raises the standard methodological problems of establishing the reliability and validity of the measurement procedures used. Precautions must be taken against the danger that only features of content consistent with the investigator's hypotheses will be perceived as relevant and coded. To deal with the problem of reliability, I used two independent coders to test the objectivity of the coding categories and criteria for their application to historical documents. After several trials to fine-tune the coding scheme, we achieved an acceptable level of intercoder agreement.[81]

---

[79] This is one possible objection to Janice Stein and Raymond Tanter's finding that Israeli decisionmakers used "analytic" (modified rational choice) procedures for handling information during the 1967 war. Stein and Tanter relied solely on memoirs, interviews, and speeches to reconstruct the decision process. See *Rational Decision-Making*, p. 315 and passim.

[80] Ole R. Holsti, "Foreign Policy Formation Viewed Cognitively," in *Structure of Decision: The Cognitive Maps of Political Elites*, ed. Robert Axelrod (Princeton: Princeton University Press, 1976), p. 45.

[81] As part of their training, a graduate student in history, Andrew Rotter, and another in political science, Jim Conrad, pretested the categories on two different samples of ten documents each, selected from a list of ninety-three documents containing relevant thematic material. The ninety-three documents were carefully selected by the author from over 2,354 pages of unpublished archival material and the Foreign Relations series from

The effect of information about Soviet actions on each man's fundamental beliefs and assumptions is traced sequentially from 1944 to 1947. To analyze the degree and direction of change, the analytical categories used in content analysis were scaled from pre-Cold War to Cold War beliefs.

PROBLEMS OF INFERENCE AND EVIDENCE

Because the information processing framework used in this study is novel and somewhat unfamiliar, the logic of causal inference should be clarified. The use of cognitive psychological theories to explain foreign policymaking is in its infancy. Previous studies have analyzed decisionmaking, that is, the search for information and policy options, revision of estimates, evaluation of policy alternatives, value integration, and choice.[82] I have focused on the way policymakers interpreted information, and its effects on their preexisting beliefs. An information processing framework has become more compatible with the concepts and hypotheses used by social psychologists since the "cognitive revolution."

What does it mean to say that an individual's cognitive processes explained the way he interpreted information? How does one determine which psychological theory provided the best explanation of the manner in which he interpreted the evidence in that particular situation?

Using historical documents, I tried to determine what information policymakers were *exposed to*, *how they interpreted it*, and its *effect on their beliefs*. The procedure is diagrammed below:

incoming information about Soviet actions	$\longrightarrow$	policymakers' interpretation of the information	$\longrightarrow$	effect of the information on policymakers' preexisting beliefs

The logic is what Alexander George has called the process-tracing mode of causal inference for the single case. That is to say, not being

---

1944-1947. For the third trial, on which reliability calculations were made, a multistage sampling design was used. The documents were first divided into different types of content: diplomatic cables, official memoranda, personal letters, private memoranda, diaries, and official minutes. Then fifteen documents were randomly selected to form a representative sample. The coders had not been previously exposed to these documents. Applying my coding rules to this sample, the two independent coders and I obtained a composite reliability coefficient of .85.

[82] See, for example, Steinbruner, *Cybernetic Theory of Decision*; and Stein and Tanter, *Rational Decision-Making*.

satisfied to show that a policymaker's response was consistent with a psychological hypothesis, I have tried to trace the intervening steps or cause-and-effect links by which the independent variable, incoming information, influenced a policymaker's beliefs and ultimately the dependent variable, his choice of policy.[83]

To determine what information policymakers had available, I used only those documents—policy memoranda, Top Secret daily summaries of current events—that the subjects actually read.[84] I also used a variety of primary sources—diaries, minutes of discussions, intragovernmental memoranda, and letters—to infer policymakers' reaction to the information they received.[85] Did the incoming information have

---

[83] Alexander L. George, "The Causal Nexus between 'Operational Code' Beliefs and Decision-Making Behavior: Problems of Theory and Methodology," in *Psychological Models and International Politics*, ed. Lawrence Falkowski (Boulder, Colo.: Westview Press, 1979), pp. 95-124.

[84] For example, the president and the secretary of state are usually too busy to read the raw diplomatic cable traffic. The information about international events that is available in diplomatic cables, the news media, or intelligence reports is reduced and distorted as it proceeds through the lower levels of the bureaucracy up to national decisionmakers. By looking at memoranda from staff members and the daily Top Secret summaries of foreign policy developments, I was able to determine an important part of the information actually received by Truman about foreign policy developments. Of course, the president and secretary of state have many other sources of information— conversations with staff members, newspapers, magazines, the radio—to which the analyst is not privy and must therefore guess at. One way of doing this is by reading the *New York Times* and *Washington Post*. Often Truman, for example, referred to some Soviet act that was reported in the major newspapers that day. Although it is possible that the subjects could have been influenced by some piece of information which did not appear in any of the examined sources, it is unlikely that such an esoteric item could have escaped mention by *someone*. Occasionally, top foreign policy officials do read important diplomatic cables. In that case, their initials will appear on the State Department copy. Where there was written evidence that one of the subjects read a diplomatic cable or memorandum, it was used to reconstruct the world as it appeared to him at the time.

[85] For the most part, this was not self-report data, that is, reasons that U.S. officials gave for their actions. The historical documentation provided an "unobtrusive" measure of their initial reactions to events when they were not being observed by the public and had no reason to slant their language.

All archival evidence is not equally useful as a basis for making inferences about policymakers' information processing. Used carefully, diaries may provide valuable evidence not available elsewhere about a leader's beliefs and perceptions. The Truman Diary, only recently opened to scholars, provided a rich source of data about the president's interpretation of ongoing events. Diaries of staff members and friends of the subject also may reveal examples of his informal response to foreign policy developments. Particularly useful for this study were the diaries of Eben Ayers, Walter Brown, and Joseph Davies. Minutes of intragovernmental discussions—where accurately transcribed—may also be sources of evidence concerning policymakers' information processing. On the other hand, when trying to advocate a particular policy option, an official

any effect on the subjects' preexisting beliefs about the Soviet Union? Did their beliefs change or remain the same?

The next step involved comparing their reaction to events with the interpretation given by other officials who received the same information. Cognitive social psychological theories explain variations in the way policymakers processed the same information. If responsible officials reached similar conclusions about the import of Soviet actions, then the logic of the situation must have been compelling, and there is no need to invoke psychological variables. Unfortunately, direct evidence of how other people responded to an incident is often not available, because unless an official was personally involved he left no tracks of his thoughts in the form of memoranda. However, one can infer whether a particular event had any impact on other policymakers' convictions by tracing their beliefs over time, and observing whether there were any significant changes at the time of that specific incident. This is what I have done.

In addition, one can also show that a hypothetical rational observer would have reached a different conclusion given the evidence available at the time, if he had not been misled or deceived by intuitive cognitive processes. I performed a mental experiment. Would the subject have reacted in that fashion if he had not used a particular schema or processed the information in a certain way? If a subject's interpretation of an event was disproportionate to, or incongruent with the information available to him, then his preexisting beliefs or cognitive processes probably were important in explaining his reaction. If a policymaker construed the facts much as anyone else would have, then psychological variables explain a trivial amount of his information processing.

If individual cognitive processes were indeed important in a particular instance, I had to select from among several possible theoretical interpretations. The Hovland approach is applicable when a foreign policymaker altered his beliefs after reading a persuasive analysis of Soviet policy for reasons unrelated to the logic, quality, or cogency of the arguments—such as the author's trustworthiness and expertise, the message's moderate discrepancy from the reader's position, or his own low self-esteem and persuasibility.

According to cognitive dissonance theory, if an individual did not change his beliefs, even when presented with logically compelling, contradictory evidence, then he must have distorted the information to maintain internal consistency among his beliefs. Or, if the person

---

may not reveal private doubts, reservations, or opposing arguments. Official policy memoranda—often dull, lifeless, written in bureaucratese—may not be at all representative of naturalistic information processing. By using multiple primary sources, the analyst can counterbalance and compensate for the deficiencies of each type of evidence.

did change his beliefs, then cognitive dissonance theory is relevant when a policymaker was forced by situational or political pressures to act contrary to strongly held, consistent beliefs, without adequate justification and in spite of his fear of negative consequences.

Attribution theory is germane when a policymaker conscientiously tried to put together whatever information was available to form an explanation of Soviet actions or make an inference about their motives. Nevertheless, even the best-intentioned policymaker will deviate in his explanations or predictions from those that would be offered by a hypothetical rational observer because of certain biases inherent to intuitive thinking—the tendency to overestimate the weight of personality dispositions relative to situational factors, susceptibility to vivid information or personal experience, or failure to consider the implications of a nonevent.

Self-perception theory is applicable when a policymaker had no well-defined, enduring, or consistent beliefs about the Soviets, but was forced to make a decision by the pressure of external events, such as a formal Soviet diplomatic proposal, the scheduling of a major foreign policy address, the need to obtain congressional appropriations. Through acting, he reached cognitive closure and developed supporting beliefs about Soviet policy. Self-perception theory also provides the best explanation when an individual was induced to take a more extreme or forceful position than his beliefs would have warranted, and subsequently adopted a more polarized position on the issue as a consequence of his actions.

Schema theory fits when a policymaker made a prediction or explanation by reasoning analogically to past situations, a metaphor, or the actions of a stereotypical character or personal acquaintance who resembled Soviet leaders.

The following narrative depicts the relative contributions of Harriman, Truman, Byrnes, and Acheson to the development of Cold War policies as their influence fluctuated. Thus, Ambassador Harriman was the "bridge" between the Roosevelt and Truman administrations, conveying to the new administration his interpretation of FDR's "grand design." Truman placed his individual stamp on U.S. policy toward the Soviet Union soon after he became president. In 1946, however, he often deferred to Byrnes' judgment, particularly in the Iranian crisis and policy toward German reunification. In late 1946, Acheson assumed a major role in developing U.S. policy toward the Mediterranean and Middle East, which culminated in his authorship of the Truman Doctrine in March 1947. Together, they helped to shape the Cold War consensus that has guided American foreign policy for a third of a century.

CHAPTER TWO

TAMING THE BEAR

EARLY IMPRESSIONS OF THE SOVIET UNION

As AMBASSADOR to Moscow from 1943 to 1946, Harriman could influence FDR's evolving policy toward the Soviet Union. President Roosevelt did not trust career diplomats in the State Department; he preferred to use personal envoys for important missions. FDR's reliance on the ambassador's judgments grew out of Harriman's active political support for the New Deal, social acquaintance, and in particular, their shared friendship with Harry Hopkins. Harriman's cables interpreting Soviet policies often went straight to the president, unfiltered through layers of the State Department or White House bureaucracy.

Further, Harriman's role as ambassador placed him in an ideal position to sway Harry S Truman after FDR's death. Harriman had formed strong opinions on U.S.-Soviet relations by the time Truman succeeded to the presidency, beliefs that were at odds with those of many other Washington officials at the end of World War II. His views were not those of an ideological hard-liner, but were based on practical experience with the Soviets in business as well as diplomacy over a span of nearly twenty-five years.

W. Averell Harriman was the eldest son of E. H. Harriman, famous Wall Street financier and railroad executive, who had personal assets valued at around $70 million. Harriman followed his father's example as an entrepreneur. His daring financial dealings with the Bolsheviks in the 1920s achieved front-page notoriety. In 1922, Harriman chose to disregard the commercial blockade imposed by Western nations on the Soviet Union and joined with representatives of the Hamburg-American Line and the Russians in forming a joint shipping company.[1]

In 1924, Harriman learned that the Bolsheviks were willing to allow foreigners to exploit the vast manganese deposits in the Caucasus. He

[1] Larry I. Bland, "W. Averell Harriman: Businessman and Diplomat, 1891-1945" (Ph.D. dissertation, University of Wisconsin, 1972), pp. 50-51.

aggressively bid for and received the rights to a concession located in Soviet Georgia.[2]

But Harriman's triumph was short-lived. World manganese prices plummeted in the mid-1920s. The costs of doing business in the Soviet Union exceeded Harriman's expectations—for example, rebuilding the mine's railroad and loading facilities and observing new Soviet labor laws that required concessionaires to provide social insurance, clothing, and housing for Soviet workers. Suddenly faced with a money-losing operation, in November 1926 Harriman journeyed to Moscow to persuade the Bolsheviks to modify the terms of the concession contract. He was courteously received by numerous high-ranking Soviet officials, including Trotsky. Though the Bolsheviks agreed to revise the contract in Harriman's favor, within a year the concession was again experiencing serious financial difficulties due to the enormous number of working hours consumed by the numerous visits and inspections of lower-level Soviet officials. To release himself from the concession arrangement, in August 1928 Harriman accepted $3,450,000 in Soviet bonds and agreed to lend Soviet mine operators $1,000,000 at 7 percent interest. Harriman concluded that the Russians were tough bargainers, and could be trusted to fulfill their financial commitments.[3]

Although he did not meet Stalin during his financial dealings of the 1920s, through his discussions with Soviet officials in Moscow Harriman formed an enduring impression of the Soviet leader. In the Yale alumni publication, Harriman reported that Russia was run by "a man known as Stalin. He is not a dictator in any sense of the word, as has been expressed, but he is a political boss in the sense of Charles Murphy of Tammany Hall."[4] The persona of "political boss" evoked a rich set of expectations. A political boss was pragmatic, someone who was not above making unprincipled political deals. He could be relied on to see that his share of the bargain was carried out, because unlike democratic politicians, he was not vulnerable to the whims of public opinion or the demands of subordinates.

Later, as ambassador to Moscow, Harriman persisted in the belief that any major difficulty in Soviet-American relations could be resolved through face-to-face discussions with Stalin. A neophyte in Russian studies, Harriman was highly susceptible to analogies drawn from the familiar. In contrast, his minister counselor at the U.S. em-

[2] Ibid., pp. 55-57.

[3] Ibid., pp. 62-69; W. Averell Harriman and Elie Abel, *Special Envoy to Churchill and Stalin, 1941-1946* (New York: Random House, 1975), pp. 48, 51.

[4] Bland, "W. Averell Harriman," p. 66.

bassy in Moscow, George F. Kennan, persistently argued against the notion that personal relationships between Western and Soviet leaders had any effect on official Russian policies.[5] Because Truman shared Harriman's confidence in the effectiveness of personal contact as a way of resolving disputes, it is not surprising that Harriman influenced Truman's unformed views, whereas Kennan did not.

Harriman's rise to influence in the foreign policymaking process began with his support for FDR in the 1932 election. Unlike other members of the Eastern plutocracy, he campaigned hard for Roosevelt and supported increased governmental regulation and reform of the American economy. It was his friendship with Harry Hopkins, the former social worker from Iowa, that eventually gained him entry into Roosevelt's circle of trusted advisers and "trouble-shooters."[6]

In 1941, Harriman was sent to London as Roosevelt's personal representative, in direct communication with the White House, to oversee and expedite the flow of lend-lease aid to Britain. When Russia entered the war against Germany, Harriman was dispatched to Moscow for about a week to negotiate the first lend-lease agreement.[7]

Harriman's experience negotiating the first Soviet lend-lease protocol convinced him of the value of face-to-face discussions with Stalin for resolving disagreements and obtaining Soviet cooperation. In a report to the president on his conversations with Stalin, Harriman commented:

> I left feeling that he had been frank with us and if we came through as had been promised and *if personal relations were retained with Stalin*, the suspicion that has existed between the Soviet Government and our two governments might well be eradicated.
>
> There can be no doubt that Stalin is the only man to deal with in foreign affairs. Dealing with others . . . was almost a waste of time.[8]

In October 1943, Roosevelt appointed Harriman ambassador to the Soviet Union. The assignment was a measure of the president's grow-

[5] See, for example, U.S. Department of State, *Foreign Relations of the United States: Diplomatic Papers, 1945*, Vol. V: *Europe* (Washington, D.C.: U.S. Government Printing Office, 1967), pp. 812-13, 858-59 (hereafter cited as *FR* followed by the appropriate year and volume or other special designation).

[6] Bland, "W. Averell Harriman," pp. 79, 81-82, 93-101; Henry Brandon, "Very Much the Ambassador at Large," *New York Times Magazine*, March 5, 1967, p. 115; Charles J. V. Murphy, "W. Averell Harriman," *Life*, December 30, 1946, pp. 62-63.

[7] Bland, "W. Averell Harriman," pp. 102-103, 110-11, 126-27; Harriman and Abel, *Special Envoy*, pp. 3-4, 76-77.

[8] Robert Sherwood, *Roosevelt and Hopkins: An Intimate History* (New York: Harper & Bros., 1948), p. 391, emphasis added.

ing respect for Harriman's diplomatic acumen. When Roosevelt first mentioned the Moscow assignment to Harriman in the spring of 1943, relations with the Soviet Union were ominously cold due to the recent decision by Churchill and Roosevelt to postpone once again the long-awaited Anglo-American invasion of France. To impress Churchill and Roosevelt with his outrage at their betrayal of Soviet trust, Stalin withdrew his ambassadors from both Washington and London. As an added slap, he rejected FDR's request for a private meeting between the two of them. According to one observer, there was "an atmosphere alarmingly reminiscent of that which had preceded the Molotov-Ribbentrop Pact of August 1939, and the fears of a separate Russo-German armistice were revived."[9]

Harriman was puzzled by the insulting tone of Stalin's cables. But he agreed with FDR that Stalin's language was probably designed to satisfy his military advisers that he had made every effort to obtain the participation of Western armies in the battle against Hitler's main forces. Then too, Stalin was often crude. Despite the recent difficulties with Stalin, Harriman described himself as a "confirmed optimist" about our long-term relations with Russia. In a private letter to Roosevelt, he explained that

> Stalin wants, if obtainable, a firm understanding with you and America more than anything else—after the destruction of Hitler. He sees Russia's reconstruction and security more soundly based on it than on any alternative. He is a man of simple purposes and, although he may use devious means in attempting to accomplish them, he does not deviate from his long run objectives.[10]

Harriman was confident that he could collaborate with the Russian leader; he had successfully extracted agreements from Stalin in tough negotiating sessions for the Soviet lend-lease protocols in 1941 and 1942. "Stalin can be handled," Harriman told the outgoing Ambassador Standley.[11]

Harriman began his tenure as ambassador to Moscow as a firm advocate of Roosevelt's policy of Soviet-American cooperation. He be-

[9] Hull to FDR, June 9, 1943, Roosevelt Papers, PSF: "Russia," FDRL; Sherwood, *Roosevelt and Hopkins*, p. 734; McNeill, *America, Britain, and Russia*, pp. 277, 323-24. Vojtech Mastny, *Russia's Road to the Cold War: Diplomacy, Warfare, and the Politics of Communism, 1941-1945* (New York: Columbia University Press, 1979), pp. 79-80.

[10] W. Averell Harriman to Franklin D. Roosevelt, July 5, 1943, Harry L. Hopkins Papers, "Harriman, W. Averell," FDRL.

[11] Ibid.; William H. Standley and Arthur A. Ageton, *Admiral Ambassador to Russia* (Chicago: Henry Regnery, 1955), p. 490.

lieved that the wartime military alliance could be nurtured into a wider collaboration to preserve the peace in the postwar period, and that difficulties could be resolved through face-to-face negotiations. Further, his personal business dealings with the Russians and the lend-lease negotiations had given him a healthy respect for Soviet negotiating skills and faith in their observance of economic commitments.

Harriman's position as liaison between Roosevelt and Stalin was critical, because U.S. policymakers attached great importance to cultivating a lasting cooperative relationship with the Soviets. Franklin D. Roosevelt's ambitious "grand design" for the postwar world order rested on the premise that Russia would be willing to undertake a constructive role in world affairs and to collaborate with the West in maintaining world peace.

As ambassador, Harriman was responsible for interpreting Soviet motivations for the president and State Department. Unlike Truman and Byrnes, he did not have the luxury of casually entertaining ideas, or changing his mind from one moment to another. Since his role required that he commit himself to a position, Harriman could not easily slough off any inconsistency between his preexisting beliefs and Soviet actions. He should have experienced cognitive dissonance when the Soviets did not live up to his optimistic expectatations about great-power collaboration in solving postwar political problems, and would therefore be under psychic pressure to distort and reinterpret the information to maintain a favorable image of the Soviet Union.

In contrast, attribution theory suggests that Harriman would be open and receptive to evidence that the Soviets were pursuing a unilateral policy in Eastern Europe to achieve their security interests. Harriman should have been motivated by no other concern than to provide the best possible explanation of Soviet behavior. In addition, the theory would suggest that Harriman would be among the first to adopt more hard-line views of the Soviet Union, because, unlike Washington officials, he was faced with the difficult job of negotiating face to face with the Russian Foreign Office. If concrete, personal experience is formative, then Harriman's inability to get the Russians to accept Western values of democracy in countries occupied by the Red Army should have been sufficient to impress him with the elusiveness of any permanent collaboration between the great powers. Further, according to attribution theory, Harriman should have been inclined to blame disagreeable Soviet acts on their national character.

For different reasons, self-perception theory also suggests that Harriman would soon revise his favorable image of the Soviets' desire for collaboration with the West. Once he found himself arguing with

Molotov on various postwar issues, Harriman should have concluded that he did not like the Russians so well after all. Contrary to cognitive dissonance theory, a self-perception interpretation suggests that Harriman could easily maintain contradictory beliefs about the Soviet Union simultaneously. Harriman should have been influenced by the most recent and salient evidence of Soviet intentions, and American relations with the Soviets during the war were on a roller coaster course.

Finally, according to schema theory, Harriman should have been prone to compare Soviet actions in Eastern Europe with Hitler's expansionist policies in the same region. In addition, schema theory would lead us to expect Harriman to base his analysis of Soviet foreign policy on metaphors and analogies drawn from his life in the United States.

ROOSEVELT'S GRAND DESIGN

Roosevelt believed as Harriman did that cooperation between the United States and the Soviet Union was feasible after, as well as during, the war. Unlike Harriman's inchoate ideas about the form it would take, Roosevelt's analysis of postwar Soviet-American collaboration was richly detailed and global in conception.

Roosevelt's design for a new, more harmonious international system was derived in part from his interpretation of the "lessons of the past." He was convinced that previous attempts by statesmen to ignore the requirements of international *Realpolitik* had been not only futile but disastrous. Woodrow Wilson's well-intentioned but misguided efforts to eliminate considerations of power politics at Versailles, for example, had contributed directly to the current world conflagration. Roosevelt was determined not to repeat Wilson's mistakes. This time the postwar settlement must be based on existing power relationships, not noble aspirations.[12]

The problem of designing a world order had challenged Roosevelt for more than two decades. A supporter of the League of Nations during the 1920 vice-presidential campaign, FDR viewed the international organization not as a panacea but as a device to institutionalize sustained American participation in world affairs. Following the Senate's rejection of membership in the League, Roosevelt urged that

[12] For an incisive discussion of Roosevelt's attempts to adjust his grand design to both international power realities and domestic political constraints, see Alexander George, "Domestic Constraints on Regime Change in U.S. Foreign Policy," pp. 233-59.

the United States cooperate with the international organization's efforts to preserve the peace. But during the 1932 presidential campaign, under pressure from William Randolph Hearst, Roosevelt repudiated his earlier support for the League of Nations because it was concerned with "strictly European national difficulties" of no interest to the United States.[13]

Though the timing of his public rejection of the League was politically motivated, Roosevelt had gradually become disillusioned with the organization during the 1920s. Complaining that the League had become "nothing more than a debating society," Roosevelt believed that keeping the peace required prompt and effective use of force.[14]

Instead of attempting to set up another world organization, Roosevelt believed that the United States, Russia, Britain, and China should police the peace after the war. All other nations should be forced to disarm. The Four Policemen could quash aggressor nations through economic blockade and aerial bombardment of selected cities. In this way, Roosevelt could sidestep the traditional American reluctance to send troops overseas. FDR was willing to concede that a world organization might someday assume the security responsibilities of the Big Four, but only in the distant, unforeseeable future.[15]

The Four Policemen would not restrict their collaboration to handling immediate threats to the peace, but would consult together frequently during the war to reach a common solution to territorial and political issues, and afterwards as a continuing peace conference.[16]

[13] Robert Dallek, *Franklin D. Roosevelt and American Foreign Policy, 1932-1945* (New York: Oxford University Press, 1979), pp. 11-15, 18-19; Robert A. Divine, *Roosevelt and World War II* (Baltimore: Johns Hopkins University Press, 1969), pp. 52-55.

[14] In 1941, Roosevelt wrote in a private memorandum: "in the present world confusion, it is not thought advisable at this time to reconstitute a League of Nations which, because of its size, makes for disagreement and inaction." In 1942, he told Molotov that he "could not visualize another League of Nations with 100 different signatories; there were simply too many nations to satisfy, hence it was a failure and would be a failure." Sumner Welles, "Two Roosevelt Decisions," in *Causes and Consequences of World War II*, ed. Robert A. Divine (Chicago: Quadrangle Books, 1969), p. 155; memorandum for Myron C. Taylor, September 1, 1941, Roosevelt Papers, PSF: "Italy, 1941"; *FR: 1941*, III, p. 472.

[15] Elliott Roosevelt, ed., *F.D.R.: His Personal Letters, 1928-1945* (New York: Duell, Sloan and Pearce, 1950), 2:1372; *FR: 1942*, III, pp. 568-69, 573-74, 580-85.

[16] He was influenced by the model of the Concert of Europe, established in Vienna in 1815, which had succeeded in preventing a general European war until Sarajevo. FDR gave the most coherent exposition of his grand design in interviews with Forrest Davis, in December 1942 and March 1944. Davis paraphrased Roosevelt's remarks in: "Roosevelt's World Blueprint," *Saturday Evening Post*, April 10, 1943, p. 20; "What Really Happened at Teheran," *Saturday Evening Post*, May 13, 1944, p. 12; "What

But domestic political pressure began to build for the creation of a new, more effective League of Nations. Internationalist groups had succeeded in arousing the guilt that most Americans felt for rejecting membership in the League.[17] During 1943 Roosevelt, too, gradually came to accept the State Department's plan for a world organization consisting of an executive council to handle security questions and a general assembly confined to discussion and debate. He was still primarily concerned with assuring continued American participation in world affairs. If the American people insisted on a new international organization as the vehicle for U.S. participation in world politics, Roosevelt was willing to go along, if the Big Four retained responsibility for enforcing the peace. In December 1943, Roosevelt asked Hull to submit a proposal for a new international organization, and in February 1944, he gave his approval to the State Department draft.[18]

Roosevelt was aware of the risks of assuming that the Soviets would be willing to submerge ideological differences and past grievances to collaborate with the West in restoring world order. He also knew that Russian ambitions had been greatly stimulated by the defeat of Hitler's armies. Roosevelt foresaw that Germany's unconditional surrender would leave a gaping power vacuum in the heart of Europe into which the Russian military juggernaut, flush with victory, could easily expand. Neither the United States nor Britain could permanently occupy the vacuum between the Russian border and the English Channel. Yet, historically, the U.S. national interest lay in preventing a single power from exercising control over the manpower and resources of the European continent. Unfortunately, the alternatives to Soviet-American

---

Really Happened at Teheran II," *Saturday Evening Post*, May 20, 1944, p. 20. Chip Bohlen told Oscar Cox that FDR had gone over Davis' article about Teheran several times before allowing it to be published. Cox diary, June 8, 1944, Oscar Cox Papers, FDRL. For additional evidence that the Davis article represented FDR's views, see Gaddis, *Origins of the Cold War*, p. 153n. On Roosevelt's preference for collective decisionmaking rather than unilateral action by the Great Powers, see George, "Domestic Constraints on Regime Change in U.S. Foreign Policy."

[17] Robert Divine, *Second Chance: The Triumph of Internationalism in America during World War II* (New York: Atheneum, 1971), p. 134; Harley Notter, *Postwar Foreign Policy Preparation, 1939-1945* (Washington, D.C.: U.S. Government Printing Office, 1949), p. 102.

[18] Dallek, *Roosevelt and American Foreign Policy*, p. 508; Divine, *Second Chance*, pp. 114, 141, 144, 184-85; Ruth B. Russell, assisted by Jeanette E. Muther, *A History of the United Nations Charter: The Role of the United States 1940-1945* (Washington, D.C.: Brookings Institution, 1958), pp. 154, 155, 221; Sumner Welles, *Where Are We Heading?* (New York: Harper & Bros., 1946), p. 5.

collaboration were either impossible to achieve or likely to have disastrous consequences.[19]

Conceivably, Roosevelt could have tried to negotiate a surrender with Germany that would leave that country able to check Russian ambitions. But there was a grave danger that the Soviets would negotiate a separate peace with Berlin *first*, since their forces were engaging the bulk of Hitler's armies. In addition, American public opinion was aroused by wartime propaganda depicting Germany and Japan as aggressor nations who must be disarmed and kept permanently under heel. Judging by the public outcry over the North African cease-fire negotiated with Admiral Darlan, vice-premier of Vichy France, the American people would not have tolerated a negotiated peace with the "outlaw" nation of Germany.[20]

Another possible solution to the problem posed by the Central European power vacuum might have been to negotiate a "gentleman's agreement" with Stalin, explicitly dividing Europe into U.S. and Soviet spheres of influence. What made this alternative impossible, in Roosevelt's thinking, was the American public's traditional aversion to involvement in internal European political affairs. At the Teheran Conference in December 1943, Roosevelt frankly admitted to Stalin that he doubted whether Congress would approve the dispatch of American troops to Europe after the war. A year later, at a private luncheon with Richard Law, the president "appeared to accept the possibility of a Europe completely disrupted by civil and social disturbances and spoke of United States withdrawal from Europe with a genial kind of fatalism which was somewhat depressing." Thus, in deference to public opinion, FDR wanted America's postwar occupation zone limited to northwest Germany, Norway, and Denmark, where there was greater political stability and less likelihood that the United States would "get roped into accepting any European sphere of influence."[21]

---

[19] Davis, "What Really Happened at Teheran," p. 37.

[20] Gaddis, *Origins of the Cold War*, pp. 8-10.

[21] In September 1944, when British Foreign Secretary Eden asked Roosevelt why he refused to allow American troops to be stationed in France after the war, the president remarked, "Anthony, frankly, because they smell . . . that is what the American people think. There is going to be a revolution there." Roosevelt thought that revolutions should be "quarantined." If people wanted to kill each other, he commented, that was an inevitable outcome of the war, and the best way for us to deal with it was to have nothing to do with it whatever. FDR said he was determined that American troops should not be mixed up with the French civil war. Divine, *Roosevelt and World War II*, pp. 63-64; Dallek, *Roosevelt and American Foreign Policy*, p. 433; Sherwood, *Roosevelt and Hopkins*, pp. 785-86; Stettinius Calendar Notes, September 21, 1944, Stettinius Papers, Box 242, University of Virginia; "Record of conversation between Mr. Richard

If an explicit spheres of influence agreement was not feasible because of American public opinion, Roosevelt might have opted for a de facto division of influence on the Continent, relying on the operation of a laissez faire, competitive, anomic balance of power system to curb Soviet ambitions. But Roosevelt feared that a world divided into rival armed blocs, maintained solely by an unsteady balance of power, would be highly unstable and forever teeter on the brink of war. Roosevelt foresaw the Cold War as a likely outcome should the U.S. and the Soviet Union fail to develop a working cooperative relationship. In Roosevelt's view, this unsteady balance of power carried too great a risk of a clash between the two great powers, a war that might destroy the world. This was unthinkable and unacceptable.[22]

The main obstacle to achieving Roosevelt's vision of postwar collaboration, as he saw it, was Soviet mistrust of the West. Roosevelt attributed occasional uncooperative or hostile-appearing Soviet actions to the suspicious Russian character, not situational exigencies or conflicting national interests. Roosevelt once observed privately that Stalin's activities as a member of a conspiratorial underground organization in Czarist Russia and his subsequent efforts at acquiring and maintaining supreme power in Communist Russia had made him abnormally suspicious and distrustful. In addition, Roosevelt recognized that previous Soviet experience in international politics—Allied intervention in the Russian civil war following the Bolshevik revolution and Hitler's surprise attack on his Russian ally in 1941—reinforced their distrust of the outside world.

FDR believed that the Russians' distrust of the outside world was a product of their experience, and could be overcome by maintaining a consistent posture of patience, generosity, and friendliness toward them. Specifically, by refraining from public criticism of Soviet actions, providing them with generous lend-lease aid, occasionally siding with Stalin against Churchill, and avoiding retaliatory actions when the Russians engaged in provocative behavior, Roosevelt hoped to convince the Soviets that America could be trusted. Once Soviet suspicions had been undermined, Roosevelt felt, as Harriman did, that he could persuade the Soviets that their security and legitimate foreign

---

Law and President Roosevelt on December 22, 1944," Earl Halifax to Foreign Office, December 29, 1944, AN 155/82/45, AN 155, FO 371/44595, PRO; "Record of conversation between Mr. Richard Law and President Roosevelt on December 22, 1944," Earl Halifax to Foreign Office, December 29, 1944, Top Secret, AN 154/82/45, AN 154, FO 371/44595, PRO.

[22] Davis, "What Really Happened at Teheran II," p. 48. For the analytical distinction between a cooperative and a competitive balance of power system, see George, "Domestic Constraints on Regime Change in U.S. Foreign Policy."

policy objectives could be most easily achieved through cooperation with the United States; thus, collaboration was in their own objective best interests.[23]

Roosevelt shared Harriman's opinion that the quickest and most effective way to break down Soviet suspicions would be to establish an intimate personal relationship with Stalin. If he could just have an opportunity to exert his powers of personal charm and persuasion on the Russian dictator, he was convinced that Stalin would be disarmed and his lasting friendship secured. Roosevelt felt he was better equipped to reach an understanding with Stalin than was Churchill, because the Russian leader was a realist, like himself. Churchill, on the other hand, was too idealistic. Roosevelt did not relax his efforts to arrange a face-to-face conference with the Russian leader until he succeeded in meeting Stalin at Teheran in November 1943, despite repeated rebuffs and postponements.[24]

Harriman enthusiastically supported Roosevelt's efforts to arrange a personal meeting with the Soviet leader, even going so far as to offer to go to Moscow himself should Davies' mission fail. But by 1943, Harriman disagreed with Roosevelt's policy of handling the Soviets with "kid gloves." Harriman thought that the United States should be "blunt and tough" with the Soviets. "When the fault lies with the Russians," he told Assistant Secretary Adolph Berle, "we ought to raise hell about it." "We are building up trouble for the future by allowing the Russians to kick us around," he warned Harry Hopkins.[25] There is no record of whether Harriman discussed his ideas about handling the Russians with the president before leaving for Moscow.

The "Spirit of Moscow and Teheran"

Harriman arrived at Moscow on October 18, 1943. He embarked on his diplomatic career with no academic training in the language, cul-

[23] Willard Range, *Franklin Roosevelt's World Order* (Athens: University of Georgia Press, 1949), pp. 183, 195; Welles, *Where Are We Heading?*, pp. 27-28; Davis, "What Really Happened at Teheran II," p. 48.

[24] Davis, "What Really Happened at Teheran," pp. 12-13; McNeill, *America, Britain, and Russia*, pp. 326-27; Range, *Roosevelt's World Order*, pp. 182-83; Cordell Hull, *Memoirs* (New York: Macmillan, 1948), 2:1249; Robert I. Gannon, *The Cardinal Spellman Story* (Garden City, N.Y.: Doubleday, 1962), p. 223; *FDR: His Personal Letters*, 2:1372.

[25] *FR: Teheran*, pp. 14-45; Harriman to Hopkins, March 12, 1943, Roosevelt Papers: Map Room File, "Hopkins Messages 1943, folder 2," FDRL; Beatrice Bishop Berle and Travis Beal Jacobs, eds., *Navigating the Rapids, 1918-1971: From the Papers of Adolph A. Berle* (New York: Harcourt Brace Jovanovich, 1973), p. 446; Harriman to Stettinius, April 16, 1943, Stettinius Papers, Box 151.

ture, or history of the country to which he was accredited. Since he had no specialized expertise in Soviet affairs, Harriman formed his impressions of Soviet aims on the basis of information acquired first-hand, through his face-to-face dealings with Soviet officials, not through tedious study of abstract ideological tracts or Russian history. As his interpreter Charles Bohlen recalled, "reading ideological books was not his forte." In several experiments, psychologist Nisbett and his colleagues have demonstrated that concrete, vivid information, par-ticularly data acquired through personal experience, has a far greater impact on social judgments and attitudes than abstract information of greater evidential value.[26] Similarly, the information he garnered from face-to-face discussions with foreign leaders and diplomats made a more lasting impression on Harriman than the more pallid, abstract information available in written analyses of Soviet foreign policy.

The successful outcome of the first Conference of Foreign Ministers, held in Moscow from October 18-30, 1943, reinforced Harriman's optimism about the prospects for postwar collaboration with the So-viet Union. Again, he based his judgments on the impressions he had acquired from observing Molotov during the discussions.

After the Moscow Conference, Harriman reiterated to Roosevelt his belief that the United States and the Soviet Union could continue to work together harmoniously in the postwar period. He recalled how Molotov had opened up, showing increasing pleasure at being ac-cepted as an equal in world councils, as he began to realize that the British and Americans had not previously settled all the issues between themselves.[27]

Harriman reported that the Soviets were determined to prevent the reestablishment of anything resembling the old "cordon sanitaire" in Eastern Europe, whereby the Western powers tried to contain Bolshe-vism by creating a belt of small countries hostile to the Soviet Union out of the remnants of the former Austro-Hungarian and Tsarist em-pires. Although they would keep us informed, the Soviets would take unilateral action if necessary to ensure that the governments of border states were "friendly" to the Soviet Union. Harriman was afraid that the Soviets might extend their political system into Eastern Europe if this proved to be the only way they could ensure that these govern-ments were not hostile. Still, the ambassador thought that the Soviets might temper their policy once they became more confident in their

---

[26] Charles E. Bohlen, *Witness to History, 1929-1969* (New York: W. W. Norton, 1973), p. 127; Kennan, *Memoirs*, pp. 243-46; Nisbett and Ross, *Human Inference*, pp. 49-50, 58-59.

[27] *FR: Cairo and Teheran*, p. 152.

ability to attain security through Big Three collaboration.[28] Although Harriman recognized Soviet security interests in neighboring areas, he hoped that it might be possible to devise a political solution which would not place the Eastern Europeans under the "iron heel" of a Soviet-style communist regime.

Harriman foresaw conflict with the Russians over Poland. "The problem of Poland is even tougher than we believed," he wrote. The Soviets regarded the present Polish government in London as unacceptable, and would establish diplomatic relations only with a government acknowledging that Polish foreign policy must center on friendship with the Soviet Union. On the other hand, Molotov had assured him that the Soviets wished Poland to be strong and independent, and that they would allow the Poles to establish whatever social and political system they wished.[29]

At this point, Harriman's assessment of the chances for postwar Soviet-American cooperation was qualified but positive. Although there were signs that the Soviets might try to communize Eastern Europe, Harriman believed that Soviet policy in the region was still evolving and amenable to influence.

For a short time, Harriman succumbed to the euphoria surrounding the first tripartite wartime summit conference held at Teheran from November 28 until December 1943. There FDR had his first opportunity to test his personal skills on the Soviet dictator.

To lay the basis for long-term cooperation, President Roosevelt did his best to accommodate Soviet security requirements. He told Stalin that he was aware that the Baltic states had originally been part of Russia. Roosevelt added with a smile that when Soviet armies reoccupied these areas, he did not intend to go to war with the Soviet Union. FDR assured Stalin that he agreed that the Soviet Union should receive part of eastern Poland; but because of the forthcoming elections, he could not participate in any frontier settlement just yet. There were six to seven million Polish-Americans in the United States, Roosevelt explained, and he did not wish to lose their votes. In this favorable atmosphere, Stalin asked what could be done for Russia in the Far East. FDR suggested that the Chinese would not object if the port of Dairen were internationalized, which would give Russia access to a warm-water port. FDR also proposed internationalizing the approaches to the Baltic Sea and the Kiel Canal. Churchill ended this discussion by saying that

[28] *FR: 1943*, III, pp. 591-92.
[29] Ibid.

it was important that the nations who would govern the world after the war . . . should be satisfied and have no territorial or other ambitions. If that question could be settled . . . he felt that the world might indeed remain at peace. . . . Hungry nations and ambitious nations are dangerous and he would like to see the leading nations of the world in the position of rich, happy men.[30]

Partly because the more contentious postwar issues were postponed or glossed over, the conference ended with an onrush of good feeling. At one of several banquets held to toast allied unity, FDR closed by saying, "So as we leave this historic gathering, we can see in the sky, for the first time, that traditional symbol of hope, the rainbow."[31]

POST-TEHERAN DISILLUSIONMENT

But as Harriman soon learned, official Soviet attitudes toward Britain and the United States could shift from smiling benevolence to bitter hostility with dizzying rapidity. In January 1944, less than a month after the Teheran Conference, *Pravda* launched a virulent attack against poor Wendell Willkie for a *New York Times Magazine* article in which he was mildly critical of Soviet aims in Eastern Europe. On January 17, 1944, *Pravda* followed up the attack on Willkie by publishing a dispatch from Cairo which charged that "two leading British personalities" had been discussing a separate peace with Ribbentrop.[32]

The sudden chill in the Soviet press was accompanied by a serious escalation in the Polish-Soviet dispute. On January 4, 1944, the Red Army crossed the 1939 Polish frontier; the Soviet government did not acknowledge, however, that Russian military forces had crossed the territorial limits of the Soviet Union. The Poles and the Soviets had quarreled over the title to these territories since the fifteenth century. Ownership had passed into Polish hands following the Polish invasion of the Soviet Union in 1920 and the treaty of Riga in 1921,[33] and

[30] *FR: Cairo and Teheran*, pp. 532-33, 553-54, 567, 594-95.

[31] Harriman and Abel, *Special Envoy*, p. 278.

[32] Ralph B. Levering, *American Opinion and the Russian Alliance, 1939-1945* (Chapel Hill: University of North Carolina Press, 1976), p. 149; Harriman to Secretary of State, January 6, 1944, Moscow Post Files, 800, RG 84, WNRC; "P.S. to Teheran," *Time*, January 24, 1944, p. 12; "Russia's Western Claims," *New Republic*, January 17, 1944, p. 72; McNeill, *America, Britain, and Russia*, p. 413; "The Bear's Way," *Time*, January 30, 1944, p. 34.

[33] Samuel L. Sharp, *Poland: White Eagle on a Red Field* (Cambridge: Harvard University Press, 1953), pp. 117-20, 122-23; W. W. Kulski, "The Lost Opportunity for Russian-Polish Friendship," *Foreign Affairs* 25 (July 1947): 676-77; Frederick L. Schu-

back into Soviet possession following the Nazi-Soviet pact of 1939. After Hitler's invasion of the Soviet Union in 1941, the Polish and Soviet governments were able to reestablish diplomatic relations only by agreeing to leave the question of frontiers open for settlement in the future.[34] Wartime cooperation between the London Poles and the Soviets ended abruptly after the Germans' announcement in 1943 of their discovery of a mass grave of 10,000 Polish officers, allegedly murdered by the Bolsheviks. When the London Poles demanded an independent investigation, Stalin angrily broke off relations, charging that his Polish allies were "striking a treacherous blow at the Soviet Union to help Hitler tyranny."[35]

When Soviet troops crossed the 1939 Polish frontier, the London government-in-exile immediately issued a public statement claiming the right to administer liberated territories as the legal and sovereign government of Poland. The Soviets charged that the London Polish government had claimed parts of the Ukraine and White Russia. But the Soviet statement also offered some hope for a negotiated settlement of the frontier issue. The Soviet government announced that it wished to see a strong and independent Poland created. Further, the Russians offered to redraw the 1939 boundaries so that districts of predominately Polish population could be incorporated into Poland, and the Poles were offered compensation in the West through annexation of German territories. Finally, the Soviets proposed an alliance of mutual assistance against the Germans.[36]

But the Poles were in what Eden described as a kind of "suicide mind." Though the Red Army was marching through Poland, the London Polish government proudly announced that they could not accept unilateral decisions or fait accompli on the frontier issue, and demanded British and American mediation of the dispute. Hull urged the Soviets to accept the Poles' offer to discuss outstanding questions, and tendered the "good offices" of the United States in arranging for resumption of diplomatic relations between the two governments. Molotov thanked Hull for the offer, but pointed out that the Soviets

---

man, "The Polish Frontier: A Test of the United Nations," *New Republic*, January 31, 1944, pp. 138-39.

[34] Kulski, "Lost Opportunity," pp. 672-75; Herz, *Beginnings of the Cold War* pp. 38-42; Feis, *Churchill, Roosevelt, Stalin*, pp. 29-32.

[35] Kulski, "Lost Opportunity," pp. 678-79; Herz, *Beginnings of the Cold War*, pp. 42-46; Stalin to Roosevelt, April 21, 1943, *Stalin's Correspondence*, 2: 60; *FR: 1943*, III, pp. 415, 420-21, 426-46.

[36] *FR: 1944*, III, pp. 1216-20.

could not deal with the present Polish government in London because it was composed of "fascist elements."[37]

At this impasse, Harriman argued that the United States should pressure Poland to eliminate anti-Soviet, reactionary members of the cabinet, as Stalin had demanded. He thought that the Soviets would recognize a government under the leadership of the current Prime Minister Mikolajczyk, if he would replace incorrigibly anti-Russian members with individuals who supported the Curzon Line and friendship with the Soviet Union. Harriman assured Hull that the Soviets sincerely wanted to see a strong and independent Poland emerge from the war—if it was friendly to the Soviet Union. He saw no evidence that the Soviets intended to impose a communist government on Poland. The Soviets would *never*, however, enter negotiations with the present London Polish government. Privately, Harriman thought that the Soviets' distrust of the Polish government was reasonable. The Polish cabinet was predominantly a group of aristocrats who wanted Britain and America to restore their landed properties and feudal privileges. They suffered from the delusion that the only future for Poland lay in having Britain and the United States fight Russia to protect Polish independence. If the London Polish government did not reach a modus vivendi with the Soviet Union soon, he believed, the Russians would set up their own committee of National Liberation as the government of Poland.[38]

But Hull was not receptive to Harriman's well-reasoned and sensible suggestions. He feared that the Russians' insistence on a hand-picked Polish government as a precondition for negotiations would be interpreted by American public opinion as a return to power politics and spheres of influence, thus jeopardizing public support for a new international organization.[39] President Roosevelt remained aloof from the Polish-Soviet dispute because of the forthcoming presidential elec-

---

[37] Ibid., pp. 1224, 1226, 1228-30.

[38] Harriman to Hull, January 22, 1944, 760C.61/2188, #214, General Records of the Department of State, Decimal File, RG 59, NA; Harriman to Hull, January 21, 1944, *FR: 1944*, III, pp. 1232-33; Memo of Mr. Harriman to Herbert Feis, February 24, 1954, Herbert Feis Papers, LC; "January 19, 1944," Feis Papers, Box 75.

[39] A State Department survey of editorial opinion found widespread concern that the Soviets' undiplomatic methods boded ill for the future of great power collaboration. The survey disclosed increasing support for Soviet territorial claims in eastern Poland, far exceeding endorsements of the Polish position. Yet most editorial writers believed that the Soviet Union should achieve its territorial aims through international agreement, not military force. Hull to Harriman, January 25, 1944, *FR: 1944*, III, pp. 1234-35; Office of Public Information, Department of State, "Public Attitudes on Foreign Policy, the Polish Russian Controversy," January 22, 1944, 760C.61/2197, RG 59, NA.

tions. Privately, however, he was sympathetic toward the Russian position and impatient with the concerns of the London Poles.[40]

On February 9, 1944, the State Department sent Harriman a cable expressing anxiety about the recent trend in Soviet actions, which suggested that the Russians intended to achieve their war aims in Eastern Europe through unilateral action, not consultation and collective decisionmaking with the United States and Britain.[41]

Because he had a more realistic understanding both of the agreements reached at Moscow and the Soviet interpretation of the amorphous concept of international cooperation, Harriman did not share Hull's concern. He believed that the basic aims of Soviet foreign policy had not changed since the Moscow and Teheran conferences. The Soviets had consistently stated in public and in private that the cordon sanitaire should be eliminated and "friendly" governments established in Eastern Europe. Harriman believed that the Soviets did not want to communize Poland or prevent it from having an independent life, and that their fear that certain elements in the Polish cabinet were hostile was certainly justified.[42]

THE FIRM BUT FRIENDLY QUID PRO QUO APPROACH

Though unconcerned by evidence that the Soviets would take matters into their own hands to ensure "friendly" governments in Eastern Europe, Harriman was worried that the Soviets would misinterpret lax and lenient treatment of them by the United States. Although much of Harriman's time and energy was consumed by discussions with the Soviets on the Polish problem, he was also involved in attempts to secure Soviet cooperation in various projects espoused by the U.S. military. When Harriman was appointed ambassador, a small mission

---

[40] During a relaxed weekend at Hyde Park, FDR complained to British Lieutenant Miles, "I am sick and tired of these people. The Polish Ambassador came to see me a while ago about this question." Here President Roosevelt mimicked the Ambassador. "Please Mr. President. . . ." FDR replied, "Do you expect us and Great Britain to declare war on Joe Stalin if they cross your previous frontier? Even if we wanted to, Russia can still field an army twice our combined strength, and we would just have no say in the matter at all." Furthermore, he thought that a fair plebiscite in those territories might just prove that the people would prefer to go back to Russia. "Yes, I really think those 1941 frontiers are as just as any." The president also objected to the Poles' protests over the Katyn massacre. "Another thing," he said, "the way these Poles fell for the graves question. Wow, what fools they were; I've no patience with them." Lt. Miles, "The President at Home," FO 371/38516, A 7/7/45, PRO.

[41] Hull to Harriman, February 9, 1944, *FR: 1944*, IV, pp. 824-26.

[42] Harriman to Hull, February 16, 1944, ibid., p. 822; Feis Notes, "Backwash from the Moscow and Teheran Conferences," February 9, 1944, Feis Papers, Box 52.

of military representatives charged with promoting Soviet-American military cooperation was set up under General John Deane and placed under the embassy's jurisdiction. His experience in negotiating with lower-level Soviet officials soon reinforced his preexisting belief that Roosevelt's policy of generous, unconditional aid should be abandoned and U.S.-Soviet relations placed on a strict quid pro quo basis.

Trading was the only language the Russians understood; once financial commitments had been made in Washington, the Russians felt themselves under no obligation to reciprocate. Harriman thought that the United States should retaliate by cutting off selected lend-lease shipments whenever the Soviets refused to cooperate on important issues. What disputes warranted sanctions Harriman did not say. His quid pro quo approach was a matter of tactics, not strategy.

Harriman believed that the Russians respected firmness, and regarded forbearance in the face of provocation as a sign of weakness. They were bluntly and brutally frank with us whenever they disapproved of our policies or actions, and they expected us to behave in the same manner. Consequently, we must be friendly and frank but *firm* in registering our objections whenever they violated our standards of international conduct. If we tried to win their good will by overlooking occasional improprieties and sharp practices, the Soviets would continue to "kick us around."[43]

As we have seen, Roosevelt sought to undermine Russian suspicions and to foster a lasting collaborative relationship with the Soviets through a policy of patience and magnanimity. Generous lend-lease aid played an important role in Roosevelt's strategy for altering Soviet attitudes and behavior. In administering the Soviet lend-lease program, concern for efficiency, prevention of waste, and short-term political advantage were subordinated to Roosevelt's overriding objective of winning Soviet friendship. To avoid alienating the Soviets by implying that we did not trust their word, U.S. officials were to refrain from asking the Soviets to furnish statistical information justifying their lend-lease requests, as the other allies were required to do. Roosevelt believed that "the only reason we stand so well with the Russians is that up to date we have kept our promises." Consequently, although lend-lease commitments to other countries were adjusted,

---

[43] Harriman and Abel, *Special Envoy*, p. 206; Harriman to Hopkins, March 14, 1943, Roosevelt Papers: Map Room File, "Hopkins Messages 1943, folder 2"; Berle diary, September 3, 1943, *Navigating the Rapids*, ed. Berle and Jacobs, p. 446; Harriman to Stettinius, April 16, 1943, Stettinius Papers, Box 151; Harriman to Hopkins, January 14, 1944, U.S. Military Mission to Moscow, Subject File, Oct. 1943-Oct. 1945, "Lend Lease," Records of the U.S. Military Mission to Moscow, RG 334, NA.

subject to availability of supplies and shipping, the annual Soviet lend-lease protocol listing the types and quantities of supplies to be delivered was to be regarded as engraved in stone by U.S. officials. Finally, Roosevelt stubbornly rejected all suggestions that he attach political conditions to Soviet lend-lease assistance. As Harriman announced to the American delegation at the Moscow Conference in 1941, U.S. policy was to "give and give and give, with no expectation of any return, with no thought of a quid pro quo."[44]

The cordiality and cooperativeness exhibited by Soviet officials at the Moscow and Teheran conferences seemed at first to demonstrate the value of Roosevelt's strategy for influencing Russian behavior. For example, the Soviets had agreed "in principle" to proposals advanced by the U.S. military mission for mutual exchange of weather information, improved signal communications, improved air transport between the Soviet Union and the West, and the establishment of air bases within the Soviet Union for the use of American bombers returning from missions over Germany. But by January 9, 1944, Harriman reported that he and Deane had gotten the "complete runaround" from Soviet officials whenever they tried to get action or even concrete discussions of these projects.[45]

To explode the bottleneck and ensure that this pattern of Soviet noncooperation did not carry over into our political relations as well, Harriman urged the use of a "firm but friendly" approach.[46]

Harriman also thought that U.S. relations should be placed on a more even, reciprocal basis and quid pro quo exacted in return for our lend-lease assistance, abandoning FDR's policy of unquestioning generosity. "You will recall that before I left Washington I requested, and you agreed, that the Military Mission should be consulted on decisions in connection with important requests for items not already approved," he wrote Harry Hopkins. "The purpose of my request was twofold and recent events have strengthened it," Harriman reminded Hopkins. First, the military situation had changed such that the Russians, as other allies, should furnish information that would allow us

[44] John M. Blum, ed., *From the Morgenthau Diaries* (Boston: Houghton Mifflin, 1967), vol. 3, *Years of War, 1941-1945*, pp. 81-82; George C. Herring, *Aid to Russia, 1941-1946: Strategy, Diplomacy, and the Origins of the Cold War* (New York: Columbia University Press, 1973), pp. 38-39, 40, 42; Standley and Ageton, *Admiral Ambassador*, p. 63; *FDR: His Personal Letters*, 2:1195.

[45] Harriman and Abel, *Special Envoy*, p. 250; John R. Deane, *The Strange Alliance: The Story of Our Efforts at Wartime Co-operation with Russia* (New York: Viking Press, 1947), pp. 19-21; Harriman to Hull, January 9, 1944, *FR: 1944*, IV, pp. 802-803; Moscow to War Dept., January 6, 1944, Hopkins Papers, "Harriman (Incoming Messages) 1943-1945."

[46] Harriman to Hull, January 9, 1944, *FR: 1944*, IV, pp. 802-803.

to judge whether their need for particular military equipment was greater than ours. Second, the Military Mission would be placed in a stronger bargaining position in obtaining cooperation from the Soviets. "Whenever I talk to Molotov on any matter that we request he immediately uses the word 'reciprocity,' " he complained. The Soviets were evidently under the impression that our lend-lease assistance was given in return for the Red Army offensive, and they did not feel obliged to be helpful to U.S. military forces in return. Harriman argued that "as you know, it is most distasteful to get a trading atmosphere into our negotiations over mutual assistance in the war, but trading seems to be the language they understand and we don't find them at all impressed by any obligation on their part to reciprocate after commitments have been made in Washington."

As a first step toward carrying out the new approach, Harriman recommended that the Moscow military mission be given authority to screen Soviet requests for lend-lease items in short supply. The mission could then delay taking action on Soviet requests for selected lend-lease items until they carried out various joint military projects, to teach the Soviets that they were expected to cooperate with the mission. Initiation of a screening procedure in Moscow would also prevent waste by forcing the Soviets to analyze their requirements more carefully. General Deane had discovered by accident that 102 naval diesel engines furnished by the United States under the lend-lease program were deteriorating from rust in open storage, when shortages of this engine threatened to delay the long-awaited Anglo-American invasion of France.[47]

The War Department and the Joint Chiefs of Staff approved the Harriman-Deane proposals with alacrity. But the Soviet Protocol Committee steadfastly resisted all efforts to modify the unconditional aid policy set down by Roosevelt. General Burns had always felt that if we were to improve our relations with the Russians, the United States must act in a "spirit of sincere friendship," without requesting any quid pro quo. Acting chairman General York warned the Joint Chiefs that any change in policy might destroy the fruits of the committee's patient efforts to win the Soviets' trust and friendship.[48]

[47] Harriman to Hopkins, January 14, 1944, U.S. Military Mission to Moscow, Subject File, Oct. 1943-Oct. 1943, "Lend Lease," RG 334, NA; Moscow to War Department, January 6, 1944, Hopkins Papers, "Harriman (Incoming Messages) 1943-1945"; Harriman to Hull, January 15, 1944, *FR: 1944*, IV, pp. 1039-40; Harriman to Hull, March 2, 1944, ibid., pp. 1057-58; Deane, *Strange Alliance*, pp. 96-98; "January 14, 1944," Feis Papers, Box 52.

[48] Admiral Leahy to the President, n.d., Subject: Policy as to Furnishing Items of

After extended discussions within the administration, Roosevelt overruled the Joint Chiefs and came down on the side of the Soviet Protocol Committee. As Roosevelt explained in a memo to Secretary of the Navy Frank Knox, the Moscow military mission had found only one example of overstocking; the evidence suggested that the Soviets had made every effort to confine their requests to reasonable levels.[49]

Adopting a "firm but friendly" approach, including the use of lend-lease as a political lever, probably would not have secured greater cooperation from the Soviets in furnishing data on their lend-lease needs or in carrying out joint military projects.

As Deane later conceded, the Soviets were simply "incapable of producing facts and figures that would justify any of their requests, because their administrative machinery was not geared to do so." The Soviet wartime bureaucratic apparatus was rudimentary: typewriters, filing systems, and mimeograph machines were almost nonexistent. The Russian wartime administrator had to carry a mass of detail around with him in his head. Deane reports that he and Harriman would have been willing to support Soviet requests based on nothing more than a "sob story."[50]

Soviet foot-dragging on projects of military collaboration was caused by a number of factors—long-standing Soviet suspicion of foreigners, insistence by the Soviets on the principle of reciprocity in all joint military operations, the high degree of centralization of authority in the Soviet bureaucracy—none of which would have been affected by a "tougher" U.S. negotiating stance or implied threats to withhold lend-lease assistance.

According to one Soviet expert, the almost pathological suspicion exhibited by the Soviets toward foreigners during the war was prompted by Stalin's recognition that after hostilities ended, the USSR would be exhausted and vulnerable to exploitation by hostile capitalist powers. Every U.S. proposal for military collaboration was carefully

Short Supply to the USSR, ABC 400.3295 Russia (19 Apr. 42), Sec. 2, Records of the War Department General and Special Staffs, RG 165, NA; Memorandum for Admiral Leahy from General York, January 21, 1944, Hopkins Papers, "USSR—Jan.-Feb.-Mar."; Herring, *Aid to Russia*, p. 130; Richard M. Leighton and Robert W. Coakley, *Global Logistics and Strategy, 1940-1943, United States Army in World War II: The War Department* (Washington, D.C.: Office of the Chief of Military History, 1969), p. 686.

[49] Memorandum for the Secretary of Navy from President Roosevelt, March 6, 1944, Roosevelt Papers, PSF: CF, "Lend-Lease Jan.-Mar. 1944," drafted by Gen. York; Herring, *Aid to Russia*, p. 130; Stettinius to Harriman, February 25, 1944, *FR: 1944*, IV, pp. 1055-56; Lubin to FDR, February 21, 1944, Roosevelt Papers, PSF: CF, "Lend-Lease Jan.-Mar. 44."

[50] Deane, *Strange Alliance*, pp. 98-99, 111, 203.

examined for ulterior motives, with the result that by the time approval was granted, the proposed project was ineffective.

In addition, the Soviet government was reluctant to allow the Russian people to be exposed to the higher living standards of the West. Thus, large U.S. military missions could not be permitted to enter the Soviet Union because the visual evidence they provided of the American way of life might arouse popular unrest. According to an official U.S. military historian, "why the Russians consented to the shuttle bombing project and allowed it to be set up remains one of the most intriguing questions of Soviet-American wartime relations." The shuttle bombing project involved stationing hundreds of U.S. servicemen on Soviet soil, while hundreds more swarmed in and out with each bombing mission. Previously, all foreigners had been granted entrance visas only after exhaustive background investigations by Soviet authorities, and they were placed under continuous surveillance during their stay in the Soviet Union. The Soviets had resisted all previous attempts by the allies to obtain permission for the entry of foreign servicemen on Russian soil. Even during the dark hours of the German siege on Stalingrad, the Soviets had refused the American offer to station a group of heavy bombers at Soviet bases in the Caucasus to assist in the defense of the city.[51]

Other delays stemmed from the Soviets' insistence on the principle of reciprocity in all joint military operations. For example, in response to the proposal submitted by Deane at Teheran for improvement of signal communications, the Soviets offered to allow Americans to operate a radio station in Moscow, if they were granted privileges in the United States. Unfortunately, foreign governments were prohibited by law from operating radio stations within the United States. The War Department proposed as an alternative that teletype machines be established in each nation's capital for use of the other country. Soviet officials, ever suspicious of any arrangement that smacked of unequal status or foreign exploitation, were disgruntled at Washington's refusal of their original offer. Marshal Stalin had waived a similar legal prohibition against foreign radio stations in Moscow. Why could not President Roosevelt do the same?[52]

[51] Adam Ulam, *Expansion and Coexistence: Soviet Foreign Policy, 1917-73*, 2nd ed. (New York: Holt, Rinehart and Winston, 1974), pp. 326-27; Deane, *Strange Alliance*, pp. 112-14; Maurice Matloff, *Strategic Planning for Coalition Warfare: 1943-44, United States Army in World War II: The War Department* (Washington, D.C.: Department of the Army, 1959), pp. 284-85, 500; Summary Report by Commanding General John Deane, "The U.S. Military Mission to Moscow, October 18, 1943 to October 31, 1945," 336, Sec. VIII, History of the U.S. Military Mission to Moscow, RG 165, NA.

[52] Deane, *Strange Alliance*, pp. 66-68; Harriman to Roosevelt, March 12, 1944, *FR: 1944*, IV, p. 950.

Still other delays in carrying out joint military projects were caused by the high degree of centralization of authority in Soviet bureaucratic organization. United States proposals for coordinated military operations were subject to approval by the highest Soviet authority. Even after a decision was made to go ahead with a specific project, supporting decisions to implement the proposal again had to be cleared with the Foreign Office, causing additional delays. Due to the stringent security practices of the Kremlin, lower-level Soviet military officers were frequently unable to answer American requests for military intelligence or information on Soviet military equipment and operations.[53]

Harriman's policy prescriptions did not touch the complex underlying causes of the Soviet bureaucracy's failure to cooperate. Although firmness might have elicited a positive response from lower-level Soviet officials in a few areas—such as issuing visas or exchanging currency—a tougher negotiating stance, including the use of tacit threats to withhold lend-lease items, might have exacerbated underlying tensions in the U.S.-Soviet alliance without achieving any compensating improvement in the Soviets' willingness to provide information or to engage in joint military projects. Harriman's interpretation of the Soviet government's delay in carrying out military cooperation was distorted by his preexisting beliefs that the United States should "get tough" with the Soviets and demand an explicit quid pro quo in return for our economic assistance.

In considering possible ways to influence Soviet behavior, Harriman did not restrict himself to the potential uses of negative reinforcements; he thought that the Roosevelt administration should employ the "carrot" as well as the "stick." Harriman had long been a vigorous proponent of a postwar reconstruction credit to the Soviets. But to be effective in influencing Soviet behavior, he believed that such a credit must be cancelled whenever they misbehaved.[54]

In November 1943, Harriman advised Mikoyan that the American people were eager to assist Soviet reconstruction, and it might be possible to begin joint discussions concerning U.S. credits and financial assistance.[55] In late December 1943, Molotov, showing the "keenest

[53] Deane, *Strange Alliance*, p. 111; Richard C. Lukas, *Eagles East: The Army Air Forces and the Soviet Union, 1941-1945* (Tallahassee: Florida State University Press, 1970), p. 210; General John Deane, "The U.S. Military Mission to Moscow, Oct. 18, 1943 to Oct. 31, 1945," 336, Sec. VIII, RG 165, NA.

[54] Harriman to Hull, February 14, 1944, *FR: 1944*, IV, p. 1055.

[55] Harriman to Welles, November 4, 1943, *FR: 1943*, III, pp. 586-88; Memorandum of Conversation, November 5, 1943, ibid., p. 781.

interest," asked Harriman what might be done about a reconstruction credit. Although he pointed out that the United States could not fulfill very sizable requests for reconstruction-related items without interfering with war production, Harriman suggested that it might be a good idea for the Soviets to draw up detailed plans and specifications now so that Russian orders could be rushed into production as circumstances permitted, even as the war continued. Several weeks later, Commissar for Foreign Trade Mikoyan returned with a concrete proposal. Mikoyan suggested as an initial credit $1 billion at 2 or 3 percent interest to be repaid over a period of twenty-five to thirty years.[56]

Harriman urged Washington officials to draft a program for U.S. reconstruction assistance promptly so that he could begin preliminary discussions in Moscow. He thought that the initial credit should be small and expansible—something in the order of $500 million at 2 or 3 percent interest, repayable over twenty-five to thirty years. But the United States should retain firm control over the unexpended balance of the credit, and should be under no obligation to accept Soviet orders.[57]

Most Washington officials viewed a credit to the Soviets as a gesture of good will, proof of our determination to cooperate with the Soviets in the postwar period. Harriman disagreed with this strategy. "There are many undetermined questions in our relations with the Soviet Union," he warned, "and we should not, therefore, put ourselves in [a] position where this credit could be used for purposes incompatible with United States interest or unless our relations are developing satisfactorily in other directions." Instead of viewing U.S. assistance as a token of our good faith, Harriman conceived of the credit as a "carrot" to induce the Soviets to play the "international game" according to our rules. The terms of the loan agreement should allow us to cancel the unpaid balance if the Soviets failed to cooperate with American goals for the postwar international system.[58]

Harriman saw several advantages to be gained from negotiating a credit upon which the Russians could begin to draw now, before the

[56] Harriman to Hull, January 7, 1944, *FR: 1944*, IV, pp. 1032-33. Harriman to Hull, January 26, 1944, ibid., pp. 1040-41; Harriman to Hull, February 1, 1944, ibid., pp. 1041-42.

[57] Harriman to Hull, January 9, 1944, *FR: 1944*, IV, pp. 1036-37; Harriman to Hull, January 7, 1944, ibid., p. 1034.

[58] Harriman to Hull, January 9, 1944, ibid., p. 1037; Harriman to Hopkins, February 13, 1944, ibid., pp. 1052-53; Harriman to Hull, February 14, 1944, ibid., p. 1055; George Herring, *Aid to Russia*, p. 53; White to Morgenthau, "Proposed U.S. Loan to the U.S.S.R.," March 7, 1944, Harry Dexter White Papers, Princeton.

war ended. First, the credit would provide a legitimate means of fulfilling Soviet requests for industrial plant and other equipment that would require many months to produce and contribute relatively little to the war effort. Washington officials were at that time in a quandary over how to handle Soviet requests for $300 million worth of industrial equipment included in the third lend-lease protocol.[59]

Second, Soviet orders for manufactured goods and capital equipment would keep American factories operating at full capacity as wartime demand eased, and would prevent a sharp postwar surge in unemployment.

Third, economic assistance was one of the few practical means available for influencing Soviet international conduct. Stalin would have to offer the Russian people the prospect of speedy reconstruction of the Soviet economy if he wished to remain in power. Consequently, a reconstruction credit offered now, but always within our power to suspend, would be of "extreme value" in persuading the Soviets to cooperate on our terms. Harriman argued that "economic assistance is one of the most effective weapons at our disposal to influence European political events in the direction we desire and to avoid the development of a sphere of influence of the Soviet Union over Eastern Europe and the Balkans."[60] However, at that same time Harriman was urging that the United States put pressure on the London Poles to come to terms with the Soviet Union and reconstruct their cabinet to the Soviets' liking. Although Harriman used the term "sphere of influence," he probably meant the extension of their political system to Eastern Europe, since he accepted the Soviets' right to have governments "friendly" to them in neighboring countries.

Secretary Hull found Harriman's arguments persuasive. Unfortunately, the administration could not grant the Soviets a credit for postwar reconstruction without congressional authorization. Hull informed Harriman that an interdepartmental committee had been formed to study possible methods of financing immediate Soviet-American trade as well as long-term reconstruction credits.[61]

Meanwhile, officials at the Foreign Economic Administration had

[59] Harriman to Hull, January 9, 1944, *FR: 1944*, IV, p. 1035; Harriman to Hopkins, February 9, 1944, ibid., p. 1050.

[60] Harriman to Hull, January 7, 1944, ibid., p. 1034; Harriman to Hull, January 9, 1944, ibid., p. 1035; Harriman to Hull, March 13, 1944, ibid., p. 951; Harriman to Hopkins, February 13, 1944, ibid., p. 1053; Harriman to Hull, February 14, 1944, ibid., p. 1054.

[61] Hull to Harriman, February 2, 1944, ibid., p. 1043; Hull to Harriman, February 8, 1944, ibid., pp. 1047-48.

discovered a loophole in the Lend-Lease Act which would allow them to ship the Soviets items useful for postwar reconstruction until some of the legal barriers to direct financial assistance could be removed. As Hopkins explained in a cable to Harriman, section 3(c) of the Lend-Lease Act provided that materials contracted for under the lend-lease program could be shipped to Russia until July 1, 1947. Accordingly, they proposed to negotiate a supplementary agreement to the next protocol whereby the United States would ship materials and equipment having both a war and postwar use if the Soviets agreed to reimburse the United States, on credit, for any dual-purpose items delivered after the war ended. Hopkins thought that we should not attempt to make any definite arrangements to finance Soviet reconstruction through long-term credits until we had determined what portion of their needs could be satisfied with this strategem.[62]

Because of the legal obstacles to granting the Soviets a credit, Harriman reluctantly conceded that lend-lease machinery should be utilized to the fullest extent possible to help the Soviets rebuild their country. But he warned that lend-lease was only a "stop gap" means of providing financial assistance to the Soviets. The Russians were planning a fifteen-year reconstruction program. Unless they were assured of receiving credits, Soviet planners might not wish to commit themselves to purchase relatively expensive American goods and services. American businessmen would then lose a competitive advantage in obtaining the Russians' business at a time when Soviet orders would be critically needed to keep American factories operating and to avoid a postwar recession. Further, it might be advantageous to begin the task of drawing up detailed plans and specifications now, so that Russian orders could be rushed into production as soon as the war ended, to "cushion the shock" of transition from wartime to peacetime production needs.

But most important, if we hoped to use reconstruction assistance as a "carrot" to persuade the Soviets to behave as civilized members of the world community, we had to put together an attractive offer. Harriman explained that

if aid for Russian reconstruction is to be of real value in our overall relations with the Soviet Government as a benefit which they can

[62] Hopkins to Harriman, February 4, 1944, ibid., pp. 1043-45; Memorandum for Harry Hopkins from Oscar Cox, January 15, 1944, Cox Papers, "Russia—Reconstruction," FDRL; Memorandum on the Furnishing of Supplies to the USSR Under 3(c) of the Lend-Lease Act, Draft, 3/6/44, Cox Papers, "Russia—Reconstruction"; Oscar Cox to Averell Harriman, March 22, 1944, Cox Papers, "Russia—Reconstruction."

obtain from us if they play the international game with us in accordance with our standards we must have a well-forged instrument to offer them. Vague promises excite Soviet suspicions whereas a precise program offered now to them but kept always within our control to suspend will be of extreme value.[63]

Harriman pleaded with Hopkins not to permit the measure to be bogged down in Hull's committee but to take energetic action to find some means of surmounting the legal obstacles to granting the Soviets a reconstruction credit during the war.[64]

THE WARSAW UPRISING

By the beginning of 1944, improvements in the mobility of the Red Army enabled them to take advantage of their numerical superiority and to conduct an uninterrupted offensive that pushed the Germans out of all but a small corner of Soviet territory by May 1944.

Harriman returned to Washington in mid-May for consultation on some of the major issues affecting U.S.-Soviet relations. During his stay in Washington, Harriman reported to the Policy Committee, an official body composed of ranking State Department officials that met regularly to advise Secretary Hull on major policy questions. Harriman assured committee members that the Soviets unquestionably wished to collaborate with the United States in a world security organization and to participate constructively in world affairs. Moreover, the U.S.-Soviet alliance continued to grow more solid, despite the existence of numerous superficial difficulties and a few more fundamental ones. The only major issue on which we would find it impossible to bring the Russians to accept our views was Poland. Harriman warned that nothing would persuade the Soviets to recognize the Polish government-in-exile. On the other hand, the Soviet government was not firmly committed to the Polish committee in Moscow. Not wishing to install a puppet regime, the Soviets hoped that they would find nonhostile groups in Poland who would set up a provisional government. But the Soviets genuinely feared a German resurgence and would insist that the Polish government look to Moscow for security. Harriman thought that U.S. "policy should be to stand on the side-

---

[63] Harriman to Hopkins, February 9, 1944, *FR: 1944*, IV, pp. 1049-50; Harriman to Hull, February 14, 1944, ibid., pp. 1054-55; Harriman to Hopkins, February 13, 1944, ibid., pp. 1052-53.

[64] Harriman to Hopkins, February 13, 1944, ibid., p. 1053; Harriman to Hull, February 14, 1944, ibid., pp. 1054-55.

lines, to make it clear to the Russians that we expect them to permit the Poles to establish a government of their own choosing, but not to deviate from the principle that the Poles must make their peace with the Russians."[65]

Harriman also warned Policy Committee members that the pattern set by the Czech-Soviet treaty of friendship and mutual assistance was the "best we can expect in Eastern Europe." Under the treaty, both nations promised not to participate in an alliance against the other, and to respect each other's independence and sovereignty. In effect, Czech Prime Minister Beneš had traded recognition of Soviet leadership in foreign affairs in return for their acknowledging Czech domestic political autonomy. Harriman assured State Department officials that "Stalin and his Government do not wish to foment revolution along their borders or to cause disorders which would threaten international stability."[66]

Soviet policy toward the Polish underground during the Warsaw uprising shook Harriman's complacency about Soviet foreign policy objectives in Eastern Europe. In late June the Red Army launched an offensive that carried them to the outskirts of Warsaw by July 31.[67] In a July 21 cable to the State Department, Harriman predicted that the Soviet Union would recognize a new Polish government formed by the National Council of Poland, the quasi parliament of the communist-led resistance movement. Without evidence of Soviet involvement in forming this new government, the United States would have no grounds for opposition. We would then be faced with a Soviet fait accompli and the difficult problem of deciding whether we should continue to recognize the London government-in-exile.

"There is no doubt the Soviet Government will have real influence in Polish affairs," Harriman observed. Nevertheless, he did not think that the Soviets would interfere with the Polish political and economic system, the status of the church, or the composition of the government, beyond ensuring that politicians hostile to the Soviet Union were not invited to participate. Indeed, the Soviets "will attempt to prove to the world that the Polish people have been granted complete freedom of political expression," he predicted.[68]

Events soon partially vindicated Harriman's warning that the Sovi-

---

[65] Policy Committee Minutes, May 10, 1944, Harley Notter File, General Records of the Department of State, Lot File, RG 59, NA; Memo for Under Secretary of State Stettinius, March 15, 1944, *FR: 1944*, III, pp. 1267-68.

[66] Policy Committee Minutes, May 10, 1944, Harley Notter File, RG 59, NA.

[67] Feis, *Churchill, Roosevelt, Stalin*, pp. 387-89.

[68] Harriman to Hull, July 21, 1944, 760C.7-2144, #2702, RG 59, NA.

ets would set up their own Polish government. On July 27, Stalin turned over the administration of liberated Polish territory to the Polish Committee of National Liberation, a rival government that had been formed at Stalin's urgings out of the National Council of Poland. Just as Harriman had predicted six months earlier, there were now two factions claiming authority to rule Poland, one in Lublin sponsored by the Polish communists and the Soviet Union, the other in London, supported by the noncommunist resistance movement and Britain and the United States. There were signs, however, that the emerging conflict among the allies over Poland was not yet irreconcilable. Stalin's decision to name the new Lublin government the "*Committee* of National Liberation" rather than the Polish Provisional *Government,* the title preferred by the Polish communists, may have been a sign that he was still willing to reach an agreement with the London Poles if they would agree to accept the Curzon Line and form a new cabinet.[69]

On July 26, Soviet troops reached the Vistula, about fifty-seven miles from Warsaw. The official Soviet war communique announced on July 29 that Marshal Rokossovsky's troops were heavily engaged with German reinforcements rushed in to stem the Russian advance about twenty miles southeast of Warsaw. Meanwhile, the Commander of the Polish Home Army, General Bor-Komorowski, anxiously monitored the progress of the Red Army, searching for an opportune moment to hurl his civilian troops into action against the Germans.[70]

Home Army leaders believed that German defeats on the Eastern Front, the invasion of Normandy, and the attempt on Hitler's life had so demoralized the Germans that they would abandon Warsaw under the first Soviet attack. The underground army in Warsaw had only enough arms and ammunition for three or four days of offensive action. Home Army generals were faced with shortages of virtually every type of light ammunition, and they possessed almost none of the heavy support weapons—mortars, bazookas, antitank and antiaircraft guns—essential for guerrilla operations against the heavily fortified German positions. On July 31, the day before the outbreak of the Warsaw uprising, General Pelczynski warned other Polish underground leaders that if the Russians did not soon enter Warsaw, the insurgents would be massacred by the Germans. Home Army leaders themselves had almost no reliable information on the progress of the battle between

[69] McNeill, *America, Britain, and Russia*, pp. 430-31; Jan M. Ciechanowski, *The Warsaw Rising of 1944* (London: Cambridge University Press, 1974), pp. 62, 106-13.

[70] Feis, *Churchill, Roosevelt, Stalin*, p. 379; Ciechanowski, *Warsaw Rising*, p. 233.

German and Soviet forces on the outskirts of Warsaw. Yet they did not try to notify the Russians before the uprising or to establish tactical liaison once the fighting had begun. General Bor-Komorowski had issued orders to underground troops in other Polish cities to conduct their operations independently of the Red Army as long as possible so that the Russians could not use their military collaboration as evidence that the Poles wished to cooperate politically as well. Possibly, similar considerations prompted his decision not to coordinate the operations of the Warsaw Home Army with the Soviet offensive.[71]

Upon receipt of an unsubstantiated report that Russian tanks were entering the suburb of Praga, Bor-Komorowski ordered the underground army to rise against the Germans at 5 p.m. the following day. The contest was pathetically unequal. The Poles suffered heavy losses when they attacked heavily fortified German objectives and were forced to withdraw. As early as the second day it was apparent that only the speedy entry of the Red Army could save the city from slaughter and destruction. But on August 1, Rokossovsky's troops were forced to retreat from Praga when the Germans brought in four additional armored divisions. The Warsaw representative of the London Polish government, however, accused the Soviets of deliberately halting their offensive. "This incomprehensible, passive and ostentatious behavior of the Soviet troops . . . has its political significance." His report to London immediately touched off rumors that the Soviets had paused on the Vistula to allow the Nazis to exterminate the noncommunist resistance movement.[72]

General Bor sent urgent appeals to London for additional men and equipment. On August 5, Churchill informed Stalin that he had decided to airdrop arms and ammunition to the Warsaw Poles, hinting that the Russian leader might wish to follow his example. In his reply, Stalin belittled the military significance of the uprising: "The Home Army consists of a few detachments misnamed divisions. They have neither guns, aircraft, nor tanks. I cannot imagine detachments like those taking Warsaw."[73]

When Polish Prime Minister Mikolajczyk, then visiting Moscow, requested arms for the Warsaw Poles, Stalin bluntly replied: "What

[71] Ciechanowski, *Warsaw Rising*, pp. 225-26, 243-49, 259-61, 265, 270-71; Alexander Werth, *Russia at War* (New York: Avon Books, 1965), p. 877; Feis, *Churchill, Roosevelt, Stalin*, p. 379.

[72] Werth, *Russia at War*, pp. 875-77; Ciechanowski, *Warsaw Rising*, pp. 237, 239-40, 262; Document No. 184, August 5, 1944, GSHI, *DOPSR*, 2:324.

[73] Churchill to Stalin, August 4, 1944, *Stalin's Correspondence*, 1:248-49; Stalin to Churchill, August 5, 1944, ibid., p. 249; Feis, *Churchill, Roosevelt, Stalin*, pp. 382-83.

can an airlift do?—We can supply a certain quantity of rifles and machine guns, but we cannot parachute cannons." Stalin added that it would be very difficult to prevent the Germans from intercepting arms and supplies dropped to the Poles, because of the great concentration of German forces in the Warsaw area. "Perhaps it could be done. We must try."[74]

In the meantime, attempts by the R.A.F. to drop supplies to the Warsaw Poles after long night flights from Italian bases proved to be, in Churchill's words, "forlorn and inadequate." On August 12 he appealed to Stalin to provide arms and ammunition to the beleagured Poles. In his reply of August 16, Stalin reneged on his August 9 promise to Mikolajczyk that the Soviets would airdrop arms and supplies to Warsaw. After probing more deeply into the Warsaw "affair," Stalin had concluded that the uprising was a "reckless and fearful gamble," which was taking a heavy toll in human lives because the Poles had not informed Soviet headquarters in advance or attempted to coordinate their military operations with the Red Army. Consequently, the Soviet government wished to disassociate themselves from the Warsaw "adventure."[75]

Harriman had sent a letter to Molotov on August 14, requesting permission for U.S. bombers to land at the Ukraine shuttle bases after making airdrops of arms and ammunition to the resistance forces in Warsaw. The next morning he received a written reply from Vishinsky stating that the Soviet government "could not go along" with the project because the Warsaw uprising was a "purely adventuristic affair."[76]

Harriman and British Ambassador Clark-Kerr demanded an immediate interview with Molotov, but were received by his deputy Vishinsky instead. The two ambassadors warned Vishinsky that the Soviet government's refusal to permit American bombers to assist Warsaw resistance forces would shock world public opinion. Vishinsky clung adamantly to the position that the Warsaw uprising was "ill-advised, not a serious matter, not worthy of assistance, and . . . would have no influence on the future course of the war." He remarked defensively that the Soviet government did not have to fear public reaction abroad

[74] Document No. 189, August 3, 1944, GSHI, *DOPSR*, pp. 335-37; *FR: 1944*, III, p. 1308.

[75] Churchill to Stalin, August 12, 1944, *Stalin's Correspondence*, 1:252; Stalin to Churchill, August 16, 1944, ibid., p. 254.

[76] Harriman to Hull, August 15, 1944, *FR: 1944*, III, p. 1374; Feis, *Churchill, Roosevelt, Stalin*, p. 385.

because the exploits of the Red Army and the Soviet people spoke for themselves.

Harriman pointed out that we were not asking the Soviets to participate in the airdrop. He failed to understand why the Soviets should object to *American* attempts to assist the Warsaw Poles. Vishinsky replied that the use by American bombers of air bases in the Ukraine amounted to Soviet participation. Besides, the Soviet government did not wish to encourage "adventuristic actions" that might later be turned against it. "It was," in Harriman's judgment, "the toughest talk I ever had with a Soviet official." Much later George Kennan remarked that he could still recall the appearance of Harriman and General Deane as they emerged from the Kremlin in the wee hours of the morning, "shattered by the experience."[77]

Vishinsky's evasive replies and stony refusals led Harriman to infer that the Soviet government was deliberately exploiting the tragedy in Warsaw to blacken the reputation of the London Polish government and eliminate its political supporters. The Soviet government's refusal to allow American pilots to assist the gallant Warsaw Poles seemingly could not be attributed to legitimate military considerations. That night Harriman cabled his impressions to Washington:

> For the first time since coming to Moscow I am gravely concerned by the attitude of the Soviet Government in its refusal to permit us to assist the Poles in Warsaw as well as in its own policy of apparent inactivity. If Vishinsky correctly reflects the position of the Soviet Government, its refusal is based not on operational difficulties or denial that the resistance exists but on ruthless political considerations.[78]

Harriman urged Roosevelt to dispatch immediately a "strong" personal message to Stalin. He thought that Stalin should be warned that the American public's faith in the chances for success of a world security organization and postwar Soviet-American collaboration would be "deeply shaken" if the Soviets continued their present policy. "Care should be taken, however, to avoid anything in the nature of a threat," Harriman warned. As yet, there was no evidence that Stalin was personally committed to the policy expounded by Vishinsky.[79]

Roosevelt was not yet willing to go so far as to send a personal

[77] Harriman to Hull, August 15, 1944, *FR: 1944*, III, p. 1375; Harriman and Abel, *Special Envoy*, p. 339; Kennan, *Memoirs*, p. 221.

[78] Harriman to Hull, August 15, 1944, *FR: 1944*, III, p. 1376.

[79] Harriman to Roosevelt and Hull, August 17, 1944, 740.0011 E.W./8.-1744, #3028, RG 59, NA.

message. Harry Hopkins felt strongly that the president should not be involved personally in a wrangle that could have unforeseen consequences. Roosevelt did instruct Harriman to inform Stalin that although the U.S. government hoped that the Soviets would assist British and American attempts to furnish aid to the Polish underground forces, the U.S. military intended to furnish such aid as was practicable—whether or not the Soviets chose to cooperate. Still Stalin did not relent.[80]

Harriman's suspicions that the Soviets had ulterior motives in denying assistance to the Warsaw resistance forces were confirmed when he learned that the Moscow radio station operated by the Union of Polish Patriots had called upon the Poles to rise against the Germans. On July 29, for example, the Kosciusko radio station had urged Warsaw residents to abandon caution and engage in active, direct struggle with the Germans:

> No doubt Warsaw already hears the guns of the battle which is soon to bring her liberation. . . . For Warsaw, which did not yield, but fought on, the hour of action has already arrived.[81]

The Soviets accused the Polish émigré government of deliberately ordering the underground forces into action prematurely, as a propaganda weapon against the Soviets. Yet it was the Soviets themselves who had ruthlessly incited the half-trained, ill-equipped men and women of Warsaw to rise against the Germans.[82] When Harriman and Clark-Kerr finally obtained an interview with Molotov, Harriman questioned Molotov about the role played by these radio appeals in encouraging the Poles to embark upon a premature uprising against the Germans. Molotov replied somewhat unconvincingly that he had

---

[80] Hull to Harriman, August 17, 1944, *FR: 1944*, III, pp. 1378-79; Feis, *Churchill, Roosevelt, Stalin*, p. 386; Memorandum by Charles Bohlen, August 17, 1944, Miscellaneous Office Files, 1910-1944, "580-407-EUR/EE," General Records of the Department of State, Lot File, RG 59, NA.

[81] T. Bor-Komorowski, *The Secret Army* (London: Gollancz, 1950), p. 212.

[82] Harriman to Hull, August 17, 1944, *FR: 1944*, III, p. 1378; Harriman to Hull, August 19, 1944, ibid., pp. 1382-83. It has since become clear that the Kosciusko radio broadcasts were not responsible for the decision of the underground resistance leaders to launch a general uprising in Warsaw. Home Army leaders regarded the broadcasts as routine propaganda, and were determined not to let Soviet appeals have any influence on the timing of the insurrection. As General Bor-Komorowski recalled, "these calls were nothing new. Soviet propaganda had continually appealed to the Polish nation for a general rising against the Germans." In 1950, General Pelczynski frankly stated that the Soviet broadcasts "did not incite us to rise." Bor-Komorowski, *Secret Army*, p. 212; Ciechanowski, *Warsaw Rising*, pp. 264-65.

not heard of such broadcasts. Under close questioning, however, he finally admitted that Stalin had promised Mikolajczyk that he would provide aid, but had changed his mind because of radio and press criticism, inspired by the London Polish government, which accused the Soviets of deliberately abandoning Warsaw to the Nazis.

Harriman and Clark-Kerr tried to persuade the Soviets to relent by reminding them of American and British public opinion. Clark-Kerr pointed out that there had already been much "irresponsible and mischievous comment" in the Western press about the Soviet government's puzzling behavior during the Warsaw uprising. Harriman reminded Molotov that the American public viewed the Polish problem as a test of the allies' ability to work together after the war in dealing with mutual problems. Harriman was deeply disturbed by Molotov's ominous rejoinder to these friendly words of advice: "We shall judge from these comments who are our friends against the common enemy." Molotov also threatened to close off the air shuttle bases established in the Ukraine for the use of American bombers, with the excuse that they were needed by the Soviet Air Force and that it was improbable that the U.S. would make many flights during the coming winter months.[83]

That evening, Harriman cabled to Washington his interpretation of this emerging, sinister dimension of Soviet foreign policy:

> As you know, I have been consistently optimistic and patient in dealing with our various difficulties with the Soviet government. My recent conversations with Vishinsky and particularly with Molotov tonight lead me to the opinion that these men are bloated with power and expect that they can force their will on us and all countries to accept their decisions without question.[84]

On August 20, Roosevelt and Churchill sent a joint personal message to Stalin, pleading with him to consider the hostile world reaction to the allies' abandonment of Warsaw to the Nazis. They politely asked that he reconsider his position: "We hope that you will drop immediate supplies and munitions to the patriot Poles of Warsaw, or will you agree to help our planes in doing it very quickly? We hope you will approve." In his reply, Stalin reviled the "handful of power-seek-

---

[83] Harriman to Hull, August 22, 1944, *FR: 1944*, III, pp. 1386-89; Document No. 192, GSHI, *DOPSR*, pp. 340-41; Feis, *Churchill, Roosevelt, Stalin*, p. 386; Harriman and Abel, *Special Envoy*, pp. 340-42; Harriman to Roosevelt and Hull, August 17, 1944, 740.0011 E.W./8-1744, #3049, RG 59, NA; "Military Cooperation, August 17, 1944," Feis Papers, Box 63, LC.

[84] Harriman to Hull, August 22, 1944, *FR: 1944*, III, p. 1389.

ing criminals" who by "playing on the credulity of the inhabitants of Warsaw, had exposed practically unarmed people to German guns, armour, and aircraft." What was worse, their irresponsible actions had created military difficulties for the Red Army by causing the Germans to concentrate their forces in the Warsaw region.[85]

Churchill strongly urged Roosevelt to send U.S. planes to Warsaw in defiance of Stalin, daring the Soviets to try to prevent American planes from landing on Soviet air bases. FDR, however, did not wish to jeopardize the outcome of talks then underway with the Soviets for American use of Siberian bases against Japan. More important, President Roosevelt was probably concerned that any attempt to pressure Stalin might damage our long-term relations with the Soviet Union. At the Quebec Conference, in a conversation with Archduke Otto of Austria, Roosevelt took out his frustrations by attacking the London Poles for placing him in such a morally compromising position. In a record of their conversation, the archduke noted: "R. is in an ill humor about Poland. Apparently there is a disposition to yield there. Sharp criticism of the Warsaw revolt, which was launched without consulting the allies."

Operational considerations alone were sufficient to cause American military officials to oppose airlifting supplies to the Warsaw Poles. The Joint Chiefs advised Hull that the great distances involved and conditions under which supplies would have to be dropped made American aid infeasible. Air Force Major General Anderson told Hopkins that even if the Soviets did permit us to conduct the operation, at best 5 percent of the supplies would reach the Poles; further, an airlift attempt would subject U.S. crews and airplanes to extensive losses from German attack. The whole situation had the makings of a serious international incident of the greatest future consequences to the United States. Since there was very little chance of aid reaching the Poles, an airlift simply was not worthwhile. Anderson thought that the British were using us as a tool against the Soviets. Hopkins agreed and said he would withhold cablegrams from Churchill to the president to make sure that the United States did not get committed to this job.[86]

---

[85] Roosevelt and Churchill to Stalin, August 20, 1944, *Stalin's Correspondence*, 1:254; Stalin to Churchill and Roosevelt, August 22, 1944, ibid., p. 255.

[86] Roosevelt to Winant, August 25, 1944, Roosevelt Papers: Map Room File, "052 Polish-Russian Relations, Sec. 2," FDRL; "Warsaw Dropping Operations," n.d., Military Mission to Moscow, Box 67, Interservice Agencies Warsaw Dropping Operations, RG 334, NA; Dallek, *Roosevelt and American Foreign Policy*, p. 464; "Roosevelt Conversation with Archduke Otto of Austria, September 15, 1944," *FR: Quebec, 1944*, p.

Hopkins believed that the "problem of Warsaw itself will be handled by the sure victories on Germany's eastern front." The president's political adviser was infuriated but not intimidated when he learned that Roman Catholic leaders were threatening to withdraw their support from Roosevelt unless aid was given to Warsaw. Hopkins wrote Ambassador Winant that "I have no patience with the efforts which the Church inspires by what amounts to almost secret and devious methods to control the political affairs of the world." "You must remember, first, that this country is overwhelmingly Protestant," he assured Winant "and, secondly, that no leader of the Catholic Church has ever been able to make his parishioners vote his political views." Further, Hopkins judged that "on the whole, public opinion here in the last few months seems quite reconciled to the type of settlement of the Polish problem that seems to be impending."[87]

Harriman's reaction to Soviet policies was less politically calculated and more emotional than that of Washington. The Soviets' callous and brutal refusal of his appeals to provide aid to the Warsaw insurgents overrode his attempts to maintain an open mind and weight available evidence carefully before drawing any conclusions about future Soviet policies. The evidence he had acquired about Soviet political motivations firsthand from his difficult, emotional negotiations with Molotov and Vishinsky had far greater and more lasting impact on his inferences about future Soviet behavior than the more abstract information he had previously received about emerging Soviet policies in Eastern Europe, historic Russian geopolitical objectives, and previous policy statements by Soviet diplomats.[88]

As Harriman saw it, the Soviet refusal to assist the Warsaw resistance fighters was only the most recent example of a new, troubling pattern in Soviet behavior. On September 10, he advised Harry Hopkins that "our relations with the Soviets have taken a startling turn" during the last two months. The Soviet bureaucracy was stonewalling urgent requests of the Moscow military mission, showing complete

---

368; Feis, *Churchill, Roosevelt, Stalin*, pp. 387-88; Roosevelt to Churchill, August 24, 1944, #605, Roosevelt Papers: Map Room File, FDRL; CCS 645/4, August 14, 1944, Memorandum by the U.S. Chiefs of Staff, ABC 452.1 Poland (26 Nov. 42), Sec. 2-A, RG 165, NA; Memorandum for the President, August 31, 1944, 740.0011 E.W./8-1344, RG 59, NA.

[87] John Gilbert Winant to Harry Hopkins, September 1, 1944, with handwritten notation, "Notified President HLH," Hopkins Papers, "Growing Crisis in Poland," FDRL; Harry Hopkins to John G. Winant, September 4, 1944, Hopkins Papers, "Growing Crisis in Poland."

[88] Harriman's response exemplifies the tendency for people to give disproportionate weight to vivid information. See Nisbett and Ross, *Human Inference*, pp. 43-62.

indifference to our military needs. For example, the Soviets had failed to take action on: the proposal for winter shuttle bombing operations; requests that U.S. photo reconnaissance missions be allowed to undertake additional missions from Soviet bases; the scheme to transport trucks to the American Air Force in China via Soviet Central Asia and Sinkiang; requests for permission for a U.S. bombing appraisal party to visit Ploesti, Rumania, to evaluate the results of recent allied bombing raids; Stalin's previous promises to begin joint planning for Soviet participation in the war against Japan. The Russians' indifference to world public opinion was best illustrated by Molotov's recent observation that the Soviets would judge their friends by whether they accepted the Soviet viewpoint.[89]

He believed that the Kremlin faction opposed to cooperation with the West was now dominant, and that they intended to force the British and United States to accept Soviet policies, backed by the strength and prestige of the Red Army. Just as he had predicted, the Russians had interpreted our generosity and patience in the face of ample provocation as a sign of weakness and tacit acquiescence to their policies. "Unless we take issue with the present policy there is every indication the Soviet Union will become a world bully whenever their interests are involved," he predicted.[90]

The ruthlessness exhibited by the Soviets toward the noncommunist Warsaw underground caused Harriman to question his earlier judgment that the Soviets did not intend to communize Eastern Europe or meddle in the internal affairs of these countries. It now appeared that the Soviets' definition of a "friendly government" was different from our own. With Czechoslovakia, they were satisfied with a military alliance and a prominent position for the Communist party within the Czech government. In the case of Poland, where there was greater political instability and anti-Soviet feeling, they were insisting on a "hand-picked" government amenable to Soviet domination. Harriman was now uncertain whether the Soviets would follow this precedent and establish puppet governments in other neighboring countries. Nor was he able to judge whether the Soviets would attempt to introduce such Soviet institutions as the secret police, censorship of the press, or controlled education into countries occupied by the Red Army.

Harriman realized that the United States had no substantial economic or political interests in Eastern and Central Europe, and that the ultimate fate of these countries was seemingly of little concern to

[89] Harriman to Hopkins, September 10, 1944, *FR: 1944*, IV, pp. 988-99.
[90] Ibid.

us. But the Soviets' lack of scruples or remorse in their relentless pursuit of a "friendly government" in Poland was reminiscent of Hitler's tactics, and elicited a script derived from the experience of the thirties:

> What frightens me . . . is that when a country begins to extend its influence by strong arm methods beyond its borders under the guise of security it is difficult to see how a line can be drawn. If the policy is accepted that the Soviet Union has a right to penetrate her immediate neighbors for security, penetration of the next immediate neighbors becomes at a certain time equally logical.[91]

Harriman did not object to the Soviets' exercising influence over the foreign policies of neighboring countries. But he did believe that the U.S. government should take an active interest in the postwar fate of countries in Eastern and Central Europe to teach the Soviets that they must refrain from interfering in the *internal* affairs of these countries.[92]

Harriman was particularly concerned about Rumania, where he feared that the Soviets might exploit the wide-ranging powers granted to them by the armistice agreement to institute secret police and censorship of the press. The Soviet representative on the allied control commission had executive powers; British and American members' responsibilities were limited to maintaining liaison with their governments. Harriman noted that the terms of the armistice agreement gave Russia "unlimited control" over Rumania's economic life, and the power to restrict political activity "hostile to the Soviet Union." He warned Hull that the failure of the U.S. to raise any major objections to the armistice terms was interpreted by the Soviets as acquiescence to Soviet domination of Rumania. "They believe," he explained, "that we lived up to a tacit understanding that Rumania was an area of predominant Soviet interest in which we would not interfere."[93]

Despite his apprehensions about future Soviet policies in Eastern Europe, Harriman was still optimistic about the prospects for successful Soviet-American collaboration after the war. He did not believe that Stalin could forgo the benefits of continued cooperation with the West—economic assistance and world peace—without alienating the Russian people.[94] But to obtain full Soviet cooperation, the United States must stop attempting to win Soviet trust by indulging their misbehavior.

---

[91] Harriman to Hull, September 10, 1944, *FR: 1944*, IV, p. 993.

[92] Ibid., p. 994.

[93] Harriman to Hull, September 6, 1944, ibid., p. 223; Harriman to Hull, September 11, 1944, ibid., p. 230; Harriman to Hull, September 15, 1944, ibid., pp. 235-37.

[94] Harriman to Hull, September 19, 1944, ibid., p. 992.

Once again, Harriman recommended that the United States adopt a "firm but friendly" quid pro quo approach in dealing with the Russians. Through selective use of rewards and punishments, Harriman hoped to strengthen the hand of those around Stalin who wished to "play the game along our lines" and to demonstrate to Stalin that his hard-line advisers only led him into difficulties. Having given several months thought to the plan, Harriman now recommended a graduated series of sanctions. He was still vague, however, on which Soviet acts should provoke what level of reprisal.

He believed that the United States must oppose the Russians promptly with the "greatest of firmness" whenever they violated our standards of international conduct. If we demonstrated the least bit of indecision or willingness to compromise, it would be impossible to build a sound foundation for postwar collaboration with this "strange country." On minor issues, it would be sufficient to register our objections while making it clear to the Soviets that we had no intention of taking any further action. On more important questions, however, the Soviets should be informed that their failure to conform to our standards would lessen our willingness to provide them with economic assistance for postwar reconstruction. In addition, "they should be made promptly to feel specific results from our displeasure." For example, Harriman and Deane had recommended that the United States threaten to cut off shipments of industrial equipment to compel the Soviet Foreign Office to take action on some of our requests for military cooperation. Since they blamed isolationist elements within the Foreign Office rather than the Red Air Force for obstructing Soviet-American military collaboration, Harriman and Deane thought that we should not try to withhold military equipment for bargaining purposes. By showing generosity toward branches of the Soviet bureaucracy that cooperated with us, and retaliating against obstreperous officials, they hoped to teach Stalin which policy was best for the Soviet Union. Finally, when vital interests of the United States were at stake, we should inform the Soviets that we were prepared to break with them over the issue rather than accept any compromise. In such cases, Harriman was confident that Stalin would back down rather than risk a rupture.[95]

Harriman asked Hopkins for permission to return to Washington as soon as possible so that he could discuss his ideas and impressions with the president. On September 11, Hopkins assured Harriman that

[95]Harriman to Hull, September 20, 1944, ibid., pp. 997-98; "Military Cooperation," September 9, 1944, Feis Papers, Box 53, LC.

President Roosevelt was eager to discuss with him personally the problems raised in his cables, but wanted him to delay his departure because the discussions at Dumbarton Oaks between Britain, the Soviet Union, and the United States were at a "critical stage." Neither Hopkins nor Roosevelt responded to the ambassador's pleas for a firm, quid pro quo approach in dealing with the Russians.[96]

On September 10, Stalin changed his mind and agreed to cooperate in supplying the Warsaw underground army by air. Prefacing this important concession with the claim that the only really effective aid to Warsaw would come from the Red Army's advance, Stalin grudgingly noted that there was another form of assistance that could "hardly be considered effective," namely, airdrops of ammunition, food, and supplies. He had information that supplies dropped into Warsaw by the Soviets on two previous occasions had only fallen into the hands of the Nazis. "If you are so firmly convinced, however, of the efficacy of this form of assistance," he grumbled, "the Soviet government is prepared to agree to it." Harriman and other U.S. and British officials immediately concluded that their firm, outspoken opposition to Soviet inaction was responsible for Stalin's change of heart. Stalin's unexpected reversal reinforced Harriman's commitment to a tougher approach in dealing with the Soviets.[97]

Beginning September 13, small groups of Soviet planes made nightly flights to drop food, arms, and ammunition to Warsaw. Most of the supplies dropped by the Soviets reached the underground forces. Since the Russians did not use parachutes, some of the ammunition was twisted into useless scrap metal by the force of the impact as it hit the ground, but the Soviet airlift operation had an electric effect on the insurgents' morale. Due to bad weather, American planes did not appear over Warsaw until September 18. Flying at high altitudes to avoid German antiaircraft fire, American bombers dropped a substantial amount of supplies. At that high altitude, however, precision bombing was impossible, and only 25 to 30 percent of the containers reached the Polish underground army. Two bombers and two fighters were shot down, and the services of 105 bombers and 62 fighters were lost for a week.[98]

[96] FR: Quebec, 1944, p. 200.

[97] Document No. 228, GSHI, DOPSR, p. 390; FR: 1944, IV, p. 997.

[98] Bor-Komorowski, Secret Army, pp. 342-43; Feis, Churchill, Roosevelt, Stalin, p. 388; Sharp, Poland, p. 182; George Bruce, The Warsaw Uprising: 1 August-2 October 1944 (London: Rupert Hart-Davis, 1972), p. 188; Memorandum to Lieutenant General Spaatz, October 15, 1944, "Frantic" File, "Warsaw Dropping Operations," U.S. Military Mission to Moscow, RG 334, NA.

On October 3, the exhausted Warsaw insurgents laid down their arms and ended their pitiful struggle. Nearly two hundred thousand of the city's inhabitants were killed; the remaining eighty thousand survivors were forcibly dispersed throughout the rest of occupied Poland by the Nazis. According to Churchill, "when the Russians entered the city three months later they found little left but shattered streets and the unburied dead."[99]

In the more relaxed and harmonious atmosphere accompanying Churchill's visit to Moscow in October, Harriman accepted Stalin's explanation of the Soviets' failure to relieve the Warsaw resistance fighters. At a Washington cocktail party the following month, Harriman defended the Russians against charges that they had deliberately abandoned Warsaw to the Nazis. Nevertheless, his newly formed impression of the Soviets as drunk with power and unwilling to consider the rights of others remained untouched.[100] Similarly, Lee Ross and his colleagues found that impressions may persevere even when the information on which they were originally based is unambiguously discredited.[101]

As Stalin later explained to Harriman, Russian troops were forced to retreat from Warsaw when the Germans brought five additional armored divisions into the Praga area. Warsaw was on higher ground than Praga, and a direct frontal attack across the Vistula would have been prohibitively costly. In addition, Soviet troops, after advancing nearly four hundred miles in less than a month, had outrun their supplies. Before they could outflank the city, the Soviets had to extinguish German forces in the Baltic states to protect their right flank and release additional divisions needed to capture Warsaw.[102]

---

[99] Ciechanowski, *Warsaw Rising*, p. 314; Winston S. Churchill, *Triumph and Tragedy* (Boston: Houghton Mifflin, 1953), p. 145.

[100] Wallace diary, November 13, 1944, *The Price of Vision: The Diary of Henry A. Wallace, 1942-1946* (Boston: Houghton Mifflin, 1973), ed. John M. Blum, p. 393. Although the evidence for Harriman's acceptance of the Soviet explanation may seem to be thin, it should be pointed out that the person transcribing Harriman's remarks was Henry Wallace—a zealous Russophile. In his diary, Wallace went to great pains to record, with implied indignation, any anti-Soviet remarks made by U.S. officials. Therefore, it is significant that Wallace perceived Harriman as supporting the Soviet point of view on the Warsaw uprising. In addition, when he cabled President Roosevelt about his October 12 conversation with Stalin on the Warsaw uprising, Harriman reports Stalin's excuses without question or skepticism—quite a change from his cables during the uprising. Finally, in *Special Envoy* (pp. 336-37), Harriman continues to hold that the Soviet halt on the Vistula was motivated by military rather than political concerns.

[101] Lee Ross, Mark Lepper, and Michael Hubbard, "Perseverance in Self-Perception and Social Perception: Biased Attributional Processes in the Debriefing Paradigm," *Journal of Personality and Social Psychology* 32 (1975): 880-92.

[102] Harriman to Roosevelt, October 12, 1944, *FR: 1944*, IV, p. 1013; Chester Wil-

THE CHURCHILL-STALIN SPHERES OF INFLUENCE AGREEMENT

Churchill shared Harriman's concern about Soviet foreign policy aims in Eastern Europe. By the fall of 1944, local communist parties had assumed a prominent position in Balkan coalition governments. Churchill feared that the Soviets would soon take steps to eliminate noncommunist members from these coalitions and impose communist governments upon the Balkan countries. At the same time, Anglo-American military victories on the Continent following the invasion of Normandy placed the West in a favorable bargaining position for the first time. But Roosevelt was unwilling to leave the United States for another tripartite conference until after the American presidential elections. Unwilling to sacrifice the fate of the Balkan states to the whimsical demands of the American political system, Churchill resolved to go to Moscow himself to reach an understanding with Stalin. Roosevelt approved, and it was arranged that Harriman would sit in on the principal conferences between Churchill and Stalin merely as an observer, without power to commit the United States.[103]

At his first meeting with Stalin on October 9, Churchill suggested a spheres of influence agreement. "Let us settle about our affairs in the Balkans," he urged Stalin. "Your armies are in Rumania and Bulgaria. We have interests, missions, and agents there. Don't let us get at cross-purposes in small ways. So far as Britain and Russia are concerned, how would it do for you to have ninety percent predominance in Rumania, for us to have ninety percent of the say in Greece, and go fifty-fifty in Yugoslavia?" Pulling out a sheet of paper, he jotted down a list of countries and the percentages of influence to be accorded Britain and Russia in each:

---

mot, *Struggle for Europe*, pp. 536-37. See also Ciechanowski, *Warsaw Rising*, pp. 250-51; Werth, *Russia at War*, p. 878; and Harriman and Abel, *Special Envoy*, pp. 336-37. Whether Stalin could have provided greater assistance to the Warsaw uprising and deliberately allowed the Germans to exterminate the Home Army is still vigorously disputed by scholars and cannot be resolved on the basis of secondary sources. Although most Western scholars scoff at the Soviets' explanation, recent books using Polish documents conclude that military reverses prevented the Soviets from giving more aid to the Warsaw uprising. See Ciechanowski, *Warsaw Rising*, pp. 250-51; Bruce, *The Warsaw Uprising*, pp. 93, 154. On the other hand, Mastny argues that although the Russian offensive was blocked by a German counterattack in early August, the Red Army could have resumed their advance at the end of the month, had Stalin chosen to do so. See *Russia's Road to the Cold War*, pp. 184-86, 189-90. For our purposes, what is important is that Harriman accepted the Soviet rationalization for their failure to aid Warsaw, but did not revise his gloomy perceptions of the Soviet Union; thus, his new image of the Soviets was autonomous from the evidence that produced it.

[103] Churchill, *Triumph and Tragedy*, pp. 219-220.

Rumania		
	Russia	90%
	The others	10%
Greece		
	Great Britain	90%
	Russia	10%
Yugoslavia		50-50%
Hungary		50-50%
Bulgaria		
	Russia	75%
	The others	25%

Stalin studied the sheet for a moment and then silently penciled a large check by the figures. After a long pause, Churchill had second thoughts.

"Might not it be thought rather cynical if it seemed we had disposed of these issues, so fateful to millions of people, in such an offhand manner? Let us burn the paper."

"No, you keep it," said Stalin.[104]

But this dramatic exchange was only the opening bell for a prolonged round of Anglo-Soviet haggling. The Russians were not satisfied with 50 percent predominance in Hungary and 75 percent in Bulgaria. Finally, Eden and Molotov agreed that Russia would have 80 percent in Hungary and Bulgaria. In a cable to the State Department, ambassador to Britain John Winant conceded that "a casual evaluation of the conversations in regard to Bulgarian armistice terms, on the evidence I have seen, might suggest that our friend Eden was having his pants traded off." "But," he explained, "when you stop to realize the advance of the Russian troops into Yugoslavia, it is clear that the primary British purpose was to continue their relationship with Greece and to maintain a sufficient degree of control in Yugoslavia to protect British Mediterranean interests."[105]

[104] Ibid., p. 227. The official British record of the Churchill-Stalin talks on Balkan spheres of influence is reprinted in "The Meaning of TOLSTOY: Churchill, Stalin, and the Balkans Moscow, October 1944," ed. Joseph M. Siracusa, *Diplomatic History* 3 (Fall 1979): 443-63.

[105] Llewellyn Woodward, *British Foreign Policy in the Second World War* (London: Her Majesty's Stationery Office, 1962), pp. 307-308; Winant to Hull, October 12, 1944, *FR: 1944*, III, pp. 451-52. Feis evidently did not have access to British documents, for he implies that the preliminary Churchill-Stalin agreement of October 9 was definitive. Thus, he accuses the Soviets of violating their part of the agreement by their refusal to accord the British and Americans an equal share in running the occupation in Hungary. See *Churchill, Roosevelt, Stalin*, p. 452.

Harriman was not present at the first Churchill-Stalin meeting where the decision was made to recognize formally, in the form of percentages, the varying interests of the great powers in each of the Balkan countries. Fearing that the United States might veto the entire arrangement, Churchill and Stalin informed Harriman of the percentages agreement only little by little, to test for Roosevelt's reaction. As Churchill explained to Stalin, "it was better to express these things in diplomatic terms and not to use the phrase 'dividing into spheres' because the Americans might be shocked."[106] Thus, on October 10, Harriman reported that

> on matters in the Balkans, Churchill and Eden will try to work out some sort of spheres of influence with the Russians, the British to have a free hand in Greece and the Russians in Rumania and perhaps in other countries. The British will attempt to retrieve a position of equal influence in Yugoslavia.[107]

Roosevelt's only comment was that

> My active interest at the present time in the Balkan area is that such steps as are practicable should be taken to ensure against the Balkans getting us into a future international war.[108]

In a joint telegram, Churchill and Stalin merely informed Roosevelt that "we have to consider the best way of reaching an agreed policy about the Balkan countries including Hungary and Turkey."[109]

On October 11, Harriman reported that on the basis of his conversations with Eden he had obtained a better understanding of the type of arrangement the British hoped to work out with the Soviets. Although Churchill had been using the term "spheres of influence," Eden assured him that their aim was to work out a practical arrangement for settling the problems of the Balkan states and the relative responsibility of Britain and Russia for each country.[110]

On the same day, in a veiled bid for approval, Churchill gave Roosevelt a slightly more explicit account of his intentions:

> It is absolutely necessary we should try to get a common mind about the Balkans so that we may prevent civil war breaking out in several countries when probably you and I would be in sympathy with one

[106] Siracusa, "The Meaning of TOLSTOY," p. 447.
[107] Harriman to Roosevelt, October 10, 1944, *FR: 1944*, IV, p. 1006.
[108] Roosevelt to Harriman, October 11, 1944, ibid., p. 1009.
[109] Churchill and Stalin to Roosevelt, October 10, 1944, ibid., p. 1008.
[110] Harriman to Roosevelt, October 11, 1944, ibid., pp. 1009-10.

side and U. J. with the other. I shall keep you informed of all this, and nothing will be settled except preliminary agreements between Britain and Russia subject to further discussion and melting down with you.[111]

On October 12, acknowledging the joint telegram from Churchill and Stalin declaring their intention to work out a common policy toward the Balkan countries, Roosevelt stated that

I am most pleased to know that you are reaching a meeting of your two minds as to international policies in which, because of our present and future common efforts to prevent international wars, we are all interested.[112]

In the context of the previous messages—particularly Harriman's October 11 message, which provided a fuller account of the British-Soviet discussions—Roosevelt must have known that his vaguely worded statement would be interpreted as tacit acquiescence to a British-Soviet sphere of influence agreement.[113]

Though the "percentages agreement" was obviously intended to be kept secret, the *New York Times* carried an accurate account of the British-Soviet division of influence in the Balkans, but without the percentages. Walter Lippmann applauded Roosevelt's policy of encouraging an agreement between the parties directly at interest in the region, instead of involving the United States in an area remote from our concerns.[114]

Harriman too was pleased that Stalin and Churchill were able to reach an amicable settlement on the limits of their respective interests in the Balkans. But he was still concerned that the Soviets might establish communist regimes in Eastern Europe. In Washington to re-

[111] Churchill to Roosevelt, October 11, 1944, ibid., p. 1010.

[112] Churchill, *Triumph and Tragedy*, pp. 230-31.

[113] That he was fully aware of the way his message would be interpreted cannot be doubted; FDR had a special memo summarizing these diplomatic exchanges in the White House Files, with the heading, "The following references were made to British and Russian spheres of influence in Balkan countries at Conference between Churchill and Stalin," Roosevelt Papers: Map Room File, "041 Balkans—Spheres of influence." On the other hand, the British record of the talks does not suggest that Churchill and Stalin considered FDR to be a *party* to the agreement. For example, Stalin complained that FDR's cable suggesting that the talks should be merely preliminary to a meeting of the Big Three "seemed to demand too many rights for the United States leaving too little for the Soviet Union and Great Britain, who, after all, had a treaty of common assistance." See Siracusa, "The Meaning of TOLSTOY," p. 447.

[114] "Balkan 'Spheres' Decided in Moscow," *New York Times*, October 27, 1944; Walter Lippmann, "Today and Tomorrow," *Washington Post*, October 14, 1944.

port on the Churchill-Stalin talks, Harriman warned Policy Committee members that the Soviet policy of ensuring that neighboring countries did not unite with foreign aggressors could easily become imperialistic. Unless the United States aggressively opposed Soviet domination of Eastern Europe, the Soviets would set up puppet governments supported by the secret police. He did not think that the Soviets would try to interfere in the internal affairs of Finland and Czechoslovakia, where there was an educated citizenry and established political system. The danger was that the Soviets might attempt to fill the political vacuum in Poland and the Balkans, to prevent hostile governments from emerging.[115]

By this time, Harriman knew that any government in Poland or the Balkans which represented the will of the people would be anti-Soviet. Otherwise, why did he so fear that the Soviets were planning to set up communist regimes? The ambassador may have been unconsciously avoiding a difficult value trade-off—the choice between promoting democracy and self-determination in Eastern Europe and attaining Soviet cooperation in maintaining world peace and security. If the Soviets genuinely believed that they needed guarantees against hostile regimes as part of their basic security requirements, how could the United States possibly alter their policy without tearing the fabric of Roosevelt's grand design?[116]

During his stay in Washington, Harriman lobbied intensively for the United States to prevent the Soviets from importing their political system into Eastern Europe; at every available opportunity he described the horrors of the Soviet secret police. Despite his monopoly capitalist background, he did not object to the communist economic system but to their political system, which he compared to that of a "city boss backed up by the strong arm of the police."[117]

But Harriman could not arouse Roosevelt to the dangers of continued noninvolvement in the political affairs of Eastern Europe. In the notes on his first meeting with Roosevelt to discuss the Churchill-Stalin spheres of influence agreement, Harriman observed that Roosevelt showed little interest in the problems of Eastern Europe—except for their effects on domestic public opinion. The president confided to Harriman that he intended to exercise a great deal of influence on

[115] Policy Committee Minutes, October 25, 1944, Harley Notter File, RG 59, NA.

[116] See, for example, Jervis, *Perception and Misperception*, p. 140.

[117] Wallace diary, *The Price of Vision*, p. 392; Stimson diary, October 23, 1944, Stimson Papers, Yale University Library (microfilm, Stanford University Library).

the postwar settlement in the Pacific, but European political problems were so impossible that he wished to avoid them if he could.[118]

In a memo summarizing his conferences with Roosevelt, Harriman recorded that he had tried to impress on the president that our principal interest in Eastern Europe was to see that the Soviets did not set up puppet governments under the Soviet system of government of a few picked men supported by the secret police. Harriman did not believe that the Soviets wanted to "bolshevize" these countries, but they did want to be sure they maintained control over their foreign relations. Roosevelt did not seem to be convinced of the importance of a vigilant, firm policy in dealing with the political aspects in various Eastern European countries. Harriman noted that the State Department, however, was fully aware of this necessity unless we wished to turn Eastern and Central Europe over to complete Soviet influence if not domination.[119]

POST-YALTA EUPHORIA

Harriman's apprehensions were temporarily assuaged by the cooperativeness and flexibility shown by the Russians at the Yalta Conference in early February 1945. The successful outcome of the Yalta Conference reassured Harriman and other policymakers that Soviet-American collaboration to maintain order in the postwar international system was still attainable. To Stettinius he confided that

> the peace and tranquillity of the world depends on the development of intimacy between the three great powers who are winning the war. This is the avowed Russian policy and I believe you have seen enough to accept its sincerity.[120]

As Hopkins later recalled, "the Russians had proved that they could be reasonable and farseeing and there wasn't any doubt in the minds of the President or any of us that we could live with them and get along with them peacefully for as far into the future as any of us could imagine." Secretary of State Stettinius received the impression that "Stalin and his government have made up their mind to take their

[118] "Important General Comment on the Views of the President and WAH on the Problems of Central and Eastern Europe," November 20, 1944, Feis Papers, Box 53, LC.

[119] Ibid.

[120] Harriman to Stettinius, February 20, 1945, *The Diaries of Edward R. Stettinius, Jr., 1943-1946*, ed. Thomas M. Campbell and George C. Herring (New York: Franklin Watts, New Viewpoints, 1975), p. 257.

place among the United Nations as one of the powerful, peaceloving states." The Russians gave "every evidence," he said, of a "desire to cooperate along all lines with the U.S."[121]

The allies reached substantive agreements on several potentially divisive issues. They agreed to coordinate their offensives to prevent the Germans from shifting their troops between the east and west. Stalin reaffirmed his earlier promise that the Soviet Union would enter the Pacific War three months after the defeat of Germany, in return for restitution of certain territories and special rights in the Far East that had been wrested away from the Tsarist government following the Russo-Japanese War in 1905, plus the Kurile Islands.

On the issue of voting in the U.N. Security Council, Stalin made a major concession to the American viewpoint by agreeing to relinquish the right to veto discussion or efforts to bring about a peaceful settlement of any dispute in which the Soviet Union was involved. The United States and the Soviet government also signed a bilateral agreement concerning the care and repatriation of liberated prisoners of war.[122]

Other agreements merely papered over gaping differences in the allies' objectives for the postwar settlement with fine phrases and equivocal wording. The problem of Poland hovered over the conference, dampening the festive atmosphere like an unwelcome, troublesome guest.

On December 31, 1944, just as Harriman had predicted six months earlier, Stalin had recognized the Lublin government (now transferred to Warsaw), leaving the United States and Britain shackled to the equally unrepresentative London government for lack of a graceful way to discharge their obligations without offending domestic public opinion. At Yalta, the British proposed establishing an entirely new provisional government that would conduct free elections to determine the final government of Poland. The Russians, however, argued that the Warsaw government should form the nucleus of any provisional government, perhaps with the addition of a few "democratic" politicians from Poland and abroad. Seeking to mediate, Roosevelt suggested that the Polish Provisional Government in Warsaw be reorganized with the addition of democratic leaders from Poland and

---

[121] Sherwood, *Roosevelt and Hopkins*, p. 870; "Notes on a Conference of Secretary of State with Bipartisan Senate Committee, March 15, 1945," Stettinius Papers, Box 224; Walter Millis, ed., *The Forrestal Diaries* (New York: Viking Press, 1951), p. 35.

[122] Feis, *Churchill, Roosevelt, Stalin*, pp. 497-500, 503-505, 550-52; Herz, *Beginnings of the Cold War*, pp. 77-78; *FR: Yalta*, pp. 985-87.

abroad. This reorganized provisional government should then pledge to hold free elections as soon as possible.

Important details were left unspecified: how many Polish politicians should be added to the government, and how they would be selected. Harriman, Clark-Kerr, and Molotov were to meet together in Moscow in consultation with Polish politicians to choose a list of names. The accord on Poland, although based on an American draft, yielded to the Soviet position by referring to the Warsaw government as *the* provisional government and recognizing it as the basis for reconstitution.[123]

The loose, nebulous phrases of the Yalta Declaration on Liberated Europe, adopted after only a perfunctory debate, concealed conflicting conceptions of how the postwar world should be organized to maintain international peace and security. This document pledged the allies to "concert" their policies during the temporary period of instability in liberated Europe to assist the peoples "to solve by democratic means their pressing economic and political problems." Specifically, the declaration obligated the three countries to help the peoples in Eastern Europe in their efforts to restore internal peace and form provisional governments "broadly representative of all democratic elements in the population and pledged to the earliest possible establishment through free elections of governments responsive to the will of the people." But this statement of lofty principles lacked any enforcement machinery. The signatories were only required to "consult" with each other "on the measures necessary to discharge the[ir] joint responsibilities." And the provision requiring consultation did not become operative unless all three powers agreed.[124]

In drafting the declaration, State Department officials had intended to nullify the Churchill-Stalin spheres of influence agreement by getting the Soviets to agree formally to the principle of tripartite responsibility for the affairs of Eastern Europe. In contrast, the Anglo-Soviet agreement was based on the traditional diplomatic principle that great power responsibilities should be limited to a particular area of predominant interest. Whatever the aim of State Department officials, one can be certain that Stalin did not believe that he was abrogating the "percentages agreement" by subscribing to the Yalta Declaration on Liberated Europe. According to one scholar, Stalin probably regarded

---

[123] Feis, *Churchill, Roosevelt, Stalin*, pp. 525-529; Herz, *Beginnings of the Cold War*, pp. 81-84; Gaddis, *Origins of the Cold War*, pp. 161-62.

[124] *FR: Yalta*, pp. 977-78.

it as a "harmless piece of rhetoric, soothing to the Americans" but without any practical implications.[125]

BREAKDOWN OF THE YALTA AGREEMENTS

The tenuous, equivocally worded Yalta agreements soon disintegrated under the strain of practical implementation. Less than two weeks after Yalta, Soviet actions in Rumania shattered any illusions State Department officials may have entertained concerning the Soviets' willingness to renounce power politics and spheres of influence. On February 27, Andrei Vishinsky, Soviet deputy commissar for foreign affairs, flew to Bucharest and demanded the installation of a new government more to the Soviets' liking. When the king temporized, Vishinsky looked at his watch, announced that he had just two hours and five minutes to announce the appointment of a new prime minister, then left the room abruptly, banging the door so hard that the plaster cracked.[126]

Invoking the Declaration on Liberated Europe, Harriman and Clark-Kerr demanded that the members of the Rumanian allied control commission consult together before the formation of any new government. But Molotov blandly replied that formal arrangements for consultation were unnecessary since Vishinsky was already discussing these matters with British and American members of the control commission.[127]

Basic differences among the allies concerning the political future of Poland also appeared. The three ambassadors meeting in Moscow to decide on a method of reorganizing the Polish government could not even agree on which Poles should be invited for consultation. Molotov contended that members of the Warsaw government should have the right to veto the names of any Poles suggested for consultation since it was their government which was to be reorganized. This effectively excluded Mikolajczyk and other members of the London Polish government. The State Department, however, insisted that the Warsaw Poles should not be allowed to dictate which Poles should be invited to Moscow, because then it would be impossible to establish a *new*, fully representative government, as envisioned in the Yalta accords.[128]

---

[125] McNeill, *America, Britain, and Russia*, p. 559; Feis, *Churchill, Roosevelt, Stalin*, pp. 549-50; Herz, *Beginnings of the Cold War*, p. 85.

[126] *FR: 1945*, V, p. 485n; Berry to Stettinius, February 28, 1945, ibid., pp. 487-88; Berry to Stettinius, March 2, 1945, ibid., p. 492.

[127] Ibid., pp. 477-78, 482-86, 491-92, 495-98.

[128] Harriman to Stettinius, March 2, 1945, ibid., pp. 134-35; Grew to Harriman, March 3, 1945, ibid., pp. 138-39; Grew to Harriman, March 18, 1945, ibid., pp. 172-

The Russians signaled their displeasure at the breakdown of the Yalta agreements on Poland by suspending all projects in which the Moscow military mission was involved. The Soviets refused to allow the United States to send contact teams into Poland to bring emergency supplies to liberated American prisoners in Poland and evacuate the sick and wounded, violating what was agreed to at Yalta. Harriman was outraged. In a conversation with Harriman, Molotov admitted that the Soviet government would remove its objections if the United States would make the necessary arrangements with the Warsaw Polish government. Harriman could only conclude that the Soviets were trying to use American prisoners of war as a "club to induce us to give increased prestige to the Polish Provisional Government by dealing with it."[129]

The so-called "Berne incident" confirmed Harriman's growing conviction that the Soviets had "arbitrarily, and in disregard of the facts, placed their own interpretation on the Yalta agreements regarding Poland, liberated areas as applied to Rumania, and liberated prisoners of war." The Soviets bitterly protested their exclusion from preliminary talks in Berne with the Germans to arrange for the surrender of German forces in northern Italy. Stalin even insinuated that an agreement had been concluded at these talks to allow British and American forces to advance to the east without substantial German opposition in return for easier armistice terms: "It is difficult to agree that lack of resistance on the part of the Germans on the Western front can be explained only that they are defeated."[130]

The Soviets also retaliated in petty ways. For example, U.S. flyers were grounded at the shuttle bases in the Ukraine in reprisal for a few attempts by American servicemen to smuggle dissidents out of Poland. A group of American servicemen previously authorized to conduct a survey in the Amur River valley for possible air bases was forced to spend three weeks in Fairbanks, Alaska, waiting for the Russians to approve their entry into Siberia. Contrary to promises made at Yalta, the Soviets withheld permission for a U.S. naval team to visit the recently captured German experimental submarine station at Gdynia. Though Stalin had agreed that the Americans could have an air base

74; Harriman to Stettinius, March 23, 1945, ibid., pp. 176-77; Feis, *Churchill, Roosevelt, Stalin*, pp. 572-73; Herz, *Beginnings of the Cold War*, p. 86.

[129] Harriman to Roosevelt, March 8, 1945, *FR: 1945*, V, p. 1075; Harriman to Stettinius, March 14, 1945, ibid., pp. 1079-80.

[130] Harriman to Stettinius, March 17, 1945, *FR: 1945*, III, p. 732; ibid., pp. 722-46; Stalin to Roosevelt, April 3, 1945, ibid., p. 742; Stalin to Roosevelt, April 7, 1945, ibid., p. 750.

near Budapest, the Russians refused to allow a U.S. mission to enter Moscow to make the necessary arrangements.[131]

Harriman believed that the Soviets were deliberately violating the Yalta agreements. Why, he did not know. Perhaps our indulgent policy had convinced the Soviets that they could get whatever they wanted if they were firm about it. Or perhaps Stalin had encountered substantial opposition from other members of the Politburo on returning from Yalta, and decided to change the agreements by placing a new interpretation on them.[132]

Yet the Soviets' interpretation of the Yalta agreements was neither arbitrary nor without adequate textual justification. In response to a perplexed query from the British Foreign Office about the proper interpretation of the Yalta Declaration on Liberated Europe, Stettinius admitted that the provision requiring consultation would not become operative unless all three governments agreed on the need for joint action. Moreover, the terms of the agreement did not specifically prohibit unilateral action by a great power in Eastern Europe.[133] Among the principals who attended the Yalta conference, there were several who agreed with the Soviets' interpretation of the Polish agreement. Roosevelt warned Churchill that "if we attempt to evade the fact that we placed, as clearly shown in the agreement, somewhat more emphasis on the Lublin Poles than on the other two groups from which the new Government is to be drawn I feel we will expose ourselves to the charge that we are attempting to go back on the Crimea decision." James Byrnes had attended the conference as Roosevelt's adviser, and made shorthand notes of the proceedings so that he could brief congressional leaders on the agreements reached. He informed Davies that "there was no intent that a new government was to be created independent of the Lublin Government." "The Lublin Government was to be reinforced with other representative democratic leaders among the Polish people." Byrnes saw "no justification under the spirit or the letter of the agreement for insistence by Harriman and the British Ambassador that an entirely new Government should be created

---

[131] Memorandum by the Chief of Staff, U.S. Army, April 3, 1945, JCS 1301, ABC 384 United Nations (14 Jul 44), Sec. 1-B, RG 165, NA; Deane, *Strange Alliance*, pp. 253-54, 293-94; Harriman and Abel, *Special Envoy*, pp. 422-23; Feis, *Churchill, Roosevelt, Stalin*, p. 598.

[132] "WAH's Changing Appraisals and Impressions of Our Relations with the Soviet Union, March 21, 1945," Feis Papers, Box 85, LC; Harriman to Stettinius, March 17, 1945, *FR: 1945*, III, p. 732; Minutes of the Secretary of State's Staff Committee, April 20, 1945, *FR: 1945*, V, p. 840; Memorandum of White House Meeting, ibid., p. 253.

[133] Stettinius to Winant, March 16, 1945, *FR: 1945*, V, p. 515-16.

and that members of the London Emigre Polish Government should be included." British Ambassador Clark-Kerr confided to Walter Lippmann that he personally did not interpret the Yalta agreements as calling for the formation of a new government by the Big Three, but Churchill had overruled him. As Clark-Kerr recalled, the three ambassadors were to enlarge the Lublin government through the selection of additional members representing important interests in Polish society.[134]

Unlike those officials, however, who could return to Washington after many toasts of champagne and vodka, Harriman had the difficult, frustrating job of implementing the Yalta agreements. The ambassador to Moscow was subject to stonewalling, complaints, and insults. In a report on the military mission, John Deane noted that those who visited Russia on special missions found themselves entertained on an elaborate scale, bathed in an atmosphere of solidarity and friendship; those who stayed behind found that the Soviets often did not consider agreements binding. Reporting to Washington on the Polish negotiations, Harriman admitted that he resented Molotov's attempts "to give as little ground as possible in the direction of bringing in elements not under Soviet control and to fight every inch of the way." Worried about Harriman's advice to Truman on the Polish issue, Secretary of War Stimson regretfully noted that

> [Harriman and Deane] have been suffering personally from the Russians' behavior in minor matters for a long time, and they have been urging firmness in dealing on these smaller matters & we have been backing them up, but now they were evidently influenced by their past bad treatment & they moved for strong words by the President on a strong position.[135]

Harriman's firsthand experience with Soviet negotiating tactics and the collapse of the hopes of Yalta left him with a bitter taste in his mouth for Soviet-American collaboration. He came to accept Cold War beliefs about the Soviet Union far sooner than other influential figures in the development of the containment policy—such as Truman, Byrnes, Acheson.

[134] Roosevelt to Churchill, March 29, 1945, ibid., p. 189; Davies diary, June 6, 9, 1945, Joseph E. Davies Papers, LC; Memorandum of Conversation, May 23, 1945, 711.61/5-2345, RG 59, NA.

[135] Stimson diary, April 23, 1945 (Stanford microfilm); Harriman and Abel, *Special Envoy*, p. 503; Summary Report by Commanding General John Deane, "The United States Military Mission to Moscow, October 18, 1943 to October 31, 1945," Part 1, 336, Sec. VIII, History U.S. Military Mission to Moscow, RG 165, NA.

Harriman's interpretation of the events surrounding the breakdown of the Yalta agreements confirmed his worst suspicions about Soviet foreign policy behavior. In a series of cables to the State Department, Harriman set forth his apprehensions about future Soviet policies.

In September 1944, Harriman felt that it was too early to judge whether the Soviets intended to impose puppet governments in Eastern Europe or to introduce secret police, censorship, and controlled education into these countries. Recent Soviet actions in Rumania, Poland, and Bulgaria, however, convinced him that "the Soviet program is the establishment of totalitarianism, ending personal liberty and democracy as we know it." "Soviet control over any foreign country does not mean merely influence on their foreign relations but the extension of the Soviet system," he declared.[136]

As late as January 1945, Harriman attributed Soviet interest in having friendly governments in neighboring countries to their need for security against a recurrence of the German invasion. He now believed that the Soviets were using their fear of Germany as a "stalking horse" to conceal their plans to establish governments obedient to the communist ideology in bordering countries; ideology had replaced security as the source of Soviet foreign policy. The centrality of ideological goals in Soviet foreign policy calculations reminded him of Hitler's plans for world conquest, and evoked an episodic script. "The outward thrust of communism is not dead," he predicted. "We might well have to face an ideological warfare just as vigorous and dangerous as Nazism or Fascism."[137]

To reestablish world order and preserve democratic institutions, the United States must reorient its policy to the containment of communism. Harriman recalled that Stalin had once remarked that communist revolution found fertile seed in capitalistic economic breakdown. Now the Soviets were attempting to apply that Marxist dogma by publicizing the difficult food situation in France, Belgium, and Italy, compared with the relative abundance existing in areas liberated by the Red Army. Harriman charged that local communist parties were exploiting the disparity in living conditions to promote Soviet concepts and policies in Western European countries. "The only hope of stopping Soviet penetration," he warned, "is the development of sound

[136] Harriman to Stettinius, April 4, 1945, *FR: 1945*, V, pp. 818-19; Memorandum of Conversation, April 20, 1945, ibid., p. 232.

[137] Harriman to Stettinius, January 10, 1945, *FR: Yalta*, pp. 450-51; Millis, *Forrestal Diaries*, pp. 47-48; Secretary's Staff Committee Minutes, April 21, 1945, *FR: 1945*, V, p. 843; Harriman and Abel, *Special Envoy*, p. 457. See also Secretary's Staff Committee Minutes, April 20, 1945, *FR: 1945*, V, p. 841.

economic conditions in these countries." Unless we were ready to live in a world dominated by the Soviet Union, the United States would have to use our economic power to help friendly, democratic countries.[138]

In inferring that the Soviets' overriding objective was world communist revolution, Harriman was primarily influenced by recent Soviet actions in Rumania and Poland. According to Lee Ross, people typically employ behavioral data in making inferences about people and events, while overlooking the potential information conveyed by an actor's *nonresponse* or the *nonoccurrence* of an event.[139] Similarly, in attempting to surmise Soviet foreign policy aims, Harriman failed to make use of the information implied by what the Soviets did not do. In Finland, the Soviet chairman of the control commission did not use the far-reaching powers granted to him by the terms of the armistice agreement to support local communists or alter the existing conservative government. In the midst of the Rumanian political crisis, free elections were conducted in a peaceable, orderly manner without Soviet interference. In the coalition government returned by these elections, communists constituted a distinct minority. In Hungary, the Soviets did not exploit the political vacuum left by the departure of the former fascist government to establish a communist regime. The provisional government established in December 1944 by members of the Hungarian underground, with Soviet assistance, allotted the communists only two cabinet posts, with the rest going to representatives of the prewar parties.

If the Soviets had intended to establish a one-party, monolithic communist regime in any Eastern European country, Rumania would have been the logical choice. In the prewar period, conservative Rumanian leaders had fomented popular fears of Russian territorial revisionism to stave off demands for much-needed socio-economic reform. Over thirty Rumanian divisions had invaded Russia during World War II, occupying the area lying between the Dniester and Bug rivers. During their occupation of the Soviet Crimea, the Rumanians carried out extensive pogroms against Soviet Jews and systematically stripped the region of all valuable assets. The Radescu government was anti-Russian, incompetent, and unwilling to carry out agrarian reform or to purge its administrative ranks of fascist sympathizers. Yet the

[138] "WAH's Changing Appraisals and Impressions of Our Relations with the Soviet Union, March 21, 1945," Feis Papers, Box 85, LC; Harriman to Stettinius, April 4, 1945, *FR: 1945*, V, pp. 818-20.

[139] Lee Ross, "The Intuitive Psychologist and His Shortcomings"; Nisbett and Ross, *Human Inference*, pp. 48-49.

Soviets did not try to replace Radescu with a communist government. In the Groza cabinet, communist members were outnumbered by representatives of the traditional parties. The Soviet choice for vice-premier was Tatarescu, who in 1936 as prime minister had sentenced communist leader Ana Pauker to ten years in prison. Had Harriman considered the actions which the Soviets did *not* take in Eastern Europe, he might have inferred that Stalin's principal aim was not the promotion of communist dictatorships in neighboring countries, but the establishment of broadly based coalition governments "friendly" to the Soviet Union.[140]

Though Harriman advocated the use of American economic power to contain the expansion of Soviet communism, he was still confident that we could establish a working partnership with the Soviet Union, if U.S. policymakers adopted his "firm but friendly" quid pro quo approach. "As you know," he wrote Stettinius, "I am a most earnest advocate of the closest possible understanding with the Soviet Union so that what I am saying only relates to how such understanding may be best attained." At the same time, Harriman believed that "our objectives and the Kremlin's objectives are irreconcilable." Harriman explained to a group of hostile and disbelieving reporters that "the Kremlin wants to promote communist dictatorships controlled from Moscow, whereas we want, as far as possible, to see a world of governments responsible to the will of the people."[141] He maintained mutually contradictory beliefs simultaneously, with no discomfort at the inconsistency.

Feeling that his arguments would be more persuasive if he could give them in person, Harriman asked permission to return home immediately. Roosevelt and Stettinius, however, felt that Harriman should stay in Moscow. Although several Washington officials were irritated and irate with the Soviets for their obstinacy and lack of civility, and there was mumbling about the need for firm dealing,[142] Roosevelt maintained that "we should minimize the general Soviet

[140] "Conspiracy Is Not Enough," *Time*, March 26, 1945, p. 24; Feis, *Churchill, Roosevelt, Stalin*, pp. 564, 568-70; Hugh Seton-Watson, *The East European Revolution* (New York: Frederick Praeger, 1951), pp. 190-91, 206; Herz, *Beginnings of the Cold War*, pp. 134-35; Stephen A. Fischer-Galati, *The New Rumania: From People's Democracy to Socialist Republic* (Cambridge: M.I.T. Press, 1967), pp. 26-29; McNeill, *America, Britain, and Russia*, pp. 534, 575n.

[141] Harriman to Stettinius, April 6, 1945, *FR: 1945*, V, pp. 822-24; Secretary's Staff Committee Minutes, April 20, 1945, ibid., pp. 841-42; Harriman and Abel, *Special Envoy*, p. 457.

[142] Harriman to Stettinius, April 6, 1945, *FR: 1945*, V, p. 821; Stettinius to Harriman, April 7, 1945, ibid., p. 824; Stimson diary, April 2, 3, 1945 (Stanford microfilm).

problem as much as possible, because these problems, in one form or another, seem to arise every day and most of them straighten out as in the case of the Berne meeting."[143]

Military officials in Washington were skeptical about the value of retaliation against the Soviets. The Joint Strategic Survey Committee pointed out a major internal contradiction in Harriman's recommendations. If the Soviets considered it essential for their security to establish the seeds of communism in Eastern Europe, then a few minor acts of retaliation, such as grounding Soviet flyers or holding up lend-lease shipments, could hardly be expected to alter their determination. The JSSC observed that the instances of military noncooperation cited by Harriman and Deane—grounding U.S. aircraft in Soviet-occupied areas, refusing permission to a British-American naval survey at Gdynia and Danzig, exclusion of American teams from Poland to help in locating American prisoners of war—all involved freedom of movement for U.S. personnel in Russian-occupied areas. Russian political interests and intentions in these territories were part of their basic conception of postwar national security. The Soviets were suspicious and considered it important to exclude foreigners from Eastern Europe to prevent Westerners from reporting on Soviet actions or the desires of the peoples. Because these were fundamental questions of national security to the Soviets, minor acts of retaliation would only increase Soviet ill-feeling and provoke additional reprisals, without influencing Russian policies. The Joint Chiefs of Staff agreed, and ruled that the military mission in Moscow should make no attempt to retaliate when the Russians refused to carry out joint military projects.[144]

But for Harriman, the vivid data provided by his own trying negotiations with the Soviets was more compelling than the logic of national interests. Confronted with Soviet rudeness and arrogance on Poland and other issues, Harriman did not weight evidence according to normative criteria. Had he been more dispassionate and analytical, Harriman would have realized that Soviet policies in Eastern Europe, although often barbaric by American standards, nevertheless were a complex tapestry in which the thread of national security appeared throughout. He might also have realized the contradiction inherent in

[143] Roosevelt to Churchill, April 11, 1945, *FR: 1945*, V, p. 210; "The Foreign Policy of the United States," April 16, 1945, Harry S Truman Papers, PSF: Subject File, "State, Secy of—Policy Manual," HSTL.

[144] Memorandum by Chief of Staff, U.S. Army, April 3, 1945, JCS 1301, ABC 384 United Nations (14 Jul 44), Sec. 1-B, RG 165, NA; JCS 1301/2, April 5, 1945, ibid.; Memorandum for the Commanding General, U.S. Military Mission to the USSR, from J. E. Hull, Assistant Chief of Staff, OPD 26 April 1945, ibid.

arguing that Soviet policy was motivated by ideological goals of communist revolution, yet at the same time asserting that the Soviets were reasonable men who would abandon their cause in return for dollars to rebuild their country. If the Soviets' aim was to promote communist dictatorships around the world, then how could the United States ever develop a collaborative relationship with the Soviet Union, no matter how many times we retaliated by cutting off aid or playing tit for tat?

Attribution theory, then, best explains Averell Harriman's changed image of the Soviet Union. The ambassador to Moscow was motivated by no other goal than to provide the most accurate interpretation of Soviet foreign policy goals and intentions. He formulated hypotheses about Soviet aims in Eastern Europe, and revised them as the Red Army advanced on the continent. Contrary to cognitive dissonance theory, Harriman did not try to distort, reinterpret, or ignore evidence to preserve his estimate that the Soviets were concerned above all else with having "friendly governments" and preventing the restoration of the cordon sanitaire; nor did he try to maintain his earlier judgment that the Soviets genuinely wanted Poland to be independent and would allow the Poles to choose their own domestic political system. Still, Harriman did not observe scientific canons of inquiry in drawing conclusions from Soviet actions in Eastern Europe. Because of his disillusioning and disturbing quarrels with Soviet diplomats over the provision of military assistance to the Warsaw uprising and the composition of the reorganized Warsaw Polish government, he leaped to the conclusion that the Soviets were determined to impose totalitarian governments in the shadow of the Red Army.

It cannot be argued that Harriman's anti-Soviet prejudices biased his reporting from the Soviet Union, because the former entrepreneur had much respect for the Soviets' willingness to observe commitments. When he became ambassador, Harriman viewed Stalin as a reasonable man, who was interested above all else in rebuilding the Soviet Union, sheltered by a new world order based on great power cooperation to preserve international peace and security.

Nor can Harriman's changed beliefs be attributed to his desire to please his superiors in Washington. Harriman's advice to adopt a "firm but friendly" quid pro quo approach was ignored by President Roosevelt; Stettinius would not allow him to return to Washington to lobby for a new policy.

Harriman's judgments about Soviet foreign policy are also consistent with a self-perception interpretation. Harriman's role as ambassador made him aware of his beliefs about the Soviet Union and world order, since he was expected to send cables to Washington analyzing

Soviet intentions and motives. If cognitive inconsistency is uncomfortable, then Harriman should have been torn and distraught. At the same time that he argued that basic foreign policy aims of Washington and the Kremlin were irreconcilable, Harriman suggested that we could still cooperate with the Soviet Union, if his firm quid pro quo approach were adopted. But Harriman showed no signs of discomfort at the inconsistency; he continued to argue for the rest of the year that cooperation with the Soviets was a feasible policy, while at the same time accusing the Soviets of harboring ambitions of unlimited expansion.

As schema theory would suggest, Harriman compared Stalin's repression of Eastern Europe to Hitler's policies in the region, and inferred that the Soviet dictator had dreams of a new Soviet age of influence over the entire world. But Harriman did not invoke this episodic script until *after* his personal experience with Soviet callousness during the Warsaw uprising and their arrogant refusal to compromise on the Polish issue.

After Roosevelt died Stettinius changed his mind and agreed that it would be "desirable" and "appropriate" for Harriman to proceed to Washington to brief the new president on the Polish issue before Molotov's forthcoming visit to the United States. In this first interview with Truman, Harriman warned that the United States was faced with a "barbarian invasion" of Europe. Soviet control over any foreign country implied not just influence on their foreign policy but the institution of secret police and the extinction of personal liberties as well. In Harriman's opinion, this alarming trend in Soviet foreign policy was caused by Roosevelt's policy of patience and generosity, which had led the Russians to believe that they could behave as they wished without any opposition from us. Truman assured Harriman that he intended to be "firm but fair," since the "Soviet Union needed us more than we needed them." Although Stettinius had invited Harriman to Washington, chagrined and jealous at Harriman's influence over Truman, he was soon complaining to his diary that "I am burned up with the way in which Harriman has been acting. He went to see the President without any of us knowing about it and has not reported to anyone yet what took place."[145]

Ill-informed about the important foreign policy issues impinging on the presidency, bewildered by the conflicting advice thrust on him, yet

---

[145] Stettinius to Harriman, April 14, 1945, *FR: 1945*, V, p. 212; Calendar Notes, April 13, 1945, *Diaries of Stettinius*, ed. Campbell and Herring, p. 318; Stettinius Calendar Notes, April 22, 1945, Stettinius Papers, Box 244, University of Virginia.

anxious to avoid appearing hesitant or indecisive, Truman quickly seized on Harriman's concrete, common-sensical suggestions. In succeeding weeks, Truman sought to implement Harriman's "firm but friendly" quid pro quo policy in such areas as lend-lease policy, the Soviet loan, and the Polish problem.

CHAPTER THREE

Truman as World Leader

TRUMAN'S ASSETS AS A WORLD LEADER

TRUMAN had a limited understanding of foreign affairs when Roosevelt's death suddenly thrust on him the overwhelming burden of winning two wars and helping to write a lasting peace settlement. As a senator, Truman had specialized in domestic issues such as transportation and defense procurement. During his brief term as vice-president, Truman was not briefed about the complex political questions stirred up by the war. Soon after he became president, Truman complained to Henry Wallace that President Roosevelt had not taken him into his confidence about anything. "They didn't tell me anything about what was going on," he said pathetically. A few days after Roosevelt died, Harry Hopkins privately warned Foreign Minister Anthony Eden that Truman knew "absolutely nothing of world affairs," and would have been "terrified" if Winston Churchill visited Washington for consultations with the new president. *Time* magazine summarized the prevailing opinion of Truman in Washington:

> Harry Truman is a man of distinct limitations, especially in experience in high-level politics. . . .
>   His knowledge of foreign affairs is limited. . . .
>   With almost complete unanimity, Harry Truman's friends—in Washington and across the land—agreed last week that he "would not be a great President."[1]

But Truman brought with him to the presidency certain resources that helped him carry out a vigorous, assertive foreign policy: a knowledge of history, political skills, and a characteristic style of leadership.

Through diligent self-study, Truman had acquired a broad, if somewhat elementary understanding of history. As a boy, Truman read biographies and history for entertainment after his "eye doctor" forbade him to play baseball or roughhouse with the boys, lest his expensive glasses be broken. Truman continued to read history as an adult,

---

[1] Wallace diary, May 18, 1945, *Price of Vision*, ed. Blum, p. 452; Anthony Eden, *The Reckoning* (Boston: Houghton Mifflin, 1965), p. 611; "The Thirty-Second," *Time*, April 23, 1945, pp. 22-23.

for relaxation. When asked what he intended to do with his spare time after he became vice-president, Truman replied, "study history."[2]

For Truman, history was more than a hobby; it was a source of rules by which to live his life. In his *Memoirs*, Truman relates that "reading history to me was far more than a romantic adventure. It was solid instruction and wise teaching which I somehow felt that I wanted and needed."[3] This didactic view of history was inculcated into Truman by the schools and by children's literature. His elementary school teachers taught "civics, U.S. History, and reverence for the Divine Law." History was philosophy expressed through examples. When he was twelve, his mother gave him a richly illustrated, four-volume set of biographies, entitled *Great Men and Famous Women*, which was one of his most prized possessions. The series was designed to teach moral lessons to youth, and each biography contained an obvious moral. Still later he studied Plutarch's *Lives* and Abbott's biographies of famous men. In a private memorandum written shortly after he became senator, Truman recalled that he was greatly impressed by the "leaders of men." "I was always timid—am yet," he explained.[4] Truman admired the military heroes most of all, especially Hannibal, Napoleon, and Lee. He resolved to become a military man, although he was "afraid of a gun and would rather run than fight." Truman never lost his childhood faith that wisdom could be gained from studying the experiences of others as recorded in histories and biographies. When he was forced to quit his job as a bank clerk and work on his grandmother's farm, he consoled himself by remembering Cincinnatus. "I thought maybe by cussing mules and plowing corn I could perhaps overcome my shyness and amount to something." Long before Truman achieved success in politics, he advised a young law student that there were ten books which any person wanting to "get ahead" should read. These included the Bible, Shakespeare, Plutarch's *Lives, Bunker Bean, Missour's Struggle for Statehood*, Benjamin Franklin's *Autobiography*, and Creasy's *Fifteen Decisive Battles of the World*. Truman also suggested that he read Plato, "especially the parts about the old fellow who took hemlock." In 1936, after learning that the Pendergast ma-

[2] Luther Huston, "The Vice President Talks of His New Job," *New York Times Magazine*, January 21, 1945, p. 13.

[3] Harry S Truman, *Memoirs* (Garden City, N.Y.: Doubleday, 1955), vol. 1, *Year of Decisions*, p. 119.

[4] Richard Eaton and La Valle Hart, *Meet Harry S Truman* (Washington, D.C.: Dumbarton House, 1945), p. 26; Bert Cochran, *Harry Truman and the Crisis Presidency* (New York: Funk & Wagnall, 1973), p. 29; Truman, *Memoirs*, 1:119-21; Harry S Truman private memorandum, "My Impressions of the Senate, the House, Washington, etc.," n.d., Truman Papers: Senatorial and Vice-Presidential Files, HSTL.

chine wished him to run for the U.S. Senate, Truman scribbled a revealing memo to himself:

> It is 4 A.M. I am to make the most momentous announcement of my life. I have come to the place where all men strive to be at my age. . . . In reading the lives of great men, I have found that the first victory they won was over themselves and their carnal urges. Self-discipline with all of them came first. . . . And now I am a candidate for the United States Senate.[5]

His press secretary Jonathan Daniels recalled that Truman "knew the kind of history that McGuffey would have put in his readers, and he liked the historical anecdote that expressed a moral."[6]

Truman believed in the "great man" theory of history, which holds that the willful actions of leaders suffice as explanations of historical events. For him, history was a set of wonderful stories about such men as "Cyrus, Alexander, Hannibal, Jenghis [sic] Khan, Tamerlane, Charlemagne, Herman, Constantine the Great and Small, Mohomet the Prophet and the Conqueror, Saladin, Charles Martel, Richard the Lion Hearted and III . . . Gustavus Adolphus, the Lion of the North, King Henry IV, Edward the Black Prince and his father, Napoleon, Charles V, Sir Francis Drake, Captain Kidd and Robert E. Lee and Stonewall Jackson, Washington and all the rest, Andrew Jackson, Thos. Jefferson, even Old Ben Franklin." In his *Memoirs*, Truman recalls that

> while still a boy I could see that history had some extremely valuable lessons to teach. I learned from it that a leader is a man who has the ability to get other people to do what they don't want to do, and like it. It takes a leader to put economic, military, and government forces to work so they will operate. I learned that in those periods of history when there was no leadership, society usually groped through dark ages of one degree or another. I saw that it takes men to make history, or there would be no history. History does not make the man.[7]

Reinforcing Truman's belief in man's ability to master social and economic forces was his simple cyclical view of history, according to

[5] Truman, "The Military Career of a Missourian," handwritten memorandum, n.d., Truman Papers: Senatorial and Vice Presidential Files, HSTL; "My Impressions of the Senate," ibid.; Alfred Steinberg, *Man from Missouri*, pp. 55, 114.

[6] Oral History, Jonathan Daniels, HSTL.

[7] Truman, *Memoirs*, 1:119-20; "My Impressions of the Senate," Truman Papers: Senatorial and Vice-Presidential Files, HSTL.

which every event had an almost exact parallel sometime in the past. By studying past events and inferring the reasons for a famous leader's success or failure, a policymaker could draw useful lessons that could be applied to analogous problems in the present. In 1941, Truman wrote his daughter Margaret:

Ancient History is one of the most interesting of all studies. By it you find out why a lot of things happen today. . . . You will also find out that people did the same things, made the same mistakes, and followed the same trends as we do today.[8]

As president, Truman often used historical analogies to understand world events and choose among alternative policies.

Truman had another asset that helped him formulate a workable foreign policy: he was a consummate politician and proud of it. "A politician is the ablest man in government, and when he's dead they call him a statesman," he often said. "I never want to be a statesman."

Truman had acute political instincts, and knew how to sniff out the direction of public sentiment. Foreign policy in the United States must have broad public support to be viable. To obtain public backing, U.S. leaders must legitimize policy by explaining and interpreting isolated actions in a wider vision of America's role in world affairs.[9] Truman was aware of the requirements of a democratic foreign policy. Indeed, he conceived of his role as being one of *persuading* the American people, rather than issuing edicts in lonely omniscience. In October 1945 Truman explained his philosophy of leadership to a *New York Times* reporter:

A politician must be in a sense a public-relations man. Most leaders have been such men. They have had the faculty of presenting the ideas for which they have stood in such a way that the people had understood them and had confidence in them. If they had not been able to make others see as they did, they would not have been leaders. The best ideas in the world are of no benefit unless they are carried out. In order to carry them out, reason and persuasion must be employed. If enthusiasm for them can be aroused, so much the better. Some men have the ability to arouse that enthusiasm more than others. They are the political leaders.[10]

---

[8] Truman, *Memoirs*, 1:119-21; Margaret Truman, *Harry S Truman* (New York: William Morrow, 1973), p. 141.

[9] See Trout, "Rhetoric Revisited: Political Legitimation and the Cold War."

[10] "Interview with Truman," *New York Times Magazine*, October 14, 1945, p. 47; Margaret Marshall, "Portrait of Truman," *The Nation*, April 21, 1945, pp. 438-40; Frank

Truman also brought to the presidency a characteristic style of leadership acquired from his wide-ranging experience.

His father, John Truman, nicknamed "Peanuts," was a diminutive but feisty livestock trader and uneducated farmer. Harry admired his father's readiness to resort to fisticuffs in defense of the family honor or the Democratic party. But he felt closer to his mother, Martha Truman, a spirited, plain-speaking woman. The product of a finishing-school education, Martha encouraged Harry to take piano lessons and read books. After family financial reverses kept him from attending college, Harry planned to apply to West Point, but was not permitted to take the exam because of his poor eyesight. Frustrated in his attempt to secure a college education at no cost to his parents, and denied any vocational training, Truman was forced to seize whatever opportunities became available. He was a railroad timekeeper, bank clerk, bookkeeper, farmer, investor in oil and lead mining, and part owner of a men's clothing store before deciding on politics as a career. In his first job as railroad timekeeper, the timid, eighteen-year-old lad lived in grubby tents with roughneck "gandy dancers," from whom he learned "all the cuss words in the English language—not by ear but by note."[11]

His military experience as an artillery captain in World War I was formative. Commanding an unruly battery of young Irish-American recruits helped shape his ideas about leadership, which he later characteristically defined as "the ability to get other people to do what they don't want to do and like it." Battery D had harassed and broken four previous captains. When he took charge, Truman was so frightened that he could not utter a word. That night, the rowdy, fun-loving Irish lads started a brawl that sent four men to the infirmary. Truman called in the sergeants and corporals. He said: "I didn't come over here to get along with you. You've got to get along with me. And if there are any of you who can't, speak up right now and I'll bust you right back right now." "We got along," Truman remembered.

Truman's control of his men was severely tested several weeks later when Battery D was unexpectedly hit by a heavy gas-shell barrage from the Germans. Two guns had become mired in the mud when a hailstorm of shells fell on the battery. A sergeant panicked, hollering,

McNaughton and Walter Hehmeyer, *This Man Truman* (New York: McGraw-Hill, 1945), p. 72; Huston, "The Vice President Talks," p. 13; "Serenade for Harry," *Time*, October 9, 1944, p. 20.

[11] Cochran, *Harry Truman*, pp. 32-33, 36-38, 45-46; Steinberg, *Man from Missouri*, pp. 29-31, 55-57; Robert J. Donovan, *Conflict and Crisis: The Presidency of Harry S Truman, 1945-1948* (New York: W. W. Norton, 1977), pp. xv-vi.

"Run fellers run they've got a bracket on us." Truman rose unhurt from a ditch where his horse had rolled over on him, and spouted out a stream of oaths which combined the best of rural Missouri and railroad-laborer profanity. The chaplain, Father Tiernan, said that Truman's language "took the skin off the ears of those boys." "It turned those boys right around," he said admiringly. "It was bea-u-ti-ful," recalled a gunner. "He called us every name west of the Mississippi. We stopped like whistled-after-rabbits and in 2 minutes were back lammin' it at the Germans."[12]

Throughout his political career, Truman followed a "give 'em hell" script when dealing with stubborn opponents ranging from Soviet Foreign Minister Molotov, labor leader John L. Lewis, and the 80th Congress to "uppity" music critics; it allowed him to conceal his diffidence and insecurity under a façade of "tough talk."[13]

In 1922, the postwar decline in farm prices forced Truman and his friend Eddie Jacobson to sell their men's clothing store and turn over the stock to creditors. Harry was nearly thirty-eight and penniless. He decided to run for Eastern Jackson county judge, an administrative position that levied taxes and maintained county roads and property.

[12] John Lewis Gaddis, "Harry S Truman and the Origins of Containment," in *Makers of American Diplomacy: From Benjamin Franklin to Henry Kissinger*, ed. Frank J. Merli and Theodore M. Wilson (New York: Charles Scribner's Sons, 1974), pp. 495-96; Cochran, *Harry Truman*, pp. 43-44; Jonathan Daniels, *The Man of Independence* (New York: J. B. Lippincott, 1950), p. 96; Steinberg, *Man from Missouri*, p. 46.

[13] It is significant that in a private, undated memorandum Truman compared his fears as a freshman senator to his feelings on taking command of Battery D: "I was as much surprised as anybody when I became a Senator. . . . I came to Washington with the same misgivings I had when I was given a battery to take to the front in 1918." "My Impressions of the Senate, the House, Washington, etc.," Truman Papers: Senatorial and Vice-Presidential Files. In *Presidential Character: Predicting Performance in the White House* (Englewood Cliffs, N.J.: Prentice-Hall, 1972), James David Barber similarly argues that Truman's "first independent political success" in the "Battle of Who Run" was the germination of his later reliance on fighting rhetoric as president (pp. 259-61, 276). Jervis also theorizes that a political decisionmaker's first experience of himself as an autonomous and valued individual influences his general beliefs about how best to cope with the environment. See *Perception and Misperception*, pp. 250-51. For examples of Truman's tendency to "talk tough" when challenged outside the Cold War context, see Donovan, *Conflict and Crisis*, pp. 115, 148, 165, 175, 214-15, 241-42, 399-400, 420, 422, 425. Whether Truman acquired the "get tough" script from the "Battle of Who Run" or the example set by his plain-spoken, feisty parents cannot, of course, be determined from the evidence on Truman's childhood. In this case, as in most other psychobiographies, perhaps the best the investigator can do is to trace recurring patterns in the subject's adult behavior, instead of trying to speculate on their origins. On this point, see Philip E. Tetlock, Faye Crosby, Travis L. Crosby, "Political Psychobiography," *Micropolitics* 1 (1981): 191-213.

Through family connections and the support of a war buddy who was the nephew of Boss Pendergast, he won the endorsement of the Pendergast machine and the election. During his first term, Truman and Presiding Judge McElroy, a fellow Pendergast Democrat, rationalized county administrative procedures, eliminated waste and financial irregularities, reduced the county debt by almost $700,000, and made substantial improvements in the county's graft-ridden, shoddily constructed road system. Elected presiding judge in 1926, Truman continued his fight against graft, bribery, and corruption. Nevertheless, he remained a loyal member of the Pendergast organization, and never failed to follow the Boss' instructions when dispensing county patronage or delivering his bloc of votes on election day.

Tom Pendergast epitomized the Big City Irish Boss. With a small, black derby perched precariously atop his bald head, bulging neck, corpulent frame, and powerful hands, Boss Pendergast could have been snipped from a Thomas Nast cartoon. Truman may have modeled his impulsive style of decisionmaking after Pendergast. The Boss used to sit in his small boxlike office, furnished only with a worn green rug, a few chairs, a brass cuspidor, and a splintered roll-top desk. He greeted supplicants with impatience, wasting no time on small talk, and demanded to know their business. Pendergast then snapped out a decision and called out "All, right, who's next?"[14]

Under the tutelage of the Pendergast machine, Truman learned the "code of the politician": a man who failed to keep his word could never again be trusted. Truman had always attached great importance to keeping his promises. When his men's clothing store went out of business, for example, Truman rejected his lawyer's advice that he declare bankruptcy; he insisted on paying off all his creditors, even though it took many years and placed a considerable burden on his meager financial resources.[15] But his experience as a member of the Pendergast machine taught Truman to give overriding importance to the principle of keeping one's word. This came to be the standard by which he judged all potential political allies.

That a machine boss always kept his word was part of an old American political script.[16] A political machine depends on the reliable ob-

---

[14] Steinberg, *Man from Missouri*, pp. 72-73.

[15] Gaddis, "Harry S Truman," p. 496.

[16] And still is. In 1980, Mayor Jane Byrne was sharply criticized for giving her endorsement to President Carter, then transferring support to Kennedy only two weeks later. Chicago political veterans recalled that Boss Daley said little, but always kept the promises he gave. Eugene Kennedy, "Hard Times in Chicago," *New York Times Magazine*, March 9, 1980.

servance of oral commitments by both the Boss and his adherents. The machine attended to the needs of each voter throughout the year—dispensing jobs, loans, coal, and free Christmas dinners—in return for his promise to support the machine slate. Although thugs could be used on election day to force compliance and punish ingrates, excessive violence might provoke a federal investigation. In return for their loyal support on election day, machine followers expected the Boss to keep *his* promises to assist them when times were bad, and provide entertainment in the form of speakeasies, baseball tickets, political rallies, and picnics. The founder of the Pendergast machine, a gregarious saloon keeper named Jim, taught his younger brother Tom to judge an individual by whether he kept his word. No matter how unsavory a man's character, if he kept his agreements, he was respected by Tom and Jim.

Boss Pendergast conformed to the script. In an interview with a reporter shortly before he died, Pendergast attempted to defend his career: "I've never broken my word. Put this down: I've never broken my word to any living human being I gave it to. That is the key to success in politics or anything else." At his funeral, the priest intoned, "We all know he was a man of his word. I have heard men say they would rather have his word than his note." Truman maintained that Pendergast "was always honest with me, and when he made a promise, he kept it. If he told me something, I knew it was the truth." Years after Pendergast died in poverty and disgrace, Truman reminisced that "his word was better than the contracts of most businessmen."[17]

As presiding judge of the county court, Truman successfully campaigned for a new bond issue to build roads. To persuade the voters that their increased taxes would not be siphoned off by the Pendergast machine, Truman pledged that he would grant road contracts only to the lowest bidder. Soon after he let a $400,000 contract to a South Dakota firm, Pendergast summoned him into his office. Standing behind Pendergast were several irate contractors who had built hundreds of miles of crumbling "piecrust roads." When they demanded an inside track, Truman firmly announced that contracts would go to the lowest bidder. Pendergast turned to his friends and said, "Get out of here."

[17] Steinberg, *Man from Missouri*, pp. 68, 229-30; McNaughton and Hehmeyer, *This Man Truman*, p. 69; William Hillman, ed., *Mr. President: The First Publication from the Personal Diaries, Private Letters, Papers, and Revealing Interviews of Harry S Truman, Thirty-second President of the United States of America* (New York: Farrar, Straus and Young, 1952), pp. 188-89; William M. Reddig, *Tom's Town, Kansas City and the Pendergast Legend* (Philadelphia: J. B. Lippincott, 1947), p. 385; Grace and Morris Milgram, "The Man from Missouri," *Common Sense* 13 (October 1944), p. 349.

After they left, Pendergast said to Truman, "You carry out your commitments." Though Truman was fond of telling this story, it has an apocryphal ring. Nevertheless, the anecdote epitomizes the script Truman had derived from his association with Pendergast.[18]

Truman followed the code in his own political dealings. "No contract should be entered into lightly," he said. "When I say I'm going to do something, I do it, or bust my insides trying to do it." Because of his conscientiousness in carrying out his commitments, Truman acquired the reputation of a man who could be trusted to keep his agreements. In a personality sketch written soon after he became president, *Time* magazine observed that "to Harry Truman, the complete politician, a promise is a promise, something to be kept."[19] The *New Republic* contrasted Truman's candor and trustworthiness favorably with FDR's equivocation and slipperiness:

> Truman has another trait which will serve the cause of smooth administration of our government, not only in the immediate task, but in others as well. He has the training of a politician, and the reputation of adhering to the code of the politician. Mr. Roosevelt was also a skilled politician, but in a different sense. He had the intuition to know where the winds of public opinion were blowing, where the centers of power lay, what line to take in arousing the people and what must be done either to conciliate or to overpower those who might block his main objective. But he did not maintain harmony in his administrative family. He made too many opposing commitments, forgot too many promises. Mr. Truman plays the game more the way Jim Farley played it. With his associates his word is his bond. He keeps his promises to those who have helped him. This is what enables even the most corrupt boss to operate his machine and win elections; it is a useful habit for any political administrator, even the most honest.[20]

After Hitler invaded the Soviet Union in June 1941, Truman told a reporter in an off-the-cuff interview: "If we see that Germany is winning we ought to help Russia and if Russia is winning we ought to help Germany and that way let them kill as many as possible, although I don't want to see Hitler victorious under any circumstances. *Neither of them thinks any thing of their pledged word*." Truman once told a journalist, "Look at Hitler. His word wasn't good, so he got nowhere,

[18] Steinberg, *Man from Missouri*, pp. 88-89; Hillman, *Mr. President*, p. 87; Cochran, *Harry Truman*, pp. 61-62.

[19] "The 'Thirty-Second,' " *Time*, April 23, 1945, p. 22.

[20] "President Truman's Task," *New Republic*, April 23, 1945, p. 540.

finally." As president, Truman applied the test of whether the Soviets had faithfully carried out their agreements to decide whether the United States could continue to work with the Soviets in the postwar world. According to his press secretary, Jonathan Daniels, "The old Jackson County political emphasis on the keeping of a word given seemed to Truman to be pertinent in foreign affairs—the politics of the world."[21]

But for a practical politician like Truman—not a statesman—it was a man's public *reputation* for keeping his promises that counted, not his private observance. Truman showed himself not unwilling to violate in private the principles he proclaimed publicly. Although personally honest and morally scrupulous, Truman was not bothered by the corruption, drug peddling, prostitution, graft, and bribery practiced by the Pendergast machine. In 1930, he wrote a memorandum to himself in which he defended Pendergast's immorality because of the public service the Boss provided:

> I am only a small duck in a very large puddle, but I am interested very deeply in local or municipal government. Who is to blame for present conditions but sniveling church members who weep on Sunday, play with whores on Monday, drink on Tuesday, sell out to the Boss on Wednesday, repent about Friday, and start over on Sunday. I think the Boss is nearer Heaven than the snivelers.

Nor was Truman concerned that his own election to public office was obtained through fraudulent voter registration. In a 1944 interview, Truman did not dispute a reporter's claim that he had won the 1934 Senate primaries by about 40,000 votes and that subsequent vote fraud convictions showed about 86,000 fraudulent registrations in Kansas City alone. "Those things were due to overzealousness by Tom's boys," Truman explained. "They were too anxious to make a good showing for the boss and they took the easiest way. Tom didn't know anything about it—he was never involved in that sort of thing. Those fake registrations weren't needed to enable the machine to win."[22]

A foreign policy leader following the "code of the politician" could be expected to carry out national commitments even when the original interests underlying them had changed. In contrast, diplomatic history

---

[21] Donovan, *Conflict and Crisis*, p. 36, emphasis added; Cochran, *Harry Truman*, p. 30; Daniels, *Man of Independence*, p. 270.

[22] M. Truman, *Harry Truman*, p. 74; Gerald Johnson, "Truman," *Life*, November 6, 1944, p. 114; Marshall, "Portrait of Truman," p. 439; Milgram, "The Man from Missouri," p. 349.

is replete with examples of states failing to carry out their obligations to defend other states, of disregarding nonaggression treaties as so many "scraps of paper," of unilaterally withdrawing from international contracts. Because Truman observed the "code of the politician," however, one would expect him to observe previous agreements with the Russians—on occupation zones in Germany, armistice arrangements in Eastern Europe, the concessions made in return for Soviet entrance into the war against Japan, and allied military strategy—even as our growing rivalry with the Soviets caused some of his advisers to question whether policies premised on great power cooperation were still appropriate. For a politician like Truman, what was most important was the bond established between two men by an agreement, not the relationship between two nations. On the other hand, since a man's public reputation for keeping agreements was more important than his legal observance, Truman could be expected to be indifferent to whether the Soviets actually complied with the spirit of lofty, idealistic proclamations such as the Yalta Declaration on Liberated Europe, or the Atlantic Charter, unlike some of his Wilsonian advisers in the State Department. For Truman, it was sufficient to invoke Wilsonian principles in public speeches; he was unconcerned about the gap between American rhetoric and policy. Truman's lack of concern for the disparity between word and deed, and his insensitivity to the danger of arousing unrealistic expectations among the American people, were frustrating and irritating to Realist advisers such as Dean Acheson and the British Foreign Office.

Since the presiding judge of the county court by tradition served no more than two terms, Truman was faced with unemployment in 1934 unless he could win Pendergast's endorsement for another political office. Fortunately, Pendergast was desperately looking for a senatorial candidate willing to challenge popular congressman "Tuck" Milligan. After several leading Democratic politicians refused to make the race, Pendergast asked Truman, who eagerly accepted. Truman was as surprised as anyone else when he, an obscure county judge, won election to the U.S. Senate. By energetically cranking out ghost votes, Pendergast's lieutenants rolled up 137,529 votes for Truman, while only 8,912 went to Milligan and 1,525 to Cochran. Years later, his experience with the flagrant voting fraud practiced under Pendergast's regime caused Truman to be skeptical about the prospects for "free elections" in Russian-occupied Eastern Europe.

Since he lacked formal education and political experience outside of county government, Senator Truman did not speak out on the questions of fascism, the Bolshevik revolution, or Stalin's purges. He compared the unknown and incomprehensible phenomenon of Stalinist Russia to a more familiar realm of experience—Jackson county politics. In 1938, Truman charged that the reappointment of Maurice Milligan as U.S. attorney for the Western district amounted to approval of "Hitler-Stalin tactics." Milligan had been almost solely responsible for the collapse of the Pendergast machine; he obtained guilty verdicts in 283 cases of ballot-box stuffing. "A Jackson County, Mo., Democrat has as much chance of a fair trial in the Federal District Court of Western Missouri as a Jew would have in a Hitler Court or a Trotsky follower before Stalin," Truman declared.[23]

Truman first won national attention as chairman of the Senate Special Committee to investigate the National Defense Program. After receiving numerous letters complaining about the widespread waste and inefficiency in the construction of Fort Leonard Wood in Missouri in early 1941, he began to worry that the vast sums allocated for defense production were being mismanaged and wasted. Truman recalled the 116 congressional committees established after World War I to expose boondoggles and corruption in war production. Reasoning from an episodic script, he concluded that an investigating committee should be set up while defense production was in progress, instead of after the war, when it would be impossible to correct abuses. "It won't do any good digging up dead horses after the war is over like last time," he argued. "The thing to do is dig this stuff up now and correct it." Truman also recalled that he had been reading the records of the Civil War investigating committee of the Union Congress, whose mistakes had been of material assistance to the Confederacy. He resolved to avoid this committee's mistakes as well.[24] In early February 1941, Truman successfully sponsored a resolution calling for a Senate investigation of defense production and procurement.

As chairman of the Senate investigating committee, Truman practiced political skills that he later used as president in dealing with foreign countries. He preferred to use quiet persuasion in place of public confrontation to induce government agencies and contractors to correct abuses uncovered by his committee's investigations. But when persuasion failed, Truman "got tough." The *New Republic* praised his

[23] For Truman's views as a senator on the American role in the world, see Wilson Miscamble, "The Evolution of an Internationalist: Harry S Truman," *Australian Journal of Politics and History* 23 (August 1977): 268-83; *Congressional Record*, 83, pt. 2:1938, February 15, 1938; George Creel, "Truman of Missouri," *Colliers*, September 9, 1944, pp. 63-64.

[24] Steinberg, *Man from Missouri*, pp. 181-82; McNaughton and Hehmeyer, *This Man Truman*, pp. 91-93; Daniels, *Man of Independence*, p. 218; Truman, *Memoirs*, 1:168.

firm handling of the "big, unwilling guys who had been telling war-production officials where to get off." On one occasion, a powerful corporation official holding millions of dollars in defense contracts barged into Truman's office to tell him to "call off his dogs." The contractor later exited meekly, crestfallen and discomfited. His interview with Truman had consisted of a series of repetitions of the following exchange:

"Are the charges true or false?"

"Well, you see—"[25]

The episode foreshadows Truman's famous "straight one-two to the jaw" interview with Molotov. Journalist Irving Brant reported that on the Senate floor, Truman was a "hard, tough fighter, tangling with his closest Democratic friends as readily as with partisan opponents, and greeting both with the heartiest friendship in the cloakroom a few minutes later."[26]

Journalists credited the committee with saving billions of dollars through timely exposure of corruption and waste in government and private industry. Though the committee's accomplishments were hyperinflated, by publicizing questionable practices of unethical contractors and "dollar a year" defense officials, Truman's committee did check many of the worst abuses. After he appeared on the cover of *Time* in March 1943, his name was increasingly mentioned as a possible candidate for vice-president.[27]

TRUMAN'S WORLD ORDER

No historian has given sustained attention to Harry Truman's foreign affairs philosophy. Many have wondered whether Truman had any ideas at all. But despite his lack of formal training in foreign affairs, Truman's mind was not a blank sheet; he had acquired a set of assumptions about the causes of war and the requirements of peace because he had lived through a tumultuous era in world politics.

During the first weeks of his presidency, Truman often vowed to carry on Roosevelt's policies—including Soviet-American collaboration in foreign affairs. "I know I can't measure up to him," he admitted humbly. "But there are some things I want to do. . . . I want to win two wars. I want to ensure getting a peace organization. And I want

---

[25] Irving Brant, "Harry S Truman: II," *New Republic*, May 7, 1945, p. 635.

[26] Irving Brant, "Harry S Truman," *New Republic*, April 30, 1945, 578.

[27] Huston, "The Vice President Talks," pp. 44-45; Daniels, *Man of Independence*, p. 223; Steinberg, *Man from Missouri*, p. 197.

to carry forward the policies of Franklin Roosevelt, just as he did, if I can."[28]

But Roosevelt's legacy was uncertain. Throughout the war, FDR refused to disclose specific war aims or his plans for the peace. As the war progressed and FDR's thinking crystallized, he revealed to the American public the essence of his "Grand Design" for a great power concert. Roosevelt left no doubt that the Big Three would dominate the new world organization and bear the burden of policing the peace. In his 1943 State of the Union Message, Roosevelt belittled the League of Nations as a "formula for permanent peace, based on a magnificent idealism" whose failure proved that peace could not be maintained by good intentions alone. To prevent future wars, he said, the United States, Britain, and the USSR "can and must remain united." In April 1943, as a "trial balloon," Roosevelt allowed the *Saturday Evening Post* to publish a tacitly authorized account of his plans for peace, based on a confidential interview with journalist Forrest Davis, which stressed the overriding importance of maintaining Soviet-American cooperation in the postwar world. In May 1944, FDR allowed the *Saturday Evening Post* to publish another two-part article on his "grand design," which revealed for the first time his plan to have the "Four Policemen"—Britain, the United States, the Soviet Union, and China—enforce the peace within the framework of an international organization.[29]

He was less candid about the price the United States would have to pay to secure Soviet collaboration—recognition of a Soviet sphere of influence in Eastern Europe. He had reason to be. Several million Polish-Americans might desert the "New Deal" coalition and vote Republican in 1944 if convinced that Poland had been delivered to Soviet domination. Disclosure of Stalin's war aims might provoke a recurrence of American isolationism. Several influential Senators had threatened to withhold endorsement of the United Nations if the peace settlement failed to live up to the principles of the Atlantic Charter. To avoid endangering his internationalist foreign policy, FDR allowed the American people to believe that the postwar settlement would be based on the principle of national self-determination. He persuaded Churchill and Stalin to sign the Yalta Declaration on Liberated Europe as a sop to American public opinion. Calling for the formation of

[28] David E. Lilienthal, *The Journals of David E. Lilienthal* (New York: Harper & Row, 1964), vol. 1, *The TVA Years, 1939-45*, p. 699; Wallace diary, May 19, 1945, *Price of Vision*, ed. Blum, p. 454.

[29] Divine, *Second Chance*, pp. 114-15; Davis, "Roosevelt's World Blueprint"; idem, "What Really Happened at Teheran, I and II."

representative governments in Eastern Europe and free elections, the Declaration lacked any enforcement machinery.[30]

After Truman became president, he continued FDR's policy of promoting Big Three collaboration, while glossing over the implications of a great power concert for the principles of self-determination and sovereign equality of all nations. In his first major presidential address, Truman stressed that continued unity of the great powers was essential for peace. But he assured the public that "the responsibility of the great states is to serve and not dominate the world."[31]

Had Roosevelt confided to Truman his deception of the American public? Not likely. During the eighty-two days that Truman spent as vice-president, Roosevelt was in Washington for less than a month. Truman had only two official appointments with the president, and much of their discussion concerned domestic politics.[32] But Truman's views on world politics happened to coincide with Roosevelt's. This should not surprise us, since both men endured the maelstrom of world politics in the 1930s.

Scholars have assumed that Truman's idealistic public pronouncements reflected his private beliefs. His beliefs about world order were a contradictory mishmash of political realism and lofty idealism. He enjoyed spinning "golden dreams" about world peace. But when it came to concrete, real-world problems, Truman was as skilled a practitioner of *Realpolitik* as any president. Dean Acheson recalled that

> he did not share the indiscriminate condemnation of power in politics, domestic or foreign, that American liberals learned from Lord Acton. Military power he had experienced in use. He knew its nature, its importance, and its limitations. He knew that its primary effectiveness was in overcoming opposing military power or deterring another's use of it, or in overawing an opponent and gaining acceptance of one's own will.[33]

Truman recognized that without world government, war was always possible. In a 1944 speech, Truman pointed out that "even if the ma-

[30] Gaddis, *Origins of the Cold War*, pp. 17, 30, 134, 149-50; Dallek, *Roosevelt and American Foreign Policy*, pp. 438-39, 478-80, 507, 516; Arthur H. Vandenberg Jr., ed., *The Private Papers of Senator Vandenberg* (Boston: Houghton Mifflin, 1952), pp. 96-97, 104-105.

[31] Message to Congress, April 16, 1945, *Department of State Bulletin* 12 (April 22, 1945): 722.

[32] Truman, *Memoirs*, 1:1-2; Steinberg, *Man from Missouri*, pp. 230-31; Daniels, *Man of Independence* pp. 256-57, 259.

[33] Acheson, *Present at the Creation*, p. 732.

jority of nations were to renounce war, it would be merely an idle pretense. As long as there exists one single nation that may make a sovereign choice of war, all other nations must be prepared to do likewise."[34]

The results of appeasement in the thirties had convinced Truman that only willingness to use preponderant force could deter aggressors. "Who can say what the results would have been if France had prevented Hitler from occupying the Rhineland as she could have done— or if England had gone along with us in preventing Japan's grab in Manchuria," Truman asked rhetorically in a 1944 speech. Very little concerted action might have deterred Italy's conquest of Ethiopia. "Timely action might have made unnecessary the cost in lives and resources now being expended by the United Nations to restore to the world peace among men," Truman declared. To prevent the rise of German and Japanese militarism, Truman supported the unconditional surrender policy and forced disarmament.[35]

But even disarmament of the Axis nations would not be sufficient to preserve the peace if the victorious powers again fell to squabbling after the war. Again, Truman was influenced by an episodic script drawn from the interwar period. In 1944, Truman said that "if we had kept together after the first World War—if we had taken common measures for the safety and security of the world—the present war need not have happened." A year later, Truman predicted that "unless there is complete understanding between [the] three great powers, there will be no peace. It will be a truce—armistice, which will be just like the one we had in 1920."[36]

The great powers would have to remain united to discharge their responsibilities for policing the peace. Wilsonian collective security had failed. The League of Nations had proved that "individual nations will not go to war or risk war simply to save the peace of the world, even though it is now clear that their own peace is involved sooner or later." Months before Roosevelt revealed his plans for the "Four Policemen," Truman publicly advocated a thinly disguised great power concert. In a January 1944 speech, Truman boldly declared that "the only logical basis for erecting a lasting peace and reconstructing a war-torn world

[34] Truman Speech before the United Nations Forum, January 17, 1944, *Appendix to the Congressional Record*, 90, pt 8: A266.

[35] Speech in Toledo, Ohio, June 14, 1944, Truman Papers: Senatorial and Vice-Presidential Files, HSTL; Harry S Truman to Mrs. Howard Wills, March 29, 1944, ibid.

[36] Speech in Toledo, Ohio, June 14, 1944, ibid.; Press Conference #13, Association of Radio News Analysts, June 16, 1945, off the record (microfilm, Stanford University Library).

must be in a new, improved league of nations . . . controlled by Britain, China, Russia, and the United States, in the name of all and for the welfare of all."[37]

Throughout much of his senatorial career, Truman had urged that the United States undertake an active role in world affairs. Although he succumbed to political pressures and voted for the neutrality laws of 1935, 1936, and 1937, he did not believe that legislated neutrality could keep the United States out of war. In 1937, Truman charged that the neutrality policy was a "farce," a misguided attempt to prevent war by sinking the U.S. Navy instead of assuming our responsibilities as a world power.[38] In 1939, Truman recommended that Congress amend the neutrality laws to allow the sale of arms to Britain. In early 1943, he worked diligently to secure passage of a Senate resolution in favor of an international security organization, when Roosevelt was still procrastinating for fear of stirring up American isolationists. That summer, Truman participated in an arduous, unpaid lecture tour of nineteen Great Plains cities, sponsored by a public interest group, to win public support for an international organization. According to Harry Hopkins, Roosevelt selected Truman as his running mate so that he could lobby the Senate for ratification of the peace settlement.[39]

Like Roosevelt, Truman viewed the United Nations not as a panacea, but as a means of ensuring continuing American participation in world affairs. Again, he was influenced by an episodic script. He believed that the Senate's repudiation of the League of Nations had led ultimately to the outbreak of World War II, and that another world war would occur unless the United States assumed responsibility for maintaining the peace. In 1943, he reminded the Senate that:

A small group of willful men kept us from assuming our world obligations in 1919-20, and the same thing can happen again. I am just as sure as I can be that this World War is the result of the 1919-20 isolationist attitude, and I am equally sure that another and a worse war will follow this one, unless the United Nations and their

[37] Speech before the United Nations Forum, January 17, 1944, *Appendix to the Congressional Record*, 90: A266; Speech in Toledo, June 14, 1944, Truman Papers: Senatorial and Vice-Presidential Files, HSTL.

[38] Truman, *Memoirs*, 1:153, 189-90; Speech Delivered at Kansas City, April 19, 1937, Truman Papers: Senatorial and Vice-Presidential Files, HSTL.

[39] Divine, *Second Chance*, pp. 92, 127-28, 148, 279-80; McNaughton and Hehmeyer, *This Man Truman*, pp. 119-20; Vandenberg diary, March 16, 1943, *Private Papers*, ed. Vandenberg, p. 39; *New York Times*, March 15, 1943; *New York Times*, March 20, 1943; M. Truman, *Harry Truman*, pp. 156-57; Daniels, *Man of Independence*, p. 259.

allies, and all the other sovereign nations, decide to work together for peace as they are working together for victory.[40]

Consequently, Truman would never admit publicly that he had written off Eastern Europe to Soviet domination. Like Roosevelt, Truman was sensitive to the hostile public reaction that would be aroused by the merest whiff of "spheres of influence" or "power politics."

Truman also shared Roosevelt's views on the importance of free trade for world peace. Consistent with his "great man" theory of history, in 1939 Truman traced the periodic recurrence of wars to the inability of Caesar, King Henry IV of France, Napoleon, and Woodrow Wilson to carry out their plans for eliminating trade barriers:

> Caesar and Napoleon wanted to place the whole continent of Europe, Asia, and Africa . . . under the same hegemony, break down the trade barriers, and use their unlimited resources for the benefit of the whole population. Caesar was assassinated before he finished his plan and no successor of his had his ability or insight.
>
> Napoleon almost succeeded, and then he went to Russia. . . .
>
> King Henry's plea was a United States of Europe with a congress and a senate to work out the difficulties of the various states, take down the trade barriers, live and let live. He also was assassinated before he could accomplish his purpose.
>
> None of you have forgotten Woodrow Wilson and his 16 points for peace. He was destroyed by European power politics as played by Lloyd George and Clemenceau, and by the United States Senate. His grand plan was almost the same one that Henry the Fourth proposed. It failed, and Europe is right back where Julius Caesar left off.

Truman believed that World War I had been caused by Germany's need for raw materials to power her industries and feed her growing population.[41]

After World War II broke out, Truman shared the Roosevelt administration's assessment that competitive currency devaluations and restrictive trade barriers had led to depression, the rise of fascist dictators, and war. In March 1944, Truman joined with two other senators

---

[40] Speech before the Senate, November 2, 1943, *Congressional Record*, 89, pt. 7:8993. See also Speech in Toledo, Ohio, June 14, 1944, and Speech in Washington, D.C., April 14, 1944, Truman Papers: Senatorial and Vice-Presidential Files, HSTL.

[41] Speech in Caruthersville, Mo., October 8, 1939, *Appendix to the Congressional Record*, 85, pt. 2:202; Speech before the National Aviation Forum, February 20, 1939, *Appendix to Congressional Record*, 84, pt. 11:642.

in sponsoring a resolution favoring international economic cooperation. The resolution read in part:

> The future peace depends on the abandonment of political nationalism and economic imperialism and autarchy. Our policy before the war of making reciprocal trade agreements with individual countries was good policy. . . . Only by expanding such a Good Neighbor policy and by doing it quickly can we forestall the growth of areas of economic disaffection which eventually enlarge into world wars.

Truman also recognized that expanding world trade would benefit the United States by providing markets for excess production. As president, Truman wholeheartedly supported the open door policy.[42]

TRUMAN'S INFORMATION PROCESSING STYLE

Like any President, Truman had his own methods of gathering and using specialized information, which shaped his approach to staffing and organizing the executive branch. Conscious of the deficiencies in his education and intellectual background, as a senator Truman often remarked wistfully, "I wish I had had a college education. I might have accomplished something better. I feel a terrible inadequacy of education." The Hovland approach predicts that Truman would be among the first to change his beliefs about the Soviet Union, since he had low self-esteem and was easily influenced by others. When a few of his closest advisers in the White House and State Department adopted Cold War beliefs about the Soviet Union, Truman should have been ready to abandon FDR's bold—and risky—"grand design."

Instead of trying to acquire (or simulate) expertise in areas of which he was ignorant, Truman preferred to organize the problem, hire experts, and back their conclusions. But he insisted on evaluating the evidence and making the final decision for himself. As chairman of the committee investigating national defense production, Truman appointed competent subcommittee chairmen, gave them a free hand in investigating, and backed them against hostile witnesses and political pressures. After he became President, Truman promised that he would get the best men available and rely on them. He told Henry Wallace that "he knew he didn't have much in the way of brains but that he did have enough brains to get hold of people who were able and give them a chance to carry responsibility." "But I shall always be President

[42] Joint Statement to the Senate by Truman, Senator Thomas, and Senator Kilgore, March 7, 1944, *Congressional Record*, 90, pt. 2:2299.

and make the final decision in matters of major policy after they give me their facts and their recommendations," he said. "He delegates!" Davies observed with surprise and pleasure. "A complete and definite contrast to F.D.R."[43]

It was a method of administration that suited his cognitive style. He read official reports rapidly but superficially, skipping over the details. Truman preferred to let others handle particulars, leaving him free to concentrate on the broad issues.[44]

Whenever possible, Truman preferred to make decisions using information he had acquired through personal experience. (As we have said, psychologists have found that people give more weight to information derived from their own experience than to abstract data obtained secondhand or from printed material.)[45] As a senator, when Truman heard rumors about widespread waste and fraud in defense production, he climbed into his Chevrolet coupe and visited camps and defense plants for himself, traveling over 30,000 miles.[46] As president, Truman loved to get away from Washington and mingle with small-town folks and farm families. A *Washington Post* reporter observed that:

> President Truman, whatever his virtues and faults, is the friendliest man who has occupied the White House in a generation. He likes people. He likes to get out where they live and shake hands with them and talk to them in their own language. He likes to know what they are thinking about and *he would prefer to know it firsthand.*[47]

Attribution theory predicts that Truman would draw too many and too permanent conclusions about U.S.-Soviet relations from his brief meetings with Stalin at the Potsdam Conference, since this was the only time he met with the Russian leader.

Truman characteristically made decisions rapidly. Shortly after he became president, Truman told Eden that "I am here to make deci-

---

[43] McNaughton and Hehmeyer, *This Man Truman*, p. 133; Brant, "Harry S Truman," p. 579; Wallace diary, June 15, 1945, *Price of Vision*, ed. Blum, p. 462; Davies diary, May 13, 21, 1945, Joseph E. Davies Papers, LC.

[44] McNaughton and Hehmeyer, *This Man Truman*, pp. 131-32; Notes on Lunch with Dean Acheson, June 2, 1966, Feis Papers, "Personal Traits and Relations with Aides," LC.

[45] Daniels, *Man of Independence*, p. 51; Nisbett and Ross, *Human Inference*, pp. 49-50, 58-59.

[46] Steinberg, *Man from Missouri*, pp. 180-81; Daniels, *Man of Independence*, p. 281; McNaughton and Hehmeyer, *This Man Truman*, pp. 91-93.

[47] *Washington Post*, October 10, 1945, emphasis added.

sions, and whether they prove right or wrong I am going to take them."[48]

In contrast to Truman's crisp decisiveness, Roosevelt had had a habit of toying with a problem, taking different positions from one minute to the next, advancing a step in one direction only to hop three steps to the side. Former Roosevelt cabinet members immediately noticed the new atmosphere of efficiency and dispatch that pervaded the White House. Secretary of War Stimson commented that:

> it was a wonderful relief to preceding conferences with our former Chief to see the promptness and snappiness with which Truman took up each matter and decided it. There were no long drawn-out "soliloquies" from the President, and the whole conference was thoroughly businesslike so that we actually covered two or three more matters than we had expected to discuss.[49]

Stimson remarked that Truman's cabinet meeting was the "quickest" he could remember since he entered the War Department in 1940. "The president kept everybody on the jump and did not spend any time talking himself but simply in snapping the whip over the others," he recorded. Assistant Secretary of State Grew wrote to a friend: "When I saw him today I had fourteen problems to take up with him and got through them in less than fifteen minutes with a clear directive on every one of them. You can imagine what a joy it is to deal with a man like that and my admiration and liking for him daily increase." House leader Rayburn said that with Truman they got more decided in fifteen minutes than Roosevelt used to decide in an hour and three-quarters. Secretary of Commerce Henry Wallace was more perceptive. He noticed that Truman "seemed eager to make decisions of every kind with the greatest promptness. Everything he said was decisive. It almost seemed as though he was eager to decide in advance of thinking." One of Truman's aides later recalled that he developed a "mania" for making decisions and was disappointed when there were none to render at the moment.[50]

This type of information processing encourages several major types of errors: the use of inappropriate generalizations or analogies, premature cognitive closure, and incomplete or erroneous causal analysis. Rapid-fire decisionmaking requires cognitive "shortcuts"; the decision-

[48] Eden, The Reckoning, p. 621.

[49] Stimson diary, April 18, 1945.

[50] Joseph C. Grew, Turbulent Era: A Diplomatic Record of Forty Years, 1904-1945 (Boston: Houghton Mifflin, 1952), 2:1485n; Wallace diary, April 27, June 9, 1945, in Price of Vision, ed. Blum, pp. 437, 459; Steinberg, Man from Missouri, p. 246.

maker does not have time to formulate his values, search for a reasonable number of alternatives, forecast the consequences of each action, and rank them according to his value hierarchy. Schematic processing does not require much cognitive labor; the person matches a situation to an analogous historical event, person, or object. The danger, of course, with analogical thinking is that the historical analogy will be incomparable, the metaphor strained, the persona laughable. Once a decisionmaker has applied a schema to an emerging problem, he will wrench information so that it fits the frame, and is apt to overlook an alternative conceptual framework that better explains the data. Finally, the policymaker under psychic pressure to make quick decisions is likely to stop at the first satisfactory explanation, instead of considering alternative interpretations.[51] Roosevelt's talent for procrastination—so maddening to his subordinates—served him well by giving him time to acquire new information bearing on the problem, a different perspective, or the luxury of not having to make a decision after all.

Truman's insecurity about his lack of formal education and expertise probably contributed to his impulsive decisionmaking. He knew that Roosevelt's former advisers could not look at him without making unflattering comparisons to their great leader. Making decisions quickly was a means of proving to Washington officials that *he* was in charge and in command of events.[52]

Truman's tendency to respond reflexively, according to well-rehearsed scripts, often got him into trouble. When he became president, members of his administration began to worry that he would make decisions based on insufficient information. Truman himself was aware of the dangers of his impulsiveness. In June 1945 he told a hometown crowd that he was not having as much trouble now making decisions as he had when he was a judge in Jackson county. Then, he explained, whenever he made a decision he had to get the agreement of at least one other judge. "Now," Truman said, grinning, "I don't have to get anybody's agreement but Harry Truman's, and sometimes I am afraid that agreement comes too quickly. Let's hope that it

[51] Taylor and Crocker, "Schematic Bases of Social Information Processing," pp. 93, 118; Hazel Markus, "Self-Schemata and Processing of Information about the Self," *Journal of Personality and Social Psychology* 35 (1977): 64; Schneider, Hastorf, and Ellsworth, *Person Perception*, p. 251; David Kanouse, "Language, Labeling, and Attribution," in *Attribution: Perceiving the Causes of Behavior*, ed. Edward E. Jones et al. (Morristown, N.J.: General Learning Press, 1971), p. 131; Jervis, *Perception and Misperception*, p. 187-95.

[52] Herbert Feis, *From Trust To Terror: The Onset of the Cold War* (New York: W. W. Norton, 1970), p. 8.

doesn't." His apprehensions proved to be well-founded. Six months later, Wallace remarked sadly, "it is more and more evident that the President arrives at decisions on the spur of the moment on the basis of partial evidence. He does *so* like to agree with whomever is with him at the moment."[53]

As Wallace's observation suggests, Truman had a predilection for agreeing with his advisers. Each of Roosevelt's former cabinet members was impressed with his influence over the new president. Henry Wallace noted that "Truman was exceedingly eager to agree with everything I said." In private, when Morgenthau mentioned Wallace's name, Truman let forth some foul language to indicate his disrespect for Wallace's opinions. "Wallace is nothing but a cat bastard," Truman said vehemently. Secretary of Treasury Henry Morgenthau wrote in his diary: "I again went away with the distinct feeling that the man likes me and has confidence in me, and I must say my confidence in him continues to grow." Two months later he was out. Truman later told Jonathan Daniels that "Morgenthau didn't know shit from apple butter." Under Secretary Grew recorded in his diary that

> The President, as usual, was exceedingly affable and, as usual, he expressed full appreciation of my recommendations and advice. He said that he welcomed all my recommendations and that if at any time he disagreed with them he would tell me so with complete frankness but, whether he agreed with them or not, he welcomed having them made. Among all the Presidents under whom I have served, I have never known one who seems so genuinely grateful for advice on any subject.

To his friend Eddie McKim, Truman growled: "Ed, I'm going to clean out that goddamn state department and get some people in there with guts and leadership." In October 1945, when Henry Wallace told Marquis Childs that his relationship with Truman was good, the columnist warned: "Well, that is one of the great difficulties with the President; he does that way with everyone."[54] Truman's decisiveness may have

[53] Wallace diary, May 4, June 9, December 11, 1945, *Price of Vision*, ed. Blum, pp. 440-441, 459, 528; *Washington Post*, June 29, 1945.

[54] Martin Weil, *A Pretty Good Club: The Founding Fathers of the U.S. Foreign Service* (New York: W. W. Norton, 1978), p. 225; Grew, *Turbulent Era*, 2:1485; Wallace diary, April 27, October 15, 1945, *Price of Vision*, ed. Blum, pp. 437, 491; Morgenthau presidential diary, May 9, June 6, 1945, Henry M. Morgenthau, Jr. Papers, FDRL; Morgenthau diary, April 14, 1945, *From the Morgenthau Diaries*, ed. Blum, 3:423; McNaughton Report, May 11, 1945, Frank McNaughton Papers, HSTL.

been his way of compensating for his propensity to agree with everyone.[55]

Truman was not an ideologue or a systematizer of ideas. Many of his beliefs were inconsistent, and the situation determined which of his many convictions became salient to Truman at that particular moment. Thus, at one cabinet meeting, Truman announced that the budget had to be trimmed, and that the place to make cuts was in the military budget. But less than half an hour later, Truman spoke against making any reductions in the army and navy. "If we had not cut our army and navy after the last war there would not have been World War II," he said. Amazed, Henry Wallace commented in his diary:

> I suspect there has never been a President who could move two different directions with less time intervening than Truman. He feels completely sincere and earnest at all times and is not disturbed in the slightest by the different directions in which his mind can go almost simultaneously.[56]

Because Truman seemed to be unaware of, much less bothered by, the inconsistency in his statements, he should not have suffered from cognitive dissonance. Thus, self-perception theory would better explain his response to Soviet behavior. A practical politician like Truman has few permanent opinions on political issues, and is more likely to use his actions and the context as a guide to his beliefs. If a self-perception interpretation is correct, then Truman should have changed his beliefs about the Soviet Union *after* he had adopted the new policy of containment, not before. In addition, Truman's beliefs should have been highly unstable, varying from one situation to another, because the United States alternately clashed and cooperated with the Soviets after the war.

[55] Robert Jervis pointed out this pattern to me.
[56] Wallace diary, July 24, 1946, *Price of Vision*, ed. Blum, pp. 601-602.

CHAPTER FOUR

Keeping Agreements

GETTING TOUGH WITH RUSSIA

ALTHOUGH excluded from policymaking under Roosevelt, Truman knew that U.S.-Soviet relations had cooled considerably since Yalta. By early April, newspaper editorials and magazines almost unanimously condemned the Soviets for establishing a puppet government in Poland. Columnist Drew Pearson pointed out that "friendly feeling" toward Russia had received a jolt because of the widespread impression that "the Yalta promises were not being kept and that the rights of little nations were being trampled on."[1]

In early April, the Russians requested that the Warsaw Poles be invited to the San Francisco Conference if a new Polish government was not agreed upon by then, which would be a tacit admission that the Yalta agreements were null and void. When the United States and Britain refused, Stalin retaliated by announcing that Gromyko rather than Molotov would head a low-ranking Soviet delegation, an action widely interpreted as a slight towards the United Nations Organization. According to *Time* magazine, "Washington, London, Paris instantly leaped to the blackest conclusion: Stalin just didn't give a damn."[2]

As Secretary of State Stettinius informed him about recent developments, Truman's anger grew. The State Department had prepared a memo outlining the background and current status of major foreign policy issues which amounted to a formal complaint against the Soviet government, giving no indication that there were legitimate differences of interpretation over the meaning of the Yalta accords. According to the memo, the Soviets had taken a "firm and uncompromising" position on every major issue since Yalta—the Polish question, application of the Crimea agreement on liberated areas, exchange of prisoners of war, and the San Francisco U.N. Conference. Negotiations to form a new Polish government were deadlocked because Soviet authorities were "consistently sabotaging" Harriman's efforts to carry

---

[1] Levering, *American Opinion and the Russian Alliance*, pp. 194-96.

[2] Divine, *Second Chance*, p. 276; *Time*, April 9, 1945, p. 23; *Newsweek*, April 9, 1945, p. 52; *FR: 1945*, I, pp. 113, 147-48, 164.

out the Yalta decisions. Using their position as head of the allied control commission, the Soviets were interfering in the political affairs of Rumania, Bulgaria, and Hungary, in conflict with the Declaration on Liberated Europe. The Soviets also refused to allow U.S. contact teams to enter Poland to assist in evacuating American P.O.Ws.[3] Truman, who scrupulously adhered to the "code of the politician," found it intolerable that the Russians should so cavalierly disregard the Yalta agreements.[4]

But Truman did not immediately adopt tough tactics. On his desk were several important cables relating to Poland that Roosevelt had been too ill to answer. On April 7, Stalin had complained to FDR that the Polish negotiations were deadlocked because the British and American ambassadors had departed from the Yalta agreements. Instead of enlarging the Warsaw government, they were trying to create an entirely new entity. To end the stalemate, Stalin suggested that they follow the "Yugoslav precedent" and add one new minister for each four ministers in the Warsaw government. This represented an entirely new negotiating position. The Soviets had increased their demands since Yalta.[5]

Churchill had been threatening to make a public statement to the House of Commons blaming the Russians for the breakdown of the Polish negotiations. FDR had asked Churchill not to make any statements without first consulting him. On the advice of the State Department, Truman also advised Churchill not to publicize their differences with the Russians until they had exhausted every possible diplomatic solution. A few days later, at Truman's suggestion, the two leaders sent a joint message to Stalin, assuring him that they never intended to deny that the Warsaw Poles would play a "prominent role" in the Polish provisional government. On the other hand, they could not accept the Warsaw Poles' right to veto candidates for consultations in Moscow in forming a new government. Nor did they see how the Yugoslav pattern could be applied to Poland.[6]

Before receiving the joint message, Stalin relented and decided to send Molotov to San Francisco, as a gesture of respect for the late president. On his way to the U.N. Conference, Molotov planned to

[3] Stettinius Memorandum, "Special Information for the President," April 13, 1945, Truman Papers, PSF: Subject File, Cabinet, HSTL.

[4] *FR: 1945*, V, pp. 235, 253, 255; Forrestal diary, 23 April 1945, *Forrestal Diaries*, ed. Millis, p. 50; Donovan, *Conflict and Crisis*, p. 42; Davies journal, April 30, 1945, Joseph E. Davies Papers, LC.

[5] *FR: 1945*, V, pp. 201-204.

[6] Ibid., pp. 158, 186, 209-12, 220-21.

stop off at Washington to meet the new president. Stalin told Harriman that Molotov's visit afforded a "splendid opportunity" to settle the Polish question.[7]

But the Russians followed up this conciliatory gesture with renewed efforts to bolster the legal status of their Polish puppets. On April 17, Truman learned that the Russians were planning to sign a mutual defense treaty with the Warsaw Polish government. Despite U.S. opposition, the Soviets continued to insist that the Warsaw government be invited to the San Francisco Conference. In addition, the Soviet government now blatantly admitted that they had handed over to the Warsaw Poles former German lands, contrary to previous occupation agreements with the United States and Britain. By his own recollection, Truman decided to "lay it on the line with Molotov."[8]

"Getting tough" was a scriptal response for Truman, an approach he had used successfully in the past when under pressure to assert his authority. He resolved to speak bluntly with the Russians. At his April 17 press conference, a reporter asked Truman if he expected to see Molotov before he went to San Francisco. Truman interrupted to say that yes, he did. "He is going to stop by and pay his respects to the President of the United States," Truman said firmly. "He should." The reporters cheered and clapped for a full minute. On April 19, crusty, outspoken Admiral Leahy briefed Truman on the Yalta Conference and gave him a copy of the cables exchanged between Roosevelt and Stalin on the Berne negotiations. Leahy noted that "the insulting language of the recent Stalin telegrams was an affront to the solid, old-fashioned Americanism possessed by Harry Truman," and predicted that "Molotov would be in for some blunt talking from the American side."[9]

Ambassador Harriman and Foreign Secretary Eden reinforced Truman's determination to "get tough." In his first meeting with Truman on April 20, Ambassador Harriman told the president that the Russians had misinterpreted U.S. generosity as a sign that they could behave as they wished. Harriman assured Truman that the United States had nothing to lose by taking a firm stand on important issues, because the Russians needed our economic assistance for postwar reconstruc-

---

[7] *FR: 1945*, I, p. 289; "President's Personal Notes," April 13, 1945, Truman Papers, PSF: Presidential Appointment File, HSTL.

[8] *FR: 1945*, V, pp. 225-27, 229-31; Truman, *Memoirs*, 1:50.

[9] News Conference, April 17, 1945, *Truman Public Papers, 1945*, p. 11; Lloyd C. Gardner, *Architects of Illusion: Men and Ideas in American Foreign Policy, 1941-1949* (Chicago: Quadrangle Books, 1970), pp. 59-60; William D. Leahy, *I Was There* (New York: McGraw-Hill, 1950), p. 349.

tion. Truman replied that he was "not in any sense afraid of the Russians" and that he intended to be "firm but fair," since the Soviet Union needed us more than we needed them. He would make no concessions from American principles to win Soviet trust. Harriman pointed out that obviously certain concessions would have to be made in the "give and take" of negotiations. Truman said he understood. While we could not get 100 percent of what we wanted, on important matters we should be able to get at least 85 percent, he declared. Harriman quizzed his pupil: just how important did he feel the Polish question was in relation to American participation in the United Nations? Truman replied immediately and decisively that unless a settlement was achieved along the lines of the Yalta decision, the U.N. treaty would never get through the Senate. Would the United States go ahead with plans for the world organization if the Soviets dropped out? Truman would not answer the question directly. The truth of the matter was that without Russia there would not be much of a world organization, he admitted.

That night, Truman stayed up late reading the Yalta agreements. The next day he complained to Stettinius that the Yalta agreement on Poland was amazingly hazy. But recognizing the ambiguity of the agreements did not shake Truman's resolve to make the Soviets accept the American interpretation. He told Eden that he would tell Molotov "in words of one syllable" the importance he attached to settling the Polish question. Congratulating his decision, Foreign Secretary Eden said that the Soviet Union still wanted good relations with the United States, and "plain speaking" might have the desired effects.[10]

Disregarding State Department requests for postponement, the Soviet government signed a friendship treaty with the Warsaw Polish government the day Molotov arrived in Washington, confronting Truman with a fait accompli. Yet, despite all his previous bluster, Truman was restrained in his first meeting with Molotov on April 22. After an exchange of pleasantries, Truman assured Molotov that he "stood squarely" behind all of the commitments and agreements entered into by President Roosevelt. He told the Russian foreign minister that settling the Polish question was the most important problem facing them, because Poland had become a symbol for the American people of our ability to cooperate with the Soviet Union. Molotov replied that he knew the importance of Poland for the United States, but

[10] *FR: 1945*, V, pp. 232-33; Calendar Notes, April 21, 1945, *Diaries of Stettinius*, ed. Campbell and Herring, p. 325; Wilson D. Miscamble, "Anthony Eden and the Truman-Molotov Conversations, April 1945," *Diplomatic History* 2 (Spring 1978): 172.

Poland was vital to the Soviet Union, since it was situated on their borders, far from the United States. Truman repeated three more times that he intended to carry out all agreements made by Roosevelt before concluding their first interview. The next morning, Truman told his staff that he had spoken "plainly" to Molotov.[11]

But Molotov was as difficult as ever. In negotiations with Stettinius and Eden, Molotov stuck to his position that the Yugoslav precedent should be applied to Poland, and that the Warsaw government should be represented in San Francisco. He refused even to consider the proposals outlined in the Churchill-Truman joint message. After a long, tiresome wrangle with Molotov on the morning of April 23, Stettinius promised Eden that he "would mobilize the President to talk like a Dutch Uncle to Molotov." Truman was furious when he heard the news. Truman feared that failure to settle the Polish problem would jeopardize the success of the San Francisco United Nations Conference. As a British diplomat observed, "the question arises whether we can really go to San Francisco to urge the adoption of a plan admittedly based on Great Power cooperation when the Great Powers are so obviously at sixes and sevens." In addition, Truman knew that the Senate would refuse to ratify the U.N. treaty unless a solution was reached along the lines of the Yalta decisions. Truman believed that "continued failure to settle this question endangered the entire U.S. position in taking its place at the world council table."[12]

The president immediately called a meeting of his military and political advisers. Truman complained that all "our agreements with the Soviet Union so far had been a one-way street and that could not continue; it was now or never." He blustered that he intended to go ahead with the plans for San Francisco, and if the Russians did not care to join us, "they could go to hell." Yet, Truman had admitted to Harriman that without the Russians, there would be no world organization.

He asked for comments. Stimson tactfully disagreed with Truman's accusation that the Soviets had failed to keep their agreements. He pointed out that the Russians had kept their word in big military matters, and that U.S. military authorities had come to rely on it. Although the Soviet Union had agreed to free elections in Poland, only the United States and the United Kingdom had any real concep-

[11] FR: 1945, V, pp. 235-36; Ayers diary, April 23, 1945, Eben A. Ayers Papers, HSTL.

[12] FR: 1945, V, pp. 237-41, 241-51; Miscamble, "Eden and the Truman-Molotov Conversations," p. 175; Cadogan diary, April 23, 1945, The Diaries of Sir Alexander Cadogan O.M., 1938-1945, ed. David Dilks (London: Cassell, 1971), p. 732.

tion of an "independent, free ballot"; the party in power always ran the election. The Soviet conception of "independence" and "democracy" in areas vital to the security of the Soviet Union was very different from ours. Stimson advised Truman to "go slowly and avoid any open break." Poland was "too big a question to take chances on." Secretary of the Navy Forrestal objected that it was obvious that the Russians intended to dominate Eastern Europe and that it was better to have a showdown with them now rather than later. Harriman agreed that the real issue was whether we were going to help the Russians dominate Poland. If the issue were handled properly, he thought that the Soviets would not break with the United States. Admiral Leahy recalled that after the Yalta Conference, he knew that the Soviets would not allow a free government to operate in Poland. Moreover, the Yalta agreement on Poland could be interpreted in two ways. It was a serious matter to break with the Russians, the old admiral warned. He hoped that we could state our position to the Russians in such a way as not to close the door to a possible compromise. General Marshall also advised caution. He said that the military was still hoping for Soviet participation in the Japanese war when it would do us some good; the Russians had it in their power to delay their entry into the Far Eastern war until after the United States had done all the "dirty work." General Deane disagreed. He said that the Russians would enter the Pacific war as soon as they were ready, regardless of what happened in other areas. From his experience in Moscow, Deane said, he had learned that if we were afraid of the Russians we would get nowhere. Truman then thanked the military representatives for their advice and said he would keep their point of view in mind. After they left, Truman said that he was "satisfied that from a military point of view there was no reason why we should fail to stand up to our understanding of the Crimean Agreements." Yet all of his military advisers, except General Deane, had urged that he handle the Polish issue cautiously, to avoid giving unnecessary offense to the Soviets and causing them to change their plans to help the United States in the war against Japan. All this indicates that Truman had already decided to lecture the Soviets about keeping their agreements before he called the meeting.[13]

That same afternoon Truman met with Molotov. The president announced that the proposals contained in the joint message to Stalin

[13] Memorandum of a meeting at the White House, April 23, 1945, *FR: 1945*, V, pp. 252-255; Stimson diary, April 23, 1945 (Stanford microfilm); Forrestal diary, April 23, 1945, *Forrestal Diaries*, ed. Millis, pp. 48-51.

were "eminently fair and reasonable" and went as far as we could to meet the wishes of the Soviet Union. Truman reminded Molotov that legislative appropriation was required for any foreign aid program, and that he could not hope to get these measures through Congress without public support. He hoped, Truman said pointedly, that the Soviet government would keep that in mind in considering the proposals contained in the joint message on Poland. But the Russian foreign minister was not cowed. In the past, Molotov explained, the three countries had treated each other as equals; there had been no case where one or two of the three had tried to impose its will on the other. This was the only basis of cooperation acceptable to the Soviet Union. Molotov said bluntly that he did not agree that abrogation of the Yalta decisions by others could be considered as a violation by the Soviet government. As Molotov spoke, Truman grew impatient. He kept interrupting the foreign minister to say that an agreement had been reached on Poland and all he was asking was that Stalin carry it out. Finally, Truman cut him off. "The United States Government was prepared to carry out loyally all the agreements reached at the Crimea," he said crisply, and "only asked that the Soviet Government do the same." He wanted the friendship of the Soviet Union, Truman said, but only on the basis of a mutual observance of agreements, and not as a "one-way street." Molotov departed in a huff.[14]

Truman had unintentionally reversed FDR's policy of conceding a sphere of influence in Poland to the Russians. He had asserted an *American interest* in Poland, and refused to accept special Soviet prerogatives based on geographic proximity and history.

Stalin's reply arrived the next day. Truman's "tough talk" had only infuriated the Russians. Stalin accused the United States and Britain of trying to "dictate" their demands to the USSR. He reminded Truman that the Russians had accepted Britain's right to establish ideologically compatible governments in Belgium and Greece, because those countries were vital to British security. Why, then, did Britain and the United States refuse to recognize the importance to Soviet security of having a friendly government in Poland?[15]

Truman showed no immediate misgivings about what he had done. The morning after his stormy interview with Molotov, Truman told his staff that he had "talked strongly" to the Russian foreign minister and was "hopeful of good effects from the meeting." On April 25,

[14] Miscamble, "Eden and the Truman-Molotov Conversations," p. 180; *FR: 1945*, V, pp. 256-58.
[15] *FR: 1945*, V, pp. 263-64.

Truman told Stettinius that the message he had received from Stalin was "conciliatory in tone." On April 30, Truman bragged to his close friend, Joseph Davies:

> I said . . . that what we wanted was that your Government should live up to your agreements made at Yalta . . . and that we would strictly live up to our agreements. . . . There is no use discussing it. I gave it to him straight. I let him have it. It was the straight-one-two to the jaw. . . . The Soviets only understand the "tough method."[16]

The news quickly spread throughout Washington that Truman had "gotten tough" with Molotov. Senator Vandenberg crowed: "This is the best news in months. FDR's appeasement of Russia is over."[17] Admiral Leahy thought that Truman's "strong American" stand left the Russians no choice but to accept our position on Poland or withdraw from the United Nations. Churchill wrote to Eden, "My appreciation is that the new President is not to be bullied by the Soviets." *Time* magazine reported that Stettinius and Molotov were not smiling when they emerged from their meeting with Truman. *Time* explained:

> From the President down, Mr. Molotov's U.S. hosts were prepared to look their guest in the eye, to be tougher with him than they had ever been before. So were the British. It was, they had discovered, the best way to make Mr. Molotov look *them* in the eye.[18]

But Truman's "toughness" was more a matter of style than substance. He had not abandoned FDR's policy of Soviet-American collaboration. He believed that there could be no lasting peace without trust and cooperation among the Big Three. Truman thought that plain speaking and the threat of withholding economic assistance would be sufficient to make the Soviets back down. The ambassador to the Soviet Union had assured him that the Soviets would not risk a break with the United States because they needed our economic assistance for postwar reconstruction. Consequently, the United States had nothing to lose by standing up for free elections and democracy in Poland. Truman had never considered whether a policy of insisting on self-determination for Poland might be incompatible with continued Soviet-American cooperation. Was Truman unconsciously avoid-

[16] Ayers diary, April 24, 1945, HSTL; Stettinius Calendar Notes, April 25, 1945, Stettinius Papers, Box 244, University of Virginia; Davies journal, April 30, 1945, LC.
[17] *Private Papers*, ed. Vandenberg, pp. 175-76.
[18] Leahy diary, April 23, 1945, *I Was There*, ed. Leahy, p. 63; Churchill, *Triumph and Tragedy*, p. 492; "Look a Russian in the Eye," *Time*, April 30, 1945, p. 25.

ing the difficult decision of choosing between great power cooperation and Polish democracy? Perhaps. But he had only been in office for ten days when he gave Molotov the famous tongue-lashing. In such a short period of time, Truman had to rely on the advice of those who presumably knew the Soviets better than he did. And Harriman had witnessed Soviet economic deprivation and the primitive condition of their railraods and roads firsthand. It was not unreasonable for Truman to accept Harriman's recommendations without reservation, particularly since the president was anxious to be decisive.

Yet, in diplomacy, style and nuance can convey substantial meaning. The Russians must have interpreted Truman's bluntness and unwillingness to accept Soviet prerogatives in Poland as evidence that he had decided to abandon the policy of collaboration now that the Russians were no longer needed to defeat Germany. Before his meeting with Truman, Molotov had confessed to Davies that the Soviets were worried that "differences of interpretation" and "complications" might arise because Truman lacked full information on the Yalta agreements. With Roosevelt alive, Molotov explained, the Soviets had felt that any differences could be worked out because they had "full confidence" in his sincerity and willingness to cooperate. The Soviets did not know Truman as they did Roosevelt.[19]

STALIN, PENDERGAST, AND EASTERN EUROPE

After Truman's blunt talk with Molotov, relations with the Soviets deteriorated rapidly. The San Francisco U.N. Conference, representing the world's hopes for an enduring peace, was disrupted by noisy, acrimonious squabbles between the United States and the Soviet Union. Molotov refused to accept the custom of allowing the host nation to serve as chairman of the conference but instead demanded rotation among four coequal chairmen representing the United States, the Soviet Union, Great Britain, and China. Truman decided that at least the secretary of state should be the senior of the four. Truman told Stettinius that he should "stand pat on this," and if Molotov didn't like it, to tell him to "go to hell."[20]

When Molotov asked for the admission of a representative from the Warsaw Polish government, Senator Vandenberg whispered into Stettinius' ear: "*This* move *must* be killed at once and in the open." He

[19] Davies journal, April 23, 1945, LC.

[20] Wallace diary, April 27, 1945, *Price of Vision*, ed. Blum, p. 436; Transcript of Telephone Conversation, April 26, 1945, *Diaries of Stettinius*, ed. Campbell and Herring, p. 339.

wrote out a short statement for Stettinius. Without hesitating, Stettinius read that the U.S. was still waiting for Russia to carry out the Yalta agreements on Poland. What Truman had said in private was now made public.[21]

In publicizing the dispute over Poland, the U.S. delegation legitimized press criticism of Soviet behavior. United States Ambassador Harriman sought to channel press commentary in the right direction. With Stettinius' permission, Harriman held off-the-record press conferences to enlighten newsmen on the nature of Soviet foreign policy. "The Kremlin wants to promote Communist dictatorships controlled from Moscow, whereas we want, as far as possible, to see a world of governments responsive to the will of the people," he said. "We will have to find ways of composing our differences in the United Nations and elsewhere in order to live without war on this small planet." By mid-May, not only the Hearst newspapers but the *New York Times* and other reputable publications were critical of Soviet actions.[22]

The Soviets defiantly tightened their grip on Eastern Europe, particularly Rumania and Bulgaria. Under Secretary Grew informed Truman that the Soviet government dominated both countries, regardless of the nominally allied character of the allied control commissions or the commitments made in the Crimea Declaration on Liberated Europe. Reports from U.S. representatives in Rumania and Bulgaria confirmed that Soviet activities were in direct violation of the spirit of the Yalta Declaration on Liberated Europe. In Rumania, the Soviets had installed a communist government representing perhaps 10 percent of the population. Under the protection of the Red Army, the Rumanian communists had appointed communists to all important judicial and municipal posts, and were systematically arresting and executing political opponents. In Bulgaria, the Soviets were establishing a communist-dominated government. Freedom of speech and the press were nonexistent. The U.S. representatives on the Bulgarian control commission were virtual prisoners. They could not receive mail or supplies without asking permission from the Russians, who inspected every shipment. Both countries were being absorbed into an exclusive Russian economic sphere through heavy reparations, requisitions by the Russians for the Red Army, seizure of "German" property, monopolization of trade.[23]

---

[21] *Private Papers*, ed. Vandenberg, p. 181; Gardner, *Architects of Illusion*, p. 64.

[22] Harriman and Abel, *Special Envoy*, pp. 456-57; I. F. Stone, "Trieste and San Francisco," *Nation*, May 26, 1945, p. 589.

[23] *FR: 1945*, IV, pp. 205-206; *FR: 1945*, V, pp. 540-41; Memorandum of Conversation by Grew, May 2, 1945, 711.00/5-145, RG 59, NA.

By the end of May, the *New York Times* commented that "developments in the Balkans point to the existence of a plan carefully preconceived and systematically applied to establish a Communist regime, or one like it, in every country in the peninsula." First, the communists gained control over the ministries of justice and interior, using their police powers to execute political opponents and break up rival parties. Before long, membership was increased by opportunists, fellow-travelers, and the fearful so that the party could claim a following of 25 to 30 percent, sufficient to wield power in the Balkans. In Bulgaria, for example, after the communists gained a position of dominance, they had 1,500 to 2,000 politicians, administrators, professors, and journalists executed. Apart from the official executions, an estimated 15,000 to 20,000 political opponents had been murdered since the communists took over. In Rumania, the communists had acquired the ministries of justice and interior, and were directing violent attacks against the opposition National Peasant party.[24]

The defeat of Germany had created an irresistible opportunity for Soviet expansion. As columnist C. L. Sulzberger pointed out, "for the first time in history there is no political backbone on the continent." Moscow had decided to take advantage of the power vacuum in Eastern Europe and the absence of any positive proposals from the West to protect its frontiers by lining up a set of friendly governments.[25]

The Soviets showed no concern for the effect of their actions in Eastern Europe on American public opinion. On May 3, Molotov casually announced just before a dinner meeting that the Soviets had arrested sixteen Polish underground leaders who had been lured out of hiding with promises of safe conduct and invited to Moscow for discussions on broadening the Warsaw Polish government. Eden and Stettinius indignantly suspended negotiations on Poland. While Molotov was touring a shipyard, Stettinius held a press conference at which he denounced the arrest of the "prominent Polish democratic leaders."[26]

Truman was still "talking tough" with the Russians. In early May, he banged his fist on the desk and declared to a visiting Labor delegation: "We have got to get tough with the Russians. They don't know how to behave."[27]

[24] *New York Times*, May 23, 1945.

[25] *New York Times*, May 21, 26, 1945.

[26] *FR: 1945*, V, pp. 281-84; I. F. Stone, "Anti-Russian Undertow," *Nation*, May 12, 1945, p. 534.

[27] Curtis D. MacDougall, *Gideon's Army* (New York: Marzani and Munsell, 1965), 1:22-23.

But Truman's toughness was more rhetorical than real. He took no action to achieve Soviet compliance with the Yalta principles of tripartite action in Eastern Europe. For a while, Truman was even thinking of withdrawing from the allied control commissions in Bulgaria and Rumania, rather than confront the Soviets. He rejected the recommendation of the U.S. representatives in those two countries that the United States use diplomatic pressure, publicity, and the threat of withdrawing economic aid to force the Soviets to observe the spirit of the Yalta agreements.[28] Similarly, Truman ignored Grew's contention that "our interests and responsibilities under the Crimea Declaration require us to take a strong stand vis-à-vis the Soviet Government in support of the principles of joint Allied action in the political sphere and nonexclusion in the economic sphere."[29] Unlike his legalistic advisers in the State Department who were unacquainted with the "code of the politician," Truman was more concerned with obtaining the *appearance* of Soviet compliance with the Yalta agreements on Liberated Europe than with forcing them to accept American involvement in the region. In addition, he was still committed to FDR's goal of obtaining Soviet cooperation with American plans for the peace.

President Truman's adherence to the "code of the politican" also brought him into conflict with Churchill. Truman rejected the prime minister's strategy of using Anglo-American troops as a bargaining lever to persuade the Soviets to honor the Yalta agreements in Eastern Europe. When the fighting stopped, U.S. troops were deep inside the German occupation zone previously assigned to the Soviets. On April 18, Churchill suggested that they settle the question of sharing food from the Soviet-occupied zones with the rest of Germany before Anglo-American forces withdrew. "These occupational zones were outlined rather hastily at Quebec in September 1944," he rationalized, "when it was not foreseen that General Eisenhower's armies would make such a mighty inroad into Germany." Under Secretary of State Grew agreed that "some hard bargaining is going to be necessary" if we were to get the Soviets to cooperate in Austria and Czechoslovakia, and that Eisenhower's troops should be allowed to advance to the Moldau to improve our bargaining position. On May 6, Churchill strongly urged Truman to hold another Big Three meeting as soon as possible, before Anglo-American troop strength in Germany melted away. Then the United States and Britain could force a settlement of

---

[28] *FR: 1945*, IV, p. 206; Lynn E. Davis, *The Cold War Begins: Soviet-American Conflict over Eastern Europe* (Princeton: Princeton University Press, 1974), pp. 274-75; Memorandum of Conversation by Grew, May 2, 1945, 711.00/5-245, RG 59, NA.

[29] *FR: 1945*, IV, p. 202.

all the major issues, using the withdrawal of Anglo-American troops as a negotiating counter.[30]

On May 9, Truman replied that the initiative for another tripartite meeting should come from Stalin. Discouraging Churchill's hopes for military leverage on Soviet policies in southeastern Europe, Truman wrote that "in the meantime, it is my present intention to adhere to our interpretation of the Yalta agreements." Throughout the month of May, Churchill badgered Truman to call for an early summit conference and to order American troops to hold their lines. He warned that withdrawal of American forces would "mean the tide of Russian domination sweeping forward 120 miles on a front of 300 or 400 miles." Churchill argued that the allies ought not to retreat until they were satisfied about Poland, Russian occupation policies in Germany, and conditions in the Russian occupied countries in the Danube valley and the Balkans. On May 15, Harriman also advised the president to settle the fate of Poland and Germany at a tripartite meeting as soon as possible. Although we would not use our troops in Europe for political bargaining, Harriman declared, our chances for success would be greatly improved if the meeting took place before we were out of Europe. On June 11, Truman put an end to the discussion by informing Churchill bluntly: "I am unable to delay the withdrawal of American troops from the Soviet zone in order to use pressure in the settlement of other problems." Instinctively, Truman followed the "code of the politician." He could not very well insist that the Soviets adhere to the Yalta agreements while reneging on our commitment to the occupational agreements worked out by the European Advisory Commission.[31]

Nevertheless, the American military presence in Germany was an organic outcome of the battlefield. To a follower of *Realpolitik* such as Churchill, a state's leaders had an obligation not to toss away influential bargaining counters without obtaining an equivalent quid pro quo. The postwar territorial and political settlement in Europe would inevitably be founded on the balance of forces among the victors, and

[30] Churchill to Truman, April 18, 1945, *FR: 1945*, III, pp. 231-32; Churchill to Truman, May 6, 1945, *FR: Potsdam*, I, pp. 3-4, Grew to Truman, May 5, 1945, *FR: 1945*, III, pp. 277-78.

[31] Truman to Churchill, May 9, 1945, *FR: Potsdam*, I, p. 4; Churchill to Truman, May 11, 1945, ibid., pp. 6-7; Churchill to Truman, May 12, 1945, ibid., pp. 8-9; Churchill to Truman, May 13, 1945, ibid., p. 10; Memorandum by Acting Secretary of State, May 15, 1945, ibid., p. 13; Churchill to Truman, June 4, 1945, *FR: 1945*, III, p. 326; Truman to Churchill, June 11, 1945, ibid., p. 133-34; Truman, *Memoirs*, 1:213-14, 217-19; Truman to Eleanor Roosevelt, May 10, 1945, Eleanor Roosevelt Papers, Box 4560, FDRL; Gaddis, *Origins of the Cold War*, p. 210.

Stalin would neither understand nor appreciate our unilateral abrogation of power. Failure to settle satisfactorily the question of Russian
aims in Germany, Czechoslovakia, Austria, Yugoslavia, Hungary, Rumania, and Bulgaria before the Western world folded up its war machines would make a third world war inevitable.[32] Had Truman not
been so intent on following the "script," he might have been more
receptive to Churchill's advice.

Truman found other reasons for rejecting Churchill's strategy. If the
United States refused to withdraw from the Soviet occupation zone in
Germany, the Soviets could retaliate by shutting us out of Berlin and
Vienna, refusing to allow the control commissions in those two coun-
tries to operate. Besides, U.S. troops in Europe were needed for the
war against Japan.[33]

V-E Day on May 8 only released a flood of new problems for Truman—adjusting lend-lease, land-grabbing by U.S. allies before the
Peace Conference, orderly withdrawal of U.S. troops to the Pacific,
securing Soviet participation in the war against Japan.

FDR had left no policy on ending lend-lease or extending loans for
postwar reconstruction. Wishing to maintain maximum personal control over an important foreign policy tool, Roosevelt forbade planning
for lend-lease adjustment, and promised that he would issue orders
himself at the appropriate time. But Roosevelt's flexibility was constrained by Republicans in Congress, who were suspicious that FDR
would bankrupt the United States by continuing "lavish" aid to other
countries after the war. FDR was forced to accept an amendment to
the Lend-Lease Act explicitly stating that lend-lease could not be used
for postwar reconstruction or relief, with certain minor exceptions.[34]
Truman was well aware of the strong sentiment within Congress in
favor of restricting lend-lease to the wartime needs of the allies. On
April 26, Truman told his budget director Harold Smith that "if we
use lend-lease for rehabilitation purposes we will open ourselves to a
lot of trouble."[35]

Averell Harriman, however, saw that the president could use these
congressional restrictions to his advantage as a lever on Soviet policy.

[32] Churchill to Truman, May 11, 1945, *FR: Potsdam*, I, p. 7.

[33] Geir Lundestad, *The American Non-Policy Towards Eastern Europe, 1943-1947: Universalism in an Area Not of Essential Interest to the United States* (Oslo: Universitetsforlaget, 1978), pp. 372-73; Herbert Feis, *Between War and Peace* (Princeton: Princeton
University Press, 1960), p. 76; Gaddis, *Origins of the Cold War*, pp. 209-10.

[34] Herring, *Aid to Russia*, pp. 181-90; Leon C. Martel, *Lend-Lease, Loans and the
Coming of the Cold War* (Boulder, Colo.: Westview Press, 1979), p. 124.

[35] Harold Smith diary, April 26, 1945, Harold D. Smith Papers, HSTL.

While he was visiting Washington, Harriman met frequently with State Department officials to argue for a new, more realistic policy toward the Soviets. Though Harriman believed that Soviet plans to establish satellite states were a "threat to the world and to us," he thought the United States could block further Soviet expansion if we utilized our economic leverage.[36]

Yet, Harriman's ideas about using economic aid as a device to extract political concessions were inchoate and inconsistent. Harriman argued that we had considerable leverage over Soviet foreign policy. The Soviets could probably rebuild their industry using their own financial resources, to be sure, but the Soviet government also was planning an ambitious new program of industrial development. The Soviets particularly needed our heavy machinery and machine tools, and our "know-how" in such fields as chemical industry, coal mining mechanization, power development, and railroad equipment. Harriman thought that the Soviets were "keen" to obtain a credit of up to $6 billion.[37]

At the same time, Harriman contended that the economic needs of our Western allies should be satisfied first, and the Russians allocated whatever was left. "Lack of sufficient food and employment are fertile grounds for the subtle false promises of communist agents," he pointed out.[38] Harriman did not say how the United States could meet the burgeoning economic needs of a devastated Europe while at the same time supplying the Soviet Union with generous reconstruction assistance.

To increase our leverage over the Soviets, Harriman recommended that Russian lend-lease aid be reduced after Germany's defeat. The United States should supply only the "absolute minimum requirements" of the Soviets for the war against Japan, after first taking care of the needs of Western Europe.

Harriman also urged that FDR's unconditional aid policy be ended to allow us to retaliate by cutting off selected lend-lease shipments whenever the Soviets behaved rudely or showed disregard for American interests. As part of his "firm but friendly" quid pro quo policy, the ambassador had planned to apply the same strategy to our economic assistance for postwar reconstruction.[39] But how could the United States cut off Soviet lend-lease shipments without hampering the war

---

[36] *FR: 1945*, V, pp. 820, 840, 846.
[37] Ibid., pp. 843-45, 994-96.
[38] Ibid., pp. 818-19.
[39] Ibid., pp. 839-42.

effort, if the Soviets were restricted to their "absolute minimum requirements?"

Then Harriman flew to San Francisco for negotiations with Eden and Molotov on Poland. On May 9, Harriman proposed to Stettinius that he go to Moscow to negotiate directly with Stalin on the members of a reorganized Polish government. "Stalin cared more for the general state of relations with the U.S. and Great Britain than Molotov," Harriman explained, and he might prefer on balance a "partially friendly Poland" to a "fully controlled Poland" gained at the expense of strained relations with the Anglo-Americans.[40] Even though the United States had just broken off negotiations in protest over the Soviet arrest of the Polish underground leaders, Stettinius agreed to a new diplomatic initiative.

The two men also decided that "no specific acts of pressure or retaliation should be suggested or considered until the end of the San Francisco Conference." To allow priority to be shifted to the economic needs of our Western European allies, lend-lease shipments to Russia should be curtailed at once, "but without any hint of relationship with the Polish or other political problems with the Soviet Union." Stettinius advised Under Secretary Grew that in our attitude toward the Soviets "we should be firm while avoiding any implication of a threat or any indication of political bargaining."[41]

This was a recommendation almost impossible to carry out. Obviously, the Soviets would connect a sudden, unexpected cutback in aid to the Polish issue. Since the Soviet government was planning to enter the war against Japan, the Soviets naturally expected to receive continuing lend-lease aid. Indeed, as late as April the U.S. government had asked the Soviets to submit their requirements for a Fifth Protocol, even though they knew the war in Europe would soon be over. The United States had also offered to conclude an agreement to finance Soviet purchases of lend-lease goods in the pipeline when hostilities ended. In sum, the Russians had not been warned that V-E Day would bring a major change in policy.[42] How aid was to be cut back "without any hint of relationship with the Polish or other political problems with the Soviet Union" Harriman did not say.

On May 10, Harriman returned to Washington to present to President Truman his ideas on ending the Polish deadlock and curtailing Russian lend-lease shipments. Truman had already agreed to the idea

---

[40] *FR: 1945*, V, p. 291-92.

[41] Memorandum of Conversation, May 9, 1945, *Diaries of Stettinius*, ed. Campbell and Herring, pp. 357-58; *FR: 1945*, V, p. 998.

[42] *FR: 1945*, V, pp. 991-93, 1018-21.

of using our postwar economic assistance to extract political concessions from the Soviets.[43] He was still in the mood to "get tough with the Russians." In addition, Truman was concerned about meeting congressional prohibitions against the use of lend-lease aid for postwar reconstruction. Consequently, the president quickly consented to reductions in Soviet lend-lease aid. At the same time, however, Truman approved of the United States making the first move to resume the stalled talks on Poland—hardly consistent with a "tough" Russian policy. As Kennan pointed out to Harriman, "there could be no better indication of the correctness, from Russia's standpoint, of the policies the Soviet Government has followed with respect to Poland since the Crimea Conference than if we were now to take the initiative in reopening talks with them particularly on a basis other than that agreed at the Crimea."[44]

Later that afternoon, Assistant Secretary Clayton called a meeting of representatives from all agencies involved in the Soviet lend-lease program. Everyone, including Harriman, agreed that the unconditional aid policy should be ended and the Soviets made to justify their requests just like everybody else. In addition, the Soviets should be furnished only those supplies necessary for operations in the Far East. In a memorandum on the meeting, General Lincoln noted that State Department representatives "were considering using lend-lease as a political weapon in connection with our difficulties with the Russians in Central Europe." Officials at the meeting endorsed a memorandum to the president embodying those suggestions, with the understanding that State Department representatives would make some minor changes in wording before giving it to Truman.[45]

In revising the presidential memorandum, an overzealous State Department official misinterpreted one of Harriman's penciled notations and added the phrase that all Russian supplies not destined for use in the Pacific should be "cut off immediately as far as physically practicable" and diverted to Western Europe. Harriman and Clayton ini-

---

[43] Ibid., pp. 232, 256-57.

[44] Ibid., pp. 295-96; Transcript of Telephone Conversation, May 10, 1945, *Diaries of Stettinius*, ed. Campbell and Herring, pp. 357-58.

[45] Lincoln to Marshall, May 11, 1945; ABC 400.3295 Russia (19 Apr. 42), Sec. 3, Records of the Army Staff, RG 319, NA; Lincoln to Assistant Sec. War Department General Staff, May 11, 1945, ibid.; Memo for the Record by Lincoln, May 14, 1945, ibid. Herring does not mention Lincoln's observation that the State Department intended to use lend-lease as a "political weapon," perhaps because it contradicts his thesis that the lend-lease cutback was not an attempt to apply economic pressure on the Soviet Union (*Aid to Russia*, pp. 209-10) Yet he cites the May 11 memo from Lincoln to Marshall (p. 331 note 50).

tialed the revised memorandum without noticing the changed wording.[46]

On May 11, Clayton presented the new policy to State Department officials at a meeting of the secretary's Staff Committee. Clayton announced that all the agencies had agreed that the lend-lease program to Russia "should be so flexible that it could be cut off at any time." Grew added that "lend-lease assistance is this Government's only leverage against the Soviet Union," and that he "would be very reluctant to sign any commitment for the future."[47]

That evening, Clayton explained the highlights of the new policy to Truman. Also present were Crowley, Under Secretary Grew, and Charles Bohlen. Before the meeting, FEA head Crowley told Grew that he "wanted to be sure that the President thoroughly understands the situation and that he will back us up and will keep everyone else out of it." Crowley said that "he would be having difficulty with the Russians and he did not want them to be running all over town looking for help." Truman signed the memorandum, according to his recollection, without even reading it.[48]

Officials in charge of shipping Soviet lend-lease had not participated in drafting the president's directive. On May 12, as one official complained, they had one "hell of a day as a result of carrying out written words without knowing what the fellow who wrote them intended to say." Shipping officials literally interpreted the phrase "cut off immediately as far as physically practicable." They stopped loading on all vessels destined for the Soviet Union, and ordered ships at sea to turn back in mid-ocean. When Harriman and Clayton found out, they were horrified. Clayton had the orders countermanded immediately. Then he tried to convince a representative from the Soviet embassy that it had all been a mistake. Harriman insisted that he had mentioned a cutoff in *production* not *supplies*. General Lincoln agreed that neither Harriman nor Acheson had mentioned "cutting off" lend-lease to Russia. The term they used was "adjust." Lincoln protested indignantly that the War Department "had not concurred and did not concur" with the sentence in the memorandum which called for "cutting off" supplies to Russia. "The lesson I have learned from this," he grumbled

[46] Memorandum for the Record by Lincoln, May 14, 1945, ABC 400.3295 Russia (19 Apr. 42), Sec. 3, RG 319, NA; *FR: 1945*, V, p. 999.

[47] Secretary's Staff Committee Minutes, May 11, 1945, Stettinius Papers, Box 236, University of Virginia. Herring omits any reference to Grew and Clayton's discussion of the use of lend-lease as a lever on Soviet foreign policy.

[48] *FR: 1945*, V, p. 999n; Truman *Memoirs*, 1:227-28.

privately, "is not to trust the Department will merely stick to editorial changes after they get a concurrence."[49]

Lend-lease policy was modified to allow ships on the dock or at sea to proceed. But lend-lease shipments to the Soviets were sharply curtailed, and supplies diverted to Western Europe. The State Department still intended to use economic assistance as a lever on Soviet foreign policy. As Under Secretary Grew explained in a briefing memorandum to President Truman: "In general, our attitude toward further lend-lease or its equivalent to Russia is that we are going to give very little without strings attached, and that we will use such shipments for our own ends and not just for Russian ends."[50]

Historians have long disagreed over whether the Truman administration's decision to cut back lend-lease was motivated by fear of congressional reaction to continuation of lend-lease in the postwar period, or by a desire to pressure Russia into making concessions in Eastern Europe. Truman and the State Department *were* concerned about the stir that would be raised in Congress if lend-lease were used to provide reconstruction assistance. But their principal aim in curtailing Soviet lend-lease aid was to allow the use of our economic assistance as a "carrot" and "stick" in controlling Soviet foreign policy; if the Soviets did not behave, their aid would be cut back even further. Had U.S. officials been solely concerned with meeting legal restrictions, lend-lease could have been reduced gradually, after prior notification and consultation with the Soviets to minimize disruptions in their economy. The U.S. government could have allowed the Soviets to purchase on credit items previously ordered; indeed, negotiations for such an arrangement were then underway. U.S. officials knew that the Soviets would be upset when lend-lease was abruptly canceled, but they made no attempt to warn the Russians or cushion the blow.

Commissar for Foreign Trade Mikoyan told Harriman that he had hoped that the Soviets would be notified before shipments ceased.

[49] Memorandum of telephone conversation between General Hull and General York, May 12, 1945, ABC 400.3295 Russia (19 Apr. 42), Sec. 3, RG 319, NA; Memorandum for General Hull, May 13, 1945, ibid.; York to Dean and Spalding, May 14, 1945, Feis Papers, Box 73, LC; Secretary's Staff Committee Minutes, May 14, 1945, Stettinius Papers, Box 236, University of Virginia; Memorandum for the Record, May 14, 1945, 400.3295 Russia (19 Apr. 42), Sec. 3, RG 319, NA; Memorandum for Marshall, May 13, 1945, ibid.

[50] York to Spalding, May 14, 1945, Feis Papers, LC; Notes Taken of Meeting of President's Soviet Protocol Committee, May 15, 1945, President's Soviet Protocol Committee Records, Box 5, FDRL; Minutes of Protocol Committee, May 15, 1945, ibid; Memorandum for the President, May 31, 1945, Truman Papers, PSF: "Current Foreign Developments," HSTL.

Mikoyan had expected that their two countries would be able to work out some modus vivendi to cover the intermediary period before the United States ceased lend-lease aid after V-E Day. The Soviets could not understand why the United States had decided to stop shipments without even trying to reach an agreement.[51]

There is some evidence that Truman could have continued lend-lease shipments to the Russians after V-E Day without violating the terms of the Lend-Lease Act. In an April 18 memo to Clayton, Collado of the Office of Financial Development admitted that "there is no provision in the Lend-Lease Act or in the Master Agreement with Russia that would require the discontinuance of lend-lease aid on V-E Day if Russia is not in the Pacific War at the time." McCloy and Lincoln pointed out that quoting the Lend-Lease Act to the Russians raised the question of how closely we were adhering to it in providing continuing aid to the British.[52]

By abruptly cutting back lend-lease, without consulting the Soviets to minimize the disruption in their economy, the State Department bluntly reminded the Soviets of their dependence on American economic aid. As *Nation* observed,

> Some bad poker is being played with Russia these days. . . . Recently, for example, when Secretary Grew announced that lend-lease shipments to Russia were being stopped or scaled down because the European war had ended, some of the boys in the backroom applauded lustily and waited for the chips to be shoved across to our side of the table. It seemed pretty clear that Russia needed our fi-

[51] *FR 1945*, V, pp. 1020-21.

[52] Collado to Clayton, April 18, 1945, 840.24/4-1845, RG 59, NA; Memorandum for General Hull, May 13, 1945, ABC 400.3295 Russia (19 Apr. 42), Sec. 3, RG 319, NA. In *Between War and Peace* (pp. 27-28) and *From Trust to Terror* (p. 228), orthodox historian Herbert Feis argues that Truman reduced lend-lease shipments to Russia to conform to congressional prohibitions against the use of lend-lease for postwar reconstruction. In *The Cold War Begins*, Lynn Davis states that the State Department "never threatened to withdraw economic and financial assistance to Russia to achieve Soviet compliance with the Yalta agreements." She bases this assertion not on primary sources but on an article by Herring, superseded by his book on the same subject. See George C. Herring, "Lend-Lease to Russia and the Origins of the Cold War, 1944-1945," *Journal of American History* 56 (June 1969): 113. In *Aid to Russia*, Herring takes the more moderate position that the Truman administration "abandoned the protocol system to allow the use of lend-lease as a diplomatic weapon," but Harriman and other officials did not intend "to apply immediate pressures on the Soviet Union to make concessions on political issues" (pp. 209-10). The interpretation set forth here is consistent with that in Yergin, *Shattered Peace*, p. 94; Paterson, *Soviet-American Confrontation*, pp. 43-44; Gaddis, *Origins of the Cold War*, pp. 217-19; Kolko, *Politics of War*, pp. 397-98.

nancial assistance so badly that it would have to make certain political concessions we had been asking for. It may turn out, however, that we have underestimated the strength of Russia's hand, and that Russia may get tired and decide to pull out of the game.[53]

The effects were disastrous. U.S.-Soviet relations cooled even further. When Harry Hopkins visited Moscow in late May, Stalin told him that the lend-lease cutback was one reason for the breakdown in U.S.-Soviet cooperation. Stalin admitted that the United States was justified in reducing lend-lease shipments after V-E Day, but charged that the manner in which the cutbacks were made was "unfortunate and brutal." If they had received some warning, Stalin said, they would not have been so offended, because the Soviet economy was based on plans. If the lend-lease cutback was intended to pressure the Russians in order to "soften them up," Stalin warned, then it was a "fundamental mistake." When the Russians were approached frankly in a friendly manner, much could be done, but reprisals had the opposite effect.[54]

Though Truman continued to give lip service to Soviet-American collaboration, by mid-May he had abandoned all of Roosevelt's methods of winning Soviet trust and friendship. Roosevelt's methods of handling the Soviets—demonstrating faith in Soviet intentions, keeping our lend-lease commitments, ignoring provocative behavior, refusing to let minor disagreements impede overall Soviet-American collaboration, mediating between Churchill and Stalin, establishing a personal friendship with Stalin—were all designed to reassure Stalin and convince him that the United States could be trusted.[55] Truman agreed that the Russians were "touchy" and "suspicious." But his way of reassuring the Soviets was to adhere scrupulously to his understanding of the agreements entered into by Roosevelt, and insist that the Russians do the same.[56]

Roosevelt acted on the Emersonian premise that "the only way to have a friend is to be one." In 1943, he told Beneš that "it was necessary to trust Russia." Truman, however, thought that the Russians should *prove* their willingness to cooperate with the United States by carrying out his interpretation of the Yalta agreements.

Roosevelt deliberately refrained from reacting to provocative Soviet

[53] "Shall America Help Russia Rebuild?" *Nation*, May 26, 1945, pp. 588-89.

[54] *FR: Potsdam* I, pp. 32-33, 35.

[55] Range, *Roosevelt's World Order*, p. 195; Davis, "What Really Happened at Teheran II," p. 48.

[56] Harry S Truman to Eleanor Roosevelt, May 10, 1945, Eleanor Roosevelt Papers, Box 4560, FDRL.

behavior. FDR once remarked that the Russians had a habit of sending him a friendly note on Monday, spitting in his eye on Tuesday, and then being nice again on Wednesday. The first time it happened, he was "sore" and "came back" at them, but this only made matters worse. Since then he had learned that if he ignored them, the Soviets "straightened out" by themselves. In contrast, Truman believed that we should scold the Russians when they were belligerent or uncooperative. He compared the Russians to people from the wrong side of the tracks whose manners were very bad.

To convince the Soviets that the United States kept its agreements, Roosevelt ordered that all lend-lease commitments to the Russians must be fulfilled, even at the expense of U.S. defense needs. Truman ended the protocol system and allowed Russian supplies to be diverted to Western Europe. Roosevelt had insisted that lend-lease should not be used as a lever on Soviet foreign policy. Truman tried to play the "lend-lease" card in a game of "stud poker" with the Russians.

Roosevelt tried hard to win Stalin's friendship. FDR believed that good relations between states were often based on warm, personal relations between their leaders. Consequently, Roosevelt placed great importance on summit meetings, particularly the informal sessions. Before Teheran, he persisted in asking Stalin for a personal meeting, despite repeated rebuffs and postponements from the volatile Soviet leader. Truman said he was willing to meet with Stalin and Churchill—but he wanted Stalin to make the first move, so that the Russians would not think we were unduly anxious for their cooperation.

To preserve his good relations with Stalin and husband his influence, Roosevelt avoided quibbling with the Russians over details. That was the business of the State Department. Roosevelt refused to become personally involved in a dispute with the Russians until it threatened to disrupt the Grand Alliance. In contrast, Truman let himself be drawn into a rancorous exchange of cables with Stalin on minor issues—the Soviets' refusal to allow U.S. representatives to enter Vienna, the Soviet request that the Warsaw Poles be admitted to the U.N. Conference—which could easily have been handled by the State Department.

Above all, Roosevelt tried to mediate between Britain and the Soviet Union. United States officials believed that the traditional British policy of maintaining a balance of power in Europe and of protecting the route to India would inevitably conflict with the Soviets' insistence on having a sphere of influence in bordering areas. This was a principal reason the State Department opposed spheres of influence. To prevent a clash between rival British and Soviet spheres of influence, the State

Department discouraged the formation of regional blocs and proposed tripartite collaboration as an alternative to power politics. It was U.S. policy to avoid identifying with either British or Soviet interests, so that the United States could act as an impartial arbiter. On a personal level, Roosevelt tried to avoid siding with either Churchill or Stalin. At Teheran, for example, Roosevelt tried to counteract the impression of an Anglo-American bloc by occasionally needling Churchill in front of Stalin. From the time he took office, however, Truman sided with the British against the Soviets on all major issues—Soviet recognition of the Renner government in Austria, admission of allied representatives into Vienna, recognition of the Lublin Poles. At the San Francisco Conference, the United States marshaled the votes of Latin American countries, while the British brought the Commonwealth into line against the Soviet Union on several important votes.[57]

Journalists perceived that the United States was no longer acting as an impartial mediator, but had been lured into defending British interests in Anglo-Saxon disputes. In the *New York Times*, columnist C. L. Sulzberger declared that

> the discussions at San Francisco and some of our reactions to the Soviets' unilateral course have given to some Russian as well as to some American observers the impression of an Anglo-American front against Moscow. . . . Today, an Anglo-American "front"—dip-

[57] Samuel I. Rosenman, ed., *The Public Papers and Addresses of Franklin D. Roosevelt* (New York: Harper & Bros., 1950) 13:524; Eduard Beneš, *Memoirs of Dr. Eduard Beneš From Munich to New War and New Victory* (London: George Allen & Unwin, 1954), p. 193; Millis, *Forrestal Diaries*, p. 50; Davis, "What Really Happened at Teheran I," pp. 37-39; Blum, *Price of Vision*, pp. 245, 452; MacDougall, *Gideon's Army*, pp. 22-23; Herring, *Aid to Russia*, pp. 38-39, 42; Blum, *From the Morgenthau Diaries*, 3:81-82. On Roosevelt's use of personal diplomacy, see Welles, *Where Are We Heading?*, p. 103; McNeill, *America, Britain, and Russia*, pp. 326-27; Range, *Roosevelt's World Order*, pp. 182-83; Davis, "What Really Happened at Teheran I," pp. 12-13, 39. For Roosevelt's unwillingness to become personally involved in minor disputes, see Welles, *Where Are We Heading?*, pp. 104, 106; and Stettinius Calendar Notes, March 12, 1945, Box 244, University of Virginia. For Truman's reluctance to take the initiative, see Woodward, *British Foreign Policy*, pp. 519-20; Feis, *Churchill, Roosevelt, Stalin*, p. 649; *FR: Potsdam* I, pp. 4, 8. For Truman's exchanges with Stalin on Austria and Poland, see *FR: 1945*, III, p. 121; *FR: 1945*, V, p. 280. For the State Department's opposition to spheres of influence because of the danger of British-Soviet conflict, see *FR: 1944*, IV, p. 1025; *FR: Yalta*, pp. 106-108; "British Plan for a Western European Bloc," n.d., Matthews-Hickerson Files, Box 17, "UNO folder," Lot File, RG 59, NA; C. W. Yost, "U. S. Policy toward Eastern Europe and the Near East," Stettinius Papers, Box 216. For Roosevelt's policy of mediating between Churchill and Stalin, see Walter Lippmann, "High Politics at San Francisco," *Washington Post*, May 12, 1945; Davis, "What Really Happened at Teheran I," pp. 12, 31; Dallek, *Roosevelt and American Foreign Policy*, p. 434.

lomatic or military—could only serve to heighten and to justify the super-suspicions that are the product of the communist mind and to convince the Soviet Union of the necessity of unilateral action and reliance upon its own strength. We must make clear our role of "mediator"—mediator within the framework of an international organization.[58]

Agreeing that "here in San Francisco the mediator position of the United States has been lost temporarily," Walter Lippmann warned that U.S. relations with Britain as well as the Soviet Union would deteriorate badly "if the United States becomes a partisan, rather than the detached and restraining partner, in the Anglo-Soviet difficulties which reach from the Balkans to Persia."[59] A delegation from the House of Representatives submitted an open letter to Under Secretary Grew asking whether the United States had become part of an Anglo-American front directed against Russia.[60]

The Russians also accused the United States of tagging along behind Britain. *Izvestia* observed that "in the opinion of a number of persons, the policy of mediation which was successfully carried out by Roosevelt has now changed to a policy of drifting which in many cases reduces the foreign policy of the United States to a subordinate role."[61]

The timing of Truman's tactical shift was particularly unfortunate. As a result of the Berne talks and rapid Western military advances in Germany, the Soviets were already suspicious that the West was preparing to join forces with West Germany against them. In mid-April, Stalin launched a major campaign against Berlin, without notifying his allies until the last minute. Stalin also had *defensive* installations constructed in Central Europe.[62] Then Roosevelt died and was replaced by an obscure Midwestern politician best remembered for his 1941 statement that the Nazis and Bolsheviks should be allowed to kill each other off. Relations with the Soviets deteriorated alarmingly.

Increasingly, the Soviet Union began to replace Germany as the Number One enemy in the minds of U.S. officials, even while the United States was still fighting Japan. On May 6, Henry Wallace anxiously wrote in his diary that "more and more it begins to look like the psychology is favorable toward our getting into war with Russia."

[58] *New York Times*, June 1, 1945, p. 4.
[59] "High Politics at San Francisco."
[60] *New York Times*, June 1, 1945
[61] Ibid.
[62] Mastny, *Russia's Road to the Cold War*, pp. 259-61, 270-71.

Davies predicted that unless the anti-Soviet atmosphere changed in San Francisco, "then our dead shall not sleep in the Flanders fields of this war; nor will our children or their children have a chance for a decent life." In mid-May, I. F. Stone wrote that "I do not wish to be alarmist, and I put this down in the utmost sobriety: it is beginning to seem as if the main business of the United Nations Conference on International Organization is not to write a charter for a stable peace but to condition the American people psychologically for war with the Soviet Union."[63] Returning from San Francisco, Vera Micheles Dean of the Foreign Policy Association observed:

> The most disquieting development at the conference was the tendency to believe that a conflict between the United States and Russia is becoming inevitable. . . . There is no fundamental reason why the two countries should not find a workable basis for postwar cooperation.[64]

Time magazine commented that "last week the possibility of World War III was more and more in the horrified world's public eye. That there were those who looked upon war between the democratic, capitalist U.S. and authoritarian, Communist Russia as 'inevitable' was no longer news."[65]

Truman was alarmed by the ominous turn in U.S.-Soviet relations. On May 13, Davies found Truman to be "anxious" and "very much disturbed" about the Russian situation. He was afraid that "Stalin was out of control and the Generals were dominating the situation." Truman also blamed the newspapers, "these damn sheets," he said, pointing to his desk, for "stirring things up" and making matters worse.[66]

Truman had invited Davies to come to the White House to discuss U.S.-Soviet relations, complaining that he got very little help from the State Department. Though Truman was following a "get tough" script in his relations with the Soviets, he was still receptive to evidence that the policy was not working. It was at this crucial juncture, when Truman began to have some misgivings, that Joseph Davies offered his advice. Davies, a trust-busting lawyer, had been appointed ambassador to Moscow in 1937. Kennan, Bohlen, Henderson, and other members of the Moscow Embassy staff despised and detested Davies. They accused him of displaying naiveté about Soviet intentions, and of ration-

[63] Blum, *Price of Vision*, p. 443; Davies diary, May 2, 1945, LC; I. F. Stone, "Trieste and San Francisco," *Nation*, May 26, 1945, p. 588.

[64] *Time*, June 11, 1945, p. 24.

[65] Ibid.

[66] Davies journal, May 13, 1945, LC.

alizing Soviet cruelties and oppression at home and abroad. Davies' wartime propaganda book, *Mission to Moscow*, received the withering title, "Submission to Moscow," from Soviet experts in the State Department. But Truman liked Davies, and often played poker with him.[67]

At Truman's request, Davies read aloud a letter he had written to the president. "I have found that when approached with generosity and friendliness, the Soviets respond with even greater generosity," Davies said. "The 'tough' approach induces a quick and sharp rejoinder that 'out toughs' anyone they consider hostile."[68]

Then Davies gave Truman the "inside story" of our troubled alliance with the Russians. In recounting the history of the Grand Alliance, Davies tried to show how the Soviets could have received the impression that Britain and the United States were in collusion to let Germany "bleed Russia white"—Churchill's and Roosevelt's friendship; conferences on military strategy held at Quebec, Casablanca, and New York from which the Russians were excluded; repeated postponements of the second front; the suspension of supply convoys to Russia in the midst of the Nazi onslaught. Relations with the Soviets had reached a nadir when FDR asked Davies to go to Moscow in the spring of 1943 to arrange a personal meeting between Stalin and himself. Then, in July, Stalin abruptly postponed the meeting.

Teheran was the turning point. Stalin and FDR formed a good personal relationship based on mutual understanding and trust. Since Teheran, Davies explained, Roosevelt had acted as a "good broker," composing differences between Britain and the Soviet Union. The Soviets did not trust Churchill. In October 1944, Churchill and Stalin had concluded a spheres of influence agreement dividing up the Mediterranean, Greece, Italy, and the Balkans. But the arrangement had not worked out because the Soviets had become convinced that the British were not living up to their agreements.

Davies warned that the situation facing them resembled the low point of Soviet-American relations in the spring of 1943; once again, the Soviets felt they were confronted with a hostile Anglo-American bloc. Recent U.S. actions in San Francisco had given the Soviets the impression that the United States and Britain were "ganging up" against them, Davies said. Truman listened intently to Davies' lecture, asking questions periodically. "What can be done?" he asked anxiously.

[67] Yergin, *Shattered Peace*, pp. 32-33; Weil, *A Pretty Good Club*, p. 92; Morgenthau Presidential diary, June 6, 1945, FDRL.

[68] Letter to the President, May 12, 1945, Davies Papers, LC.

Davies suggested that he follow Roosevelt's example and cultivate Stalin's friendship. "Events," Davies said, "are more frequently influenced by personalities than by argument." Davies showed Truman a recent letter from Molotov in which the Russian foreign minister wrote, "I think that personal contact of the heads of our governments could play in this matter an extremely positive part." Impressed, Truman asked Davies if he would go to Moscow to arrange a meeting between Stalin and himself. Davies explained that he could not go to Moscow because of his health, but he did offer to send a personal message to Stalin suggesting a meeting between the two leaders. "What if Stalin won't come?" Truman asked. "It is no wonder," Truman said, "that I am concerned over this matter. It is a terrible responsibility, and I am the last man fitted to handle it. . . . But I shall do my best."[69]

Truman began to see that the change in strategy and tactics that he had initiated was endangering the success of Roosevelt's "grand design." He began to blame his advisers for the breakdown in U.S.-Soviet cooperation. On May 16, Truman conceded to Roosevelt's daughter that the "get tough" policy had been a mistake. He excused himself by claiming that all his advisers had urged him to "get tough" with Russia. Two days later, Truman told Wallace that he had no confidence in the State Department whatsoever, and planned to get new leadership as soon as possible.[70]

Harriman had also begun to have second thoughts about the "get tough" policy he had been urging on the president. He was afraid that Truman's natural combativeness had given the Russians the impression that he had abandoned Roosevelt's policy of cooperating with the Soviet Union. Harriman wanted the Russians to understand that our new "toughness" was the result of Stalin's failure to keep his agreements, not a change in American leadership. Flying back to Washington from the San Francisco Conference, Harriman and Bohlen gloomily discussed the rapid cooling off of U.S.-Soviet relations. Bohlen observed that if Roosevelt were alive, he would ask Harry Hopkins to go to Moscow. Harriman seized upon the idea with great enthusiasm. What better way to demonstrate continuity than to send the former president's most intimate, trusted adviser to Moscow as the new president's personal representative? When Harriman first mentioned the idea to Truman on May 10, he said no. Truman retorted tartly that Harriman himself could convey any messages to Stalin; he wanted no

[69] Davies journal, May 13, 1945, LC.

[70] Ibid.; Truman to E. Roosevelt, May 10, 1945, Eleanor Roosevelt Papers, Box 45600, FDRL; Wallace diary, May 16, 18, 1945, *Price of Vision*, ed. Blum, pp. 448, 450.

more special envoys. But after his meeting with Davies, Truman began to reconsider Harriman's suggestion.[71]

Hopkins was a prominent advocate of Soviet-American collaboration. Truman hoped that FDR's former adviser would be able to convince Stalin that the United States sincerely wished to cooperate with the Soviets in maintaining world order, and would not be maneuvered into an anti-Soviet alliance with Britain. On May 19, Truman asked Hopkins to go to Moscow to meet with Stalin. Truman now believed that the Soviets were uncooperative and hostile because they perceived that the United States and Britain were "ganging up" against them. He was determined to correct this "misperception" of American foreign policy. To avoid the appearance of a united Anglo-American front, Churchill was not consulted about Hopkins' mission, nor were any British representatives present at his talks with Stalin.[72]

Still mindful of the "code of the politician," Truman instructed Hopkins to inform Stalin that the United States would carry out the Yalta agreements and expected him to fulfil his commitments "to the letter." On the other hand, Truman wanted to reassure Stalin that he did not expect *literal* compliance with the Yalta agreements. He would be content with a cosmetic arrangement in which the Eastern European governments were given the appearance of independence. Remembering how he had won election to the U.S. Senate by carrying the graveyards, Truman did not expect any elections held under Soviet occupation to be genuinely free. Truman summed up his meeting with Hopkins in a diary he kept sporadically:

> He said he'd go, said he understood my position and that he'd make it clear to Uncle Joe Stalin that I knew what I wanted—and that I intended to get it—peace for the world for at least 90 years. That Poland, Rumania, Bulgaria, Czechoslovakia, Austria, Yugoslavia, Latvia, Lithuania, Estonia et al. made no difference to U.S. interests only so far as World Peace is concerned. That Poland ought to have a "free election," at least as free as Hague, Tom Pendergast, Joe Martin, or Taft would allow in their respective bailiwicks. That Tito should be restrained at Trieste and Pola and Uncle Joe should make

[71] Interview with Averell Harriman, December 8, 1945, Truman Papers: Post-Presidential Files, HSTL; Harriman and Abel, *Special Envoy*, p. 459; Bohlen, *Witness to History*, p. 215; Sherwood, *Roosevelt and Hopkins*, pp. 885-86; President's Appointment File, Daily Sheets, May 15-17, 1945, Truman Papers, PSF: Presidential Appointment File, HSTL.

[72] Woodward, *British Foreign Policy*, p. 521; Wallace diary, May 29, 1945, *Price of Vision*, ed. Blum, pp. 454-55; Truman diary, May 22, 1945, Truman Papers, PSF: "Longhand Memos," HSTL.

some sort of jesture [*sic*]—whether he means it or not to keep it before our public that he intends to keep his word. Any smart political boss will do that.[73]

There is no evidence that Truman discussed with other advisers his plan to appeal to Stalin's understanding of the "code of the politician." Certainly Harriman and other State Department officials would have been horrified at Truman's cynical treatment of the Atlantic Charter principles and the Yalta Declaration on Liberated Europe. At the San Francisco Conference, for example, Ambassador Harriman declared that "while we cannot go to war with Russia, we must do everything we can to maintain our position as strongly as possible in Eastern Europe." Chip Bohlen argued to Secretary of State Stettinius that it was our *obligation* to invoke the Yalta Declaration in Bulgaria, because the scheduled elections would only permit candidates from the leftist Fatherland Front to participate. And Grew argued to Truman that our responsibilities under the Yalta Declaration required us to take a "strong stand" with the Soviet Government to ensure that Rumania and Bulgaria were independent in both political and economic affairs.[74]

Truman perceived Stalin as just another machine politician, like his mentor in Missouri politics, Boss Pendergast. People have stored within memory a wide collection of "personae," or cognitive structures representing the personality characteristics of stereotypical characters—the hooker with a heart of gold, the truck-stop waitress, the "urban cowboy," Archie Bunker. Often people assimilate casual acquaintances or public figures to these stereotypical characters, on the basis of a superficial resemblance. Influenced by the Pendergast persona, Truman expected Stalin—a revolutionary fanatic who had never visited the West—to understand American public opinion.[75]

The same day, Truman asked Davies to go to London as his personal envoy to Churchill. Truman wanted Davies to persuade Churchill that he and Stalin should have an opportunity to get to know one another. Truman hoped he could win Stalin's confidence, as Roosevelt had done, through frank, informal discussions. After trying the

[73] Truman diary, May 23, 1945, Truman Papers, PSF: "Longhand Memos," HSTL: President's Appointment File, Daily Sheets, May 19, 1945, Truman Papers, PSF: Presidential Appointment File, HSTL. In *Mr. President*, William Hillman omits the second half of this quotation, beginning with "That Poland ought. . . ."

[74] *FR: 1945*, I, pp. 389-90; Memo by Charles Bohlen to Secretary of State, *FR: 1945*, V, pp. 834-35; Memo by Acting Secretary of State Grew to President Truman, May 1, 1945, *FR: 1945*, IV, pp. 202-203.

[75] Nisbett and Ross, *Human Inference*, p. 35.

"tough" approach, Truman had decided to return to Rooseveltian "personal diplomacy."[76]

President Truman did not have great fondness for the Soviet government. "I've no faith in any totalitarian state be it Russian, German, Spanish, Argentinian, Dago, or Japanese," he wrote in his diary. "They all start with a wrong premise—that lies are justified and that the old, disproven Jesuit formula—the ends justifies the means is right and necessary to maintain the power of government." But ideological differences should not be allowed to obscure the reality that Soviet-American collaboration was essential for world peace. On May 22, he reflected in his diary:

> To have a reasonably lasting peace the three great powers must be able to trust each other and they must themselves honestly want it. They must also have the confidence of the *smaller* nations. Russia hasn't the confidence of the small nations, nor has Britain. We have. I want peace and I'm willing to fight for it. It is my opinion we'll get it.[77]

Truman had Stettinius announce to the American public his decision to return to Roosevelt's policy of mediation. On May 28, in the midst of the San Francisco Conference, Stettinius made a major foreign policy speech listing the goals of American foreign policy: the defeat and disarmament of Germany and Japan, the promotion of the principles of justice and fair-dealing among nations, removal of the economic and social causes of war, and maintenance of great-power collaboration. "The interests of the United States extend to the whole world," Stettinius said. "We must maintain those interests in relation with the other Great Powers and we must mediate between them when their interests conflict among themselves."

American journalists quickly perceived the significance of these remarks. In the *New Republic*, Thomas Reynolds observed that "from a parochial American viewpoint, the enunciation this week of the firm policy that this country's interests extend around the world and the American assumption of the role of mediator may well dwarf the not too brilliant accomplishments of the fifth week of the conference of United Nations." The *New York Herald Tribune* pointed out that Stettinius' address constituted "a formal and almost point-by-point reversal of course on all those issues of policy concerning which Mr. Stettinius' pilotage has been most severely criticized." James Reston judged that

[76] Davies diary, May 21, 1945, LC; *FR: Potsdam* I, pp. 65-66.
[77] Truman diary, May 22, 23, 1945, HSTL.

the speech was an attempt to answer charges that President Truman had abandoned President Roosevelt's role of "mediator" between Marshal Stalin and Prime Minister Churchill. I. F. Stone interpreted Stettinius' address as evidence that Truman did not "see eye to eye" with the State Department's Russian policy. The *New Republic* observed that the statement constituted a "new orientation" in that it placed the United States in the "role of mediator between Britain and Russia, in a position to accept responsibilities and act as conciliator in any situation in which those interests may clash."[78]

RETURN TO ROOSEVELTIAN DIPLOMACY

Hopkins succeeded in his mission because he returned to FDR's policy of trying to reach an agreement with the Soviets on their vital interests as the basis for a great power concert. At their first meeting, Hopkins reminded Stalin that "the cardinal basis of President Roosevelt's policy which the American people had fully supported had been the concept that the interests of the United States were world wide and not confined to North and South America and the Pacific ocean." Roosevelt had realized that the Soviets also had worldwide interests, and he had hoped that the two countries could work out any differences over their political and economic interests. Hopkins also emphasized that the United States wished to see "friendly countries all along the Soviet borders." Marshal Stalin replied, "If that be so, we can easily come to terms in regard to Poland."[79]

Consistent with Truman's instructions, Hopkins lectured Stalin on the need to consider American public opinion in carrying out his policy toward Eastern Europe. Hopkins informed Stalin that millions of Americans who had "supported to the hilt Roosevelt's policy of cooperation" had become seriously disturbed largely because of the allies' inability to carry out the Yalta agreement on Poland. He warned that continued deterioration in public opinion of Russia could endanger the entire structure of world cooperation which Roosevelt and Stalin had labored so hard to create. Without public support, Truman could not carry forward Roosevelt's policy.[80]

Hopkins explained that the Polish question was not important in itself but as a "symbol of our ability to work out problems with the

---

[78] *New York Times*, May 29, 1945; I. F. Stone, "Truman and the State Department," *Nation*, June 9, 1945, p. 637; Thomas Reynolds, "The U.S.A. at San Francisco," *New Republic*, June 11, 1945, pp. 809-10.

[79] *FR: Potsdam*, I, p. 27; Sherwood, *Roosevelt and Hopkins*, pp. 889-90.

[80] Sherwood, *Roosevelt and Hopkins*, pp. 889-90.

Soviet Union." He stressed that the United States had no special interests in Poland and no desire for any particular form of government. "We would accept any government which was desired by the Polish people and was at the same time friendly to the Soviet government"— as if such a combination were possible![81]

At another discussion, Hopkins listed the fundamental human rights that the American people expected to be observed in Poland: freedom of speech, right of assembly, right of movement, freedom of worship, competitive free elections, right to a fair trial, and right of habeas corpus. But he did not object when Stalin affirmed his intent to suppress them. "Those freedoms," Stalin argued, "could only be applied in full in peacetime and even then with certain limitations."[82]

Stalin understood that Hopkins was proposing a Soviet-American condominium, and showed his approval. "Whether the United States wished it or not," Stalin said, "it was a world power and would have to accept world-wide interests." For this reason, Stalin said, he fully recognized the right of the United States as a world power to participate in the Polish question.

Hopkins volunteered that the United States had no desire to see members of the London government or its agents involved in the consultations. That *was* good news, Stalin replied. With that concession, which went beyond Yalta, the London Polish government lost any role in determining the political future of Poland. The marshal withdrew his earlier demand that the Warsaw Poles be allowed to veto any Pole invited for consultations, and he and Hopkins were able to agree on a list of names. Truman accepted Hopkins' assurances that the compromise fulfilled the Yalta agreement, and cabled his approval. Poland's future was thus settled without the participation of the British, who had acted as representatives of Polish interests in Big Three negotiations throughout the war.

Truman was delighted that the Polish imbroglio was finally going to be settled. He bragged to Secretary of the Treasury Morgenthau: "I just put across all by myself the most wonderful thing without any help from Stettinius. I just finished talking to Harry Hopkins, and I am the happiest man in the world over what I have been able to accomplish." After Hopkins left Moscow, the Poles were quickly able to agree on a reorganized Warsaw government which provided token representation of the noncommunist opposition.[83]

[81] *FR: Potsdam*, I, p. 38.

[82] *FR: 1945*, V, pp. 302-303; Sherwood, *Roosevelt and Hopkins*, pp. 905-907.

[83] Sherwood, *Roosevelt and Hopkins*, pp. 900, 907; *FR: 1945*, V, pp. 304-14; Morgenthau Presidential diary, June 1, 1945, FDRL; Ayers diary, June 1, 1945, HSTL.

In return for a Polish settlement that met Soviet objectives, Stalin recognized the predominant interests of the United States in the Far East. He admitted that no communist leader was strong enough to unify China, and promised to do everything he could to promote the leadership of Chiang Kai Shek. The marshal approved of America's "Open Door" policy in China. He emphasized that the United States was the only power with the resources to aid China economically after the war; Russia would have all it could do to provide for its own economy. Truman later told Hopkins that China was the most important issue as far as the United States was concerned. Stalin also agreed to an international trusteeship for Korea.[84]

With the Polish issue out of the way, the Russians suddenly began to cooperate in other areas of the world. Stalin announced that he was appointing Marshal Zhukov to the control council for Germany; and Molotov agreed that the control machinery could come into force when the allied commanders met to sign the declaration on Germany's surrender. U.S. representatives were finally allowed to enter Czecho-slovakia after weeks of delay; and the American embassy opened in Prague. Stalin also agreed to meet with Churchill and Truman near Berlin in mid-July. The San Francisco Conference was saved from imminent fiasco when Stalin agreed at the last minute to the U.S. position that the Security Council veto should not apply to discussion. On June 11, Stalin even sent Truman a gracious note thanking him for the contribution made by lend-lease to the defeat of Germany. On July 4, the European Advisory Commission succeeded in reaching agreement on the control machinery for Austria. "After weeks of tension, Big Three relations improved," *Time* magazine reported. The *New York Times* noted that U.S.-Soviet relations had taken a "distinct turn for the better" since Hopkins' visit to Moscow.[85] As historian William McNeill observed, "having won a clear path to his appointed goal—a "friendly" government in Poland—Stalin was willing and anxious to conciliate the West on other issues."[86]

The ambassador to the London Polish government, Jan Ciechanowski, tried to persuade Washington to withhold *de jure* recognition until the new Polish government held free elections. But State Department officials were "too busy" to see him.[87] The head of the Polish

[84] Sherwood, *Roosevelt and Hopkins*, pp. 902-903; Davies journal, June 13, 1945, LC.

[85] "Improvement," *Time*, June 18, 1945, p. 24; *Washington Post*, June 14, 1945; New York Times, June 17, 1945, sec. 4.

[86] McNeill, *America, Britain, and Russia*, p. 588.

[87] Jan Ciechanowski, *Defeat in Victory* (Garden City, N.Y.: Doubleday, 1947), pp. 383-84; De Santis, *Diplomacy of Silence*, p. 142.

Congress Rozmarek pleaded with Truman to insist on allied supervision of the free elections called for in the Yalta agreement. Truman did nothing.[88] He had achieved a "cosmetic solution" to the problem of Poland. By the end of June, the American public favored withdrawing recognition from the London Poles and transferring official ties to the new, reorganized Warsaw government. A State Department survey of public opinion concluded that:

> the tenor of recent press and radio comment suggests that American opinion accepts the present solution as a necessary condition for preserving Allied unity. It thinks the solution to be "less than perfect" justice; and sympathy for the London Poles is stronger than support for them. But there is considerable acceptance of the necessity for establishing a Polish government able to get along with the Soviet Union, even one at least partially subservient to the latter.[89]

Thus, on July 5, Britain and the United States established diplomatic relations with the new "provisional" Polish government.[90]

But Truman would not admit publicly that the overall improvement in U.S.-Soviet relations was brought about by the U.S. recognition of Soviet predominance in Poland. Truman claimed that there had been "no change in American policy" but rather "a very pleasant yielding on the part of the Russians."[91]

From the success of the Hopkins mission, Truman developed an exaggerated idea of Stalin's power to set Soviet foreign policy, independent of geographic or bureaucratic constraints. He inferred that any conflict, however intractable, could be resolved in personal face-to-face discussions with Stalin. "If you could sit down with Stalin and get him to focus on the problem," he hypothesized, "Stalin would take a reasonable attitude, whereas if the problem never got around to Stalin ... it might be handled by the Molotov clique." Difficulties between the United States and the Soviet Union arose because "Stalin didn't know half the things that were going on."[92]

Truman was not the only one who personalized the improvement in U.S.-Soviet relations. Harriman cabled Truman:

---

[88] Richard Lukas, *Strange Allies: The United States and Poland, 1941-1945*, (Knoxville: University of Tennessee Press, 1978), p. 163.

[89] Ibid., pp. 162-63.

[90] *FR: Potsdam*, I, p. 735.

[91] News Conference, June 13, 1945, *Truman Public Papers, 1945*, p. 123.

[92] Report from Col. Bernstein, June 5, 1945, Senate Judiciary Committee, *Morgenthau Diary (Germany)*, 90th Cong., 1st sess., 1967, 2:1554-55; Press Conference #11, June 9, 1945, off-the-record (microfilm, Stanford University Library).

> It is clear . . . that Molotov is far more suspicious of us, and less willing to view matters in our mutual relations from a broad stand-point, than is Stalin. The fact that we were able to see Stalin six times and deal directly with him was a great help. Many of our difficulties could be overcome if it were possible to see him more frequently.[93]

Truman blamed the press for stirring up anti-Soviet hysteria. On June 7, he complained in his diary:

> Every time we get things going halfway right with the Soviets some smart aleck has to attack them. If it isn't Willie Hearst, its Bertie McCormack or Bert Wheeler [or] it is some other kid who wanted to appease Germany but just can't see any good in Russia.

Propaganda, he reflected, was our greatest foreign relations enemy. "Russians distribute lies about us," he wrote in his diary. "Our papers lie about and misrepresent the motives of the Russians—and the British out lie and out propagandize us both."[94]

After he had reassured Stalin, Truman tried to educate the American people on the overriding importance of Soviet-American cooperation. He used his power to shape press coverage by holding a series of off-the-record briefings in early June.

President Truman emphasized to newsmen that cooperation with the Soviets was essential for world peace. "It's very vital for us to try to understand the Russians' point of view and try to get them to understand ours," he said. "What we are after is world peace." Truman indicated his support for FDR's policy of establishing a great power concert. "And if the British and the American Governments . . . apparently gang up against Russia, or Russia and Britain against us, or we and Russia against Britain," he warned, "there isn't any possible way but to go back to old line power politics." "I don't want to have any alliance with Britain or with Russia, either one," Truman declared. "I want to have the friendship of Russia and Britain, without joining up with either one against the other."

To the American Society of Newspaper Editors, Truman complained that "half of the editorials in this country are suspicious of Russia, and it's bad business for our endeavor to get along with them." The president thought that many misunderstandings arose out of the

[93] *FR: Potsdam*, I, p. 61.

[94] Truman diary, June 7, 13, 1945, HSTL. In Hillman's *Mr. President*, the June 13 entry reads as follows: "Propaganda seems to be our greatest foreign relations enemy. Russians distribute lies about us" (p. 122).

American fear of communism. "I don't give a damn about what kind of government the Russians have if they are satisfied; and they seem to be or some thirty million of them wouldn't die for them," Truman reasoned. He wanted the press to convey the idea that differences in domestic political systems had no bearing on our ability to cooperate with the Soviets on an interstate level. "And I hope we can get a viewpoint here, that the Russians' business is their business, as far as their domestic business is concerned; but in world affairs we want their cooperation and support to maintain the peace of the world."

He told the newspaper editors that the Soviets were entitled to a sphere of influence in Eastern Europe. "I don't feel like falling out with Russia over the fact that they want friendly people around them," Truman remarked. "You know they've had that 'cordon sanitaire.' " At the same time, Truman continued FDR's policy of attempting to conceal the nakedness of Soviet domination and our acceptance of it. He asked the newspaper editors to be patient with Russia's policies in Eastern Europe. He informed them that the object of Hopkins' visit to Moscow was to reach a secret agreement on our problems with the Soviets in Poland, Rumania, Bulgaria, Austria, and Hungary, and we had opened the door. "We have opened the door," Truman repeated, "and I think if we . . . can be a little patient for a little while, we can get that door all the way open." Truman held out vague hopes of securing greater freedom in Eastern Europe through use of our economic leverage. The Russians were anxious for our help in developing their natural resources to become a great nation. "And we will use that," Truman promised.[95]

Truman was content with an arrangement in which the Eastern European countries were given the appearance of independence, because he did not agree with Harriman that Soviet hegemony in Eastern Europe endangered the West. Privately, Truman confided to Col. Bernstein that the Russians had their "hands full dealing with the problems of Poland, Hungary and Eastern Europe, and for that reason he did not think they were going to attempt to spill over into Western Europe."[96]

But Truman did expect Stalin to at least go through the motions of

[95] Press Conference #11, June 9, 1945, off-the-record (Stanford microfilm); undated memorandum, Ayers Papers, General File, "Foreign Policy (folder 1)," HSTL; Press Conference #13, June 16, 1945, off-the-record (Stanford Microfilm).

[96] Report from Col. Bernstein, June 5, 1945, Senate Judiciary Committee, *Morgenthau Diary (Germany)*, 2:1555. For other examples of Truman's lack of concern about Soviet expansion into Western Europe, see Forrestal diary, July 28, 1945, James V. Forrestal Papers, Princeton; Truman diary, July 7, 1945, HSTL.

holding elections in Eastern Europe for the benefit of American public opinion. Consequently, he refused Stalin's request that they establish diplomatic relations with Rumania, Bulgaria and, at a later time, Hungary. Truman said he was willing to exchange diplomatic representatives with Finland because that country had held free elections. But in Hungary, Rumania, and Bulgaria the governments were neither representative nor responsive to the will of the people. Stalin reminded Truman that both the United States and the Soviet Union had recognized Italy, which was no more democratic than Rumania or Bulgaria. In reply, Truman suggested that they discuss the issue at the forthcoming Big Three meeting.[97]

Due to the success of the Hopkins mission, Truman was hopeful about the future of U.S.-Soviet collaboration. Though he would often waver in the months ahead, for now Truman believed that the Russians sincerely wished to cooperate with the United States to preserve world peace.[98] And the two countries had no conflicting interests. "I'm not afraid of Russia," Truman wrote in his diary. "They've always been our friends and I can't see any reason why they shouldn't always be."[99]

The Russians were expansionist, to be sure, but no more than any other great power—including the United States. The United States and the Soviet Union each tried to impose their domestic structure and political ideology on the rest of the world, out of a sense of mission and the desire to create a congenial international environment. In his diary, Truman reflected on the parallels between Soviet and American use of propaganda:

> You know Americans are funny kids. They are always sticking their noses into somebody's business which isn't any of theirs. We send missionaries and political propagandists to China, Turkey, India and everywhere to tell those people how to live. Most of 'em know as much or more than we do. Russia won't let 'em in. But when Russia puts out propaganda to help our parlor pinks—well that's bad—so we think. There is not any difference between the two approaches except one is "my" approach and the other is "yours." Just a "moat [*sic*] and beam" affair.[100]

[97] *FR: 1945*, V, pp. 550-51, 554-55, 558-59; Kolko, *Politics of War*, p. 409.

[98] News Conference, June 13, 1945, *Truman Public Papers, 1945*, p. 123; Press Conference with the American Society of Newspaper Editors, off-the-record, June 16, 1945, Ayers Papers, General File, "Foreign Policy," HSTL.

[99] Truman diary, June 7, 1945, HSTL.

[100] Ibid.

POKER AND POTSDAM

Truman learned poker in the army and continued to play frequently after he became president. He enjoyed a friendly game with his old buddies—unpretentious, mediocre men who shared his bawdy sense of humor. Throughout his political career, Truman often applied analogies from poker to his dealings with other people. "Luck always seems to be with me in games of chance and in politics," he reflected.[101]

It is not surprising that Truman tried to apply the lessons he had learned from poker to his unspoken rivalry with Stalin. A few weeks after he became president, Truman told a friend from Kansas City that there was one thing he was not going to do—he was not going to let Stalin beat him at a poker game. In early May 1945, a close friend of Truman's told a *Time* correspondent that in the administration's dealings with Russia, they "would be playing stud instead of draw poker." "There will always be at least four cards laying face up on the table," he predicted.[102] The implication was that the United States would not be shy about using its power to win Soviet concessions.

The United States was in a good bargaining position vis-à-vis the Soviets, Truman believed. Truman viewed the forthcoming summit conference as a poker game in which he held the highest cards—U.S. economic and technical assistance, the atomic bomb, and the American plan for Germany. In early June, Truman confided to a Treasury aide that he wasn't at all pessimistic about his relations with Russia because "we held all the cards." He explained that the Soviets would need U.S. credits and financial assistance to rebuild their country. Truman said that Russia was "pretty much destroyed," and there would be widespread starvation unless something was done promptly. That was why he felt he had the cards in American hands, Truman continued, and he proposed to play them as American cards. In late June, the American representative in Bulgaria cabled the Secretary of State that

> if we are in the poker game of world affairs, and I assume we are, then we should play the game to the best of our ability. I believe that we have more chips than any one at the table. Circumstances in this area suggest that we should play our cards close to the chest but that when we do have a good hand we should not fail to make a bet. It seems, then in the case of elections in Bulgaria we do have

[101] Truman diary, May 27, 1945, HSTL.
[102] Eaton and Hart, *Meet Truman*, p. 64; *FR: 1945*, IV, pp. 698-99; *Time*, May 14, 1945, p. 33; Donovan, *Conflict and Crisis*, p. 34.

a good hand, not four aces but enough to justify a call or even to make a modest bet. If we refuse to play the cards that come our way it hardly seems that we have the right to stay in the game.

Before Truman left for the Potsdam Conference, the head of the Office of War Mobilization and Reconversion, Fred Vinson, advised him that a program of economic assistance for the Soviet Union and Eastern Europe was America's "ace in the hole," which could be used to obtain our objectives of tripartite collaboration and genuine democracy in Eastern Europe. But many experts disputed that assessment. A *Nation* editorial warned that "if we refuse to extend economic aid to Russia, it does not follow that Russia's economic program is completely stymied or that Russia will come to us on bended knee asking what concessions it must make to get credits." *Nation* pointed out that the Soviet Union was capable of carrying out its economic reconstruction program without assistance from the West. In contrast to 1918, the Russians had ended the war with internal stability, experience in large-scale economic planning, millions of skilled workers, and a sizable industrial plant. In addition, the Russians had acquired the use of forced German labor and the vast coal mines and industries of Silesia. The *New York Times* agreed that it would be a mistake to believe that "the Soviet Union . . . will be dependent upon foreign commerce or upon foreign credits and might therefore be willing . . . to alter any major points of policy."[103]

Truman also had the atomic bomb. On April 25, Secretary of War Stimson informed the new president that American scientists had discovered "the most terrible weapon ever known in human history," a bomb capable of destroying an entire city. Like Truman, Stimson believed that "this was a place where we really held all the cards." Stimson thought that the United States had a "royal straight flush and we musn't be a fool about the way we play it." Stimson advised Truman to postpone the Big Three meeting until after the first atomic bomb test: "We shall probably hold more cards in our hands later than now." Truman agreed. He proposed to the Russians that they meet in mid-July, which would roughly coincide with the first atomic bomb test. On June 6, Truman discussed with Stimson possible quid pro quos for forming a nuclear partnership with the Russians. Truman sug-

[103] Report from Col. Bernstein, June 5, 1945, *Morgenthau Diary (Germany)*, 2:1555; Barnes to Secretary of State, June 23, 1945, *FR: Potsdam*, I, p. 383; Paterson, *Soviet-American Confrontation*, p. 47; Martel, *Lend-Lease, Loans and the Coming of the Cold War*, p. 187; "Shall America Help Russia Rebuild?" *Nation*, May 16, 1945, pp. 588-89; *New York Times*, May 24, 1924, p. 10.

gested that we might ask the Russians to help settle the "Polish, Rumanian, Yugoslavian, and Manchurian problems" in return for the Bomb.[104]

Another card in his hand was the American plan for Germany. Whether allied policy stressed rehabilitation or revenge would have a multimillion dollar impact on the flow of reparations to Russia. Truman asked Treasury Secretary Morgenthau to wait until after Potsdam to publish his plan for Germany. "I have got to see Stalin and Churchill," Truman explained, "and when I do I want all the bargaining power—all the cards in my hand, and the plan on Germany is one of them." "I don't want to play my hand before I see them."[105]

The poker-playing metaphor distorted Truman's thinking and led him to adopt a short-sighted diplomatic strategy. Truman tried to get all he could from the Russians because it was good poker playing to bet high when you had a good hand. On the way over to Potsdam, Truman wrote in his diary:

> How I hate this trip! But I have to make it—win, lose or draw—and we must win. I'm not working for any interest but the Republic of the United States. I['m] giving nothing away except to save starving people and even then I hope we can only help them to help themselves.

In contrast, the "smart boys in the State Department, as usual are against the best interests of the U.S. if they can circumvent a straightforward hard hitting trader from the home front." But this time, Truman vowed to himself, "Byrnes and I shall expect our interests to come first."[106]

Truman did not consider the potential effects of his betting strategy on our long-range relationship with Russia. Because he viewed the summit conference as a poker game, not an attempt to negotiate a lasting postwar settlement, Truman failed to think through several critical issues. In the opening stages of a negotiation, it is important that the parties have a clear understanding of their common objectives as well as competing interests. Truman might have considered whether

---

[104] Stimson diary, April 25, 1945 (Stanford microfilm); Memorandum Discussed with the President, April 25, 1945, Stimson Papers (ibid.); Stimson diary, May 14, June 6, 1945 (ibid.); Stimson to Truman, May 16, 1945, Truman Papers, PSF: Subject File, Cabinet, HSTL; Davies journal, May 21, 1945, LC; Richard G. Hewlett and Oscar E. Anderson, Jr., *A History of the United States Atomic Energy Commission*, vol. 2, *The New World, 1939-1946* (University Park: Pennsylvania State University Press, 1962), p. 352.

[105] Morgenthau Presidential diary, May 9, 1945, FDRL.

[106] Truman diary, July 7, 1945, HSTL.

the great powers would have any mutual concerns once Germany had been defeated, and if so, what they were. Joseph Davies advised Truman to obtain an agreement in principle from the other two leaders on the "big matters" relating to their national security. Otherwise, he warned the president, the "heat and conflict of personalities" would create a combative setting hardly conducive to world peace, and which would poison public opinion. Davies also argued that the most important threat to future peace would be a failure to define the basic foreign policy of the three Great Powers. What was the United States prepared to fight for? Consideration of this issue would lay the basis for the next analytical task: was a reconciliation between the conflicting aims of the United States and the Soviet Union possible? Did the Soviets' insistence on having a sphere of influence in Eastern Europe jeopardize the United States' interest in maintaining a balance of power on the Continent and preserving the independence of Britain? As Davies pointed out, formulation of our policy toward Soviet domination of the Balkans was entangled with determining our basic aims in *Europe*. How serious were the issues that divided the allies?

After defining common and conflicting objectives, a negotiator usually tries to discern the opponent's minimum demands, the least he would be willing to settle for. Truman should have tried to ascertain what the Soviets' irreducible aims in Eastern Europe were. Would the Soviet government be satisfied with anything less than ironclad Stalinist control over the domestic regimes of the Eastern European states? Could Soviet security requirements be reconciled with open coalition governments in neighboring countries? A State Department official recommended to Truman that the United States strive for a Polish solution that met minimal Soviet needs: "While this government may not want to oppose a political configuration in Eastern Europe which gives the Soviet Union a predominant influence in Poland, neither would it desire to see Poland become in fact a Soviet satellite and have American influence there completely eliminated." Truman might also have analyzed the vital interests underlying Soviet repression in Eastern Europe to see whether the United States might loosen the Soviet grip by providing alternative routes to the same end. For example, since the United States opposed the Soviets' practice of meeting their economic needs through one-sided, exploitive trade pacts, expropriation of capital equipment, requisition of economic resources to pay for the occupation, and heavy reparation demands in countries occupied by the Red Army, Truman might have offered Stalin a postwar credit as an inducement not to pursue avaricious policies. Though the State Department recommended that a credit to the Soviet Union be placed on the agenda at the Potsdam Conference, Truman said nothing to Stalin on the subject. Similarly, if the Soviets' demand for control in Eastern Europe was derived from fear of reborn German aggression, the United States might have moderated their policies by offering the Soviet Government a twenty-five-year treaty for the permanent demilitarization of Germany, backed up by a commitment to use United States troops if necessary. Truman's briefing book prepared by the State Department cogently discussed the potential advantages of a German demilitarization treaty:

> It would greatly reduce Soviet fears that Germany will one day be permitted to regain its strength and be used by the Western Powers in an anti-Soviet combination. If the demilitarization of Germany is secured by such a commitment no combination of European powers could effectively threaten the Soviet Union and the latter could afford to adopt a more liberal policy, particularly in Eastern Europe, thus making it possible to break the vicious circle in which [the Soviet Union] moves to insure its own security and which tends to bring about the very combination of powers against it that it is seeking to avoid.

Though Truman asked the State Department to prepare him a memorandum on a four-power guaranteed demilitarization of Germany before the conference, he did not broach the idea to Stalin for his informal reaction.[107]

Instead, viewing the Potsdam conference as analogous to a poker game, Truman pushed our cards to the front of the table and waited for Stalin to make concessions. But in international politics, it is possible to win all the chips but lose the game. Like Truman, foreign policy analysts have often used metaphors taken from poker to describe international relations. For example, after normalization of Sino-American relations in 1979, commentators wrote about "playing the China card" in our relations with the Soviets. There are a few superficial similarities between poker and relations between nation-states. For example, the outcome of a dispute is often determined by the relative power of two nations as measured by territory, population, resources, and so on—the functional equivalents of the card values in a poker hand. A skillful negotiator may "bluff" the opponent into conceding even though he is holding a "poor hand." But the dissimi-

---

[107] Davies diary, July 30, 1945, LC; *FR: Potsdam*, I, pp. 163, 181, 214, 220, 263, 450, 715. For a concise, lucid discussion of negotiation theory, see Gordon Craig and Alexander George, *Force and Statecraft: Diplomatic Problems of Our Time* (New York: Oxford University Press, 1983), pp. 157-71.

larities between poker and international relations are more important. In the real world, a mere show of cards—or power sources—may fail to persuade the other nation to "turn in its chips" and concede defeat. For one thing, the "point value of the cards" or relative power of the contestants, is often in dispute. Wars have been fought to determine the relative power of nations. For another, no country has to follow the rules of the game.

On July 3, James F. Byrnes was sworn in as secretary of state. The secretary of state was next in the line of succession if Truman should die, and Truman had no great respect for the photogenic but intellectually shallow Stettinius. Byrnes had an unparalleled record of experience in politics, having served in both houses of Congress, on the Supreme Court, and as director of the Office of War Mobilization and Reconversion. FDR had recognized Byrnes' talents as a political strategist and used him in Congress as a legislative "trouble-shooter," a "fixer," a "handyman" for the president. If a bill was about to be lost, Byrnes could always come up with a compromise that would save at least part of it through subsequent "interpretations." During the war, FDR created the position of director of War Mobilization for Byrnes, giving him far-reaching authority over production, procurement, transportation, and distribution of civilian and military supplies. The powers delegated to Byrnes were so extensive that the press dubbed him "Assistant President." Further, Byrnes had taken shorthand notes at Yalta, the decisions of which were assuming greater importance as the basis of the structure of the postwar world. In addition, Truman wanted to make amends to Byrnes for his failure to win the vice-presidential nomination in 1944. Truman had promised to place Byrnes' name up for nomination at the convention before he himself was drafted by FDR.[108]

More relevant to Truman's immediate concerns, Byrnes was a vigorous supporter of Roosevelt's policy of Soviet-American cooperation. On May 13, Truman had acknowledged to Davies that the State Department was prejudiced against the Soviets, and promised to appoint Jimmy Byrnes to be the next secretary of state. In early June, Byrnes told Davies that "there was only one hope for peace and that was to hold the confidence of the Soviets in our good faith." "Every possible

[108] Joseph Alsop and Robert Kintner, "Sly and Able," *Saturday Evening Post*, July 20, 1940, pp. 13ff.; McNaughton Report, September 4, 1945, McNaughton Papers, Box 7, HSTL; Memorandum for James F. Byrnes from FDR, June 10, 1944, James F. Byrnes Papers, folder 637(1), Clemson; George Curry, *James F. Byrnes*, vol. 14 of *The American Secretaries of State and Their Diplomacy* (New York: Cooper Square Publishers, 1965), p. 101.

effort should be made to preserve the unity after the war to save the peace," he emphasized.[109]

Still, unlike Truman or Acheson, Byrnes' commitment to Soviet-American cooperation was not well-grounded in a network of supporting beliefs or even scripts. Consequently, self-perception theory suggests that Byrnes' dedication to Big Three collaboration would be easily shaken by the practical problems inherent in establishing a working partnership with a nation as different in political tradition, culture, and ideology as the Soviet Union. As Ambassador Halifax commented, "he seems in sum to be a man of accommodating temper, imbued with a genuine desire to serve his country and to work for a better world, but not of a strong character, settled convictions or capacity to fight too hard for them against strong odds." Like Truman, Byrnes had few enduring convictions. He constructed his attitudes on the spot, based on his most recent experience with a subject or what was politically expedient. Byrnes was not a great social or economic thinker. During his legislative career, he did not conceive of any major legislative programs; he executed the ideas of other people. Soon after he was appointed secretary of state, the *New York Times Magazine* commented that "his fixed opinions on world matters are very few indeed, and stem mostly from the national policies with which he has been associated." Byrnes had the politician's ability to shift with prevailing winds, and a knack for picking the winning side of any argument. Byrnes' lack of any firm beliefs or principles contributed to his objectivity in dealing with new information, but made it difficult for him to reach cognitive closure on any issue. According to Ambassador Halifax, "he is said to find it difficult to make up his mind, seeks advice very widely, tries to please the greatest number, and is quick to resent insufficient attention or persistent opposition." Byrnes' former law partner and long-term assistant, Donald Russell, described him this way: "I would say that Jimmy Byrnes is first a man with an inquiring and receptive mind. He doesn't start into anything with preconceived notions."[110] As secretary of state, he was able to shift course with bewildering speed whenever he received evidence that a particular approach was not working.

---

[109] Davies journal, May 13, 1945, LC; McNaughton Report, May 11, 1945, Mc-Naughton Papers, HSTL; Byrnes to Walter Lippmann, April 30, 1945, Byrnes Papers, folder 199, Clemson; Joseph Davies to Byrnes, May 10, 1945, Davies Papers, Box 16, LC; Davies diary, June 5, 1945, LC.

[110] Halifax to Foreign Office, July 3, 1945, FO 371/44620, AN 2136/245/45; Turner Catledge, "Secretary Byrnes: Portrait of a Realist," *New York Times Magazine*, July 8, 1945, pp. 12ff.; McNaughton Reports, January 2, 1943, HSTL.

Because Byrnes had no strong convictions about foreign affairs, self-perception theory predicts that the secretary of state would vacillate and waver in his approach to the Soviet Union. His beliefs should have been highly transient and contingent on the atmosphere of the moment. On the other hand, Byrnes should not have distorted or ignored information about Soviet actions to preserve his favorable image of the Soviet Union. Lacking a coherent, elaborated belief system, Byrnes should have felt no internal pressures to maintain consistency at the cost of his grasp of reality; cognitive dissonance theory would not apply to an extrovert such as Byrnes, a "born politician."

Byrnes had little time or energy for anything other than politics. He often said that his wants were confined to "two tailor-made suits a year, three meals a day, and a reasonable amount of good liquor." His joviality and ingratiating manner played no small role in his rise to success, which was based on his relationship with powerful patrons. It was often said of Byrnes that he was the best-liked man in the Senate. Unfortunately, Byrnes' success as a legislative negotiator was not easily transferred to his diplomatic dealings with the Soviets. Having no experience in diplomacy, as secretary of state Byrnes relied on analogies from his career as a legislative negotiator in domestic politics. Indeed, before his first foreign ministers' conference, Byrnes confidently told other members of the U.S. delegation that he knew just how to deal with the Russians. "It's just like the U.S. Senate," he said. "You build a post office in their state and they'll build a post office in our state." Schema theory predicts that Byrnes would apply negotiating scripts and personae derived from his experience negotiating with Republicans in the Senate to the task of obtaining peace treaties from the Soviets. Byrnes would thus not have formulated a negotiating strategy by analyzing the causes of Soviet behavior, inferring their negotiating objectives, and making predictions about their reactions to alternative U.S. negotiating positions—as attribution theory would suggest. Instead, he should have followed routinized scripts, without much thought or planning.

There were important differences, however, in the negotiating techniques likely to be successful with the Soviets from those that worked with his colleagues in the Senate. Since every member of the U.S. Senate shared "democratic-capitalist" values, Byrnes could usually resolve major policy differences through minor adjustments at the margin, or appeals to concrete personal interests. In his head, he carried a card file of information about each senator, listing his personality traits, friendships, enmities, idiosyncracies, political base, and his state's agricultural products and industries. A legislator's vote was often determined by his feelings about the president, a law's effect on the price of peanuts, or his allegiance to a prominent party leader. Byrnes would calculate whether a particular senator was more likely to be influenced by personal, sectional, or partisan considerations. When negotiating with the Soviets, however, true ideologues, Bynres had great difficulty finding workable compromises. Soviet negotiators were faceless, implacable in their devotion to the interests of the Soviet state. Conflicts of values are less easily adjusted than competition between sectional or partisan interests.[111]

During the voyage to Potsdam, Truman, Leahy, and Byrnes put the finishing touches on the U.S. agenda, using memoranda and proposals prepared by the State Department. On the way over, Truman studied his briefing book carefully, and tried to reduce each policy statement to a few handy phrases that he could memorize and recite during the negotiations. He was not inclined to challenge any of the State Department's recommendations. Nor did he question why the United States should adopt a particular policy. As Herbert Feis observed, Truman's method of study was "not the way of a patient student of pondering mind, but rather the way of a person who habitually sought simple versions from which he could arrive at quick decisions."[112]

His enjoyment of the voyage to Berlin was spoiled by the knowledge that he would soon have to test his untried diplomatic skills. Perceiving himself as a "country boy from Missouri," he was understandably nervous about having to negotiate at the same table with such legendary figures as Churchill and Stalin.[113]

The significance of Potsdam for U.S.-Soviet relations lay not just in the agreements reached, important as these were, but in the personal impressions Truman and Stalin formed of each other. Like most political leaders, Truman placed greater reliance on information acquired through his own experience. On the basis of several private conversations, journalist C. L. Sulzberger later observed that "President Truman used Potsdam as a symbol of all relations with Russia because this was his own personal experience of Russian methods."[114]

[111] Alsop and Kintner, "Sly and Able," pp. 18-19; Tris Coffin, *Missouri Compromise* (Boston: Little, Brown, 1947), pp. 245-46; McNaughton Reports, January 2, 1943, HSTL; Robert L. Messer, *The End of An Alliance: James F. Byrnes, Roosevelt, Truman and the Origins of the Cold War* (Chapel Hill: University of North Carolina Press, 1982), p. 92.

[112] Feis, *Between War and Peace*, p. 160; *FR: Potsdam*, I, pp. 239-41; Bohlen, *Witness to History*, p. 226.

[113] Truman diary, July 7, 1945, HSTL.

[114] Nisbett and Ross, *Human Inference*, pp. 49-50, 58-59; C. L. Sulzberger, *A Long Row of Candles: Memoirs and Diaries (1934-1954)* (Toronto: Macmillan, 1969), p. 364.

On July 16, Truman met the formidable Churchill. "He gave me a lot of hooey about how great my country is and how he loved Roosevelt and how he intended to love me etc. etc.," Truman wrote. "I am sure we can get along if he doesn't try to give me too much soft soap."[115]

On July 17, Truman looked up from his desk and saw Stalin standing in the doorway. "I am here to be your friend," Truman said. "I'm no diplomat," he admitted, "so I won't beat around the bush but say yes or no to questions after hearing all the argument." Stalin said he appreciated that and would always try to accommodate the views of the United States. Stalin mentioned that the Soviet agenda included the dismissal of Franco and division of former Italian colonies and other mandates. Truman thought Stalin's demands were "dynamite," but the thought of the atomic bomb comforted him. "I have some dynamite too, which I'm not exploding now," he said to himself. After they discussed some of the items on the agenda, Truman asked Stalin to stay for lunch. The two most powerful men in the world dined on liver and onions. The marshal was extremely polite and friendly to his host. Truman was greatly impressed with Stalin, and talked to him freely. He liked the way Stalin looked at him straight in the eye when he spoke. When asked about the visit, Truman replied: "He is direct. We can get along." Later, Truman wrote to himself: "I can deal with Stalin. He is honest—but smart as hell."[116]

Stalin promised to enter the war against Japan on August 15. Truman had achieved his principal objective—before the conference even began. He told Davies that even if nothing further came of the meeting, he could go home now. It is not clear why Truman was so anxious to have the Russians enter the Pacific War. He had already received news of the successful atomic bomb test. Moreover, that same day he wrote in his diary: "Believe Japs will fold up before Russia comes in. I am sure they will when Manhattan appears over their homeland."[117]

Stalin seemed like a fellow "politician" to Truman, a "big man" with whom he could bargain and make deals. "It is always easy to understand and to get along with big men," Truman explained to Davies. It was the "little fellows" who were hard to deal with, because of "their egotism and desire to show off their knowledge and 'strut their stuff.' "

[115] Truman diary, " 'Today Has Been a Historical One': Harry S Truman's Diary of the Potsdam Conference," ed. Eduard Mark, *Diplomatic History* 4 (Summer 1980): 320.

[116] Truman diary, July 17, 1945, ibid.; *FR: Potsdam*, II, pp. 43-44, 1584-85; Leahy, *I Was There*, p. 399; Davies diary, July 18, 1945, LC.

[117] Truman diary, July 18, 1945, "Truman's Diary of the Potsdam Conference," ed. Mark, p. 320; Davies diary, July 18, 1945, LC.

Truman said that there were many "big men" in the Senate—Senators George, Tydings, Austin, Borah, and Tobey. He could get along with them.[118]

His meeting with Stalin reinforced Truman's belief that the Russian dictator was like Boss Pendergast. Truman remarked admiringly to an aide: "Stalin is as near like Tom Pendergast as any man I know." Truman went beyond Stalin's superficial resemblance to Pendergast to infer that the Russian shared personality characteristics with the Missouri boss. Truman told his staff that "Stalin was one, who, if he said something one time, would say the same thing the next time . . . he could be depended upon." Truman inferred that Stalin, like Pendergast, could be trusted to keep his word. "I got the impression Stalin would stand by his agreements and also that he had a Politburo on his hands like the 80th Congress," Truman recalled. Although Truman later felt betrayed by the Russians, he maintained his favorable image of Stalin. In 1947, after he had inaugurated the Truman Doctrine to contain Soviet expansion, Truman told his staff that if Stalin were the only person he had to deal with on the Russian side, everything would be all right. "I like the 'old guy,'" Truman said. On a whistle-stop tour during the 1948 campaign, at the height of the Berlin crisis, Truman reminisced about Potsdam:

I got very well acquainted with Joe Stalin, and I like old Joe. He is a decent fellow. But Joe is a prisoner of the Politburo. He can't do what he wants to. He makes agreements, and if he could he would keep them. But the people who run the government are very specific in saying that he can't keep them.[119]

Byrnes, who had to negotiate with "Iron Pants" Molotov on the issues that the Big Three could not resolve, received a much less benign impression both of Stalin and the Soviets' willingness to observe commitments. He thought that Molotov purposely made extreme demands so that Stalin could yield, conveying the image of a reasonable man. After the conference, Byrnes told Stimson of a "number of acts of perfidy" committed by Stalin at Potsdam, which suggested that "we could not rely upon anything in the way of promises from them." Byrnes was afraid that ideological differences would make impossible any long-term program of Soviet-American cooperation.[120]

[118] Davies journal, July 25, 1945, LC.

[119] Ayers diary, October 18, 1947; Steinberg, *Man from Missouri*, p. 255; Ayers diary, August 7, 1945, HSTL; Daniels Interview, August 30, 1949, Daniels Papers, HSTL; Donovan, *Conflict and Crisis*, p. 400.

[120] Thomas G. Paterson, "Potsdam, the Atomic Bomb, and the Cold War: A Discus-

In general, Byrnes' commitment to Soviet-American cooperation was vacillating. Having few related beliefs supporting his views on Soviet-American cooperation, Byrnes was readily swayed by evidence of Soviet repressive and exploitative occupation policies; at Potsdam, Byrnes was far more suspicious of the Soviets than Truman. In addition, Byrnes was exposed to a different "slice" of Soviet behavior. Soon after arriving at the conference site, Byrnes admitted to Davies that he was disturbed by reports that the Soviets had stripped the German countryside of all movable goods. He was also worried by State Department briefing memoranda that accused Soviet occupying authorities and local communist parties of collaborating to establish one-party communist-dominated regimes in Rumania and Bulgaria.[121] Yet, Byrnes observed that he and Truman would have to preserve the relationship of trust between the Soviet Union and the United States if they were to win the new struggle to maintain world peace.[122]

The Big Three met in a Tudor manor constructed for the crown prince of the Hohenzollerns. The dark-paneled main meeting room was furnished with red carpet and plush oriental rugs; overhead a plaster galleon in bas-relief sailed through white clouds lit by a red star painted in by the Russians. At the first meeting, Stalin suggested that Truman act as chairman. He briskly "banged through" four major proposals: establishment of a Council of Foreign Ministers to draw up the peace treaties; a political program for occupied Germany; relaxation of the Italian armistice terms; and implementation of the Yalta Declaration on Liberated Europe. He let it be known that he expected prompt action. "I don't want just to discuss," Truman said. "I want to decide." Though he appeared to be in full command of the issues, Truman admitted in a letter to his mother that presiding over the meeting was a "nerve-wracking experience," and the worst was yet to come. "I have several aces in the hole I hope which will help on results," he wrote.[123]

The three leaders readily agreed to Truman's proposal for a Council of Foreign Ministers, composed of Britain, the United States, and Russia, with limited participation by France and China. The Big Three

sion with James F. Byrnes," *Pacific Historical Review* (May 1972): 227-30; Stimson diary, September 4, 1945 (Stanford microfilm).

[121] Davies diary, July 15, 16, 1945, LC; Briefing Book Paper, June 29, 1945, *FR: Potsdam*, I, pp. 357-58.

[122] Davies diary, July 15, 1945, LC.

[123] *FR: Potsdam*, II, pp. 52-54, 63, 609-10, 775-78, 1080-81; Truman diary, July 18, 1945, "Truman's Diary of the Potsdam Conference," ed. Mark, p. 323; M. Truman, *Harry Truman*, p. 269.

also had no difficulty in approving general political and economic principles to guide the occupation of Germany, which could be summarized as demilitarization, denazification, and democratization.[124]

Truman's other two proposals, however, were rebuffed by Stalin. When Truman suggested that they relax the armistice terms for Italy, Stalin demanded in return that the United States and Britain establish diplomatic relations with the former Axis satellites in Eastern Europe. "I cannot agree," Truman said bluntly. "Then we cannot go ahead," Stalin replied sharply. Truman retorted that the U.S. government was unable to recognize the satellite governments. When these governments were established on a "proper" basis, the United States would recognize them, and not before. The air was tense. Truman suggested that they pass over the issue.

Stalin regarded Truman's position as a betrayal of the spheres of influence agreed on at Teheran and Yalta. Stalin reminded Truman that he had recognized Italy, though no elections had been held. "Was the Italian government really more democratic than the governments of these countries?" Stalin asked. "Was the Italian government more responsible?"[125]

Stalin also brusquely rejected Truman's proposal for carrying out the Yalta decisions in Rumania and Bulgaria. The title of the U.S. proposal—Implementation of the Yalta Declaration on Liberated Europe—reflected Truman's obsession with holding the Soviets to their agreements. The draft proposal circulated by the U.S. delegation accused the Soviets of failing to honor their obligations under the Yalta Declaration. Truman proposed that the governments of Rumania and Bulgaria be reorganized and the Big Three consult on how they might assist the new interim governments in holding free elections. Truman wished to apply the Polish precedent to the rest of Eastern Europe.[126] Cosmetic changes would be made in the satellite governments by adding a few opposition members and elections staged for the benefit of the American public. But Stalin acted offended at any implication that the Bulgarian and Rumanian regimes were not democratic. When Byrnes submitted a proposal for allied supervision of elections in Italy, Greece, Rumania, Hungary, and Bulgaria, Truman suggested that the word "supervise" be softened to "observe"; he emphasized that he had

[124] McNeill, *America, Britain, and Russia*, pp. 617-18; Feis, *Between War and Peace*, p. 244.
[125] *FR: Potsdam*, II, pp. 174, 207, 358-59; Davies journal, July 21, 1945, LC.
[126] *FR: Potsdam*, II, pp. 643-44.

no desire to superintend elections in those countries.[127] But the Soviets would not agree to that, either.

At Potsdam, U.S. aims for Eastern Europe were limited to salvaging whatever remained of Western influence in the area. As the State Department briefing book pointed out, "it must be recognized that the Russians have already gone far to establish an effective sphere of influence in Eastern Europe."[128]

For all his bluster about nonrecognition, Truman showed little interest in Eastern European affairs. He did not wish to become involved in lengthy debates with Stalin on the Balkans. Whenever agreement could not be reached, Truman referred the dispute to the Foreign Ministers, and took up an easier question. In the diary he kept at Potsdam, Truman made no mention of the issue of free elections in Eastern Europe. The State Department opposed recognition of the Eastern European regimes because it would imply approval of the Soviet practice of setting up puppet governments and might encourage the Soviets to repeat the process further west. In contrast, Truman believed that the Soviets would have trouble digesting their gains in Eastern Europe and would not therefore be tempted to spill over into the western half of the Continent. Before leaving for the Potsdam conference, Truman privately scoffed at the warnings of a delegation of senators that France, Germany, Italy, and Scandinavia would go communist, and that Russia was a "big bad wolf." During the Berlin meeting, he remarked to Navy Secretary Forrestal that as a result of Hitler's egomania, "we shall have a Slav Europe for a long time to come. I don't think it is so bad."[129]

Following FDR's precedent, Truman hinted that Stalin should make some pretense at holding elections in Poland to satisfy American public opinion. "There are six million Poles in the United States," he explained. "A free election in Poland reported to the United States by a free press would make it easier to deal with these Polish people." As a gesture to Truman, Stalin agreed to a statement that representatives of the allied press would be allowed "full freedom" both before and during the Polish elections.[130]

In contrast, Truman was greatly aroused by the issue of Poland's western frontier because it was an egregious violation of the Yalta agreement on German occupation zones. At the Yalta Conference, the

[127] Ibid., pp. 155, 166.

[128] FR: Potsdam, I, pp. 256-57, 359-60.

[129] Forrestal diary, July 28, 1945, Forrestal Papers, Princeton; Truman diary, July 7, 1945, HSTL.

[130] Davies diary, July 21, 1945, LC; FR: Potsdam II, pp. 94, 206.

three leaders had agreed that Poland should receive German territory in the north and west to compensate for loss of the area east of the Curzon Line. But Stalin wished to transfer a bigger section of Germany than seemed prudent to either Roosevelt or Churchill. In the end, the three leaders decided that the issue should be postponed until the peace conference. But when the Red Army marched through Germany, the Soviets unilaterally handed over to the Poles the additional territory without consulting the United States or Britain. The transfer of this much territory would make the Poles dependent on the Soviet Union for protection against German revanchism. Truman was outraged by the "Bolsheviki land grab." "Just a unilateral arrangement without so much [as] a by your leave," Truman complained to himself. "I don't like it."[131]

Truman bluntly criticized the Soviet fait accompli. He pointed out that another government had been assigned an occupation zone in Germany, without consultation with the Americans or British. Simply stated, were the occupation zones valid until peace, or were we giving Germany away piecemeal? Truman said he wanted it "distinctly understood" that the occupation zones would be as previously agreed. "Any other course will make reparations very difficult," Truman said pointedly. The Soviet Union was not afraid of the reparations question, Stalin replied haughtily, and would if necessary renounce them. The next day Truman stated his position even more forcefully. He read the portion of the Yalta agreement concerning Poland's western frontier. "This agreement had been reached between President Roosevelt, Marshal Stalin, and Prime Minister Churchill." He was in complete accord with it. Truman said he did not like the manner in which Poland was assigned an occupation zone without any discussion. "That was his position yesterday, that was his position today, and that would be his position tomorrow," Truman announced dramatically.[132]

On the issue of reparations, the United States and Britain also reached an impasse with the Russians. The Soviets insisted on a guaranteed amount of German production as restitution for the damage done to them by the Nazis; the United States and Britain favored a flexible formula that took into consideration Germany's ability to pay for essential imports.

Had not the wily Byrnes used logrolling tactics learned in the Senate cloakroom, the conference might have broken up without settling the

[131] Truman diary, July 25, 26, 1945, "Truman's Diary of the Potsdam Conference," ed. Mark, pp. 324-25.
[132] *FR: Potsdam*, II, pp. 208-15, 251-52.

most pressing issues. The meeting was briefly interrupted so that Churchill could fly home to Britain to await the outcome of the British parliamentary elections. Contrary to everyone's expectations, the Conservatives lost by a landslide. While they waited for the new British prime minister, Clement Attlee, and his foreign secretary, Ernest Bevin, to arrive, Byrnes worked out the details of a "package deal." After some grumbling about Byrnes' decision to link the three issues of the Polish frontier, Italy, and reparations, the Big Three agreed to the entire package. The Soviets gave up their demand for a guaranteed amount of reparations. In return for this concession, the United States and Britain agreed to allow the Poles to administer German territory as far as the Oder-Neisse line until the issue was settled at the peace conference. This qualification fooled no one; Truman was aware that the Poles were already treating the territory as a part of Poland, expelling millions of Germans and sending in Polish settlers. On the issue of recognizing the Axis satellites, Byrnes accepted Molotov's formula that each nation examine separately the question of establishing diplomatic relations. There was no reference in the communiqué to free elections as a precondition for recognition of the Balkan states. The Potsdam agreements did not even mention the Yalta Declaration on Liberated Europe.[133]

Truman's apparent decisiveness was a cover for irresolution; his firm manner barely concealed his propensity to totter to and fro. Sir Archibald Clark-Kerr, British ambassador in Moscow, gave journalist Edgar Snow this off-the-record impression of Truman at Potsdam:

> On first contact Mr. Truman made a very good impression, with those blue eyes magnified under heavy lenses, his energy and vitality, his directness and candor, his forthright sub-altern air of do or die. But as the conference wore on his vacillations became rather trying. He would take up a point one day and say, "No, no, no!" beating the table with the sides of his hands. Then everything would come to a halt. But the next morning, after he had talked to his advisers, he would come back and pass over the same point with a mere nod of approval. Pretty soon people stopped taking his snap judgments seriously.[134]

Even Byrnes, however, could not come up with language concealing the allies' conflict over the Turkish Straits regime. Beginning with

---

[133] McNeill, *America, Britain and Russia*, pp. 622-25; Feis, *Between War and Peace*, pp. 259-71, 349-50; W. B.'s Book, July 23, 1945, Byrnes Papers, Folder 602, Clemson; *FR: Potsdam*, II, pp. 439-40, 473, 480-83, 511-14, 1485-86, 1509-10.

[134] Edgar Snow, *Journey to the Beginning* (London: Gollancz, 1959), p. 358.

Alexander I, the Russian tsars sought assured passage through the Straits and a base on the Dardanelles. But Britain was determined to keep the Russians bottled up in the Black Sea, to protect the Mediterranean route to India. During the Russian civil war, Britain and France had sailed through the Straits and occupied strategic points along the Black Sea, which enabled them to supply Denikin's White Russian armies. The 1936 Montreux Convention gave Turkey control of the Straits and the right to exclude all warships whenever Turkey was at war or threatened by aggression. "The result," Stalin complained, "was that a small state supported by Great Britain held a great state by the throat and gave it no outlet."[135]

The Russians may have felt that they were entitled to some spoils at the expense of pro-Axis Turkey. The Turks had reneged on repeated promises to the British to enter the war against Germany in return for arms and munitions. Turkey had supplied Germany with the strategic commodity chrome. Worse, the Turks had liberally interpreted the Montreux Convention to allow German warships to sail through the Straits into the Black Sea; allied warships were excluded from the Straits until late 1944, when the tide of war had turned their favor.[136]

In early June, when the Turkish ambassador proposed renewing the 1921 Turkish-Soviet friendship treaty, Molotov gave three conditions: return of Russian territory ceded to Turkey in 1921; Soviet bases on the Straits; preliminary agreement between Turkey and Russia on revision of the Montreux Convention.[137]

Soon after this conversation, the Soviets initiated a "war of nerves" against Turkey. Soviet troops massed in Bulgaria and Rumania along the Turkish border while Russian pilots repeatedly encroached on Turkish airspace. When Truman found out, he angrily scrawled on the margin of his briefing memo: "Tell Russia matters such as this should be settled by San Francisco document and that we're getting damned tired of direct action."[138]

[135] Anthony R. De Luca, "The Montreux Conference of 1936: A Diplomatic Study of Anglo-Soviet Rivalry at the Turkish Straits" (Ph.D. Dissertation, Stanford, 1974), pp. 1-22, 262-67; Jonathan Knight, "America's International Guarantees for the Straits: Prelude to the Truman Doctrine," *Middle Eastern Studies* 13 (May 1977): 241-50; *FR: Potsdam*, II, p. 303.

[136] Anthony R. De Luca, "Soviet-American Politics and the Turkish Straits," *Political Science Quarterly* 92 (Fall 1977): 503-24; Stephen G. Xydis, "The 1945 Crisis over the Turkish Straits," *Balkan Studies* 1 (1960): 67-68.

[137] Memoranda for the President, June 15, 19, 1945, Truman Papers, PSF: Subject File, "Current Foreign Developments," HSTL; Memorandum for the President, June 21, 1945, 711.00/6-2145, RG 59, NA.

[138] Memorandum for the President, June 21, 1945, 711.00/6-2145, RG 59, NA;

The British also thought that we should protest to the Soviets. But the State Department did nothing. Members of the Office of Near Eastern and African Affairs argued that the Turkish-Soviet talks were exploratory; the Soviets had not made any formal demands. Willingness to discuss Soviet desiderata on the Straits at the Potsdam Conference should be sufficient to head off any further demands for bases and territorial concessions. Besides, it would not be a good idea to give the Soviets the impression that we were "ganging up" with the British on the eve of the Big Three meeting.[139]

The State and War Departments and the Joint Chiefs of Staff were opposed to Soviet bases on the Straits because military fortifications would project Soviet influence and military power into an area vital to British interests. But there was a strong undercurrent of sympathy for the Soviet viewpoint in the U.S. government. John Hickerson felt that the United States should not oppose a "realistic solution" that met minimum Soviet security needs—assured passage for Soviet war vessels and the right to install bases in the area. The army representatives on the Joint Strategic Survey Committee argued that Soviet control of the Dardanelles was "morally justified," based on history and geography. Further, it was hypocritical for the United States to oppose Soviet bases on the Straits while we were at the same time negotiating for base rights in Iceland, the Azores, and the Pacific islands.[140]

According to a member of the U.S. delegation, "Truman's favorite project at that time was the internationalization of inland waterways—rivers, canals, straits," Before the conference, Truman told Admiral Leahy that "he considered future free and equal rights of all nations to transport on the waterways of Europe—the Rhine, Danube, Dardanelles, and the Kiel Canal—would be advantageous if not essential to the preservation of peace in Europe."[141]

At the Potsdam Conference, Churchill vigorously took Stalin to task

---

Memoranda for the President, July 2, 3, 1945, Truman Papers, PSF: "Foreign Affairs File," HSTL.

[139] Memorandum Regarding Soviet-Turkish Relations, June 29, 1945, 761.6711/6-1845, RG 59, NA.

[140] Memorandum to Matthews and Dunn, July 5, 1945, 767.68119/7-545, RG 59, NA; "U.S. Policy Concerning Dardanelles and Kiel Canal, JCS 1418/1, July 12, 1945, Enclosure "a" and Appendix, Report by Lt. Gen. Embick and Major General Fairchild of the JSSC, ABC 093 Kiel (6 Jul 45), Sec. 1-A, RG 165, NA; Briefing Book Paper, June 30, 1945, *FR: Potsdam*, I, pp. 1014-15; U.S. Position re Soviet Proposals on Kiel Canal and Dardanelles, July 8, 1945 (Expanded Draft of Letter from Secretary of War to Secretary of State) ABC 093 Kiel (6 Jul 45), Sec. 1-A, RG 165, NA.

[141] Robert Murphy, *Diplomat among Warriors* (Garden City, N.Y.: Doubleday, 1964), p. 277; Leahy, *I Was There*, p. 392.

for alarming the Turks with demands for bases, propaganda attacks, and the concentration of Soviet troops in Bulgaria. In response, Molotov circulated a memo proposing joint Soviet-Turkish control and the right of the Soviets to build bases on the Straits. Churchill objected that the Soviet demand for bases went "far beyond" their previous discussions.[142] The president did not object to the Soviets' "war of nerves" against Turkey or to their demand for bases on the Dardanelles. Instead, he used the opportunity to present his plan for internationalizing inland waterways.

Truman said that he agreed that the Montreux Convention should be revised; but he thought that the Straits should be a free waterway open to the world and defended by the Big Three. Truman believed that all the wars of the last two hundred years had originated in the area from the Black Sea to the Baltic and from the eastern frontier of France to the western frontier of Russia. He thought that it ought to be their business to see that this did not happen again. Many wars arose out of disagreements over the control of water routes. "European waterways [have] been a hotbed for breeding wars," Truman contended. To a great extent, therefore, future wars could be prevented by arranging for the free passage of goods and vessels on inland waterways. He pointed out that free navigation on American rivers and canals had helped unify our country—as if Europe were comparable to the United States! Truman then read a proposal for internationalization of inland waterways, beginning with the Rhine and the Danube. "I do not want to engage in another war twenty-five years from now over the Straits or the Danube," Truman declared.[143]

It might be argued that Truman's interest in internationalization of inland waterways reflected the liberal internationalist outlook that pervaded the U.S. government at the time, instead of his idiosyncratic reading of the "lessons of history." Wilson had included internationalization of the Dardanelles as one of his fourteen points. During Potsdam, liberal columnist Heinz Eulau, writing in the *New Republic*, suggested that placing the Straits under the control of an international commission would be the best way to satisfy Russia's traditional aspirations for an outlet to the Mediterranean. But there is no evidence that anyone else within the Truman administration favored internationalizing the Dardanelles. State Department officials present at the Potsdam Conference were embarrassed by Truman's evidentl earnest-

[142] *FR: Potsdam*, II, pp. 256-58, 1427-28.
[143] *FR: Potsdam*, II, pp. 303-304, 527; Murphy, *Diplomat among Warriors*, p. 277; Truman diary, July 26, 1945, "Truman's Diary of the Potsdam Conference," ed. Mark, p. 326.

ness, and his intense interest in a proposal that had not the slightest chance of being accepted. When asked about the president's reference to internationalizing the Straits after Potsdam, the Division of Near Eastern Affairs chief, Gordon P. Merriam, patronizingly told a United Press correspondent that Truman was new to his job and had not had sufficient time to study the problem; since then his division had prepared a report that enlightened the president.[144]

Truman's initiative caught the State Department off guard. The State Department had recommended to Truman that he support *minor* revisions in the Montreux Convention, which would still allow Turkey to close off the Straits to Soviet warships. The Joint Chiefs and the War Department opposed internationalization of the Straits because it would set a precedent for the Panama and Suez Canals.[145]

Internationalization was even less acceptable to the Soviets than the existing Straits regime. It was proposed that responsibility for defending the Straits be given to an international commission; the League of Nations had proved that a collective guarantee was equivalent to no protection at all. Worse, Truman's proposal would have placed the United States, the one power capable of threatening the Soviet Union, at Russia's underbelly. Stalin and his advisers must have wondered whether Truman's aims were confined to preventing wars. For, as Molotov pointed out, if it was such a good system, why not apply it to Suez?[146] Stalin curtly refused to discuss Truman's proposal each time he brought it up. Nevertheless, Truman continued to be fascinated with the idea of internationalizing inland waterways. He included the proposal in his speech to the nation on the Potsdam Conference, and listed it as a major foreign policy objective in his first major foreign policy address in October.

Besides their demands for bases in Turkey, the Soviets showed other signs that they intended to move into the vacuum left by the decline of the British empire in the Mediterranean and Far East. Unexpectedly, the Soviets requested a trusteeship over one of Italy's former African colonies, a base on the African coast of the Mediterranean, joint action to remove the Franco regime in Spain, a share in the

[144] Heinz Eulau, "Turkey and the Straits," *New Republic*, July 23, 1945, pp. 100-101; Murphy, *Diplomat among Warriors*, pp. 277-78; Bohlen, *Witness to History*, p. 235; R. H. Shackford, UP Correspondent, "President's Dardanelles Designs down the Spout," *Washington Post*, October 12, 1945, attached to Truman to Byrnes, October 13, 1945, Truman Papers, PSF: Subject File, Cabinet, HSTL.

[145] *FR: Potsdam*, I, pp. 1014-15; U.S. Position re Soviet Proposals on Kiel Canal and Dardanelles, July 8, 1945, ABC 093 Kiel (6 July 1945), Sec. 1-A, RG 165, NA.

[146] *FR: Potsdam*, II, p. 365.

control of Tangier, part of the German fleet, and a trusteeship over Korea. The demands for a position on the Mediterranean could not be rationalized as Soviet security interests, unlike their claims in Eastern Europe. One of Byrnes' aides complained that "it is becoming more apparent that [the] Russians have gone imperialistic and are out to extend their sphere of influence in all directions and wherever possible." Secretary of War Stimson worried that the Russians "are throwing aside all their previous restraint as to being only a Continental power and not interested in any further acquisitions, and are now apparently seeking to branch in all directions." But Truman believed that most of the new Russian claims were "bluff." As with other contentious issues, Byrnes succeeded in having discussion of Soviet demands postponed until the Foreign Ministers' Conference.[147]

From July 16 through 21, Truman received information in stages about the successful atomic bomb test in Alamogordo, New Mexico. The full report, which arrived at Potsdam on July 21, described the explosion poetically: "For a brief period there was a lightning effect within a radius of 20 miles equal to several suns in midday; a huge ball of fire was formed which lasted several seconds." A massive steel tower was ripped from its concrete foundations and laid flat by the force of the blast. A blind woman saw the light.[148] Awestruck, Truman wrote in his diary: "We have discovered the most terrible bomb in the history of the world. It may be the fire destruction prophesied in the Euphrates Valley Era after Noah and his fabulous Ark."[149]

Truman was "tremendously pepped up" and excited by this report. He told Stimson that it "gave him an entirely new feeling of confidence." Knowledge that he had the Bomb brought assurance and vigor to Truman's negotiating style. Churchill noticed that Truman was "evidently much fortified by something that had happened" and that "he stood up to the Russians in a most emphatic and decisive manner, telling them as to certain demands that they absolutely could not have." After reading the atomic bomb report, Churchill said, "Now I know what happened to Truman yesterday. I couldn't understand it. When he got to the meeting after having read this report he

[147] William O. McCagg, Jr., *Stalin Embattled, 1943-1948* (Detroit: Wayne State University Press, 1978), p. 192; Mastny, *Russia's Road to the Cold War*, pp. 293-94; Feis, *Between War and Peace*, pp. 306-309; Stimson diary, July 23, 1945 (Stanford microfilm); W. B.'s Book, July 22, 1945, Byrnes Papers, Clemson.

[148] Michael Sherwin, *A World Destroyed: The Atomic Bomb and the Grand Alliance* (New York: Random House, Vintage Books, 1973), p. 308.

[149] Truman diary, July 25, 1945, "Truman's Diary of the Potsdam Conference," ed. Mark, p. 323.

was a changed man. He told the Russians just where they got on and off and generally bossed the whole meeting." Knowledge that he had the bomb may have made Truman less willing to compromise. But it did not alter his diplomatic objectives, for these were set on the voyage to Berlin.[150]

In contrast, news that the Bomb "worked" altered Byrnes' perception of U.S. diplomatic priorities. Initially, the primary aim of the U.S. delegation was to secure a firm Russian commitment to enter the war against Japan. United States military authorities believed that Russian entry into the Pacific War might eliminate the need for the bloodbath of a U.S. invasion of Kyushu. But by July 18, Byrnes realized that the atomic bomb might force the Japanese to surrender without the need for an American invasion or Russian intrusion into the Far East.[151]

Although the United States could not prevent the Soviets from moving into Manchuria, an early Japanese surrender would remove much of the basis for excessive Soviet claims on China at the postwar peace conference. There were ominous signs that the Russians had expanding ambitions in the Far East. When Chinese Ambassador Soong arrived in Moscow in late June to negotiate the terms of Russian involvement in the Pacific War, he was confronted by Soviet demands for territory and influence going far beyond the conditions agreed on at Yalta.[152]

Preserving Chinese territorial integrity from Russian depredations was a major preoccupation for Byrnes throughout the conference. Stalin had repeatedly said that Soviet entry into the Pacific War was contingent on China's approval of Soviet claims. Byrnes hoped that Chinese-Soviet negotiations would drag on without results, so that the United States could drop the Bomb before the Soviets had a chance to move their troops deep inside China.[153]

The successful atomic test raised the problem of whether Truman should tell Stalin about the new weapon before dropping the Bomb on Japan. Truman had appointed an interim committee of scientists and officials to advise him on the use and control of atomic energy.

[150] Davies diary, July 16, 1945, LC; Stimson diary, July 16, 18, 21, 22, 23, 1945 (Stanford microfilm); Truman diary, July 25, 1945, "Truman's Diary of the Potsdam Conference," ed. Mark, p. 323.

[151] Stimson diary, July 16, 1945 (Stanford microfilm); W. B.'s Book, July 16, 18, 1945, Clemson.

[152] Lisle A. Rose, *Dubious Victory: The United States and the End of World War II* (Kent, Ohio: Kent State University Press, 1979), pp. 235, 310; Gabriel Kolko, *Politics of War*, p. 556.

[153] W. B.'s Book, July 20, 24, 1945, Clemson; Forrestal diary, July 28, 1945, Forrestal Papers, Princeton; Meeting with Byrnes, February 27, 1948, Feis Papers, LC.

The committee decided that failure to warn the Soviets at Potsdam, only a few weeks before using the atomic bomb against Japan, would arouse their suspicions and make it impossible to enlist Soviet cooperation in the control of atomic energy. As Stimson explained to Truman, the committee recommended that he inform Stalin that we were working on the Bomb, intended to use it against Japan, and would like to discuss methods of controlling atomic weapons so that this new force could help preserve peace rather than destroy civilization. If Stalin should ask for details, Truman could say that the United States was not yet prepared to give them that information. Truman listened closely and said that he thought that was the best way to do it.[154]

At Potsdam, Truman consulted with Churchill on what he should say to Stalin, but he was determined to inform the Russian leader about the Manhattan project. Both men agreed that Stalin should be informed in rather general terms that the United States had a new weapon, without being told any of the details about U.S. atomic research. After the July 24 meeting, Truman sauntered over to Stalin unaccompanied by any interpreter, to give the Russian the impression that this was a chance encounter. The president remarked casually that the United States had a new weapon of "unusual destructive force." Stalin's face betrayed no sign that he was aware of the significance of what he was being told. The Russian dictator said only that he was glad to hear of it, and hoped they would "make good use of it against the Japanese." While they were waiting for their cars to arrive, Churchill asked Truman: "How did it go?" "He never asked a question," Truman assured him. Privately, Truman reflected that "it is certainly a good thing for the world that Hitler's crowd or Stalin's did not discover this atomic bomb."[155]

Truman's revelation of the atomic secret to Stalin did not go far enough to secure future Soviet cooperation with a program of controlling atomic weapons. Contrary to Stimson and the Interim Committee's advice, Truman did not suggest negotiations on controlling the new weapon. The president did not even use the word "atomic bomb." Truman told Stalin just enough to protect the United States from later accusations that we had not dealt frankly with our ally.

[154] Hewlett and Anderson, *New World*, pp. 357, 360, 369, 371-72; Stimson diary, June 6, July 3, 1945 (Stanford microfilm); Sherwin, *A World Destroyed*, p. 306.

[155] Truman diary, July 18, 25, 1945, "Truman's Diary of the Potsdam Conference," ed. Mark, pp. 322, 324; Churchill, *Triumph and Tragedy*, pp. 640-41, 669-70; Leahy, *I Was There*, p. 429; Hewlett and Anderson, *New World*, p. 394; Walter Brown Notes, July 16, 1945, Byrnes Papers, Folder 54(1), Clemson; Ayers diary, August 8, 1945, HSTL.

Despite his sincere determination to carry out FDR's "grand design" for Soviet-American cooperation, Truman did not trust the Soviets enough to share information on the atomic bomb. Yet he realized that Stalin had to be informed before we used the weapon against Japan. He resolved this dilemma, at least in his own mind, by equivocating.

Actually, Stalin had little reason to be shocked by Truman's "revelation" because the Russians had been spying on U.S. atomic research since 1942. The Russians had an atomic bomb project of their own beginning in 1943, although they had not given it much priority. That evening, Molotov complained to Stalin, "They're raising the price." "Let them," Stalin replied with a laugh. "We'll have to have a talk with Kurchatov today about speeding up our work."[156]

The experience of negotiating with the Russians caused Byrnes to have serious doubts about the feasibility of U.S.-Soviet cooperation. Since he had no strong convictions about foreign affairs, it was not the substance of the Soviets' position that bothered him, but Molotov's style of negotiation. Molotov was rude, challenged assertions of fact, attacked Byrnes personally for deliberately misunderstanding the Soviets' need for "friendly governments," and at every opportunity, cast aspersions upon the United States' good faith. As attribution theory would predict, Byrnes generalized from his personal difficulties in collaborating with Molotov to relations between the two states. Discussing the reparations issue with Davies, Byrnes complained that the Russians were "hard to get along with." On July 24, Byrnes told Brown flatly that somebody "made an awful mistake in bringing about a situation where Russia was permitted to come out of a war with the power she will have." "England should never have permitted Hitler to rise," Byrnes said, "the German people under a democracy would have been a far superior ally than Russia." He was afraid that there was too much difference in the ideologies of the United States and Russia to work out a long-term program of cooperation. In contrast, Truman commented to Navy Secretary Forrestal that he was being very realistic with the Russians and found Stalin not difficult to do business with.[157]

The Potsdam agreements were hardly a triumph of negotiation. There was no real adjustment of vital interests; the agreements merely ratified the existing distribution of power. Events in Western Europe

---

[156] David Holloway, "Entering the Nuclear Arms Race: The Soviet Decision to Build the Atomic Bomb, 1939-1945," International Security Studies Program Working Paper, Wilson Center, Washington, D.C., July 25, 1979; Mastny, *Russia's Road to the Cold War*, p. 298.

[157] W. B.'s Book, July 24, 1945, Byrnes Papers, Clemson; Forrestal diary, July 28, 1945, Forrestal Papers, Princeton.

would be determined by the United States and Britain, in Eastern Europe by the Soviet Union. No one made any *real* concessions. While superficially agreeing to Soviet hegemony over Eastern Europe, the United States kept the option of reopening the issue of free elections. Similarly, the United States and Britain refused to recognize Poland's western frontier. The Soviets had not given up their aspirations in the Mediterranean. All these issues would continue to disrupt the Grand Alliance.

Yet public reaction to the Potsdam communiqué was generally favorable. Editors, radio commentators, and congressmen expressed relief that the Big Three were able to agree on so many issues. But the provisions on Eastern Europe were sharply criticized. Journalists recognized that the Potsdam communiqué ceded Eastern Europe to Soviet domination. *Time* magazine commented that "subterfuge no longer obscured Russia's intention to dominate Eastern Europe. The communiqué tacitly recognized the new Poland's status as a satellite of Russia." A *New York Times* editorial pointed out that "if some of the agreement appears to ignore the Atlantic Charter it should not be forgotten that the Soviet Union holds some pretty important cards in the game of European diplomacy and that its foreign policy is guided by preoccupation with the idea of security." Some commentators pointed out that there was no assurance that the Russians would live up to their pledges to allow the Western press to report freely before and during the Polish elections, and to admit correspondents into the Balkans. *Time* magazine observed that "U.S.-Russian understanding on a free press was still unfinished business." Senator Vandenberg demanded that the Big Three specifically guarantee free access for American correspondents to Poland and other "blacked out areas of Europe." The "rhetorical reference" in the Potsdam communiqué to "free elections" and a "free press" was not enough, Vandenberg complained.[158]

In his report to the nation on the Potsdam Conference, delivered in a nationwide radio address on August 9, Truman equivocated about the meaning of the Potsdam agreements on Eastern Europe:

> At Yalta it was agreed, you will recall, that the three governments would assume a common responsibility in helping to reestablish in the liberated and satellite nations of Europe governments broadly

[158] Daily Summary of Opinion Developments, August 3, 1945, RG 59, NA; Raymond Daniell, Editorial, *New York Times*, August 5, 1945; *Time*, August 13, 1945, pp. 27, 29.

representative of democratic elements in the population. That responsibility still stands. . . .

It was reaffirmed in the Berlin Declarations on Rumania, Bulgaria, and Hungary. These nations are not to be spheres of influence of any one power.[159]

[159] *Truman Public Papers, 1945*, p. 210.

CHAPTER FIVE

Power Politics

HOW MANY DIVISIONS HAS THE POPE?

ON AUGUST 6 and 9, atomic bombs were dropped on Hiroshima and Nagasaki. On August 14, Japan formally surrendered. But the release of this undreamed-of power unleashed new threats to world peace. Truman could no longer postpone deciding whether the USSR should be invited into the Anglo-American atomic partnership, sealing the permanency of the wartime alliance, or whether the Russians must be excluded because of their appetite for expansion. In his August 9 radio report to the nation on the Potsdam Conference, Truman indicated his policy on sharing atomic energy information with our erstwhile Soviet ally:

> Great Britain, Canada, and the United States, who have the secret of its production, do not intend to reveal that secret until means have been found to control the bomb so as to protect ourselves and the rest of the world from the danger of total destruction.[1]

Retiring Secretary of War Henry L. Stimson formally raised the issue of the bomb as it affected our future relations with Russia. On September 12, Stimson handed Truman a memorandum urging that the United States enter negotiations with Russia on the control of atomic energy. To exclude the Soviet Union from the Anglo-American atomic partnership would confront them with a hostile bloc, Stimson argued, and cause the Soviets to launch a "secret armament race of a rather desperate character." "If we fail to approach them now," Stimson wrote, "and merely continue to negotiate with them, having this weapon rather ostentatiously on our hip, their suspicions and their distrust of our purposes and motives will increase." Relations with the Soviets would be "irretrievably embittered"; there would be no possibility of obtaining an international control agreement that could save civilization, not for the four to twenty years it would take the Soviets to construct their own bomb, but forever.

Stimson recommended that the United States agree with Britain and

[1] *Truman Public Papers, 1945*, pp. 212-13.

Russia to halt scientific research on the atomic bomb. Then the United States could agree to impound all weapons in its possession in return for a pledge by the three countries to forego the use of atomic energy for military purposes.

Stimson emphasized that the United States must approach Russia directly, not through the United Nations. The international organization would only become embroiled in endless debates; and the Soviet Union would never take seriously any proposal produced by an organization made up of many small nations of no demonstrable power or responsibility.[2]

Truman agreed with Stimson that we should share basic scientific information on atomic energy with the Russians while withholding the technological information used to construct the Bomb. The only question in his mind was whether the United States should approach the international control of atomic energy through a Big Three agreement or through the untried United Nations.[3]

In contrast, Byrnes was "radically opposed to any approach to Stalin whatever" on the sharing of atomic energy information. The secretary of state was getting ready for the London Foreign Ministers' Conference, and he "wished to have the implied threat of the bomb in his pocket" to obtain a postwar settlement from the Russians that would be consistent with American goals. In addition, Byrnes simply did not trust the Russians to observe the restrictions of any international agreement on the control of atomic weapons; since he did not see the resemblance between Stalin and a machine boss, the secretary of state used his personal experience with the Soviets' unwillingness to carry out the Yalta agreements as the criterion for judging whether international control was feasible. Before leaving for London, Byrnes "begged" Stimson not to recommend to Truman that we begin discussions with our allies on control of atomic weapons.[4]

Because Byrnes was so adamantly opposed to even discussions on international control of atomic weapons, Under Secretary of State Dean Acheson was timid about raising the issue with the president. But the domestic political environment left him no choice. A few hours after the September congressional session opened, congressmen began competing with each other to introduce bills to ban the bomb or keep the deadly "secret." Few congressmen understood the techni-

---

[2] Stimson diary, September 12, 1945, *FR: 1945*, II, pp. 42-44.

[3] Forrestal diary, September 18, 1945, Forrestal Papers, Princeton; Wallace diary, September 18, 1945, *Price of Vision*, ed. Blum, p. 481.

[4] Stimson diary, August 12-September 4, 1945 (Stanford microfilm); Minutes of the Committee of Three, October 10, 1945, RG 59, NA.

cal problems involved in atomic energy control, and their legislative proposals were wildly impractical. Senator Vandenberg warned Acting Secretary Acheson that there would soon be a "rush to get somebody's pet Bill reported" unless the administration introduced legislation of its own. Though he was reluctant to take any action while Byrnes was absent in London, Acheson finally was persuaded that unless President Truman immediately submitted a bill for control of atomic energy to Congress, the lawmakers would take matters into their own hands, severely compromising the president's freedom of action. On September 20, Truman agreed that he should present a plan for both domestic and international control to Congress.[5]

The September 21 cabinet meeting was reserved for discussion of retiring Secretary of War Stimson's proposal that the United States approach Russia to work out an agreement for the control of atomic weapons. Speaking extemporaneously, Stimson opened the meeting. He emphasized that the scientific knowledge underlying the atomic bomb could not long remain the exclusive property of the United States. "We do not have a secret to give away," Stimson said. "The secret will give itself away." Therefore, he felt there should be free exchange of scientific information among members of the United Nations. This obviously raised the question of Russia. Stimson pointed out that "the Russians have been our traditional friends; they have never fought us, and in many cases in the past, notably during the Civil War and the question of the sale of Alaska, they have demonstrated fundamental good will." He thought we should give the Soviets the benefit of the doubt.

Acheson, who was sitting in for Byrnes, expressed his full agreement with Stimson. With impeccable logic, Acheson deduced his recommendation from the basic premises of American policy: we could not hope to secure Soviet cooperation in maintaining world peace if we confronted them with evidence of an Anglo-American bloc and sported the atomic monopoly. Acheson "saw no alternative except to give full information to the Russians, however for some *quid pro quo* in the way of a mutual exchange of information." He simply "could not conceive of a world in which we were hoarders of military secrets from our Allies, particularly this great Ally upon our cooperation with whom rests the future peace of the world."[6]

[5] Hewlett and Anderson, *New World*, pp. 424-27; Vandenberg diary, September 20, 1945, *Private Papers*, ed. Vandenberg, p. 222; McNaughton Report, September 23, 1945, McNaughton Papers, HSTL.

[6] Wallace diary, September 21, 1945, *Price of Vision*, ed. Blum, pp. 482-84; Stimson diary, September 21, 1945, dictated December 11, 1945 (Stanford microfilm); Forrestal

The reputation Dean Acheson later acquired as an ideological hardliner has clouded his earlier views; he was a Realist. Acheson had an unusually articulate and consistent set of beliefs about international politics and the requirements of world order. Because of his leisure-time reading of English history and biography, Acheson had acquired a lasting admiration for British foreign policy in the Victorian period, when the Royal Navy enforced a *Pax Britannica* and the transfer of British capital overseas powered world economic development. Acheson attributed the rise of the "totalitarian military state" and war to the collapse of the nineteenth-century world economic order. He viewed with nostalgic admiration the major features of the *Pax Britannica* that had made possible an unprecedented rise in the world's standard of living—large areas of free trade, credits extended by the financial center of London, British naval power that guaranteed "security and investment in distant parts of the world," and immigration to the United States as an outlet for surplus population. The totalitarian state arose in response to the absence of investment capital, the closing off of markets, the shortage of essential raw materials, and overpopulation.

But now that British hegemony was but a historical memory, Acheson realized that world order could only be maintained by the joint effort of the successors to Britain's leadership, the United States and the Soviet Union. "We want to be sure that the purposes and policies of the great powers are not in conflict," Acheson remarked in February 1945. "If they are in conflict we cannot prevent war." Acheson believed that peace could only be maintained by a great power concert. Without the cooperation of the Soviet Union, there could be no real peace, merely an armed truce between hostile blocs.[7] This conviction he shared with FDR.

With the exception of Stimson and Acheson, no one present at the September 21 meeting understood the technological issues or diplomatic complexities associated with the control of atomic weapons. The discussion rapidly degenerated into a heated free-for-all on the false

---

diary, September 21, 1945, Princeton; Notes on Cabinet Meeting, September 21, 1945, Matthew J. Connelly Papers, HSTL.

[7] David S. McLellan, *Dean Acheson: The State Department Years* (New York: Dodd, Mead, 1976), pp. 30-31, 38-39; Dean Acheson, *Morning and Noon* (Boston: Houghton Mifflin, 1965), pp. 218-22, 267-78; Gaddis Smith, *Dean Acheson*, vol. 16 of *The American Secretaries of State and Their Diplomacy* (New York: Cooper Square Publishers, 1972), pp. 13-14; Secretary's Staff Committee Minutes, February 9, 1945, Stettinius Papers, Box 235, University of Virginia; Dean Acheson, *Present at the Creation*, p. 111; Acheson to Truman, September 25, 1945, *FR: 1945*, II, p. 49.

issue of whether the United States should "give away the Bomb." Stimson had not proposed anything of the kind. What he had suggested was that the United States share fundamental scientific information on atomic energy with Russia, excluding for now the technology used to manufacture the Bomb.

Members of the group invoked racial slurs, historical analogies, and irrelevant personal scripts to support their predilections. Treasury Secretary Vinson drew an analogy between sharing atomic energy information and the sinking of U.S. ships after World War I. Secretary of the Navy James Forrestal agreed that sharing atomic information with Russia was comparable to the naval disarmament treaties of the interwar period. Whereas the United States and Britain had observed treaty limitations, Forrestal pointed out, the Japanese had not. "The Russians, like the Japanese, are essentially Oriental in their thinking," Forrestal said, "and until we have a longer record of experience with them on the validity of engagements . . . it seems doubtful that we should endeavor to buy their understanding and sympathy." Invoking another historical analogy, he reminded his listeners that "we tried that once with Hitler. There are no returns on appeasement." Commerce Secretary Henry Wallace advocated free exchange of scientific research. Influenced by a different historical analogy, Wallace argued that if the United States tried to suppress "scientific information . . . we would develop for ourselves a scientific Maginot line type of mind, thinking we were secure because of our past attainments, while at the same time certain other nations were going beyond us." Agriculture Secretary Anderson pointed out that Russia sold Alaska to the United States not out of good will but because their efforts to gain control of the West Coast had been frustrated. From this he concluded, with doubtful logic, that "the Russians have not yet demonstrated any reciprocal attitude of trust toward us." Truman closed the meeting by asking all the participants to submit their views in writing.[8]

Acheson's September 25 memorandum to the president is valuable for the light it casts on his views about Russia and world peace. Acheson began by arguing that the theoretical knowledge underlying the atomic bomb was already widely known; foreign research could come abreast of ours in a short period of time. The Soviet Union could probably construct its own bomb within five years. Further, there was little prospect of developing effective defensive measures against the

---

[8] Memorandum by James Forrestal, 21 September 1945, Forrestal Papers: Forrestal diary, 21 September 1945, Princeton; Notes on Cabinet Meeting, September 21, 1945, Connelly Papers, HSTL; Wallace diary, September 21, 1945, *Price of Vision*, ed. Blum, pp. 482-85.

Bomb. "The advantage of being ahead in such a race is nothing compared with not having the race," Acheson concluded. He pointed out that our joint development of the atomic bomb with Britain and Canada must appear to the Soviets as evidence of an Anglo-American bloc directed against them. "To their minds," Acheson warned, "there is much other evidence of this."

A Realist, he believed that it was foolish to be under any illusions that the Soviet Union would allow the United States to maintain an exclusive "trusteeship" over the atomic bomb. "It is impossible that a government as powerful and power conscious as the Soviet Government could fail to react vigorously to this situation," Acheson warned. "It must and will exert every energy to restore the loss of power which this discovery has produced," he predicted. Long-range cooperation with the Soviet Union, based on mutual recognition of each other's vital interests, would be impossible under a policy of Anglo-American exclusion of Russia from atomic development. "If it is impossible," Acheson wrote, "there will be no organized peace but only an armed truce." Like FDR and Truman, he foresaw a "Cold War" if the Soviet Union and the United States could not harmonize their basic purposes.

Acheson agreed with Stimson that the United States ought to approach the Soviets directly instead of tossing the unresolved issue to the United Nations, where it would be endlessly debated. After all, the United Nations could not function in this field without agreement between the United States, Britain, and the Soviet Union. Privately, Acheson had contempt for the proposed United Nations Organization. The Under Secretary of State regarded as pernicious the illusion that bringing together representatives of all nations would somehow eliminate conflicts of interest and war. In a June 1946 speech, Acheson made this acid response to the suggestion that international problems be left to the United Nations: "In the Arab proverb, the ass that went to Mecca remained an ass, and a policy has little added to it by its place of utterance." In conclusion, Acheson recommended that the United States approach the Soviet Union, after consulting with the British, to work out a program of mutual exchange of scientific information and collaboration in the development of atomic power, to proceed gradually and on condition that the two countries agree not to produce atomic weapons and to provide adequate opportunities for inspection. Eventually the plan could be opened to other nations.[9]

[9] Acheson to Truman, September 25, 1945, *FR: 1945*, II, pp. 48-50; "Random Harvest," *Department of State Bulletin* 14 (June 6, 1946): 1045-47.

Acheson asked his assistant Herbert Marks to draft the president's message to Congress on domestic and international control of atomic energy. The White House made one change in the draft speech submitted by the State Department: the president's speechwriter added the phrase that the president "would initiate discussions, first with our associates in this discovery, Great Britain and Canada, and then with other nations." He had rejected Stimson's advice to make an immediate, direct approach to the Soviet Union. In the October 3 speech, President Truman emphasized that the discussions would not concern disclosure of the "manufacturing processes leading to the production of the atomic bomb" but arrangements for the "exchange of scientific information."[10]

Truman expressed his intentions more plainly at a press conference at Reelfoot Lake in Tiptonville, Tennessee. In an interview with reporters at his hunting lodge, Truman acknowledged that the theoretical knowledge that resulted in the bomb was already well known. But the secret of producing the bomb would not be shared with any other nation, he declared.[11]

Truman believed that successful diplomacy required the backing of military power. "In order to carry out a just decision, the courts must have marshals," he argued. "In other words, any decision requires the power to insure its application." But American troop strength was declining rapidly in response to overwhelming public demands for demobilization. The atomic bomb, therefore, was the only means of countering Soviet strength on the European continent. Until an international police force was established and functioning, the United States would have to maintain a balance of power among the Big Three. As Truman commented to Davies,

And when we get down to cases, is any one of the Big Powers—are we, going to give up these locks and bolts which are necessary to protect our house—the U.S.A.—in this shrunken world community, against possible outlaw attack which might destroy our homes and lives, until experience and good judgment say that the community is sufficiently stable and decent, and the police force sufficiently reliable to do that job for us. Clearly we are not. Nor are the Soviets. Nor is any country if it can help itself.[12]

[10] Special Message to the Congress on Atomic Energy, October 3, 1945, *Truman Public Papers, 1945*, p. 165; Hewlett and Anderson, *New World*, pp. 424-47.

[11] Coffin, *Missouri Compromise*, pp. 19-20; *New York Times*, October 9, 1945; President's News Conference at Tiptonville, Tenn., October 8, 1945, *Truman Public Papers, 1945*, p. 382.

[12] Davies journal, September 18, 1945, LC.

If the United States shared the Bomb with Russia, Truman believed, he would not be able to obtain a peace settlement acceptable to the American people. Defending Truman's decision to keep the atomic bomb, Forrestal wrote to a friend: "The President is passionately desirous of getting the foundations for peace built just as soon as possible, but I believe he is equally aware that an element of our influence in being able to build that house is going to be the possession of military power." Stimson's September 11 memorandum had acknowledged that many Americans perceived the bomb as a counterweight to the growth of Soviet influence in Europe. But achieving our immediate peace council objectives, Stimson argued, was not worth jeopardizing the chances of enlisting Soviet cooperation in the control of atomic weapons.[13]

Yet, Truman had not abandoned the idea of negotiating an agreement with the Soviet Union to renounce atomic weapons. At the September 21 cabinet meeting, the president pointed out that to achieve a lasting peace, Russia, Great Britain, and the United States had to maintain a mutual trust. A few days later, Truman agreed with George Allen that if the United States tried to keep the bomb to itself, it would mean the end of the United Nations organization. Truman occasionally commented that he favored "outlawing" atomic bombs, just as the nations of the world had prohibited the use of poison gas.[14]

The international control of atomic weapons was a complex, unfamiliar, recondite issue. Truman did not foresee all the ramifications. He did not see that using the atomic monopoly as a negotiating lever in postwar negotiations with the Soviets would destroy the mutual trust on which FDR's "grand design" was premised. Truman did not understand that the longer he delayed approaching the Soviets directly, the more difficult it would be to establish the foundation of mutual trust and observance of agreements that would be absolutely critical to success in negotiating the world's first nuclear arms control agreement. Unlike Truman, Acheson had an intricate network of beliefs about international politics, grounded in years of reading and experience in foreign affairs. Acheson was absolutely consistent in his response to the problem. He pointed out that excluding the Soviets from

[13] Notes on Cabinet Meeting, September 7, 1945, Connelly Papers, HSTL; Forrestal to E. Palmer Hoyt, 1 November 1945, Forrestal Papers, Princeton; *FR: 1945*, II, pp. 42-44.

[14] Davies journal, September 18, October 26, 1945, LC; Notes on Cabinet Meeting, September 21, 1945, Connelly Papers, HSTL; Ayers diary, September 24, 1945, HSTL; Calendar Notes, October 22, 1945, *Diaries of Stettinius*, ed. Campbell and Herring, p. 439.

the Anglo-American atomic partnership was incompatible with a world order founded on great power cooperation. Further, secrecy was futile, because the Soviets would mobilize all their resources to catch up with the United States; a terrifying arms race between the two superpowers would be the inevitable outcome.

Privately, Truman feared that even atomic weapons would not deter Soviet aggression. What concerned him most were Soviet moves against Turkey and Iran. In 1941, British and Soviet troops had invaded Iran and divided the country into northern and southern occupation zones, to protect allied supply lines from German sabotage. In late August 1945, the U.S. ambassador in Iran reported that Soviet authorities in the northern zone prevented Iranian police from pursuing army deserters or putting down a riot between farm and town workers. When the Iranian Foreign Office formally protested Soviet interference in their internal affairs, the Soviets brazenly reiterated a previous demand for an oil concession. On September 22, the *New York Times* reported that besides hindering Iranian troop and police movements, the Soviets had been inciting separatist sentiment among the Azerbaijanis, Kurds, and Armenians, urging them to seek union with their ethnic brethren in the Soviet Union. The U.S. ambassador in Iran warned that the Soviets wished to establish a "friendly" government in Iran, similar to the Groza regime in Rumania.[15]

Then, the failure of the London Foreign Ministers' Conference proved that U.S. possession of the Bomb would not make the Soviets more manageable. Molotov was as intractable as ever. At the first opportunity, the Soviet Union submitted draft treaties on Finland and the Balkan states. Against the advice of the majority of the U.S. delegation, Byrnes resolved to continue the policy of withholding formal recognition and peace treaties from the Balkan countries until the Russians agreed to the formation of "representative" regimes pledged to hold truly free elections. Soviet expert Bohlen, who interpreted at some of the more acrimonious Byrnes-Molotov meetings, concluded that the recognition issue was "explosive," and urged the adoption of a less provocative policy. John Foster Dulles told Byrnes that he had some doubts about the long-range efficacy of nonrecognition in a situation such as that of Rumania. "I said that it seemed like starting over again our policy of non-recognition of the U.S.S.R—and on much the same grounds—which had proved a barren policy," Dulles

[15] *FR: 1945*, VIII, pp. 400, 406, 411; Daily Top Secret Staff Summary, September 20, 27, 1945, RG 59, NA; Secretary's Summary, September 27, 1945, RG 59, NA; *New York Times*, September 22, 1945.

recorded in a private memorandum. But Secretary of State Byrnes was determined to push for some solution that would satisfy the unrealistic public expectations of democracy and free elections. By signing the armistice agreements, it could be argued that the the United States had tacitly acquiesced to Soviet hegemony over the Balkans, and that it was Byrnes who had violated an understanding with the Soviet Union. Yet, by the second day of the conference, Byrnes was complaining that "the Russians were welching on all the agreements reached at Potsdam and at Yalta."[16]

Byrnes decided to "lay it on the line" with Molotov about the U.S. position on the Balkans. He arranged a private meeting with Molotov so that he could talk man-to-man with the Soviet foreign minister, as if he were a recalcitrant senator in need of personal persuasion. Adopting a pleading tone, Byrnes appealed to Molotov to relax his position on the Balkans for the peace of the world; he had asked for this meeting so that he would not have to say around the table certain things that he would be compelled to say unless Russia shifted its demands. He assured Molotov that the United States wished to see "friendly" governments in countries bordering the Soviet Union. Byrnes said that he was pleading for some arrangement whereby the Rumanian government could be both "friendly" and "representative of all democratic elements." He suggested that they could reorganize the government as in Poland—clearly a hint that the United States would be satisfied with the appearance of compliance with the Yalta accords.

But Molotov was not a "practical politician," and was unmoved by personal appeals that he consider American public opinion. He pointed out that if the United States refused to consider the Balkan peace treaties the *Soviet* public would be offended. Refusing to give Byrnes the "out" of a cosmetic solution to the problem of Eastern Europe, Molotov objected that the Polish precedent was inapplicable to Rumania since the two situations were different; Poland had been an ally and two governments were already in existence. It was a question of "friendly governments." If the United States had been invaded by Mexico and the Mexicans had occupied a part of the United States, as the Soviets had suffered at the hands of Rumania, the American government would not tolerate a hostile government in Mexico. When it became apparent over several meetings that Byrnes would not change his position, the Soviet foreign minister angrily charged that

[16] "John Foster Dulles Comment on Reservation re Groza Government," *Council of Foreign Ministers*, 2, pt. 1: 232-33, John Foster Dulles Papers, Princeton; Calendar Notes, September 12, 1945, *Diaries of Stettinius*, ed. Campbell and Herring, pp. 618-19.

Byrnes had abandoned Roosevelt's policy of friendship toward the Soviet Union. The reason that the United States was opposed to the
Rumanian government, Molotov said repeatedly, was that the latter
was friendly to the Soviet Union.[17]

Contrary to Byrnes' expectations, U.S. possession of atomic weapons had no effect on Molotov's willingness to make concessions to
American ideals in Eastern Europe. Indeed, the Soviet foreign minister
deliberately adopted a jocular tone when referring to the Bomb, to
show that the Soviets were not intimidated. At a September 13 reception, Byrnes buttonholed Molotov in "typical senatorial fashion" and
asked when the Soviet foreign minister was going to finish "sightsee-
ing" so that the negotiators could get down to business. Molotov in-
quired if Byrnes had an atomic bomb in his side pocket. "You don't
know Southerners," Byrnes replied. "We carry our artillery in our hip
pocket. If you don't cut out all this stalling and let us get down to
work, I am going to pull an atomic bomb out of my hip pocket and
let you have it." Molotov laughed uproariously, as did the interpreter.
At a gala dinner party several days later, Molotov commented that not
only was the secretary of state more gifted in speechmaking than he,
but he also had an atomic bomb. The Soviets even contrived an elaborate charade. At a Soviet embassy reception, Molotov, pretending to
be intoxicated, made a toast: "Here's to the Atom Bomb! We've got
it." At this point, Gousev placed his hand on Molotov's shoulder, and
ushered him out of the room.[18]

When Byrnes continued to refuse to recognize Bulgaria and Rumania, Molotov retaliated by raising a procedural issue as an excuse to
break off negotiations. The foreign ministers could not even agree on
a communiqué, however vague and equivocally worded, to conceal the
cracks in the alliance.[19]

Truman was greatly disturbed by this evidence of the Bomb's im-
potence as a weapon of influence. On October 5, 1945, Truman told
Budget Director Harold Smith that he had begun to wonder whether
the United States was demobilizing too fast. "There are some people
in the world who do not seem to understand anything except the
number of divisions you have," Truman complained. "Mr. President,"

[17] FR: 1945, II, pp. 194-97, 243-44, 246-47, 291-92; W. B.'s Book, September 19,
1945, Clemson.

[18] W. B.'s Book, September 13, 17, 1945, Clemson; Hugh Dalton diary, October
17, 1945, Feis Papers, Box 78, LC.

[19] FR: 1945, II, pp. 313-15, 487-88; Teletype between Byrnes and Leahy, September
22, 1945, Byrnes Papers, folder 96; Council of Foreign Ministers, 2, pt. 2: 348, Dulles
Papers, Princeton.

Smith pointed out, "you have an atomic bomb up your sleeve." "Yes," Truman said, "but I am not sure it can ever be used." Smith noticed that Truman was very disturbed by the London fiasco. In a November 16 letter to a congressman, Truman expressed himself more bluntly:

> Now the settlement of the results of the [two world wars] is not in any sense of the word near completion—the only language those people understand is the language of force. At the rate we are demobilizing troops, in a very short time we will have no means with which to enforce our demands—a just and fair peace—and unless we have that means we are heading directly for a third world war.[20]

As a result of his difficulties with Molotov, Byrnes was more firmly opposed than ever to sharing atomic energy information with the Soviets or entering any agreement to control the spread of atomic weapons. "In view of the way the Russians were behaving now, as emphasized in this Council of Foreign Ministers," he told Stettinius, "he would be opposed to giving the secret to anybody at the present time." At a meeting with the secretaries of state, war, and navy, Byrnes argued that before "any international discussion of the future of the bomb could take place, we must first see whether we can work out a decent peace," he said.

Byrnes had some doubts whether the Soviets could be trusted to keep any international agreement for the control of atomic energy. Appealing to familiar episodic scripts, he pointed out that though "they had a formal treaty of nonaggression with Japan, the Russians, as far back as Yalta, were making definite plans for their attack on Japan." "Stalin and Molotov would probably be insulted today if you implied that they had intended to keep their solemn treaty with Hitler," Byrnes continued. By the same reasoning, he did not think we could rely on their word today.[21]

Publicly, Truman maintained his usual optimism about U.S.-Soviet relations. At Reelfoot Lake, he remarked that difficulties between the United States and the Soviet Union were caused by misunderstandings. "Russia's interests and ours do not clash," he said firmly, "and never have. We have always been friends and I hope we always will

---

[20] Harold Smith diary, October 5, 1945; Davis R. B. Ross, *Preparing for Ulysses: Politics and Veterans during World War II* (New York: Columbia University Press, 1969), p. 187.

[21] Minutes of the Committee of Three, October 10, 16, 1945, RG 59, NA; *FR: 1945*, II, pp. 55-56, 60-61; Forrestal diary, October 16, 1945, *Forrestal Diaries*, ed. Millis, p. 102.

be."[22] But the same day Truman received word of substantial Soviet troop reinforcements along the Turkish border. The Soviets tightened the screws in their "war of nerves" against Turkey. The Moscow embassy reported that Communist party agitators were spreading rumors among the Russian people that the USSR would soon go to war against Turkey.[23]

Following Potsdam, Byrnes tried to persuade Truman to give up his pet scheme for internationalization of the Dardanelles. Byrnes pointed out that Turkey would never agree to neutralization of the Straits unless the United States promised to defend Turkey in case of attack. Before undertaking such a responsibility, the administration should consult congressional leaders, who would be exceedingly reluctant to assume additional defense burdens. John Foster Dulles, for example, "was somewhat wary about our undertaking a guarantee of passage in waters so far distant from our shores."[24]

Fearing imminent Soviet aggression against Turkey, Truman was reluctant to give up his plan to place the Dardanelles under the jurisdiction of the U.N. On October 13, he wrote Byrnes:

> My position on Dardanelles has never changed. I think it is a waterways link with the Black Sea, the Rhine and the Danube, as the Kiel Canal is an outlet to the Baltic Sea, which must eventually be internationalized. I am of the opinion if some means isn't found to prevent it, Russia will undoubtedly take steps by direct action to obtain control of the Black Sea Straits.
>
> It seems to me that an international control would be much more satisfactory to Turkey than to lose Provinces over in the northwestern corner of the country and lose the straits too, which undoubtedly would be the final result.[25]

But as a practical politician, Truman recognized his inability to undertake a commitment to defend Turkey without public support. A week later, he agreed to give up the idea of internationalizing the Dardanelles, "although I think we ought to keep pushing the program so as to prevent Russia from taking the Straits over."[26]

Rather than acting as a responsible partner with the United States in maintaining world order, the Soviets were using crude military pres-

---

[22] *Truman Public Papers, 1945*, p. 387. See also S. J. Woolf, "Interview with Truman," *New York Times*, October 14, 1945.

[23] Daily TS Staff Summary, October 8, 9, 10, 1945, RG 59, NA.

[24] *FR: 1945*, VIII, pp. 1242-43, 1255-56.

[25] Truman to Byrnes, October 13, 1945, Truman Papers, PSF: Subject File, HSTL.

[26] Truman to Byrnes, October 20, 1945, ibid.

sure to force Turkey and Iran to accede to their demands for bases, oil concessions, and territorial cessions. In mid-October 1945, Truman came to believe that the Soviets only respected brute military strength. The president expressed his new feelings about the Soviets by telling staff members an anecdote. Truman said that during the Potsdam conference, Churchill had warned Stalin that the Pope was concerned about Poland. "How many divisions does the Pope have?" Stalin retorted. That ended the discussion, Truman said. Truman subsequently told this story many times, adding embellishments and graphic details. Yet, the incident probably never happened. There is no record of this exchange in the minutes of the Potsdam Conference. Charles Bohlen, who was the translator at Potsdam and all the wartime conferences, said that the story had been circulating years before the war, and was probably apocryphal. *Time* printed another version of the story long before the Potsdam Conference. Yet, the script has psychological if not factual importance: it expressed Truman's new belief that the Russians could be influenced only by conventional military power.[27]

Truman's fear that the Soviets would take over the Dardanelles was idiosyncratic; he had received no memoranda from his advisers warning of Soviet military action. Like Truman, the secretaries of state, war, and navy were worried and preoccupied with public pressures for demobilization. Byrnes was afraid that if congressional demands for speedy demobilization left us with nothing but a token force in Japan, and the Soviets secured their demand for an allied control council, the Russians might use their military forces to take control over Japan. But Byrnes showed no comparable concern for Turkey; he persuaded the president not to offer Turkey guarantees of assistance if the Soviets attacked. Although reluctant to offend the president, State Department officials were also opposed to internationalization of the Turkish Straits, both because of the precedent it set for the Suez and Panama, and because the United States could not honor any commitment to defend the neutrality of the Straits should the Russians attack.[28] President Truman's unusual interest in Turkey and the Dardanelles was derived from the script he had formed from his reading of history: wars were often fought to gain control over strategic inland waterways.

[27] Ayers diary, October 16, 1945, HSTL; "Yalta Doctrine," *Time*, February 26, 1945, p. 23; Bohlen to Byrnes, April 26, 1957, Byrnes Papers, Clemson.

[28] Minutes of Committee of Three, October 16, November 6, 1945, RG 59, NA; Forrestal diary, October 16, November 6, 20, 1945, *Forrestal Diaries*, ed. Millis, pp. 102, 110; Knight, "America's International Guarantees for the Straits," pp. 247-48; *FR: 1945*, VIII, pp. 1289-90.

Yet, the president made no attempt to signal to the Russians that they should restrain themselves in the Near East. He did not have any conception of how the United States might use its military power to deter Soviet expansion. All he had were some simple notions to the effect that military preparedness was a safeguard against war, and diplomacy must have the backing of military power.

More important, there was little Truman could do to arrest the hemorrhaging of American troop strength. Though men were being discharged from the army at the rate of 15,200 a day in September, Truman was besieged by criticism for not bringing the boys home fast enough. At an October cabinet meeting, he complained that the program the United States was following was no longer demobilization—it was disintegration of our armed forces. On October 23, he appeared before Congress to propose a system of Universal Military Training, but the legislators were unreceptive.[29] The atomic bomb seemed to eliminate the need for conventional military forces. To slow down the rate of demobilization, Truman would have had to create a "Red Scare" when he was still hopeful about "getting along" with the Russians, even if we could not cooperate on all issues.

Truman could afford to postpone a confrontation with the Soviets, because they did not pose any *immediate* threat to U.S. security. Truman viewed the Soviet Union not as a revolutionary power with unlimited ambitions, but rather as a traditional imperialist power, bent on obtaining warm-water ports, territorial concessions, and other spoils of war. Since he had not been exposed to Molotov's tenacious, irritating, and dilatory negotiating tactics, Truman viewed the breakdown of the London Conference with relative equanimity. He told Stettinius that during the war we had been able to work with the Russians because of the overwhelming military necessity. All of the really difficult problems had been postponed until the end of the war, and now that we were running into them, it was inevitable that there would be difficulties with the Russians. Truman thought that we should not take these problems too seriously; he had every hope that we could work out our differences amicably if we gave ourselves some time. The president said that the Russians were probably having problems at home; we certainly had our internal problems and they were bad enough. This might explain some of the things that the Russians had been doing, he said. But whereas Truman attributed Soviet intransigence to the difficult circumstances in which they found themselves, Byrnes' explanation was dispositional. Although the United

[29] Truman, *Memoirs*, 1:507-509; Donovan, *Conflict and Crisis*, pp. 136-37.

States had reversed its policy of tacitly accepting Soviet dominance over Eastern Europe, Byrnes blamed the breakdown in Soviet-American cooperation on Russia. Secretary Byrnes told Stettinius that

> there was no question but that we were facing a new Russia, totally different than the Russia we dealt with a year ago. As long as they needed us in the war and we were giving them supplies, we had a satisfactory relationship, but now that the war was over, they were taking an aggressive attitude and stand on political and territorial questions that was indefensible.[30]

Privately, Byrnes expressed considerable bitterness at his treatment by Molotov. As at Potsdam, Byrnes was disgruntled by Molotov's rude and insulting behavior, quite apart from the substance of the Soviets' negotiating position. He told Davies that the London Conference and Molotov in particular were much worse than he could imagine. "Molotov was insufferable," Byrnes complained. He "was almost ashamed of himself for having taken what he did from Molotov." Even Harriman, who was outraged at being excluded from the London negotiations, admitted that Molotov's manner had been difficult in dealing with Bevin and Byrnes, as was his position on substantive issues. As Walter Brown commented in his diary, Molotov's "game" at these conferences was to conduct a "war of nerves," throwing out this question and that, hoping to wear the others down.[31] Consistent with the attribution theory hypothesis that people are influenced more by concrete, firsthand experience than more abstract analyses, Byrnes based his estimate of Soviet aims and methods on his impressions of the Soviet foreign minister.

Truman still hoped that he could work with Stalin. Truman believed that the Kremlin was divided on the issue of whether to cooperate with the West, and that Stalin was a moderating influence. "Stalin is an honest man who is easy to get along with—who arrives at sound decisions," he told Henry Wallace. Truman thought it would be a catastrophe for the United States if Stalin should die or retire because "nobody on earth can get along with Molotov."[32] The personal impressions he had acquired at Potsdam continued to influence his

[30] Calendar Notes, September 28, October 22, 1945, *Diaries of Stettinius*, ed. Campbell and Herring, pp. 426, 437, 440.

[31] Davies diary, October 9, 1945, LC; Stettinius Calendar Notes, September 25, 1945, Box 247, University of Virginia; W. B.'s Book, September 28, 1945, Clemson.

[32] Truman to Davies, October 6, 1945, Truman Papers, PSF, HSTL; Wallace diary, October 15, 1945, *Price of Vision*, ed. Blum, p. 490; Calendar Notes, October 22, 1945, *Diaries of Stettinius*, ed. Campbell and Herring, pp. 439-40.

thinking, despite the lack of any firm evidence that Stalin was warmly disposed to the United States. Like Truman, Byrnes had also succumbed to the illusion that Stalin was a benevolent statesman concerned only with world peace, whereas Molotov was intransigent and impossible to reason with; he failed, or refused, to see that Molotov would not take any negotiating position that Stalin had not previously approved. At the London conference, Byrnes predicted that unless Molotov was "ousted he would lead Russia to the same fate that Hitler led Germany and Mussolini Italy." Explicating a strained analogy, Byrnes pointed out that "Molotov was trying to do in a 'slick dip' way what Hitler had tried to do in domineering small countries by force." Unfamiliar with Soviet negotiating tactics, Byrnes blamed his difficulties in negotiating a postwar settlement with the Russians on Molotov's personality. Repeatedly, Byrnes complained that he saw no possibility of reaching an agreement with Molotov and that the only hope for peace lay in holding the next foreign ministers' meeting in Moscow, where he could talk with Stalin.[33]

Truman was unwilling to dramatize recent difficulties with the Soviets to win public support for maintaining a favorable military balance with the Soviet Union. On October 26, Truman told his cabinet that "we were not going to let the public know the extent to which the Russians had tried our patience but that we were going to find some way to get along with the Russians."[34] For all his suspicions of Russian intentions, Byrnes was also not ready to abandon FDR's policy of cooperation. To do so would be to admit failure as a negotiator and peacemaker. Byrnes assured his cabinet colleagues that he was not pessimistic about the future of our relations with Russia. His experience in dealing with the Russians, he said, led him to believe that they always tried to see if they could stand pat and compel their allies to yield to them. Once they see we are not yielding, Byrnes predicted, they may at any time decide to come along.[35] But it was Byrnes who first made concessions.

Consistent with his conviction that the Soviets only respected divisions, Truman tried to "rattle a few sabers." Truman's October 27 Navy Day speech in Central Park was promoted by a White House press aide as "the most important speech" the president had made since taking office. The setting of the speech dramatized America's overwhelming military power. Forty-seven fighting ships were an-

[33] W. B.'s Book, September 16, 17, 20, 21, 1945, Clemson.
[34] Wallace diary, October 26, 1945, *Price of Vision*, ed. Blum, pp. 501-502.
[35] Minutes of the Committee of Three, October 16, 1945, RG 59, NA.

chored along the Hudson River, stretching for a distance of seven miles. As he cruised up the river, all forty-seven gave Truman a twenty-one gun salute while navy bands played the national anthem. Overhead, 1,200 planes roared across the sky. Before going to Central Park, Truman dedicated the new aircraft carrier, Franklin D. Roosevelt, at the Brooklyn Navy Yard. Then, standing hatless before an audience of over a million, his topcoat whipped by the cold gray wind, Truman set forth his administration's foreign policy.

The *Washington Post* described Truman's speech as "compounded partly of Theodore Roosevelt's philosophy of 'walk softly but carry a Big Stick' and partly of FDR's 'Four Freedoms.' " The crowd cheered when Truman declared that the United States, even after demobilization, would still be the "greatest naval power on earth." The audience also applauded Truman's statements that all talk about scrapping the U.S. army and navy because of the Bomb was "100 percent wrong"; that the United States would not share the information needed to manufacture the atomic bomb; that armed strength was the only guarantee of American security; and that the United States in its foreign policy would not approve "any compromise with evil." Truman declared that possession of the atomic bomb had not altered the fundamentals of United States foreign policy. Proceeding to list these principles, Truman did not go beyond the generalizations of the Four Freedoms and the Atlantic Charter.

Some journalists commenting on Truman's speech speculated that his statement that the United States would refuse to recognize any government imposed by a foreign power meant that the United States would refuse to recognize Soviet-installed governments in the Balkans. The *Washington Post*'s correspondent noticed that Truman was "especially precise and emphatic" in enunciating the nonrecognition policy, suggesting that the United States would "breathe life" into the Atlantic Charter and strive for its conception of democracy. According to the *New York Times*, Truman had offered American friendliness and idealism to the world while making it clear that the United States would not pursue a policy of appeasement toward Soviet-imposed regimes in the Balkans.[36]

But response to Truman's speech was not completely favorable within the diplomatic community. The British embassy ridiculed Tru-

[36] Ayers diary, October 26, 1945, HSTL; Leahy diary, October 25, 1945, William D. Leahy Papers, LC; *Washington Post*, October 28, 1945; *New York Times*, October 28, 1945; Barnet Nover, *Washington Post*, October 30, 1945; James Reston, *New York Times*, October 30, 1945; Ernest Lindley, *Washington Post*, October 29, 1945; *Truman Public Papers, 1945*, pp. 433-34.

man's statement referring to no territorial changes without the consent of the people; this was a "fantastic absurdity," juxtaposed with insistence in the same speech on the right of the United States to establish bases wherever they were a strategic necessity. Even the president's statements on nonrecognition were contradicted a few days later when Secretary of State Byrnes threw a "bouquet" to Russia's Eastern European policies in a speech declaring that the United States recognized the Soviet Union's special security interests in neighboring countries. In sum, British official J. B. Donnelly observed, "the danger is that Mr. Truman will be unable to lead his country along any consistent path whether economic or political."[37] The British did not understand that a practical politician like Truman was not bothered by the gap between verbal commitments and reality: mere declaration that we were carrying out the ideals of the Atlantic Charter and the Four Freedoms had "magical force" equivalent to action.

Truman also struck a conciliatory note. He advised against letting the search for perfection hinder progress toward Soviet-American cooperation. In the past, alliances had disintegrated when the common danger was past. Truman declared that the former allies must take control of history and mold it in the direction of continued cooperation. There were no conflicts of interest among the Great Powers that could not be solved. The American people would have to learn to understand the legitimate security needs of other nations.[38]

In late October, the Soviets stepped up their war of nerves against Turkey. On October 22, the *Washington Post* reported that Soviet troops were conducting maneuvers in southern Bulgaria near the border with Turkey. The Russians had over 200,000 troops in Bulgaria. The Soviets were also active on Turkey's eastern flank, in Iran. Russian military commanders refused to allow Iranian gendarmes to enter northern Iran to put down continuing disorders among Kurdish autonomists. On October 22, the *Post* reported that new contingents of Russian troops had been sent into Tabriz, 200 miles east of the Turkish-Iranian border. On November 1, General Marshall sent Truman a memorandum stating that the Russians had recently increased their forces in the Transcaucasus from five to twelve divisions, and had also built up their troop strength in northern Iran. Marshall confirmed that the Soviets had been conducting extensive maneuvers along the Bulgar-Turkish border. All this occurred at a time when the Soviets were demanding that the Turks return the Kars Plateau area to the USSR

[37] Halifax to Foreign Office, October 27, 1945, FO 371/44/600, AN B301/84/85.
[38] *Truman Public Papers, 1945*, pp. 435-36.

and grant them bases on the Dardanelles and the Bosporus. The Turks were alarmed and asked for British aid in case of a Soviet attack. Ominously, the Turkish-Soviet treaty of nonaggression was scheduled to expire on November 7, 1945. On the other hand, on October 29, Molotov assured Harriman that a war between Turkey and the Soviet Union would be "unthinkable." United States officials judged that the Soviet troop maneuvers were part of the "war of nerves," which would probably intensify once the Turkish-Soviet pact expired. On November 2, Truman opened a large folder on his desk and showed his staff a map of Turkey marked with many small tabs representing Russian divisions.[39]

Then, just as abruptly, the Soviets relieved the tension. On November 2, the Turkish minister of foreign affairs informed the U.S. ambassador that the Turkish government was no longer concerned about Soviet troop movements, because in the last few days the new Soviet divisions had been offset by withdrawals.[40]

The same day, the State Department presented to Turkey the U.S. proposals for revising the Straits regime, handing additional copies to the British and Soviet embassies. Since Potsdam, State Department officials had gone to greater lengths to meet perceived Soviet security needs. The latest proposal contained the important concession that Black Sea warships could sail through the Straits at all times. Stalin had complained bitterly at Potsdam about Turkey's ability under the current regime to close the Straits to Soviet warships. At his November 7 press conference, Secretary of State Byrnes took the unusual step of explaining the U.S. note to Turkey in great detail. He pointed out that under the U.S. proposals, Turkey could no longer bottle up Soviet ships in the Black Sea, which should remove the main justification for Soviet bases on the Straits.[41]

But the Soviet government thought otherwise. When the Soviet ambassador to Turkey, Vinogradov, read the U.S. note, he objected bitterly that there was no guarantee that warships of non-Black Sea powers would be excluded from the Straits in wartime, because Turkey was weak and untrustworthy. Vinogradov vigorously denounced Turkey's wartime record of allowing Axis warships free passage through the Straits. Moreover, he pointed out, by refusing to enter the war, Turkey had forfeited any claims to good will from the Allies. The U.S.

[39] *Washington Post*, October 22, 23, 1945; *New York Times*, October 22, 1945; Marshall to Truman, 1 November 1945, Leahy Files, RG 48, NA; Ayers diary, November 2, 1945, HSTL.

[40] *FR: 1945*, VIII, p. 1270.

[41] Ibid., pp. 1265-66; *New York Times*, November 8, 1945.

proposals for the Straits did not meet Soviet security requirements. Vinogradov spoke with such bitterness and hostility that U.S. Ambassador Wilson suspected that Soviet desiderata on the Straits were merely a façade for their plans to control Turkey.[42]

From November 11 to 15, Truman met with British and Canadian prime ministers Attlee and MacKenzie King to discuss international control of atomic energy. No attempt was made to consult with the USSR before the meeting. As a warning to the West, in a November 6 speech Molotov stressed that the Soviets wished to collaborate with the United States, but warned against attempts to exploit the atomic monopoly for political gain. Molotov's fiery peroration brought his Kremlin audience to their feet cheering: "We shall have atomic energy too, and many other things."[43]

The meeting was hastily improvised. Byrnes had pressured Truman to delay discussions on international control until he could see whether the United States could obtain a "decent peace." President Truman complained to Henry Wallace that he had been having a "hell of a time" with the State Department in trying to begin discussions with England and Canada preparatory to having conferences with Russia.[44]

Truman, Attlee, and King worked with their staffs on a communiqué until well past midnight. On November 15, Truman read the three-power agreement to the press in a hoarse voice, while Attlee and King slumped in their chairs behind him, looking up occasionally to reveal bloodshot eyes. Truman announced that the three countries would share fundamental scientific information on atomic energy with any nation willing to reciprocate. But they would not disclose information on the industrial applications of atomic energy until effective, enforceable safeguards had been devised to prevent its use for destructive purposes. An atomic energy commission would be set up under the aegis of the United Nations. The work of the commission would proceed by stages, "the successful completion of each one of which will develop the necessary confidence of the world before the next stage is undertaken."[45]

It was a plan that the Soviets were not likely to accept. As Henry Wallace pointed out to Truman, the step-by-step provision "suggested that Russia would have to pass the first grade in moral aptitude before

[42] FR: 1945, VIII, pp. 1271-72.

[43] New York Times, November 7, 1945; "The World Outside," Time, November 19, 1945, p. 30.

[44] Minutes of the Committee of Three, October 10, 1945, RG 59, NA; Wallace diary, October 15, 1945, Price of Vision, ed. Blum, p. 490.

[45] New York Times, November 17, 1945.

she would be allowed to enter the second grade in moral aptitude."[46] During the many years required for the commission to carry out the tasks of sharing basic scientific information, implementing an effective inspection system, and devising enforceable safeguards, the United States would retain its atomic monopoly. The Soviets would receive no information they did not already have until "effective enforceable safeguards" could be devised (if ever).

Indeed, Truman showed surprisingly little concern for obtaining Soviet acceptance of the plan. The Soviet government was in effect handed an arms control agreement as a fait accompli and instructed to abide by it. The *New Republic* pointed out the contrast to Roosevelt's policy of consulting the Soviets whenever their interests were involved, instead of confronting them with a united Anglo-American front.[47]

The Soviets responded bitterly to this departure from FDR's policy. On the eve of Truman's conference with Attlee and King, *Pravda* accused the West of engaging in "atomic diplomacy." After Truman read the three-power declaration to the press, the Soviet embassy made no official comment, but let it be known that they were expecting a more substantial offer. On November 19, what was described as the "strongest and frankest" attack yet on American foreign policy appeared in *New Times*. A. Sokoloff charged that the Bomb had "altered the views of some foreigners who formerly advocated international collaboration," encouraging "attempts to use the atomic bomb in the game of foreign power politics."[48]

On November 19, large-scale uprisings broke out in the Azerbaijan province in northern Iran, directed by the newly organized Democratic party, a reincarnation of the Iranian Communist party. The insurgents had seized all roads leading into the province, and cut off all telegraph communications with the rest of the country. An Iranian government spokesman charged that Russian trucks were distributing rifles and machine guns to the rebels.[49]

The president remarked to his staff that the situation in Iran was reverting to the "old power line-up." Truman felt that there was a strong possibility that the Russians would grab control of the Black Sea Straits. The president insisted, however, that "we must get along with Russia," and he assured his staff that "there was not going to be any war with Russia."[50]

[46] Wallace diary, November 16, 1945, *Price of Vision*, ed. Blum, p. 516.
[47] "Sixty Days to War or Peace," *New Republic*, November 26, 1945, p. 692.
[48] *New York Times*, November 16, 17, 19, 1945.
[49] *New York Times*, November 19, 1945.
[50] Ayers diary, November 19, 1945, LC.

Truman found it hard to believe that his good friend Stalin would betray him. He remarked to his staff that "things are most unsettled in Russia, although we have little information as to what actually is going on and are unable to get any information." He wondered aloud whether he should send a personal envoy to Stalin, and asked who he might send. Hopkins' name came up, but Judge Rosenman pointed out that Hopkins was in the hospital. Admiral Leahy was also mentioned as someone who could "talk with Stalin." The same day, Truman informed Leahy that he was considering sending him on a special mission to Moscow to straighten out some of the "misunderstandings" that existed between our two governments. But nothing came of it.[51]

The following day, Iranian officials reported that Russian troops had accompanied the insurgents and participated in the fighting. Armed contingents of the rebels were marching toward Teheran. The State Department informed Truman that the American embassy in Iran felt that the "Soviets obviously hold the key to the situation and could easily stop all disturbances." The Russian commander-in-chief halted a 1,500-man Iranian relief column sent to aid the beleaguered Azerbaijani gendarmes, warning the Iranians that any attempt to advance would be considered an attack on the Soviet Union.[52] The Democratic party was claiming the right of self-determination and autonomy within the framework of Iranian sovereignty.[53]

The State Department sent the Soviets a mild note recommending that allied forces be withdrawn from Iran by January 1, 1946. Offering the Soviets a way to concede gracefully, the note suggested that Soviet commanders who had interfered with Iranian armed forces might have been acting without the sanction of the Soviet government.[54]

On November 30, the Soviet government rudely replied that U.S. references to an armed uprising in Iran "did not correspond to reality." Disturbances had been caused by "reactionary elements" seeking to deny national rights to the population of northern Iran. The Soviets denied that they were interfering with Iranian military forces, and refused to withdraw their troops before the treaty deadline of March 2, 1946.[55]

At a November 29 press conference, Truman was asked if he planned to hold another Big Three conference. He said no categori-

---

[51] Ibid.; Leahy diary, November 19, 1945, LC.

[52] Daily TS Staff Summary, November 20, 21, 23, 1945, RG 59, NA; *New York Times*, November 21, 1945.

[53] Daily TS Staff Summary, November 26, 1945, RG 59, NA.

[54] *FR: 1945*, VIII, pp. 448-49.

[55] Ibid., pp. 468-69.

cally. "I am not in favor of special conferences," Truman said firmly, "because I want to see the United Nations do its job. The League of Nations was ruined by a lot of special conferences." President Truman went on to say that if the United Nations Organization worked as it should, there would be no need for a summit conference or any other sort of conference outside the U.N.[56]

But Truman had not informed his own secretary of state about his spur-of-the-moment decision to use the United Nations as a forum for settling great power differences. On the same day that the State Department had dispatched a note to the Soviet government on Iran, Byrnes had suggested to Molotov that they hold another meeting of the Big Three foreign ministers in Moscow on December 11. Indeed, it is doubtful whether Truman had given the matter much prior thought before he opened his mouth.

On Thanksgiving Day, Byrnes was alone in his office catching up on unfinished business when he recalled the Yalta agreement providing for regular consultations between the Big Three foreign ministers. The next day he cabled Molotov, reminding him of the Yalta provision and suggesting they hold their next conference in Moscow. Harriman reported that Molotov was "obviously much pleased" at the suggestion, commenting that "it is a good thing Mr. Byrnes recalled that the three of us could meet independently."[57]

Byrnes proposed negotiations without first consulting with the British, to "make Molotov feel good." British Foreign Secretary Bevin, however, was incensed. Bevin had serious misgivings about holding a conference without adequate preparation in the form of private meetings where they could explore each other's position informally. Whereas British Foreign Secretary Bevin was following the traditional diplomatic practice of having preliminary conferences of lower-level official experts to prepare for major summit meetings, Byrnes wished to treat the Soviets as if they were recalcitrant senators in need of private "arm twisting" and bribery. Byrnes believed that a small, informal meeting in Moscow where he could intercede with Stalin had good chances for success. As host, even Molotov might be "more pliable." Byrnes suggested that the agenda be left wide open, to permit free-wheeling talks on all issues disturbing allied relations. "If some-

[56] *Truman Public Papers, 1945*, pp. 511, 513; *New York Times*, November 30, 1945; *Truman Public Papers, 1945*, p. 388.

[57] *FR: 1945*, II, pp. 578-79; James F. Byrnes, *Speaking Frankly* (New York: Harper & Bros., 1947), p. 109; Curry, *Byrnes*, p. 162; Patricia D. Ward, *The Threat of Peace: James F. Byrnes and the Council of Foreign Ministers, 1945-1946* (Kent, Ohio: Kent State University Press, 1979), pp. 52-53; W. B.'s Book, Thanksgiving Day, Clemson.

thing comes up that seems like a decent trade," Byrnes said, and if he could "get Truman on the phone," he would proceed according to their combined judgment.

Though Bevin was "desperately anxious" to talk with Byrnes before the Moscow Conference, the secretary of state politely declined. "While our Government is eager to work in closest cooperation with yours, I think you will agree that it is not necessary or desirable that we should reach agreement on every detail before discussion with the Soviet Union," Byrnes explained. In fact, Byrnes intended to assume FDR's role of mediator between Britain and the Soviet Union."[58]

Secretary Byrnes called prominent members of the Senate Foreign Relations and Atomic Energy committees into his office to brief them on his negotiating strategy at Moscow. Byrnes told the senators that his principal objectives were to stimulate greater Russian interest in the United Nations, secure Soviet participation in the atomic energy commission, and settle the question of Japanese occupation machinery. He was afraid that the United Nations would be a "pretty stale chicken" unless the Soviets demonstrated greater enthusiasm for the organization. Thus far, the Russians had not "risen to the bait" implicit in the Truman-Attlee-King Declaration. As an inducement for the Soviets to cooperate, Byrnes would offer to exchange atomic scientists and basic scientific information. He argued that this initial step was necessary to allay Soviet suspicions of American "atom politics," and to create a favorable atmosphere for negotiation. Byrnes planned to abandon the "bomb in the pocket" tactics, which had been so counterproductive in London, in favor of a radically new approach. Instead of using the atomic bomb as an implied "threat," Byrnes would offer to share scientific information on atomic energy as an inducement for the Soviets to cooperate with the United States on *other* issues. As a result of recent Soviet rhetoric about "atomic democracy" and warnings against U.S. attempts to exploit the atomic monopoly politically, Byrnes had concluded that the Soviets would not cooperate as long as they believed that the United States was using the Bomb as a diplomatic weapon in power politics. The main purpose of the Moscow Conference was to "keep our skirts clean" on the atomic bomb, he explained. Since the offer to exchange information was not made contingent on any Soviet quid pro quo, in effect Byrnes was extending the Soviets a "bribe." Moreover, Byrnes planned to follow Stimson's

[58] W. B.'s Book, Thanksgiving Day, Clemson; *FR: 1945*, II, pp. 582-88, 590-91, 593-95, 597; Byrnes to Harriman, November 24, 1945, 740.00119 Council/11-2445, RG 59, NA; Davies journal, December 11, 1945, LC; McNaughton Report, December 13, 1945, HSTL.

suggestion that we approach the Russians directly, instead of through an international organization. Byrnes recalled that time and time again Molotov had complained that the United Nations placed the Soviet Union and Honduras on the same footing. It was to avoid a similar reproach that Byrnes had decided to seek Soviet approval of the atomic commission proposal *before* presenting it to the United Nations.[59] In sum, in his negotiating tactics, Byrnes had come full circle from Cold War confrontation to Rooseveltian accommodation.

Trying to avoid the impression of inconsistency in the administration's foreign policy that was created by Truman's off-the-cuff statement, Byrnes disingenuously told the press that in referring to the "Big Three," Truman meant the heads of state instead of their countries, and that the president was not ruling out another meeting of the Council of Foreign Ministers.[60] Then Byrnes wrote Truman a condescending letter recounting his explanation to the press. "I am advising you about this," Byrnes concluded, "because the way these questions were asked, I assumed that they might go back at you to have you specify and if you cannot avoid answering, I at least wanted you to know what I had said." This letter was the beginning of the end for Byrnes.[61]

The reporters regarded Byrnes' explanation as less than credible. Truman's off-the-cuff remarks seemed to fit in with his earlier decision to turn the problem of atomic energy control over to the United Nations. *Time* magazine judged that "there was ample evidence that the President had carefully considered his remarks in advance. They were clearly in line with the Truman-Attlee-King atomic bomb statement that UNO, if it is to work, must be entrusted with important matters."[62] Liberal journalists accused the president of abandoning FDR's policy of Soviet-American cooperation. "One can imagine what a shock would have swept this country if Russia had bluntly announced that she was not interested in meeting with the United States and Britain again," Samual Grafton complained. The *New Republic* wrote:

> It is time for [Truman] to go back to the basic premises on which the late Franklin Roosevelt first forged the unity of the United

[59] McNaughton Report, December 10, 1945, Visson File, HSTL; McNaughton Report, December 13, 1945, HSTL; *Time*, December 17, 1945, p. 25; Vandenberg diary, December 10, 1945, *Private Papers*, ed. Vandenberg, pp. 227-28.

[60] Secretary's Press Conference, December 5, 1945, Verbatim Reports of the Secretary's Press Conferences: 1945, RG 59, NA.

[61] Memorandum for the President, December 6, 1945, Truman Papers, PSF: General File, "Meetings—Big Three," HSTL.

[62] "Change of Tactics," *Time*, December 10, 1945, p. 17.

States, Great Britain, and Russia—unity on which the entire structure of the United Nations must stand or fall.

These premises, whether or not the President likes special conferences, impel consultation and conferences of the four great powers.[63]

TROUBLE WITH BYRNES

In December, the Iranian Democrats, with Soviet support, moved rapidly to consolidate their control over northern Iran before the Moscow Foreign Ministers' Conference. On December 12, the "Governmental Assembly of Azerbaijan" met, and selected a "cabinet" representing each of the portfolios of the Iranian government except Foreign Affairs and War. On the opening day of the conference, Moscow radio proclaimed the establishment of a new "national government" in Azerbaijan. The *New York Times* printed an eyewitness report by an Iranian general, who charged that the Azerbaijani capital Tabriz was lost because Russian occupation troops confined governmental troops to their barracks. An administration source told the *New York Times* that the timing of the announcement on the eve of the Moscow Conference was unmistakably intended to confront Byrnes and Bevin with a fait accompli.[64]

On December 17, the same day that the *Times* story appeared, Truman complained to his staff that the "Russians confront us with an accomplished fact and then there is little we can do." "They did that in the case of Poland," he pointed out. "Now they have 500,000 men in Bulgaria and some day," he said, "they are going to move down and take the Black Sea straits and that will be an accomplished fact again."

"There's only one thing they understand," the President said.

"Divisions?" Press Secretary Charley Ross asked.

Truman nodded, and added that "we can't send any divisions over to prevent them from moving into Bulgaria. *I don't know what we're going to do*," he said.[65]

Truman had no policy in reserve in case FDR's "grand design" proved to be infeasible, unrealistic, or unwise. A new bipolar world

---

[63] Thomas Reynolds, "Pulmotor Needed for UNO," *New Republic*, December 17, 1945, p. 828.

[64] Daily TS Staff Summary, December 4, 14, 1945, RG 59, NA; *New York Times*, December 17, 1945.

[65] Ayers diary, December 17, 1945, HSTL, emphasis added.

was emerging, divided between an atomic power and a revolutionary, revisionist power. The only alternative to great power cooperation and the U.N. appeared to be armed rivalry between two hostile blocs—the Cold War.

But Truman felt unable to oppose Soviet expansionism with military power, because of U.S. public opinion. Members of Congress were under heavy pressure from constituents to increase the rate of demobilization. Over two hundred "bring back Daddy" clubs were organized by servicemen's wives to lobby Congress. In December, these women deluged congressmen with baby shoes with notes attached, pleading "please bring back my daddy." When a shortage of ships for troop transport developed, servicemen in the Far East sent thousands of letters to their representatives stamped with the slogan "No boats, No votes."[66] General Carl Spaatz complained publicly that there had been such a rapid demobilization of Air Force personnel under public pressure to "bring the boys home," that the Air Force was now substandard and deteriorating at an accelerating pace. "At this very moment," General Spaatz warned, "our overseas Air Force commanders have insufficient usable personnel to carry out the responsibilities assigned, and considered essential, by the Joint Chiefs of Staff." On December 19, a *New York Times* editorial lamented that the American people, for whom "no sacrifice was too great" to win the war, now were not content with an orderly demobilization that would enable us to carry out our responsibilities in Europe and Asia.[67]

Soviet subversion in northern Iran appeared to be aimed at Turkey. Beginning in December, the Soviets also stepped up their "war of nerves" against Turkey. On December 18, *New York Times* columnist C. L. Sulzberger wrote that the Big Three talks on Iran were "another case of closing the barn door after the horse is gone." The new Azerbaijani government was moving so rapidly to consolidate its position through land reform and administrative purges that even if the foreign ministers were able to reach an agreement, it would be difficult to dislodge them. Sulzberger noted that Soviet pressure against Turkey had intensified once they had established a foothold in northern Iran. Sulzberger surmised that since the "Iran business is working according to schedule, the gardener is looking at another ripe tree."[68]

The next day, in talking with Davies about the Moscow meeting, Truman deplored the Soviets' "unilateral action" in Azerbaijan. "They

[66] R. Alton Lee, "The Army 'Mutiny' of 1946," *Journal of American History* 53 (December 1966): 555-71.

[67] *New York Times* editorial, December 19, 1945.

[68] *New York Times*, December 18, 1945.

should not confront us with a 'fait accompli,' " he complained. "It disturbed faith as to their peaceful intent." Davies demurred that the Soviets were only trying to protect their vital interests. They were interested in protecting the Baku oil fields and securing an Iranian oil concession, he asserted. Truman objected that the Russians were not so much interested in oil as in the Dardanelles.[69]

There were other signs that the Soviets intended to use northern Iran as a springboard into Turkey. On December 21, the *New York Times* reported on page one that two Soviet Georgian intellectuals had demanded that the Turks "restore" to Georgia over 10,000 miles of territory in northern Turkey, including a strategic 180-mile stretch of Black Sea coast. *Izvestia, Red Star,* and *Pravda* prominently published the Georgian claim. The *New York Times* pointed out that during the war the Soviet press had accurately forecast the territorial claims of the Soviet government. These new demands were far more extensive than previous claims raised by Molotov in June. State Department sources attributed the latest Soviet demands to Stalin's desire to control more territory adjacent to the strategic port of Batum, from which the Russians shipped considerable quantities of oil, and, more generally, to his insistence on having "friendly" governments in countries bordering on the Soviet Union. On the European–Middle East periphery of the Soviet Union, Turkey was the one gap in the Soviet security belt.[70] Meanwhile, the Soviet embassy in Istanbul was recruiting Armenians for Soviet Armenia, which was already overcrowded and incapable of supporting a new influx of refugees. The Turks believed that the Soviet government would use the additional population as an excuse to seize Turkish territory.[71]

British power was contracting throughout the globe, leaving a tempting vacuum in the Mediterranean. It was only natural that the Soviet Union would respond to the same geopolitical considerations that motivated Tsarist attempts to expand into the area. Whereas Truman viewed Soviet subversion in Iran and territorial demands on Turkey as a campaign for the Dardanelles, the State Department adopted a broader geopolitical perspective. As Loy Henderson pointed out in a December 28 memo to Acheson, Great Britain was pursuing its traditional policy of using the Near East as a dam to hold back the flow of Russia and maintain its line of communications to India. At the same time, the Soviet Union was determined to break through the

[69] Davies journal, December 19, 1945, LC.
[70] *New York Times*, December 21, 1945.
[71] *New York Times*, December 22, 1945.

structure built by Britain so that Soviet influence could flow un-impeded into the Mediterranean and Indian Ocean. Weakened by the war, however, Britain could no longer maintain its Near Eastern ram-parts, battered by a series of unilateral Soviet acts.

But no one in Washington seriously considered filling the vacuum with U.S. military and economic power. The State Department was faithfully following FDR's policy of tripartite political cooperation and the open door for economic competition. Henderson suggested hold-ing a summit conference representing Britain, the Soviet Union, France, and the United States to work out a common policy toward the Middle East. In January 1946, Gordon Merriam, chief of the Di-vision of Near Eastern affairs, reiterated the principles underlying U.S. policy in the Near East:

> Our own ideas, as I understand them, are along the lines of free competition in trade and communications matters, complete liberty on the part of independent countries of the Middle East to select advisors and experts, and, in general, a friendly vying among the Powers in the course of which each will put its best foot forward to help the Middle East countries get ahead on a basis of complete respect for their independence and sovereignty.[72]

Lacking the State Department's geopolitical categories or Truman's "script" about inland waterways, Byrnes' reaction to Soviet pressure on the Northern Tier countries was erratic and inconsistent. When the uprisings first broke out in Azerbaijan in late November, Byrnes was sure that they had been fomented by the Russians. His suggested re-sponse, however, was to withdraw U.S. troops as soon as possible. By the Moscow Conference, Byrnes concluded that the Soviets could probably obtain their aims in Azerbaijan through underground meth-ods after their troops had been withdrawn; the inhabitants of the province had "real grievances" and had not been given the provincial autonomy they had requested. Secretary Byrnes privately sent a mes-sage to the Iranian prime minister requesting that concessions be made to some of the Azerbaijanian demands, such as the use of Turkish in schools and the creation of provincial councils as provided for in the Iranian Constitution. Byrnes warned Stalin that the Iranians planned to submit a complaint to the U.N. Security Council about Soviet in-terference in their internal affairs, and the United States would find it hard to support the Soviets on the issue. But when Stalin refused Byrnes' request that foreign troops be withdrawn immediately, the

---

[72] FR: 1946, VII, pp. 6-7; FR: 1945, VIII, pp. 488-90.

secretary of state did not harp on the subject. Byrnes did not bring up the most recent Soviet demands for Turkish territory or the "war of nerves" being conducted against Turkey.[73]

Truman began to blame his inability to formulate a coherent policy toward the Soviets on his secretary of state, James Byrnes. Truman consciously tried to avoid FDR's bad example of becoming involved in the details of policy implementation. He resolved early on that he would delegate authority while maintaining presidential decisionmaking responsibilities.[74] But he had not yet learned how to use subordinates to carry out details while maintaining some control over the overall direction of policy. He did not understand that relying on the "best men available" was not equivalent to giving them a "blank check."

In Byrnes' case, the problem was exacerbated by the secretary of state's independent style. Throughout his political career, Byrnes had always operated as a loner, relying only on a small retinue of loyal advisers. In addition, he preferred to negotiate without any fixed strategy, using his instincts and intuition to achieve the best agreement possible. Furthermore, Byrnes was unable to accustom himself to the change in Truman's and his relative status. He continued to treat the president condescendingly as if he were still a Senate leader instructing a junior member. Acheson recalled that Byrnes picked up a telephone and asked to speak to the president. "Harry?" he said. When he had finished, Acheson gently scolded him, "Mr. Secretary . . . no one does anything like that. No matter who you are, he is 'Harry' to no one except Mrs. Truman. . . . Not any more." The amiable Byrnes replied, "Dean, of course you are right. I shouldn't do it." But he did it, Acheson related.[75]

In early December, Truman complained to Budget Director Harold Smith that "I would have a pretty good government, don't you think, if I had a good Labor Department and a good State Department?" On December 8, Truman took a cruise on the presidential yacht *Williamsburg* to escape from incessant appointments and pressures. Tired and haggard, he took Davies aside and pleaded with him to find out from Byrnes what he was going to do at Moscow. He was fond of

[73] Wallace diary, November 23, 1945, *Price of Vision*, ed. Blum, p. 519; Notes on Cabinet Meeting, November 23, 1945, Connelly Papers, Box 1, HSTL; Memorandum of Conversation, December 17, 1945, *FR: 1945*, II, pp. 630-61; "December 17, 1945," Feis Papers, Box 86, LC; *FR: 1945*, II, pp. 684-87.

[74] Davies journal, May 13, 21, 1945, LC.

[75] Interview with Acheson, February 18, 1955, Truman Papers: Post-Presidential Files, HSTL.

Byrnes, Truman said, but Byrnes was a "conniver."[76] Several days later, Truman complained to his staff that he should not have to read the newspapers to get U.S. foreign policy. That morning he had read in the *New York Times* for the first time a statement by Byrnes on U.S. economic policy toward Germany.[77] But he said nothing to Byrnes about his unhappiness with the secretary's failure to consult with him. During the Moscow Conference, Byrnes' cables to the State Department were as terse and uninformative as if hastily scrawled on a postcard.

To be fair, Byrnes had not suddenly usurped the president's authority to set foreign policy. During the London Conference in September, Byrnes' cables to Washington were also extraordinarily brief, and Truman made no attempt to involve himself in the negotiations. Throughout the London Foreign Ministers' Conference, Truman gave Byrnes no more substantive advice than "Give 'em Hell" or "Stick to your Guns."[78]

On December 27, Truman was in Independence when a coded message began to come in from Moscow informing him of the end of the conference and the agreements reached. Before he had received the full text, the conference results were announced in the press and radio. When reporters asked his opinion of the communiqué, Truman was forced to say that he would have to talk with Secretary Byrnes—a remarkable admission.[79]

The next day, Truman returned to Washington and boarded the presidential yacht *Williamsburg* with a group of his closest advisers. When he arrived from Moscow, Byrnes told reporters that he did not plan to see the president. The first word Truman received from his secretary of state was a message telephoned from Byrnes' office to the White House Secret Service and relayed to the ship. It was a peremptory request for Truman to have Charlie Ross arrange radio time for Byrnes to make an address to the nation on the conference. Then, as an afterthought, Byrnes expressed hope that Truman was having a pleasant trip and added that he would see him on his return to Washington. The Secret Service agent in charge of relaying the message was so taken aback by Byrnes' rudeness that he "tamed down the tone" of the message before letting it go to Truman.

---

[76] Harold Smith diary, December 5, 1945, HSTL; Davies journal, December 8, 1945, LC.

[77] Ayers diary, December 12, 1945, HSTL.

[78] Messer, "The Making of a Cold Warrior," pp. 378-79; Ward, *Threat of Peace*, pp. 72-73.

[79] *New York Times*, December 28, 1945.

Truman and the members of his party were outraged by Byrnes' arrogance. The president immediately cabled back:

Happy to hear of your safe arrival. Suggest you come down today or tomorrow to report on your mission. . . . We can then discuss among other things the advisability of a broadcast by you.[80]

Byrnes was dead tired after all-night negotiating sessions with Molotov. But he stayed in Washington just long enough to shave, have lunch with Mrs. Byrnes, and glance at a few cables before boarding a plane for Quantico, Virginia, where the presidential yacht was anchored. Before Byrnes arrived, Truman complained bitterly about the commitments made without consulting him.

On boarding the yacht, Byrnes greeted the president warmly and the two men headed for Truman's quarters, where they were closeted for over two hours. Blithely arriving without even a briefcase, Byrnes brought with him no documents or papers. Several of Truman's advisers complained that it was a rather casual way to report to the president. Before Byrnes arrived, Truman was so angry that he was inclined *not* to give his secretary of state permission to make a radio broadcast. But Byrnes was able to convince Truman that his failure to receive the communiqué was a mixup, the result of time pressures and poor telegraph communications from Moscow.

On December 30, Byrnes reported on the Moscow Conference over a nationwide radio hookup. Truman could not have seen the final draft of Byrnes' speech because it was not completed until shortly before he went on the air.[81]

At Moscow, Byrnes had agreed to recognize Bulgaria and Rumania in return for the addition of a few opposition members to the cabinet. Before the conference even began, Byrnes was prepared to abandon U.S. insistence on "free elections" as a condition for recognizing Rumania and Bulgaria. He was aware that continued delay in concluding peace treaties with Hungary, Rumania, or Bulgaria worked to the Soviets' advantage by allowing them to consolidate their position in those countries. Further, his firm policy toward Soviet domination of Eastern Europe was having decidedly mixed results. To be sure, free elections were held in Hungary on November 4, and the conservative Smallholders won a resounding victory. A *New York Times* corre-

[80] Ayers diary, December 29, 1945, January 1, 2, 1946, HSTL; copy of messages exchanged between Byrnes and Truman, December 19, 1945, Ayers Papers, "Byrnes, James F.," HSTL.

[81] Leahy diary, December 29, 1945, LC; McNaughton Papers, January 4, 1946, HSTL; *Time*, January 7, 1946, p. 20.

spondent observed less election-day violence and intimidation than in Tammany-dominated New York City. Stalin also refrained from interfering in the Austrian elections held in early November. On the other hand, in elections held in Bulgaria on November 18, the Fatherland Front racked up an unbelievable 88 percent majority amid charges of "wholesale" election frauds and terrorism. In Yugoslavia, Tito's People's Front won the elections by an even larger majority.[82]

At Moscow, when he got nowhere with Molotov, Byrnes tried a private audience with Stalin late on a snowy night. To break the ice, Byrnes remarked to Stalin that he "had had a difficult time with Mr. Molotov." Stalin replied with a smile that "this was unexpected news." Stalin showed some irritation over accusations in the Western press that Soviet troops stationed in the Balkans had interfered in the elections of those countries. He maintained that all the Soviet Union asked of neighboring countries was that they should not be hostile. What parties ran the countries was of no concern to the Soviets. Then Stalin conceded that "perhaps the Bulgarian parliament could be advised to include some members of the loyal opposition" and that "in the case of Rumania . . . since no elections had been held, it might be possible to make some changes in the Government there which would satisfy Mr. Byrnes and Mr. Bevin." Byrnes snapped up Stalin's offer and within minutes it was decided that a tripartite commission would go to Rumania to recommend the addition of two ministers from the National Peasant and Liberal parties. Stalin himself promised to "advise" the Bulgarians to broaden their government. When this had been carried out, the United States and Britain promised to recognize Rumania and Bulgaria. Obviously, the addition of a few ministers would not disturb Soviet control over the two countries. George Kennan described the agreements as "fig leaves of democratic procedure to hide the nakedness of Stalinist dictatorship." The American mission in Rumania regarded the Moscow agreements as a "sell-out" and considered resigning en masse.[83]

Some journalists criticized Byrnes for his concessions in the Balkans and his failure to restrain Soviet pressure on Iran and Turkey. On December 28, C. L. Sulzberger observed that "the most glaring fact

[82] *New York Times*, November 6, 20, 21, 1945; Schoenfeld to Byrnes, November 9, 1945, *FR: 1945*, IV, p. 904; McNeill, *America, Britain, and Russia*, pp. 702-703; Memorandum from Harriman to Byrnes, December 22, 1945, Bohlen Files, "Memos (CEB) 1945" folder, RG 59, NA; McNaughton Report, December 10, 1945, Visson File, HSTL.

[83] *FR: 1945*, II, pp. 700-702, 732-33, 752-56; Kennan, *Memoirs*, pp. 299-300; Sulzberger diary, January 26, 1946, *Long Row of Candles*, p. 292.

that emerges from the communiqué on the Moscow talks is the complete failure of the U.S., British, and Soviet governments to reach an agreement on the delicate Iranian situation, which the Soviet Union apparently insists on regarding as a fait accompli and which is developing into what appears to be a ramified Middle Eastern crisis, shifting its dynamism toward Turkey." A few days later, Arthur Krock reported that influential members of Congress had many questions about the Moscow agreements, such as "why was nothing settled about Russia's activities in Iran and its demands on Turkey?"[84]

Truman continued to have problems with Byrnes. On January 4, the president told Admiral Leahy that he had first learned of our formal recognition of Yugoslavia from the newspapers and that no one had discussed it with him previously. The next day, Truman received a copy of a letter from Mark Ethridge, publisher of the *Louisville Courier-Journal*, summarizing the results of his investigation into Soviet rule in Bulgaria and Rumania. Byrnes had sent Ethridge, a New Deal liberal, to investigate whether foreign service personnel were exaggerating Soviet activities in the Balkans. The secretary of state had received Ethridge's report in late November, but he had decided to bottle it up and use the threat of its publication as a negotiating lever at the Moscow Conference. Byrnes made no attempt to excuse his delay in sending the report to Truman. Instead, he attached a casual note, "This is the letter from Mark Ethridge I promised to send you for your files." Truman complained to his staff that the Ethridge letter was dated December 8, but he had received a copy of it only that morning, January 5. Then, strangely, he added that he didn't want a controversy with the State Department at that time.[85]

As he read the Ethridge letter, Truman's anger grew. Far from being "representative" as called for by the Yalta Declaration, the governments of Rumania and Bulgaria were communist dictatorships, Ethridge reported. Recent elections in Bulgaria were rigged; Ethridge knew the results a month before they were held. In Rumania, the government was hand-picked by the Soviet Vice-Commissar for Foreign Affairs Vyshinsky. Truman was so indignant that he immediately sat down and wrote out in longhand a seething letter to Byrnes. But he later decided not to send it, instead retaining it for his files. Attached to the letter was the note, "read to the Secretary of State and discussed—not typed or mailed." More likely, Truman conveyed his

[84] *New York Times*, December 28, 30, 1945; *Time*, January 7, 1946, pp. 18-19.

[85] Leahy diary, January 4, 1946, LC; Ayers diary, January 5, 1946, HSTL; Byrnes to Truman, January 2, 1945, Truman Papers, PSF: Subject File, "Bulgaria and Rumania," HSTL.

ideas more diplomatically. Despite his reputation for giving opponents "hell," Truman was a gentle, considerate man. He hated personal confrontations, and would so tightly rein in his temper when chastising subordinates that they sometimes failed to detect any criticism of their actions. The emotions and anger so carefully controlled by Truman would then spill forth in personal memoranda he wrote for his own use. In addition, Truman was still intimidated by Byrnes, whose Washington experience as a Supreme Court justice, "assistant president" for domestic affairs, and legislative "fixer" greatly outranked his own. In March, Baruch complained that Byrnes had Truman so "terrorized" that he didn't know where to turn.[86]

Regardless of whether he read the letter to Byrnes, it is a valuable record of Truman's thinking. Truman began by lecturing Byrnes on the president's responsibility for making foreign policy decisions. That meant that he must be informed on the progress of negotiations. Unwilling to admit that he had been lax in overseeing his secretary of state, Truman acted as if Brynes had only recently overstepped his authority: "At London you were in constant touch with me and communication was established daily if necessary. That procedure did not take place at this last conference."

Truman noted that he had received the Ethridge letter only that morning, confirming their previous information on those two "police states," Rumania and Bulgaria. "I am not going to agree to the recognition of those governments unless they are radically changed," he declared firmly. Truman then expressed concern about the Soviets' resort to fait accompli to achieve their objectives:

> At Potsdam we were faced with an accomplished fact and were, by circumstances almost forced to agree to Russian occupation of Eastern Poland and the occupation of that part of Germany east of the Oder River by Poland. It was a high handed outrage. . . .
>
> When you went to Moscow you were faced with another accomplished fact in Iran. Another outrage if ever I saw one.

Mindful of the intensified Soviet "war of nerves" against Turkey, Truman wrote, "there isn't a doubt in my mind that Russia intends an invasion of Turkey and the seizure of the Black Sea Straits to the Mediterranean."

"Only one language do they understand," he reiterated.

"How many divisions have you?"

[86] Stettinius Calendar Notes, March 22, 1946, University of Virginia.

"I'm tired babying the Soviets," Truman concluded.[87]

Many scholars have accepted Truman's claim that this memorandum was "the point of departure of our policy."[88] But, as we shall see, Truman had not given up trying to reach an accommodation with the Soviets. Although his hopes for Soviet cooperation had been severely shaken, he was not prepared to give up FDR's policy of Soviet-American cooperation without something to replace it. A refusal to "baby the Soviets" hardly constituted a workable policy.

The State Department could not formulate a policy for Truman because they could not agree on an "accepted interpretation of Soviet intentions." As a result, U.S. policy toward the Soviets was fundamentally inconsistent. In early January, Joseph and Stewart Alsop commented that it was obvious that "there is no well-defined policy towards Russia." Recent actions such as the creation of a Far Eastern Commission for Japan presumed at least a working relationship with the Soviets. Yet, U.S. defense planning was aimed against Russia; the chain of air bases the United States was striving to create from Okinawa to the Aleutians and Iceland would encircle the Soviet Union.[89]

---

[87] Truman to Byrnes, January 5, 1946, Truman Papers: PSF, "Longhand Memos," HSTL.

[88] Truman, *Memoirs*, 1:552. See, for example, Yergin, *Shattered Peace*, p. 162; Gaddis, *Origins of the Cold War*, pp. 289-90; Donovan, *Conflict and Crisis*, pp. 161-62.

[89] Joseph and Stewart Alsop, "We Have No Russian Policy," *Washington Post*, January 4, 1946.

CHAPTER SIX

Drift and Indecision

THROUGHOUT 1946, Truman improvised, following no consistent policy toward the Soviet Union. According to Louis Halle, then a member of the State Department, it was already apparent by the end of World War II that FDR's vision of great power unity could not be realized, at least in the near future. State Department officials were faced with the awesome realization that "the official foreign policy that had been projected for the postwar world could not be made to work." As a result, Halle recalls, the United States was without a workable foreign policy until the spring of 1947.[1]

By early 1946, Truman had abandoned FDR's tactics of securing Soviet cooperation—conciliation, patience, satisfaction of legitimate Soviet security needs through territorial appeasement, generous economic assistance—without having any clear ideas about what should replace them. He had *not*, however, given up Roosevelt's foreign policy objective of persuading the Soviets to cooperate with Britain and the United States in maintaining world order. Desperately, Truman tried several expedients as they occurred to him, none well thought out or part of any consistent strategy: abolishing the Security Council veto, rallying world public opinion against Soviet expansion, offer of a U.S.-Soviet alliance, military force demonstrations, and personal diplomacy. Repeatedly, Truman told his aides that *he did not know what he would do* if nothing worked in persuading the Soviets to cooperate.

What he did not do, however, was enunciate an anti-Soviet policy. Truman deliberately refrained from making any public statements that could be construed as an attack on Soviet policies. He was not yet willing to close the door to a possible accommodation with the Soviet Union. Truman was still eager to cooperate with the Soviets *if* they stopped meddling in third areas and started observing their commitments more religiously. But he was no longer willing to appease the Russians or make unilateral concessions to allay Soviet suspicions. Truman adhered to the "code of the politician"—keep your agreements and insist that your allies do likewise.

Truman's hopes for accommodation with the Soviets relieved his

[1] Louis Halle, *Cold War as History*, pp. 102-103.

anxiety and warded off the specter of arms race and war. Recent experience and conventional wisdom had convinced him that unless the great powers remained united, there could be no lasting peace. A world divided into two hostile armed blocs must teeter on the brink of war, he believed. Truman did not want to be responsible for another world war, especially in an era of atomic weapons. Repeatedly, Truman gratuitously asserted that he did not want war, that we were not going to war with Russia, that he was no warmonger, even though no one had suggested the possibility of Soviet-American conflict.[2]

Truman was particularly sensitive to any implication that he was a warmonger, because of liberal criticism that he was no FDR. Many liberals blamed Truman for opening up an alarming rift with Russia by abandoning Roosevelt's policies. Had Roosevelt lived, they believed, he could have held the Grand Alliance together through diplomatic skill and the force of his personality. As newspaper columnist Samuel Grafton wrote on the first anniversary of Roosevelt's death:

It is because he is gone that the West, squealing legalisms, is now forlornly on the defensive, whereas if he had lived, blessed bad lawyer that he was, we might now be trying for a new level of international understanding.

For he, more than any other, was the coalition, he who could deal with Mr. Churchill as a country squire and with Mr. Stalin as a commoner.[3]

Journalists who covered the White House perceived that Mr. Truman's favorite word was "hope." When asked about the international situation at a time of great East-West tension brought on by the Iranian crisis and Churchill's "iron curtain" speech, Truman replied: "Would it help any if I said that I am not alarmed about this?" "The President only hoped," *Time* harrumphed. During one press conference, Truman by actual count used the word "hope" seven times.[4]

In early January, Truman considered abolishing the United Nations Security Council veto. At Truman's request, Byrnes asked two members of the U.S. delegation, Senators Vandenberg and Connally, for their views on eliminating the Security Council veto, without letting them know that it was the president's idea. The two senators pointed

---

[2] See, for example, Wallace diary, September 16, 1946, *Price of Vision*, ed. Blum, p. 621; Truman to John Garner, September 21, 1946, Truman Papers, PSF: Subject File, HSTL; M. Truman, *Harry Truman*, p. 323.

[3] Alonzo L. Hamby, *Beyond the New Deal: Harry S Truman and American Liberalism* (New York: Columbia University Press, 1973), pp. 142-43.

[4] *Time*, March 25, 1946, pp. 19-20; Coffin, *Missouri Compromise*, pp. 26-27.

out that the almost unanimous vote in the Senate for ratification could not have been secured without the veto clause. When Byrnes informed Truman over teletype of the senators' objections, he quickly backed down. "The suggestion was merely for your consideration," Truman assured Byrnes. "From what you say I think it would be best to let it rest."[5]

By the end of January, Truman had abandoned his original optimistic assessment of the results of the Potsdam Conference. He told staff members that the meeting would probably go down in history as a bad conference. Truman rationalized that nothing more could have been done because they were confronted with so many Russian faits accomplis. Plain-speaking Admiral Leahy contradicted the president. There was really only one accomplished fact, he said, and that was the Polish situation.[6]

A POSITIVE FOREIGN POLICY

On February 9, the eve of elections to the Supreme Soviet, Stalin made a speech that has been called the Soviet "declaration of Cold War."[7] Stalin began with the orthodox Marxist thesis that the capitalist system contained within itself the elements of general crisis and military catastrophe. World War II had occurred because of the uneven rate of development in capitalist economies. He concluded by stressing that three more five-year plans would be essential to prepare the country "against any eventuality."

Stalin's references to the hostile international system constituted about one-tenth of an address devoted largely to explaining and justifying past Stalinist economic policies.[8] Nevertheless, some American observers interpreted the speech as signifying Soviet remilitarization, a return to isolationist policies, and a renewed commitment to world revolution. Justice William O. Douglas called Stalin's election speech "The Declaration of World War III."

More knowledgeable observers interpreted the address as an attempt to mobilize the war-weary Soviet populace for the additional sacrifices required by a return to Stalin's policy of capital-intensive industrial development, which implied continuing shortages of food and con-

[5] Conference between Truman and Byrnes, 12 January 1946, Truman Papers, PSF: "United Nations—James Byrnes," HSTL.

[6] Ayers diary, January 24, 1946, HSTL.

[7] Walter LaFeber, *America, Russia, and the Cold War, 1945-1980*, 4th ed. (New York: John Wiley & Sons, 1980), p. 39.

[8] Trout, "Rhetoric Revisited," p. 269.

sumer goods. In a memorandum for Byrnes and Acheson, Elbridge Durbrow pointed out that the Soviet people were reluctant to face another series of five-year plans and further postponements of any rise in their standard of living. In emphasizing the weaknesses of capitalism and reviving the logic of capitalist encirclement, Stalin was trying to rally the Soviet people to the tasks ahead, while discouraging demands for an easier life. "The speech was therefore for internal consumption," Durbrow wrote, "and reflects the seriousness of the problems facing the regime in reconstruction, reconversion, and rehabilitation." He assured the secretary that "it does not necessarily mean that the Soviet Government has given up its type of collaboration in the international field, which will undoubtedly continue as long as it appears to be in the interest of the Soviet Government."[9]

Similarly, the recently retired ambassador to Moscow, Averell Harriman, told reporters that it was important to remember that public statements by high Soviet officials were "directed primarily to their own people." After making great sacrifices during the war, the Russian people were being asked to support another five-year plan.[10] Recommending that the United States take the initiative in extending to Russia a postwar credit, the *Washington Post* flippantly dismissed Stalin's election day speech:

> It is taken for granted, especially since Stalin's speech of February 8, that any kind of credit would subsidize a potential enemy. This is because Stalin has launched his country on a mammoth industrialization plan. What of it? If such a plan had been announced by Britain or France, we should have welcomed it. It would have been regarded as a sign of economic health.[11]

Other Americans were ambivalent and undecided. *Time* magazine observed that the "world communist line, 'soft' during the war, has been gradually hardening into a return to the tactics and slogans of world revolution." "Comrades everywhere could be expected to take a tip from Uncle Joe's speech and sharpen their opposition to non-Communist governments," the magazine predicted. On the other hand, *Time* pointed out, Stalin may have had "purely Russian reasons for pointing outward toward imagined enemies." Restless Russians had been asking for more food, clothes, and luxuries, and the foreign men-

[9] Forrestal diary, February 17, 1946, *Forrestal Diaries*, ed. Millis, p. 134; Elbridge Durbrow, "Comment on Stalin's Election Speech," February 11, 1946, Matthews-Hickerson Files, "Russia," Lot File, RG 59, NA.

[10] Harriman and Abel, *Special Envoy*, p. 547.

[11] *Washington Post*, March 7, 1946.

ace was Stalin's "handiest excuse for low living standards."[12] The *New York Times* conceded that Stalin's speech was disappointing to many of those who felt that the close wartime partnership of Russia and the democracies had provided a solution of the old prewar problems. "But if a solution is to be found," the *Times* continued hopefully, "it will be necessary to face the facts." And the facts were that "despite the new Russian policy and party line . . . Russia has been collaborating with the socialist and capitalist nations in the United Nations organization."[13] *Newsweek* speculated that the speech was a response to the Russian public's demand for more consumer goods and some relaxation of the rigorous regimen imposed by the war. "By raising again the specter of capitalist encirclement," *Newsweek* reasoned, "and by emphasizing the need for a powerful Red Army, the Soviet leaders apparently hope to explain why conditions have not improved more rapidly." *Newsweek* went on to make a prescient observation: "Now the danger to Moscow is that the revival of the old line will not be believed at home and may well help alienate friends abroad."[14]

Truman leaned toward the "domestic politics" interpretation of Stalin's election speech. As a politician trying to cope with reconversion, inflation, and high wage demands, he could understand Stalin's predicament. At the Women's Press Club Dinner, he commented that Stalin's speech reminded him of an amusing story about a fellow senator who said, "Well, you know we always have to demagogue a little, before elections."[15]

Like Truman, the British Foreign Office was not concerned by Stalin's election day speech. Speculating on why the speech provoked so much comment in the United States while it was generally ignored by the British people, J. B. Donnelly of the British Foreign Office theorized that "Americans attach more importance to speeches and decla-

[12] *Time*, February 18, 1946, pp. 29-30.

[13] *New York Times* editorial, February 11, 1946, p. 28.

[14] *Newsweek*, February 18, 1946, p. 47. Through selective quotation, Gaddis exaggerates the fearful reaction of U.S. officials and the public to Stalin's election speech. Most responsible journalists and officals were reluctant to accept Stalin's rhetoric at face value or to draw any firm conclusions from it. For example, describing the reaction of *Time* magazine, Gaddis (p. 300) states that the magazine concluded that *Russia* was returning to the slogans and tactics of world revolution, when the article refers instead to the "*world communist line*." In addition, Gaddis omits the second half of the quotation, which attributes Stalin's speech to domestic political considerations. Similarly, Gaddis misrepresents the meaning of the February 20, 1946 *New York Times* editorial by "summarizing" it in this manner: "Stalin's address would disappoint those who assumed that communism and capitalism could coexist peacefully in the postwar period."

[15] Davies diary, February 9, 1946, LC.

rations than do the more realistic and empirical inhabitants of the United Kingdom." In addition, "Capitalism, which is regarded as synonymous with Free Enterprise, is still the nearest thing to a universal religion in the United States." "It was therefore inevitable," Donnelly reasoned, "that most Americans should be keenly affected by the Marshal's strong denunciation of so cherished a creed."[16]

In contrast, Stalin's speech stimulated excited speculation in the State Department. The director of the Office of European Affairs, Freeman Matthews, advised Byrnes in a memorandum that Stalin's election speech constituted the "most important and authoritative guide to postwar Soviet policy" and "should be required reading for everyone in the Department." "It will henceforth be the Communist and fellow-traveler Bible throughout the world," Matthews predicted. At Matthews' suggestion, Byrnes cabled George Kennan at the Moscow embassy, asking him to provide an "interpretive analysis of what we may expect in the way of future implementation" of policies outlined in the preelection speeches of Stalin and his associates.[17]

Depressed at his lack of influence on U.S. policy toward Russia and ready to resign, Kennan responded with one of the longest and certainly most well-known diplomatic dispatches in the history of the Foreign Service. According to Kennan, the Soviets perceived the world as divided between socialist and capitalist centers, between which there could be no permanent peaceful coexistence. Kennan argued that the Soviet party line was not based on objective analysis of the world situation, but arose out of traditional Russian insecurity, created by repeated nomadic invasions. To this geopolitically based insecurity was later added the Kremlin's fear that the Russian people would make unfavorable comparisons if permitted contact with the superior political and economic systems of the West. Out of necessity, Russian rulers "learned to seek security only in patient but deadly struggle for total destruction of rival power, never in compacts and compromises with it."

The fluid and constant pressure exerted by Russian rulers to extend the limits of their police powers reflected traditional Russian nationalism, but in the guise of Marxism, with its "honeyed promises to a desperate and war-torn world," Russian expansionism was more dan-

[16] "Political Situation in the United States," 21 February 1946, FO 371/51606, AN 423/1/45.

[17] HFM to Acheson and Byrnes, February 11, 1946, Hickerson-Matthews Files, "Russia," RG 59, NA; Byrnes to Kennan, February 13, 1946, 868.001/2-1246, drafted by HFM, signed by Byrnes, RG 59, NA.

gerous to the West than ever before. Kennan's conclusions were frightening:

> We have here a political force committed fanatically to the belief that with [the] U.S. there can be no permanent *modus vivendi*, that it is desirable and necessary that the internal harmony of our society be disrupted, our traditional way of life be destroyed, the international authority of our state be broken, if Soviet power is to be secure.

To cope with this political force, Kennan recommended that the United States build up the cohesion and resistance of the Western bloc, and counter Soviet expansion through possession of superior force.[18]

The reaction to this discursive, somewhat academic discussion of Soviet policy was astonishing. The State Department aide charged with preparing a summary of incoming cables for Byrnes gave him a copy of the entire telegram with the note: "This telegram from George Kennan in Moscow is not subject to condensation. You will wish to read it in full." Copies were circulated to Under Secretary Acheson, Counselor Cohen, Assistant Secretaries William Benton, William Clayton, and James Dunn, and each of the State Department offices. The State Department sent copies of the "long telegram" to diplomatic missions around the world. Secretary of War Robert Patterson was "much impressed" with Kennan's analysis. Secretary of the Navy James Forrestal had the text reproduced, and made it "required reading" for hundreds of military officers.[19]

If the Hovland approach to attitude change is correct, then Byrnes should have adopted Cold War beliefs and given up trying to work out a modus vivendi with the Soviet Union as a basis for the postwar settlement. Kennan's telegram provided an authoritative, gracefully crafted, and convincing analysis of the sources of Soviet conduct that had the imprimatur of the nation's foreign policy professionals in the State Department. Byrnes informed Kennan that he had read the telegram with the "greatest interest" and thanked him for his "splendid analysis."[20] Nevertheless, the "long telegram" left no lasting impression on Byrnes' fundamental beliefs or his basic approach to dealing

[18] *FR: 1946*, IV, pp. 696-709.

[19] C. Ben Wright, "George F. Kennan, Scholar-Diplomat: 1926-1949" (Ph.D. dissertation, University of Wisconsin, 1972), p. 410; Curry, *Byrnes*, p. 368n; Kennan, *Memoirs*, p. 310; Matthews to Kennan, February 25, 1946, 861.00/2-2246, RG 59, NA.

[20] Byrnes to Kennan, February 27, 1946, 861.00/2-2246, RG 59, NA.

with the Soviet Union. Byrnes was still unwilling to admit publicly that Soviet-American differences over the outlines of the postwar order were basic and irreconcilable, or to take any action that might close the door to an accommodation with Russia. The implication of Kennan's analysis was that Soviet-American differences could not be resolved through personal meetings with Stalin, mutual adjustment of interests, give-and-take politics or, indeed, through any form of diplomatic negotiation. Byrnes simply was not prepared to accept such a pessimistic assessment. And, indeed, his previous experience with the Russians did not lead him to that mental impasse, for he believed that he had been quite successful at Moscow in using quid pro quo diplomacy. There is no evidence that Truman even read the "long telegram."

Oddly, Under Secretary of State Acheson did not bestow glowing praise or even any comment on Kennan's interpretation of Soviet motives and methods. Acheson may have privately preferred an alternative analysis of the policy alternatives facing the administration. In December, Acheson had commissioned a study of "The Capabilities and Intentions of the Soviet Union as Affected by American Policy" from the department's experts on Soviet affairs and academic specialists recruited during the war. The final installment of the report, written by Chip Bohlen, was circulated among interested officials at about the same time that Kennan's "long telegram" arrived; Acheson wrote marginal comments. Bohlen defined three alternative policies that the United States could pursue toward the Soviet Union: cooperation based on a division of the world into spheres of influence; limiting Soviet expansion through acquisition of U.S. military bases and use of economic pressure; and persuading the Soviets to support the principle of world cooperation and collective solution of political and territorial issues in the United Nations. Bohlen thought that the collective solution to political problems was infinitely preferable, but to allay Soviet suspicions that coalitions were being formed against them, he recommended that Britain and the United States meet with the Soviets before any international meetings so that their differences could be settled privately and on a preliminary basis, subject to later revision by the international community. Acheson's only criticism was that "could such talks remain only *preliminary* and not become definitive?"[21]

In late February, Truman became concerned about Soviet activities

---

[21] Robert L. Messer, "Paths Not Taken: The United States Department of State and Alternatives to Containment, 1945-1946," *Diplomatic History* 1 (Fall 1977): 297-319; "Draft," 711.61/2-1446, RG 59, NA.

in their occupation zone in North Korea. At the Moscow Conference, Byrnes, Bevin, and Molotov had agreed that a joint commission, representing the Soviet and American military commands, would establish a provisional Korean government. Soviet and American commanders each selected a group of "representative" Koreans from their occupation zone for consultation with the Joint Commission. On February 25, at his daily White House staff meeting, Truman pulled a handful of diplomatic cables out of the holder on his desk and announced that "we were going to war with Russia." "The situation looks bad," he said, "and there are two fronts, one Korea."[22]

General Hodge had just cabled that the Russian-sponsored "Korean Central Government" of North Korea was composed entirely of "violent Communists" or "unknown Koreans brought in from Russia or Manchuria." Hodge predicted that the Russians would force us to accept their government as the democratic representatives of North Korea, while trying to secure enough communist representation in South Korea to obtain control of the Korean provisional government for the Communist party.[23]

On February 28, Truman told his staff that the night before he had edited a speech of Byrnes and written one of his own. Truman bragged that he had "told Byrnes to stiffen up and try for the next three months not to make any compromises." He added that the United States was sending the battleship *Missouri* and a task force to Constantinople "to honor a dead Turk." "And impress Russia??" Eben Ayers wrote in his diary.[24]

Truman returned the speech to Byrnes with a handwritten comment: "Jim, I've read it and like it. See last page." On the last page, Truman scrawled, "Jim: A good speech—I think. I've marked some phrases I particularly like." The passages Truman underlined or highlighted reflected his determination to speak plainly to the Russians: "a just and lasting peace is not the inevitable result of victory"; "we must break that vicious circle of suspicion and distrust. That requires plain speaking"; "we must make it clear in advance that we do intend to act to prevent aggression"; "the Charter forbids aggression and we cannot allow aggression to be accomplished by coercion or pressure or subterfuges such as political infiltration"; "we must not conduct wars of nerves to achieve strategic ends."[25]

[22] Ayers diary, February 25, 1946, HSTL.
[23] Daily TS Staff Summary, February 1, 18, 19, 1946, RG 59, NA; Secretary's Summary, February 25, 1946, ibid.; Hodge to Secretary of State, February 24, 1946, *FR: 1946*, VII, pp. 640-62.
[24] Ayers diary, February 28, 1946, HSTL.
[25] Overseas Press Club Speech Draft, Byrnes Papers, folder 626, Clemson.

Forrestal was the one who first suggested that the United States send a task force to the Mediterranean. Byrnes approved, adding that it could accompany the battleship *Missouri*, which was returning the body of the former Turkish ambassador as a gesture of respect.[26] Oddly enough, the Truman administration had decided to make what would be interpreted as a forceful gesture of support for Turkey at a time when the Soviet "war of nerves" had abated.[27]

On the evening of February 28, Byrnes told the Overseas Press Club that the United States wished to continue to be friends and partners with the Soviet Union, but we intended to defend the U.N. Charter. Plainly referring to Soviet practices in Iran, Manchuria, Germany, and Turkey, Byrnes denied that any country had the right to maintain troops in other states without their consent; to help itself to enemy properties before a reparations settlement; or to conduct a war of nerves to achieve strategic ends.[28]

According to John Lewis Gaddis, the period of late February and early March 1946 marked a turning point in American foreign policy. Byrnes' speech was "the first open manifestation of the tougher Russian policy toward which the Truman administration had been moving since the Moscow Conference." Before then, U.S. officials had tried to resolve differences with the Soviets through negotiation and compromise, on the assumption that our common interests were more significant than transitory difficulties. "From this time on," Gaddis contends, "American policymakers regarded the Soviet Union not as an estranged ally, but as a potential enemy, whose vital interests could not be recognized without endangering those of the United States."[29] He attributes this reorientation of American policy to the combined effects of domestic public pressure for a "tougher" policy and external events which seemed to indicate that the Soviet Union was motivated by ideology rather than security.[30] But, as Gaddis himself admits in another context, "with industry and imagination, any event in history can be made into a turning point of one sort or another."[31]

Did Truman have in hand a new policy toward the Soviet Union, which he was only waiting to unveil to the American public? Was Byrnes' Overseas Press Club speech a manifestation of the reorienta-

[26] Forrestal diary, February 28, 1946, *Forrestal Diaries*, ed. Millis, p. 141.

[27] See, for example, *FR: 1946*, VII, pp. 812-13, 815-16.

[28] *New York Times*, March 1, 1946.

[29] Gaddis, *Origins of the Cold War*, pp. 284, 304-306, 312-15.

[30] Historians who have accepted Gaddis' thesis and incorporated it into their narrative include Donovan, *Conflict and Crisis*, pp. 185, 189; Yergin, *Shattered Peace*, pp. 163-64, 186-87; Ward, *Threat of Peace*, p. 80.

[31] Gaddis, "Was the Truman Doctrine a Real Turning Point?" p. 402.

tion of American policy toward the Soviet Union from cooperation to containment? According to James Reston, Byrnes' speech raised several questions among Washington observers, among them, "Was this a speech or a policy?" Reston reported that "the general feeling among those who know the habits of Mr. Byrnes, his colleagues at the State Department, the pressure of work on him in many areas, and his political approach to national and international problems is that the pronouncement . . . was something in between a speech and a policy." While Byrnes' address might "result in a firmer policy," the general conclusion was that "the speech preceded the policy and not vice versa." *New York Times* columnist Edwin L. James agreed that "it is too early to say that this country has worked out an all-embracing policy vis-à-vis the vigorous foreign policy of the USSR." J. B. Donnelly of the British Foreign Office commented pessimistically that "it would of course be wrong to expect that the United States will live up to Mr. Byrnes's declarations immediately and in a firm and consistent manner. With Mr. Truman and Mr. Byrnes at the helm that would be far too much to hope."[32]

Further, domestic public opinion did not pressure Truman into abandoning FDR's "grand design" of Soviet-American cooperation.[33] In support of his argument, Gaddis cites a February 1946 opinion poll to show that only 35 percent of a national sample believed that Russia could be trusted to cooperate with the United States[34] In fact, throughout 1946 public opinion was highly volatile, responding reflexively to each event that seemed to portend future Soviet-American conflict or cooperation. Thus, after resolution of the Iranian crisis in early April 1946, 45 percent of a national sample thought Russia could be trusted to cooperate.[35] In any event, the American people gave little sustained attention to foreign affairs. Americans were more concerned with problems affecting their daily lives—strikes, inflation, food shortages, price controls, and the housing crisis. "Foreign Affairs!" one worker grumbled. "That's for people who don't have to work for a living."[36]

[32] *New York Times*, March 3, 1946; Halifax to Foreign Office, March 2, 1946, FO 371/51606, AN 587/1/45.

[33] Gaddis, *Origins of the Cold War*, pp. 289-90, 313, 360.

[34] Ibid., p. 328.

[35] Hadley Cantril and Mildred Strunk, eds., *Public Opinion, 1935-1946* (Princeton: Princeton University Press, 1951), p. 371.

[36] Lester Markel et al., *Public Opinion and Foreign Policy* (New York: Council on Foreign Relations, 1949), p. 54; *New York Times* editorial, June 13, 1946; Richard M. Freeland, *The Truman Doctrine and the Origins of McCarthyism: Foreign Policy, Domestic Politics, and Internal Security, 1946-1948* (New York: Schocken Books, 1970), pp. 64-65; Paterson, *On Every Front*, pp. 119-20.

Of greater concern to the Truman administration were the views of "opinion leaders," those who kept informed and could command attention and respect for their positions on foreign policy issues. They included journalists, businessmen, labor leaders, leaders of various interest groups, and intellectuals. And in February-March 1946, almost no one favored confrontation with the Soviet Union, the division of the world into two armed blocs, arms race, and the near certainty of war. Speeches by Byrnes, Senator Vandenberg, and John Foster Dulles, given within the space of a few days, were widely interpreted as evidence of the Truman administration's unfolding new policy. It is instructive to examine what each man said on the subject of Soviet-American cooperation. "We have openly, gladly, and wholeheartedly welcomed our Soviet Ally as a great power, second to none in the family of the United Nations," Byrnes said. "Only an inexcusable tragedy of errors could cause serious conflict between us in the future."[37] More dramatically, Senator Vandenberg declared that "two great rival ideologies—democracy in the West and communism in the East—here find themselves face to face with the desperate need for mutual understanding in finding common ground upon which to strive for peace for both."[38] John Foster Dulles judged that "it ought to be possible to find ways which will, in fact, stop our present tendency to drift apart and set up, within the framework of the United Nations, a trend toward fellowship. . . . We shall have to keep trying."[39] Ambassador Halifax observed that "amongst many thoughtful people there is at the same time an anxiety lest America should be manoeuvred into an anti-Russian position." "Along with the growing public awareness of the ideological differences that separate the United States and the Soviet Union there is, moreover, a continuing hope, disclosed in the speeches of both Vandenberg and Byrnes, that there are no basic reasons why the two countries should ever come into headlong collision with one another," Halifax commented.[40]

Byrnes' speech was an answer to public pressure of a different sort. Truman's foreign policy was criticized as weak, inconsistent, incoherent, and reactive to initiatives of Britain and the Soviet Union. For example, Senator Vandenberg spoke pointedly of "the need for positive foreign policies as our constant guide." "The situation calls for patience and good will but not for vacillation," Vandenberg said bluntly. Dulles stressed that "we must remember that a problem as

[37] Overseas Press Club Speech, February 28, 1946, *Department of State Bulletin* 14 (March 10, 1946): 358.
[38] *New York Times*, February 28, 1946.
[39] *Newsweek*, March 11, 1946, p. 27.
[40] Halifax to Foreign Office, 2 March 1946, FO 371/51606, AN 587.

hard as that we face cannot be solved by last-minute improvising."
J. B. Donnelly of the British Foreign Office rejoiced that Byrnes and
Vandenberg's speeches were a "remarkable example of the democratic
force at work because the driving force has come not from the top but
from below." "Events and public opinion have forced the obviously
uncertain and reluctant Administration into affording to the world at
least some measure of the leadership which the United States ought
to be providing," he concluded.

Byrnes' address was interpreted as an attempt to set down a clear
policy line. "Where stood the U.S.?" *Time* magazine asked. "As long
as its leaders could not make up their minds, the nation blundered
down a dark road." Making a less-than-flattering reference to Byrnes'
speech, *Time* rejoiced: "Last week the blunderer made a sudden turn."
New York Times columnist Edwin James pointed out that "up to the
present, any definite, consistent, and thought-out policy has been lacking." The speeches of Byrnes, Senator Vandenberg, and Mr. Dulles
indicated a distinct move toward a "more positive and clearer attitude
on Russian ambitions."[41]

Flushed with the heady knowledge of America's overwhelming economic and military power, the American people were no longer willing to play the passive role of mediator, merely responding to the
initiatives of Britain and Russia. As James observed, "the U.S. government represents a powerful nation, perhaps the most powerful in the
world." Surely the proper role for the United States did not lay in
acting as an honest broker between Great Britain and Russia. According to *Time*, "to many a U.S. citizen, to most of the world, the nation
seemed to have shrunk farther and farther from responsibility in world
affairs." "Was it a great power, with a voice and a goal of its own,"
Time asked rhetorically, "or just a nervous broker between an implacable Russia and an impoverished Britain?"[42] Americans wanted the
United States to assert its moral leadership, to stand for something
positive in world affairs. Columnist Anne O'Hare McCormick wrote
that "sensing a drift toward new troubles and dangers, the American
people want the U.S. to speak up and assert her power." "This is the
pressure," she noted, "reflecting an instinct rather than any real feeling
of danger, to which Mr. Byrnes responded with his thus-far-and-no-
farther declaration."[43]

The American people did favor a "firmer" policy toward the Soviet
Union. But what did that mean? One thing for certain, it did not mean

[41] *Time*, March 11, 1946, p. 19; *New York Times*, March 3, 1946; Halifax to Foreign
Office, 2 March 1946, FO 371/51606, AN 587.
[42] *Time*, March 11, 1946, p. 19.
[43] *New York Times*, March 2, 1946.

a policy of increased arms expenditures and "saber rattling." Members of Congress applauded speeches calling for "tough" talk to the Soviets, while viewing with equanimity the almost complete disintegration of American armed forces, under pressure to "bring the boys home." "Few members of Congress or press commentators followed through their demands for a more vigorous stand with a protest against the present wholesale dismantling of the United States military machine," Halifax pointed out. General Eisenhower announced that it would take the army over one year to get back to the level of efficiency which it had one year before Pearl Harbor. When asked "Get tough with what to back it up?" congressmen merely shrugged.[44]

Although press commentators demanded a more positive United States line in dealing with the Russians, none had any concrete recommendations about what such a policy might be. In the Overseas Press Club speech, Byrnes' substantive contribution was limited to asserting that the United States would defend the U.N. Charter.[45]

If Truman did not know what he would do if world opinion failed to restrain Soviet expansion, he was not about to let the Soviets sense any irresolution on our part. He tried to maintain a calculated ambiguity in the minds of the Soviets about what the United States might do.

On March 5, when that venerable Cold Warrior Winston S. Churchill spoke at Westminster College in Fulton, Missouri, Truman introduced him by saying "I know that he will have something constructive to say to the world." His weary, wrinkled, cherubic face framed by a flaming scarlet academic robe, Churchill looked like a fallen angel. Coming to the crux of his speech, he pleaded for a "fraternal association of the English-speaking peoples," that is, an Anglo-American alliance. Lowering his voice to a whisper, Churchill slowly and dramatically measured his words: "Nobody knows what Soviet Russia and its Communist international organization intends to do in the immediate future, or what are the limits, if any, to their expansive and proselytizing tendencies." President Truman sat behind Churchill idly playing with the tassel on his mortarboard.

Then Churchill coldly and deliberately bit out his words:

From Stettin in the Baltic to Trieste in the Adriatic, an iron curtain has descended across the Continent. Behind that line lie all the capitals of the ancient states of Central and Eastern Europe. Warsaw,

[44] C. P. Trussel, *New York Times*, March 31, 1946, sec. 4; Halifax to Foreign Office, March 2, 1946, FO 371/51606, AN 587; Halifax to Foreign Office, March 10, 1946, FO 371/51606, AN 656.

[45] Halifax to Foreign Office, March 2, 1946, FO 371/51606, AN 587.

Berlin, Prague, Vienna, Budapest, Belgrade, Bucharest, and Sofia, all these famous cities and the populations around them lie in what I must call the Soviet Sphere, and all are subject in one form or another, not only to Soviet influence but to a very high, and in many cases, increasing measure of control from Moscow.

The audience sat in silence. Only when Churchill said "I do not believe that Soviet Russia desires war," did his listeners applaud. "What they desire is the fruits of war," he continued, "and the indefinite expansion of their power and doctrines."[46]

Truman's private reaction to Churchill's speech was an enigma. His presence on the same platform as Churchill seemed to indicate his tacit endorsement of the former prime minister's remarks. Immediately after the speech, Truman refused to comment for publication, and his travelling companions would give no hint of any opinion he may have expressed in private. At a press conference on March 8, Truman left open Churchill's proposal for an Anglo-American alliance, explaining that he would have something further to say about it later. He also refused to take advantage of an opportunity to "disavow" the proposal. At the same time, Truman insisted that he had not seen a copy of the speech beforehand.[47]

Truman also denied to Henry Wallace that he had seen Churchill's speech in advance. He went into great detail about how he had been "sucked in" and how Churchill had "put him on the spot." Then, as if to excuse himself for the tension in U.S.-Soviet relations, Truman brought out a map of Europe and the Near East, explaining that he had tried at Potsdam to get the Rhine and Danube internationalized, as well as the Dardanelles, the Suez Canal, and the Kiel Canal.[48] Despite his "inside sources" at the State Department, Arthur Krock was forced to write that "what the President thinks of Winston Churchill's speech at Fulton, Missouri . . . is known to very few in Washington."[49]

But reporters were skeptical about Truman's claim that he had not seen Churchill's speech in advance. They pointed out that Churchill had spent an evening with the president at the White House before the speech was delivered, and British officials announced the next day that he had discussed his remarks with Truman.[50] Truman could have

[46] *Vital Speeches* 12 (March 15, 1946): 329-32; Coffin, *Missouri Compromise*, pp. 277-78.

[47] *New York Times*, March 7, 9, 1946.

[48] Wallace diary, March 12, 1946, *Price of Vision*, ed. Blum, pp. 558-59.

[49] Arthur Krock, *New York Times*, March 13, 1946.

[50] *New York Times*, March 7, 1946; Arthur Krock, ibid., March 13, 1946.

refrained from applauding if he had wished to disassociate himself from the substance of Churchill's remarks.[51] *Time* magazine's initial conclusion was that the "iron curtain speech" was a "magnificent trial balloon." One week later, however, after Truman's denials, *Time* complained that "if he had any decisive foreign policy of his own, he kept quiet about it, except that he still talked of UNO as if he still regarded it as the world's one hope of peace."[52]

Subsequent evidence shows that the reporters' suspicions were correct. A month before he was to deliver the Fulton speech, Churchill flew to Washington and discussed the contents of his address with Truman. Moreover, Truman knew that his presence on the same platform would be interpreted as tacit endorsement of Churchill's remarks because Democratic party Chairman Robert Hannegan and Joseph E. Davies warned Truman to read the speech in advance to prevent Churchill from putting him in a "box." But the president nonchalantly assured them that all Churchill would say was the usual "hands across the sea" stuff. Byrnes recalled that Truman had initially decided not to read an advance copy of the speech so that he could truthfully say he had not seen it beforehand if the Soviets charged Britain and the United States with "ganging up" on them. On the train, however, Truman changed his mind and read a mimeographed copy.[53]

But it would be oversimplifying matters to say that Truman privately endorsed the contents of Churchill's speech and that he was launching a "trial balloon." It is more likely that Truman wished to warn the Russians that there were limits to our patience, and that the United States had other alternatives to cooperation with the Soviets. By refusing to comment on Churchill's speech, however, he could continue to hold out the carrot of Soviet-American collaboration if the Soviets moderated their ambitions. Thus, Truman wrote to his mother and sister that he was "not yet ready to endorse Mr. Churchill's speech." *Newsweek* columnist Ernest K. Lindley wrote that governmental officials speaking off the record called the Anglo-American alliance an "alternative or reserve policy." Administration officials did not believe that the American people would support such a policy; more importantly, they hoped that Russia would be interested enough in heading off an Anglo-American alliance to heed our warnings. "The behavior of the Russians," Lindley reported, "will determine how soon and to what extent, if at all, Mr. Churchill's proposal is acted upon."

[51] *Newsweek*, March 18, 1946, p. 30.

[52] *Time*, March 18, 1946, p. 19; ibid., March 25, 1946, pp. 19-20.

[53] Leahy diary, February 10, 1946, LC; Davies diary, February 11, 1946, LC; Byrnes, *All in One Lifetime*, p. 349; Gaddis, *Origins of the Cold War*, p. 308.

Similarly, Arthur Krock reported that in the State Department and the Capitol, those who privately defended the speech agreed that it was time to impress the Soviet government that the Western democracies had "powerful alternatives" to which they could turn if Russia pursued a course of aggression. If Moscow suspected that the president knew the contents of the speech in advance, then that was a good psychological weapon on our side in the "war of nerves" with the Soviets.[54]

The reaction in Congress and the press to Churchill's speech was decidedly hostile. Although most "opinion leaders" agreed with Churchill's condemnation of Russia, they firmly rejected his alliance proposal. An Anglo-American alliance was criticized because it would intensify Russia's suspicions and end any hope of composing differences between her and the United States, require the United States to support Britain's empire, including traditional British spheres of influence, and effectively destroy the United Nations. In sum, although most Americans agreed with Churchill's diagnosis of the tension in great power relations, they were more optimistic about the prognosis for settling our differences with the Soviets. Analyzing the American reaction to Churchill's speech, Ambassador Halifax concluded that "profound as the uneasiness is about Soviet policies, there is still a reluctance to face the full implications of the facts." Among the American people, there was "still a strong underlying anxiety if possible to find a way of cooperation with the Russians."[55]

---

[54] M. Truman, *Harry Truman*, p. 312; Ernest K. Lindley, "What Mr. Churchill Meant," *Newsweek*, March 18, 1946, p. 36; Arthur Krock, *New York Times*, March 13, 1946. Historians who have viewed the "iron curtain" speech as Truman's "trial balloon" include Gaddis, *Origins of the Cold War*, p. 307; and Feis, *From Trust to Terror*, p. 78. Other historians have suggested that Truman privately agreed with Churchill's proposal for an Anglo-American alliance, but wished to protect himself from criticism within the United States and from the Soviet Union. See, for example, Yergin, *Shattered Peace*, pp. 174-75; and Kuniholm, *Origins of the Cold War in the Near East*, pp. 316-17. Lloyd Gardner correctly points out that Truman and Byrnes were not interested in an Anglo-American alliance, preferring to rely on public diplomacy and collective security. See *Architects of Illusion*, p. 104.

[55] *New York Times*, March 6, 7, 1946; Ernest K. Lindley, "What Mr. Churchill Meant," *Newsweek*, March 18, 1946, p. 36; *Time*, March 11, 1946, p. 19; Halifax to Foreign Office, March 10, 1946, FO 371/51606, AN 656. The American public's rejection of Winston Churchill's address belies Gaddis' thesis that domestic public opinion compelled Truman to abandon the goal of Soviet-American cooperation and adopt a "tough" policy. Gaddis attempts to gloss over the contradiction: "While the American people were anxious to 'get tough' with Russia, they were not yet fully prepared to accept the responsibilities, in the form of closer ties with Britain and other noncommunist nations, which 'getting tough' entailed" *Origins of the Cold War*, p. 309. But a careful review of the press suggests that the American people were not willing to give up the hope of reaching an accommodation with the Soviets.

INVITATION TO STALIN

The Truman administration had its first opportunity to carry out a "firmer" policy in Iran. The treaty deadline for Soviet withdrawal, March 2, 1946, came and went. The Soviets showed no signs of leaving. The Soviet press announced that a portion of Russian troops would be withdrawn from "relatively peaceful" districts in northern Iran; others would remain "pending examination of the situation." Kennan reported that the Soviets were putting "tremendous pressure" on Iranian Prime Minister Qavam for recognition of Azerbaijani autonomy, oil concessions, and agreement that Soviet troops remain indefinitely in northern Persia. Soviet troops might be withdrawn if oil concessions were granted.[56]

Over the next few weeks, Byrnes met with State Department and military officials, and formulated policy toward the Iranian crisis, while Truman sat on the sidelines. On March 5, Secretary Byrnes sent the Soviets two diplomatic notes protesting Soviet seizure of Japanese industrial equipment in Manchuria and their failure to withdraw Soviet troops from Iran. The note on Iran stated that the United States could not "remain indifferent" to the Iranian situation, and expressed hope that the Soviet government would immediately withdraw its forces from Iran.[57]

On March 6, Byrnes told the secretaries of war and navy that if the Soviet answer to our protests was not satisfactory, he would ask the British to join with us in presenting the problem to the Security Council. "If the Soviets decline to come before the Security Council on this issue," he predicted, *the United Nations Organization may well be gone and a different world be in the making.* "If this occurs," Byrnes emphasized, "it means the end of cooperation."[58]

The Soviets made no reply to the March 6 note. Meanwhile, the U.S. vice-consul at Tabriz, Robert Rossow, reported "exceptionally heavy Soviet troop movements" going toward Teheran. Two officials from the Division of Near Eastern Affairs prepared a blown-up map of Azerbaijan for Byrnes, with arrows representing Soviet troop movements in the direction of Turkey, Iraq, Teheran, and Iranian oil fields in the south. After NEA officials showed Byrnes the map and Rossow's cable, Byrnes remarked indignantly that the Russians were adding military invasion to political subversion in Iran. Beating his fist

[56] *FR: 1946*, VII, p. 335; *New York Times*, March 3, 1946; White House Daily Summary, March 4, 1946, RG 59, NA.

[57] *FR: 1946*, VII, pp. 340-42.

[58] Minutes of the Committee of Three, March 6, 1946, RG 59, NA, emphasis added.

into the other hand, Byrnes vowed "now we'll give it to them with both barrels."[59]

On March 8, Byrnes demanded an explanation from Molotov for the movement of additional Soviet forces into Iran. The Soviets again did not reply. Several days later, Byrnes told the press that Soviet troops in Iran had been heavily reinforced and were moving in three prongs toward Teheran, Turkey, and Iraq. On March 15, the *New York Times* reported that the Russians had doubled their troops in Azerbaijan to 60,000. Embarrassed by the publicity, the Soviet news agency Tass stated that the published reports of Soviet troop movements "absolutely" did not "correspond to reality."[60]

Truman told Adolf Berle that the Russians were bluffing in the sense of not being willing to risk a new world war, but they would carry on local aggression unless world opinion stopped them. He said he hoped to do this through the United Nations Organization; *beyond that he could not see.* Averell Harriman agreed that the Russians were weak, and did not want war. Like Truman, he thought Russia was making a bluff that should be called. Whenever the United States made a stand, the Soviets would retreat, although they would continue probing for opportunities to expand.[61]

As the Iranian crisis heated up, there was a groundswell of support among the policy elite for a Truman-Stalin meeting. In a speech to the Senate, Senator Tom Connally called for a resumption of the Big Three meetings of the heads of state. He explained: "In frank conversations face to face—in candid explanations eye to eye—in language clear and plain and, if need be, blunt, many questions which might otherwise result in serious international friction could be adjusted."[62] Columnist Anne O'Hare McCormick endorsed Connally's proposal for another Big Three meeting. If face-to-face discussions offered some hope of breaking the jam that blocked peacemaking, no other consideration should be allowed to stand in the way. On March 14, Walter Lippmann added his influential voice to the chorus. "Never before after a great war have the leading men of the leading powers thought they could make peace at a distance, by occasional and breathless interviews, or through minor officials," he pointed out. Lippmann rec-

[59] Daily TS Staff Summary, March 7, 1946, RG 59, NA; *FR: 1946*, VII, pp. 346-47.

[60] *New York Times*, March 13, 15, 1946; *FR: 1946*, VII, pp. 348, 356-57.

[61] Berle diary, March 15, 1946, *Navigating the Rapids*, ed. Berle and Jacobs, p. 573, emphasis added; Halifax to Foreign Office, March 19, 1946, FO 371/56840, N4152/971/38.

[62] *New York Times*, March 13, 1946.

ommended that the president make a move to reestablish direct contact with Stalin.[63]

The next day, Truman confided to Berle that he had decided on a policy toward Russia; to keep every agreement we make and to expect them to keep every agreement they make. Having no policy, the "code of the politician" served for Truman as a guide to action. In contrast, Byrnes was saying privately that he could not go on talking to the Soviet Union in defense of our principles, as he had in Iran, if the United States continued its rapid demobilization. Either the United States would have to make concessions or stop demobilization. For Byrnes, unilateral adherence by the United States to international commitments was no guarantee that the Soviets would do the same.

Truman told Berle that he was not looking to another meeting of the Big Three. He was ready to have it, but was not prepared to go out and beg for it.[64] But Truman was prepared to go very far indeed to obtain a meeting with Stalin. On March 19, the *New York Times* reported that tensions in Teheran had subsided, and there were no new reports of Russian troop movements. But the crisis was not over, because Soviet troops were still in Iran. Yet, Truman made a gesture that would undercut the firm policy his administration had initiated toward the Soviet Union. He composed a cordial letter to Stalin:

> When leaving you at Potsdam, I expressed the hope that you would find it possible to visit the United States and be my guest. You were kind enough to say that you would like to do that. Why can you not arrange to come at this time. I certainly would be delighted to have you do so.[65]

He gave the letter to the new ambassador to Moscow, General Walter Bedell Smith.[66] There is no evidence that Truman consulted with his secretary of state before deciding on a new diplomatic initiative. Byrnes probably would not have approved of inviting Stalin to visit Washington, in the midst of an explosive international crisis. That same day, Byrnes abruptly refused Gromyko's request that the Security Council's discussion of the Iranian complaint be postponed for a few weeks. He intended to place Soviet subversion and blackmail in Iran

---

[63] Walter Lippmann, *Washington Post*, March 14, 1946; *New York Times*, March 13, 1946.

[64] Berle diary, March 15, 1946, *Navigating the Rapids*, ed. Berle and Jacobs, p. 573; Minutes of the Committee of Three, March 6, 1946, RG 59, NA.

[65] Truman to Stalin, March 19, 1946, Truman Papers, PSF: "Russia: Stalin," HSTL.

[66] Daily TS Staff Summary, March 19, 1946, RG 59, NA; Walter Bedell Smith, *My Three Years in Moscow* (Philadelphia: J. B. Lippincott, 1950), pp. 27-28, 47.

under the bright glare of public diplomacy in the United Nations, instead of trying to work out a deal privately with Stalin as he had at the Moscow Conference.

In contrast, Under Secretary of State Acheson shared Truman's perception that despite Soviet aggression in Iran, the United States could not afford to break off diplomatic contact with the Soviet Union or stop trying to develop a cooperative relationship. In the atmosphere of tension and fear brought about by the exposure of a Soviet atomic spy ring in Canada, Stalin's February 9 speech, and the Iranian crisis, Acheson worked with a special committee to devise a plan for international control of atomic energy that would have some chances of Soviet acceptance. In January 1946, Byrnes had asked Acheson to head a special committee on international control of atomic energy, whose other members included Dr. Vannevar Bush, former director of the Office of Scientific Research and Development; Dr. James B. Conant, president of Harvard; General Leslie R. Groves, commander of the Manhattan Project; and John J. McCloy, former assistant secretary of war.[67]

Acheson persuaded the committee to appoint a board of consultants that would investigate and report on methods of control and inspection of atomic weapons. David Lilienthal, chairman of the Tennessee Valley Authority, was appointed chairman of the board of consultants because he was "experienced in statecraft as well as familiar with technological and scientific matters." The most influential consultant was J. Robert Oppenheimer, the brilliant physicist who had played an indispensable role in the development of the atomic bomb. It was Oppenheimer who provided the core of an elegant, innovative approach to the problem of controlling atomic energy. Instead of charging an international agency with the impossible task of policing the world to ensure against the clandestine production of atomic weapons, Oppenheimer proposed the creation of an atomic development authority that would have a monopoly on all "dangerous" activities related to atomic energy, maintaining exclusive ownership of the world's sources of uranium and thorium. The agency would be responsible for mining and refining atomic raw materials, leasing measured amounts of uranium to nations for peaceful use of atomic energy in research, medicine, and commercial power plants. Inspection of other nations' atomic research facilities would be an integral part of the international agency's activities in research, development, and production of atomic energy. But

[67] Interview with Acheson, 16 February 1955, Truman Papers, Post-Presidential Files, HSTL; Hewlett and Anderson, *New World*, p. 531.

the agency would not rely solely on inspection to prevent nations from building atomic bombs. Through its ownership of uranium and thorium, the international authority could determine if a state were illegally diverting atomic materials for unauthorized research. The key phrase, the consultants felt, was "security through cooperative development," as a substitute for "control."[68]

The final Acheson-Lilienthal report was drafted at several joint meetings of the Acheson committee and the panel of advisers in early March 1946. Lilienthal recorded in his diary that at times an "unimaginable gloom" hung over the committee, brought about by the "the terrible realities of the bomb, so close to us in our work, and the constant fear of a long, bitter period of antagonism and strain and perhaps war with the Russians." Acheson warned committee members of the "Russian situation and how it may disintegrate in the Middle East in the very near future." Yet, he firmly and unequivocally quashed one member's suggestion that Russia should be asked to "open up" its society or disarm as the price for international control of atomic energy. Change of the Russian system was not subject to negotiation, Acheson said. Acheson predicted that the United States was in for a long period of tension with the Soviets. The best we could do was to hope for Russia's "gradual civilization." Reminding his listeners of an episodic script, Acheson said that the situation facing them was much like the Washington Disarmament Conference of 1921-1922. The idea of preventing a naval race was a good one, even though the content of the treaties was flawed. Similarly, the consultant's proposal for atomic energy control might be faulty; but that was no reason to discard the approach.[69]

Publicly, Truman maintained a firm posture toward the Soviets. On March 21, President Truman flatly refused Gromyko's request for postponement of the Security Council meeting in what was described as the first application of the American posture of "firmness" toward the Soviet Union. With some irritation, Truman also discouraged suggestions for another meeting of the Big Three. Truman's excuse was that the U.N.O. was supposed to take over questions discussed by the

[68] Lilienthal diary, January 16, 20, 22, 24, 1946, David E. Lilienthal, *The Journals of David E. Lilienthal* (New York: Harper & Row, 1964), vol. 2, *The Atomic Energy Years, 1945-1950*, pp. 10-14; Hewlett and Anderson, *New World*, pp. 533-34, 536-38, 543-44; Acheson, *Present at the Creation*, p. 152; Gregg Herken, *The Winning Weapon: The Atomic Bomb in the Cold War, 1945-1950* (New York: Alfred A. Knopf, 1980), pp. 155-56; McLellan, *Dean Acheson*, p. 78; Smith, *Dean Acheson*, p. 41.

[69] Hewlett and Anderson, *New World*, pp. 545-46; McLellan, *Dean Acheson*, pp. 79-80; Lilienthal diary, March 9, 17, 1946, Lilienthal, *Atomic Energy Years*, pp. 28, 30.

Big Three, and it was time that the organization assumed that responsibility if there was to be peace in the world. Truman added that the next meeting of the Big Three—if any—would have to take place in the United States.[70]

In northwestern Iran, the Kurds launched a large-scale uprising against the Iranian government. There were reports that the Soviets were arming and training Kurds in Iran and smuggling arms to Kurds in Iraq and Turkey. If the Kurdish revolt succeeded, the Soviets would have two buffer states in northern Iran.[71]

Then Stalin made a conciliatory gesture, vindicating Truman's faith that he could do business with the Russian dictator. On March 22, in answer to questions submitted by an Associated Press correspondent, Stalin declared that he attached "great importance to the UNO as it is a serious instrument for the preservation of peace and international security." He added that no nations wanted war. President Truman and members of Congress hailed Stalin's statement. Truman said he always knew that Premier Stalin intended to place his full confidence and support behind the United Nations.[72]

The same day, Truman held a long, informal meeting with Ambassador Smith to discuss what he should say to Stalin. Afterwards, Truman jotted in the margin of his appointment book: "Told him to tell Stalin I had always held him to be a man to keep his word. Troops in Iran after March 2 upset that theory. Also told him to urge Stalin to come to U.S.A." Despite his worry over Soviet troops in Iran, Truman was not prepared to give up his belief that Stalin, like Pendergast, could be trusted to keep his promises.[73] Meanwhile, Byrnes was trying to "nail the Russians" to a promise before the Security Council that they would withdraw their troops in six weeks, vowing that he had "nursed" the Soviets for the last time.[74]

Truman's invitation to Stalin was not an empty gesture to appease public opinion, because it was kept secret. Ambassador Smith denied to reporters that he was carrying any instructions about a possible meeting between Truman and Stalin.

On March 27, the *New York Times* reported that Soviet troops had withdrawn from Karaj, twenty-four miles outside Teheran. Soviet forces were leaving other parts of Iran as well. Tensions that had been

[70] *New York Times*, March 22, 1946.

[71] Ibid., March 21, 1946.

[72] Ibid., March 23, 1946.

[73] Smith, *Dean Acheson*, pp. 27-28; Daily Sheets, March 23, 1946, Truman Papers, PSF: Presidential Appointment File, HSTL.

[74] Stettinius Calendar Notes, March 24, 1946.

at a peak for two weeks suddenly eased.[75] But Iran was not "saved" from the Russians. The Iranians had to agree to a joint Soviet-Iranian oil company in return for withdrawal of Soviet troops within six weeks. The Soviets still had a buffer zone in northern Iran. Further, Prime Minister Qavam was pro-Russian, and State Department officials feared that he was following a policy of appeasement toward the USSR.[76] As the *New York Times* military analyst Hanson Baldwin pointed out,

> we must recognize, then, that Northern Iran, Manchuria, and Northern Korea are and will be Russian in all but name. They are definite spheres of Soviet influence. . . . Russian interest in these areas is not a product of the Communist regime; it is centuries old. The chief difference is that today Russia has the power to support her interests in these areas, and no one else has the power to stop her.[77]

On April 4, Ambassador Smith had a long, late-night interview with Stalin at the Kremlin. The interpreter Pavlov read Truman's invitation to Stalin, but the Russian dictator said nothing.

"What does the Soviet Union want and how far is the Soviet Union going to go?" Smith asked bluntly. Although the United States could understand and appreciate the Soviet Union's desire for security and raw materials, Soviet *methods* were creating some apprehension. As Truman had instructed him, Smith said that both the president and Secretary of State Byrnes had always believed that when the Generalissimo made a promise he intended to keep it. But it would be misinterpreting the character of the American people to assume that because we were basically peaceful and deeply interested in world security that we were divided, weak, or unwilling to face our responsibilities. If faced with a wave of aggression by any powerful nation, the American people would respond as they had in the past.

When Smith had finished, Stalin refuted his arguments at length, speaking quietly and pleasantly. Stalin claimed he had made known to President Truman and Secretary Byrnes the reasons why the Soviet Union could not withdraw its troops by March 2, and had encountered no objections at the time.

"You don't understand our situation as regards oil and Iran," Stalin

[75] *New York Times*, March 27, 1946.

[76] Barry Rubin, *The Great Powers in the Middle East, 1941-1947: The Road to the Cold War* (London: Cass, 1980), p. 179; *FR: 1946*, VII, pp. 405-407; Daily TS Staff Summary, April 5, 1946, RG 59, NA.

[77] *New York Times*, March 27, 1946.

explained. "The Baku oil fields are our major source of supply. They are close to the Iranian border and they are very vulnerable. Beria and others tell me that saboteurs—even a man with a box of matches— might cause us serious damage."[78]

Smith reminded Stalin that he had not answered his original question: "How far is Russia going to go?" "We're not going much further," Stalin answered.

"You say 'not much further,'" Smith pressed him, "but does that 'much' have any reference to Turkey?"

"I have assured President Truman and have stated publicly that the Soviet Union has no intention of attacking Turkey nor does this intention exist," Stalin said. On the other hand, the Soviet Union was conscious of the danger of foreign control of the Straits, which Turkey was too weak to protect. That was why the Soviets demanded a base in the Dardanelles. Smith objected that this was the kind of problem which should be handled by the United Nations. Surprisingly, Stalin then said that the USSR could possibly agree that as an alternative the Security Council of the United Nations might be able to undertake this responsibility. But the State Department did not respond to this overture, if indeed it was genuine. The Soviet Union had never responded officially to the U.S. note of November 1945 proposing a new regime for the Turkish Straits.

At the end of the interview, Stalin finally got around to Truman's invitation. He said he would very much like to visit the United States, but "age has taken its toll." His doctors told him not to travel long distances and kept him on a strict diet. "I will write to the President and tell him why I cannot now accept his invitation." But he never did.[79]

At a May press conference, Truman revealed that he had twice invited Stalin to come to the United States for a social visit, but the Russian premier had to decline for reasons of health. Because of Stalin's consistent refusals, Truman did not see any prospects for a summit meeting soon.[80]

Publicly, Secretary of State Byrnes maintained a "firm" policy toward the Soviet Union in the wake of the Iranian crisis. At an April

[78] Contrary to later Cold War historians, Stalin's explanation may not have been entirely disingenuous. The Soviets recalled that after World War I, British troops had invaded Soviet Azerbaijan from Iran and occupied the oil center of Baku. Faramarz S. Fatemi, *The U.S.S.R. in Iran* (South Brunswick and New York: A. S. Barnes and Co., 1980), pp. 171-72.

[79] Smith, *Dean Acheson*, pp. 48-54; *FR: 1946*, VII, pp. 732-36.

[80] *New York Times*, June 1, 1946.

19 cabinet meeting, Byrnes predicted that the Russians would deliberately obstruct the peace treaty for Italy at the forthcoming Council of Foreign Ministers meeting in Paris, to force the United States to meet their demands for a Soviet trusteeship over the Dodecanese Islands and Tripolitania. "Russia is extremely anxious to maintain a military base in the Mediterranean," he said.[81]

Byrnes also frankly described to the press the difficulties he foresaw with the Russians. In a series of off-the-record briefings, he emphasized that there would be no peace treaties unless the Russians withdrew their demands in the Mediterranean. Harriman told columnist C. L. Sulzberger that "we are not going to yield at Paris." Byrnes let it be known that he intended to be "patient but firm" with the Russians.[82] To back up our diplomatic stance, Byrnes took steps to improve the military balance on the European continent. In a top secret briefing, Secretary Byrnes informed the Senate Foreign Relations Committee that the 300,000 "green" draftees stationed in Europe were undergoing rigorous combat training. In addition, the United States had recalled combat-efficient B-29s from the Pacific, and was deploying them in Western Europe and Britain.[83]

At the same time, however, Byrnes authorized Ben Cohen to discuss with U.S. military authorities the possibility of offering the Soviets a base on the Dardanelles, Tripolitania, or the Dodecanese Islands, in return for a twenty-year cooling-off period in which the Soviets would promise not to make any further demands in the Mediterranean. As Cohen explained in a memorandum to Byrnes, the United States and the Soviet Union were in a state of continual struggle and contention over areas where the Russians had the power to obtain their objectives unilaterally. For example, after all the ill feeling and political uproar caused by Russian actions in Iran, in the end the USSR had attained all that they had set out to achieve. Since we were not ready to fight for Iran, Cohen reasoned, it was worth considering a policy by which the United States acceded to Russian proposals in areas where the Soviets could achieve their objectives anyway, and thereby avoid all the political turmoil. Admiral Leahy commented drily that the proposal would have merit if Soviet agreements had any value. Colonel

[81] *FR: 1946*, VII, p. 130; Notes on Cabinet Meeting, April 19, 1946, Connelly Papers, HSTL; McNaughton Report, April 20, 1946, HSTL; Notes on Cabinet Meeting, April 19, 1946, Forrestal Papers, Princeton.

[82] Ward, *Threat of Peace*, pp. 88-89; "Conversion of Our Three Peace Bargainers to Tough Attitude," *U.S. News*, May 3, 1946, p. 54; Sulzberger diary, April 22, 1946, *Long Row of Candles*, p. 311.

[83] McNaughton Report, April 20, 1946, HSTL.

McCormack and General Lincoln pointed out that the official State Department estimate was that the Soviet Union was an expansionist totalitarian state. Should there be a war, they continued, the United States would need a "cushion of states" between Russia and vital strategic areas such as Suez and Gibraltar to prevent Eurasia from being subjugated by a rapid Russian blitz.[84]

As yet, Byrnes had no fixed opinions or set beliefs regarding Soviet foreign policy objectives or the best means of accommodating Soviet power within the U.S. vision for world order. Thus, if a "tough" policy toward Soviet demands in the Mediterranean failed, Byrnes was willing to try "appeasement" in the classical diplomatic sense of acceding to an opponent's limited and legitimate demands as a means of stabilizing a troubled area.

In addition, Byrnes was prepared to acknowledge Soviet predominance over Eastern Europe, although he hoped to persuade the Soviets to open up their sphere to normal political and commercial intercourse with the West. Byrnes told the Senate Foreign Relations Committee in closed session that the United States would no longer withhold provisional recognition simply because we did not approve of a regime. Byrnes rationalized the change in U.S. policy with the argument that keeping a minister or ambassador on the ground would enable us to keep informed and make stronger representations concerning unsatisfactory developments.[85]

The Paris Conference of the Council of Foreign Ministers opened on April 25, then adjourned in mid-May for a month's recess. Still unresolved were such issues as the disposition of the Italian colonies, Italian reparations, the Dodecanese Islands, Trieste, and the Balkan treaties. In the meantime, the U.S. delegation hoped that Stalin would instruct Molotov to adopt a more moderate position on which a settlement could be based. In return, Byrnes was prepared to recede from the maximum American position. He did not yet regard as inevitable the division of Europe along the lines of the occupation frontiers.[86]

---

[84] Memorandum for the Record, General Lincoln, 16 April 1946, ABC 334.8 Iran (30 Oct. 43), RG 165, NA; Leahy diary, April 17, 1946, LC; Memorandum by Matthews to SWNCC, April 1, 1946, *FR: 1946*, I, pp. 1167-71; Weil, *A Pretty Good Club*, pp. 235-36. See also Memorandum for General Hull, 19 April 1946, ABC 336 Russia (22 Aug. 43), Sec. 1-C, RG 165, NA; Memorandum by General Lincoln for General Hull, "The Turkish Straits," n.d., Matthews-Hickerson Files, "Turkey," RG 59, NA; Lincoln to Cohen, June 22, 1946, ABC 381 (1 Sept. 45), Sec. 1-A, RG 165, NA.

[85] McNaughton Report, April 20, 1946, HSTL.

[86] Ibid., May 18, 1946.

THE CLIFFORD-ELSEY REPORT

On June 15, the Council of Foreign Ministers met in Paris for what the *New York Times* described as "one more chance" at restoring allied cooperation. The results of the conference would determine whether there would be One World or a marked acceleration of the trend toward splitting the world in two.[87] But the meeting ended with acrimonious disputes over the future of Germany and Austria, the heart of Europe.

On July 9, Molotov read a statement attacking Byrnes' proposed four-power German demilitarization treaty on specious grounds. He criticized Western occupation authorities for their failure to eliminate German economic war potential and to eradicate fascism. Molotov renewed the Soviet demand for $10 billion in German reparations, which supposedly had been heard for the last time at Potsdam. Then, the next day, Molotov made a startling about-face. He advocated loosening the restrictions placed on German economic production. Hinting that the Western powers still favored dismemberment and agrarianization of Germany, he claimed that the Soviet government felt that the spirit of revenge was a poor guide to policy. Before discussions could begin on a German peace treaty, a unified democratic government should be set up. Thus, Molotov posed as the defender of German political unity against the vengeful Western powers.[88] The Soviet foreign minister also refused to begin work on the Austrian peace treaty until 437,000 foreign citizens, including Russian White Guards, were forcibly repatriated.[89] The conference adjourned on July 12 after several days of bitter wrangling over the German and Austrian treaties.

The same day, the president was relaxing in the late afternoon with close advisers Matt Connelly, Charlie Ross, and Clark Clifford. Truman began to think aloud about U.S. policy toward the Soviet Union. "Now is the time to take a stand on Russia," he declared. He was tired of our being pushed around, "here a little, there a little." "They are chiseling from us," Truman complained. He vowed that the "Paris Conference will bust up—be a failure if Russians want too much because we are not going to back down." If it did fail, he intended to go on the air to present the facts to the world.

Although Byrnes was not ready to "get tough" with Russia, he was discouraged by his inability to negotiate or even communicate with

[87] *New York Times* editorial, June 13, 1946.

[88] McNeill, *America, Britain, and Russia*, p. 726; Ward, *Threat of Peace*, pp. 119-21; *FR: 1946*, II, pp. 842-47, 869-73.

[89] *FR: 1946*, II, pp. 913-16, 928-37, 939-40.

the intransigent Molotov. The secretary of state no longer believed that negotiating with the Soviets was analogous to arranging cloakroom deals with the Republicans. He wrote to Joseph Ball:

> We cannot hope to change the thinking of the people of the Soviet Union. That is our trouble. Ordinarily when you can agree with one on a statement of facts you can expect to reach a conclusion. That is not true when mental operations of people differ as widely as in the case of the gentleman who represents the Soviet Union and ourselves.

Truman asked Clifford to draft a speech and plan out a campaign to educate the public. As the body of the speech, Truman requested that Clifford compile a list of U.S.-Soviet agreements and the manner in which the Soviets had violated their commitments. He was still following the "code of the politician" in his foreign policy. Truman also sketched out a few rough ideas. He could talk about the attitude of appeasement and its results, renewed demands. Was it true that our "firmness" had made Russia live up to its agreements? The next day, Clifford farmed out the assignment to George Elsey, his assistant. Elsey wanted to go beyond Truman's original assignment to prepare a report on the nature and motivation of Soviet foreign policy. Not sharing Truman's belief in the "code of the politician," Elsey felt that Soviet violations of their agreements were only a symptom of the malady; our concern was *why* the Soviets violated their agreements, not *how*. Clifford was reluctant but finally acceded to Elsey's logic.[90]

Elsey drafted memoranda under the president's signature requesting information on Soviet activities affecting U.S. security and sent off copies to the joint chiefs, the attorney general, and the secretaries of state, war and navy. He also studied numerous diplomatic cables drafted by George Kennan from January through April 1946. Acheson shared Elsey's feeling that whether the Soviets violated their agreements was not so important as the underlying conflict of objectives that made it impossible for the Soviet Union and the United States to have a common understanding of the basic concepts and terms of their agreements. In a letter transmitting the State Department's list of Soviet treaty violations, Acheson observed:

> Much of the difficulty regarding the implementation of agreements to which the United States and the U.S.S.R. are signatories results

---

[90] Handwritten memorandum by Elsey, 12 July 1946, George M. Elsey Papers, "Foreign Relations—Russia 1946 Report," HSTL; Telephone Memorandum, CMC Instructions, 13 July 1946, ibid.; Memorandum by Elsey to Clifford, 8 August 1946, ibid.; James Byrnes to Joseph H. Ball, July 22, 1946, Byrnes Papers, folder 225, Clemson.

from the divergence of objective with which the two countries approach postwar problems. As a result, many of the acts of the Soviet Government appear to the United States Government to be violations of the spirit of an international agreement although it is difficult to adduce acceptable evidence of literal violations.

From time to time, Truman prodded Clifford to make sure he was working on the Russian report.[91] He was anxious to have an authoritative interpretation of Soviet policy. Truman was still fundamentally undecided and ambivalent toward Russia. He told Henry Wallace that the United States had to be patient with Russia because it had come a long way in a short period of time. Truman said he hoped that it would not be many years before the USSR became a democracy. As an indication that he was still interested in Soviet-American cooperation, the president said he had been reading about the 1815 Congress of Vienna in his spare time. Then, within the same hour, Truman agreed with the anti-Soviet jibes made by Secretary Byrnes at a cabinet luncheon. Amazed, Wallace commented in his diary that:

> I suspect there has never been a President who could move two different directions with less time intervening than Truman. He feels completely sincere and earnest at all times and is not disturbed in the slightest by the different directions in which his mind can go almost simultaneously.[92]

On August 7, 1946, the Soviets escalated their pressure against Turkey by formally requesting a share in the defense of the Dardanelles, and sole determination by the Black Sea powers of a new regime for the Straits.[93] At the Potsdam Conference in July-August 1945, the United States and Britain had agreed that the Montreux Convention was outdated and in need of revision. But the Soviet proposals would have completely overturned the Montreux Convention, establishing an entirely new regime dominated by the Soviet Union. Under the Soviet plan, Britain, France, Greece, and Yugoslavia—all signatories to the Montreux Convention—would be excluded from having any voice in formulating the Turkish Straits regime. Further, State Department officials interpreted the reference to joint Soviet-Turkish de-

---

[91] Handwritten memorandum, 17 July 1946, Elsey Papers, "Foreign Relations—Russia 1946 Report," HSTL; Handwritten memorandum, undated, approx. early September, ibid.; Acheson to Clifford, "Comments on Soviet Compliance with International Agreements Undertaken since January 1941," August 6, 1946, 711.61/7-1846, RG 59, NA.

[92] Wallace diary, July 23, 24, 1946, *Price of Vision*, ed. Blum, pp. 587-88, 602-603.

[93] Daily TS Staff Summary, August 9, 1946, RG 59, NA; *FR: 1946*, VII, pp. 827-29.

fense of the Dardanelles as a pretext for Soviet naval bases on the Straits.[94]

Acting Secretary of State Acheson devised and orchestrated a forceful American response to the Soviet démarche. On August 14, Acheson called a State-War-Navy conference in his office. A briefing memo prepared in advance by the State Department concluded that the Soviet demands provided further evidence of their determination to expand into the Mediterranean. Soviet control over the Turkish Straits would not be sufficient to afford the USSR assured access to the high seas, because they would also have to control both the Aegean Islands and either the Suez Canal-Red Sea littorals or the Gibraltar Straits. The Soviets did not need a base on the Dardanelles for defensive reasons either, because the Straits could be useful to a hostile state only after the destruction of Soviet air power.

Military officials had independently arrived at similar conclusions about Soviet motives in demanding a base on the Straits. According to an analysis prepared in the War Department's Operations Division, it would be possible to close the Straits by air action launched from several hundred miles away, or by naval action some distance from the exits of the Straits. Hence, there was no military rationale for the Soviet demand for fortifications on the Straits to assure free passage for Russian ships during war. "No such rights could be effective as a *defensive* measure." But, the operation of a base would enable the Soviets to exert intolerable pressure on Turkey, transforming that country into a Soviet satellite. A Russian military presence in Turkey could also be used to threaten Crete, Cyprus, and Greece. "From the above, it can only be concluded that from the military point of view, Soviet demands for military rights in the area of the Straits are long range and strategic in nature and *essentially aggressive*."[95]

Having excluded possible security considerations involved in their request for a share in defending the Straits, U.S. officials inferred that the Russians had long-range plans to expand into the Mediterranean. Yet, the Soviets were asking for no more than the privileges enjoyed by the United States in the Panama Canal and the British in the Suez and Gibraltar Straits. Indeed, the State Department briefing memo conceded that while "no consistent policy has been established under

---

[94] Jonathan Knight, "American Statecraft and the 1946 Black Sea Straits Controversy," *Political Science Quarterly*, 90 (Fall 1975): 460; *FR: 1946*, VII, p. 830.

[95] "USSR Proposes Restrictive Revision of Straits Convention," August 14, 1946, Source: SD, August 13, 1946, ABC 093 Kiel (6 July 45), Sec. 1-B, RG 165, NA; "Military Considerations Involved in the Problem of the Turkish Straits," ABC 093 Kiel (6 July 45), Sec. 1-B, RG 165, NA.

international law regarding control over Seaway passages analogous to the Straits . . . in general in practice the special interests of particular states has [*sic*] been recognized." American policymakers assumed that American control over the Panama Canal was justified because of U.S. security requirements, while inferring that the Soviets' demand for a comparable position in the Turkish Straits was evidence of aggressive intent.[96]

This reasoning also assumed that the Soviets' calculation of their security interests was identical to that of U.S. military officials, and ignored the recent Russian wartime experience. During the early part of the war, when the Germans were winning, Turkey had allowed Axis warships and naval auxiliaries to sail through the Straits. The Soviet note of August 7, 1946, cited these infractions of the Montreux Convention as proof that the existing regime "does not meet the interests of the safety of the Black Sea Powers." But U.S. officials were unable to adopt the perspective of the Soviets.[97]

Further, the Soviets may well have believed that their demands on Turkey were justifiable and acceptable to the West. Britain's power was no longer sufficient to support the empire, and the British would soon be forced to retrench in the Mediterranean. Since the age of classical imperialism, the territories and spheres of influence of a declining power had been regarded as fair game for a stronger military power. The only other rival to the Soviets had laid no claims to a sphere of influence in the Middle East. Indeed, in November 1945, the United States in effect recognized Russia's special rights in the Turkish Straits, based on geographical proximity, when the State Department proposed to the Soviet Union and Britain that the Dardanelles be closed to all warships but those belonging to the Black Sea powers. This would have transformed the Dardanelles into a Soviet naval lake. Further, the Soviet "war of nerves" against Turkey—conducted through military force demonstrations, shrill propaganda, and diplomatic pressure—occasioned not a word of protest on the part of the United States.[98]

At the August 14 meeting, Acheson presented a brief for a U.S. commitment to defend Turkey against Soviet political and even mili-

[96] "USSR Proposes Restrictive Revision of Straits Convention," 14 August 1946, Source: SD, 13 August 1946, ABC 093 Kiel (6 July 45), Sec. 1-B, RG 165, NA. This is an example of the "actor-observer" fallacy described by Jones and Nisbett, "The Actor and Observer"; Jones, "How Do People Perceive the Causes of Behavior?"

[97] De Luca, "Soviet-American Politics and the Turkish Straits," pp. 507-508, 523; *FR: 1946*, VII, pp. 827-28.

[98] Ulam, *Expansion and Coexistence*, pp. 430-31.

tary pressure. He pointed out that Turkey was the only country that could serve as a useful military bastion between the USSR and Soviet domination of the eastern Mediterranean and penetration into Africa. Hence, Turkish independence must be preserved for reasons of Middle Eastern strategy. "For *global reasons*," Acheson said, "Turkey must be preserved if we do not wish to see other bulwarks in Western Europe and the Far East begin crumbling at a fast rate." Acheson argued that "the only real deterrent to Soviet plans for engulfing Turkey and the Middle East will be the conviction that the pursuance of such a policy will result in a war with the United States." Military representatives at the meeting agreed with Acheson's analysis and the draft policy he presented.[99]

On August 15, Acheson, accompanied by representatives of the War and Navy Departments, presented the proposed policy to the president. Acheson told President Truman that it was the consensus of the group that the principal objective of the Russian request for a military base on the Straits was to gain control of Turkey. He then advanced a version of what would later be called the domino theory. "In our opinion," Acheson said, "the establishment by the Soviet Union of bases in the Dardanelles or the introduction of Soviet armed forces into Turkey on some other pretext would . . . [result] in Greece and the whole Near and Middle East, including the Eastern Mediterranean, falling under Soviet control and in those areas being cut off from the Western world." Once the Soviet Union had obtained full mastery of this territory, which was strategically important in terms of natural resources and communications, it would be in a much stronger position to expand into India and China. It was unfortunate that the Soviet Union had made a formal proposal to Turkey for revision of the Straits regime, because once the Soviets were committed to a position, it was almost impossible to persuade them to retreat. "The only thing which will deter the Russians will be the conviction that the United States is prepared, if necessary, to meet aggression with force of arms," Acheson declared flatly. Therefore, "the time has come when we must decide that we shall resist with all means at our disposal *any Soviet aggression*." The USSR should be made to understand that the United States would not hesitate to use its armed forces to defend Turkey.[100]

[99] Notes made by John McCloy, ABC 093 Kiel (6 July 45), Sec. 1-B, RG 165, NA, emphasis in original; Memorandum for General Eisenhower, August 15, 1946, ABC 093 Kiel (6 July 1945), RG 319, NA; "Possible Program in Connection with Turkey," General Lincoln, August 15, 1946, ABC 093 Kiel (6 July 45), Sec. 1-B, RG 165, NA.

[100] *FR: 1946*, VII, pp. 840-42, emphasis added; Memorandum for General Eisenhower, August 15, 1946, ABC 093 Kiel (6 July 45), RG 319, NA.

President Truman quickly gave his approval to the policy suggested by Acheson. "We might as well find out whether the Russians were bent on world conquest now as in five or ten years," Truman said. He added that he was prepared to pursue the policy "to the end." The president also approved the dispatch of a powerful U.S. naval task force to the Mediterranean, including the carrier *Franklin D. Roosevelt*.[101]

On August 19, Acheson informed the Soviet government that the Turkish Straits regime was a matter of concern to the United States as well as the Black Sea powers. And the United States firmly believed that Turkey should continue to be responsible for defending the Straits.[102]

When confronted by American resolve, demonstrated through the U.S. note and naval force demonstrations, the Soviets quickly backed off. The Soviets waited a month to reply, and the tone of their newest note on the Dardanelles was viewed as much "softer." Nothing more was heard about Soviet ambitions in the Turkish Straits.[103]

Though the Russians had quickly retreated from their demands on Turkey, the Turkish Straits crisis had a lasting impact on Acheson's beliefs about the Soviet Union. Acheson now believed that the Soviets would not be content with a limited sphere of influence in Eastern Europe, but had unlimited expansionist goals. The Soviet Union would flow into any tempting political vacuum. Further, the international system was "tightly coupled," such that expansion of Soviet influence into one country would have immediate repercussions on neighboring areas and eventually around the world. In an August 25 article in the *New York Times Magazine*, James Reston documented the change in Acheson's beliefs about the Soviet Union. "With Archie MacLeish he fought in the policy committees of the State Department . . . for a liberal policy toward the Soviet Union," Reston wrote. "He was never doctrinaire about it, and when the facts seemed to him to merit a change—as he seems to think they now do in the case of the Soviet Union—he switched with the facts."[104]

He had reached these conclusions on the basis of the military opinion that Soviet fortifications on the Turkish Straits were neither nec-

[101] *FR: 1946*, VII, p. 840; Forrestal diary, 15 August 1946, *The Forrestal Diaries*, ed. Millis, p. 192; Jones, *Fifteen Weeks*, p. 62; Acheson, *Present at the Creation*, p. 195; Knight, "American Statecraft and the 1946 Black Sea Straits Controversy," p. 467.

[102] *FR: 1946*, VII, pp. 843-44, 847-48.

[103] Ibid., pp. 860-66; Daily TS Staff Summary, September 30, 1946, RG 59, NA.

[104] James Reston, "The No. 1 No. 2 Man in Washington," *New York Times Magazine*, August 25, 1946, p. 8.

essary nor sufficient to prevent a hostile power from forcing the Dardanelles. Yet, the Soviets were requesting the same rights enjoyed by the United States and Britain in waterways adjacent to their areas of vital interest. A week before the Soviet government presented its desiderata on the Straits regime, Gromyko posed this question to Joseph Davies:

> What if your neighbors, Mexico and Panama, were to claim the right to control the Panama Canal, and establish military bases for such control so as to enable them to determine whether the use of the canal should be denied to the United States? What if Russia and Britain were to sustain Mexico and Panama in that position, on the ground that it would serve to preserve World Peace? Would your country permit it?[105]

Thus, Acheson was guilty of the "actor-observer" fallacy identified by attribution theorists: he attributed the actions of the Soviet Union to the "internal" expansionist ambitions of its leaders, while inferring that comparable policies of the United States were a response to "external" geopolitical factors. Instead of resorting to a facile historical analogy, making an off-the-cuff judgment, or trying to preserve a favorable image of the Soviet Union by distorting the evidence, Acheson deliberately tried to infer the reasons for Soviet pressures on Turkey. As attribution theory would predict, he acted as any good scientist in developing alternative hypotheses—defense, access to warm water, domination of Turkey—about Soviet motives and matching them to the available evidence. But Acheson and other U.S. officials succumbed to the actor-observer fallacy because they could not adopt the perspective of the opponent.

It might be argued that Acheson's response exemplifies self-righteousness or the inability of a state's leaders to perceive how its actions might be viewed as threatening. But the reality is more complex. It was his *explanation* of the Soviet "war of nerves" on Turkey that led to a change in Acheson's image of the Soviet Union. A good Realist, Acheson acknowledged and accepted Soviet security interests in Eastern Europe. In a November 1945 speech, for example, he declared: "We understand and agree with them that to have friendly governments along her borders is essential both for the security of the Soviet Union and for the peace of the world." But although Soviet domination of Eastern Europe was a legacy of the war and justifiable by geography and Russian security requirements, Soviet demands in Turkey

---

[105] Davies diary, July 30, 1946, LC.

were an entirely new and dangerous manifestation of Soviet postwar goals.[106]

Acheson also failed to make use of the information conveyed by a *nonevent*, the "extraordinarily mild" response of the Soviet Union to the unprecedented assertion by the United States of an interest in the Turkish Straits regime. The failure of the Soviets to respond belligerently to the U.S. note of August 19 should have suggested that the Soviet bargaining position was quite weak. The Soviets had no troops stationed in Turkey, the Turkish government was stable, and the Communist party had no base of support.[107] In short, there was little the Soviets could do but engage in "bluff and bluster." In pressing the Turkish government for a naval base, the Soviet government was undoubtedly probing, albeit clumsily, for the U.S. reaction to their inclusion of Turkey in the Soviet "security belt"; there had been no serious discussions between the two countries concerning the division of influence in the Near and Middle East.

At about the same time, Byrnes resigned himself to the division of the world into "two blocs," but in response to a different set of events. Largely at Byrnes' insistence, the deliberations of the Paris peace conference were opened to the press. The secretary of state commented privately that "the more hell raised by small powers the better." Harold Nicolson, a veteran of Versailles, aptly characterized the proceedings as a "public performance, not a serious discussion."[108]

Yet, the public tableau did much to shape Byrnes' changed outlook toward the Soviet Union. The U.S. proposals for equality of economic opportunity in the Axis satellites and international control of the Danube provoked new heights of polemic from the Russian delegation. The theme of the Soviet propaganda was that the United States, having enriched itself during the war, now sought to enslave the countries of Eastern Europe through economic penetration. "Not a single argument of any sense at all," Nicolson commented, "just the old utterly meaningless slogans trotted out again. It is very depressing."[109]

[106] David S. McLellan, "Who Fathered Containment? A Discussion," *International Studies Quarterly* 17 (June 1973): 205-26; *Department of State Bulletin* 13 (November 18, 1945): 787-89.

[107] Jonathan Knight, "America's International Guarantees for the Straits," pp. 240-47.

[108] Ward, *Threat of Peace*, p. 133; Sulzberger diary, August 3, 1946, *Long Row of Candles*, p. 316; Nicolson diary, 5 August, 6 September 1946, *Diaries and Letters*, vol. 3, *The Later Years, 1945-1962*, ed. Nigel Nicolson (New York: Atheneum, 1968), pp. 71, 75.

[109] Notes on Cabinet Meeting, October 11, 1946, Connelly Papers, HSTL; Nicolson diary, October 11, 1946, *Diaries and Letters*, ed. Nigel Nicolson, 3:78.

On August 15, Vyshinsky charged that "the United States was trying to dominate the world with 'hand outs.' " Byrnes noticed that Vyshinsky's accusations of "dollar diplomacy" were heartily applauded by two members of the Czech delegation. The secretary of state was aware that Czechoslovakia had been given a $50 million surplus property credit, of which only $9 million had been used. Infuriated, Byrnes ordered that the unused portion of the credit be cancelled, citing the Czech delegation's applause as justification. He did not wish to continue "subsidizing the Communist control of Czechoslovakia." "The time has come when we should endeavor by all fair means to assist our friends in western Europe and Italy," Byrnes wrote, "rather than to continue to extend material aid to those countries of eastern Europe at present engaged in the campaign of vilification of the United States and distortion of our motives and policies." Two months later, a State Department official approvingly described Byrnes' cable as having "acquired a unique significance as a charter of our present policy." Two weeks later, still rankled by Czech support for Soviet charges that the United States was trying to "enslave" Eastern Europe through economic assistance, Byrnes ordered the suspension of a pending $50 million reconstruction loan to Czechoslovakia. When a Czechoslovak chargé asked why the United States was suspending sales of surplus property to Czechoslovakia, John Hickerson reminded him that several weeks ago Vishinsky had made a speech accusing the United States of trying to enslave Eastern Europe through a policy of handouts, and that the Czechoslovak delegation had applauded this statement. Under these circumstances, the United States government felt that it might embarrass the Czechs to receive further credit for sales of surplus property. In mid-October, Byrnes wrote the State Department that "I should wish to see much more substantial evidence of Czechoslovak independence and friendship towards the United States before resuming any form of economic assistance which some members of its delegation here profess to believe may lead to Czechoslovakia's 'economic enslavement.' "[110]

The Czech hand-clapping incident led to a fundamental reorientation of U.S. foreign economic policy. In the past, U.S. economic assistance was granted on the basis of a country's need, ability to repay,

[110] Byrnes to Clayton, August 30, 1946, DELSEC #877, Records of World War II Conferences, RG 43, NA; James Riddleberger to Laurence A. Steinhardt, October 3, 1946, Laurence A. Steinhardt Papers, LC, emphasis added; Byrnes to Clayton, September 17, 1946, *FR: 1946*, VI, p. 220; Byrnes to Clayton, September 24, 1946, *FR: 1946*, VII, p. 223; Minutes of the Committee of Three, September 25, 1946, RG 59, NA; Byrnes to Steinhardt, October 14, 1946, *FR: 1946*, VI, p. 233.

and acceptance of U.S. multilateral trade principles. But from now on, the establishment of a liberal international economic system would be subordinated to the task of rebuilding Western economic and political strength against the threat of communist penetration. The U.S. government granted no further substantial economic assistance to Eastern European countries other than Finland, which occupied a special position then as now. Finland was able to maintain a democratic government while conducting a foreign policy acceptable to Moscow. In early 1947, the State Department concluded several agreements with Hungary in a belated, last-ditch effort to save the conservative Smallholders government, but little of the promised assistance had been received before the Hungarian coup.[111]

A fundamentally pragmatic man, Byrnes was influenced more by what he saw than what he read. It was the staged drama of the peace conference—the Eastern European countries docilely mouthing Soviet slogans, the bloc voting along East-West lines, vitriolic Soviet attacks against Greece—that caused him finally to accept the "two worlds" thesis. It is otherwise difficult to explain why Byrnes should have chosen to make an example of Czechoslovakia. Far from being "communist-dominated," in May 1946, Czechoslovakia held elections that even hard-liner Ambassador Steinhardt conceded to be an "expression of the will of the people in a democratic manner." The Soviet commander Marshal Konev blocked a Czech communist scheme to have 80,000 Soviet troops move across Czechoslovakia a few days before the election, arousing feelings of betrayal from the Czechoslovakia Communist party. In the newly elected Czech government, nine out of twenty-six top positions in the government were filled by communists. Although Prime Minister Gottwald was a communist, Steinhardt reported that he was a man of common sense and shrewdness, a Czech patriot, and unlikely to embark on any extremist policies.[112]

Byrnes did not change his views about the Soviet Union because he misperceived the consolidation of a Soviet security glacis in Eastern Europe as the first step in a drive for world communist domination. By April 1946, Byrnes was resigned to Soviet domination over Eastern Europe, as evidenced by his readiness to conclude peace treaties with the former Axis satellites, without guarantees of free elections. He recognized that there was at least the possibility that Soviet actions in Eastern Europe might be motivated by genuine fears of another Ger-

[111] Lundestad, *The American Non-Policy towards Eastern Europe*, pp. 139-45, 392-94.
[112] Daily TS Staff Summary, May 20, 22, 23, 28, 1946, RG 59, NA; Steinhardt to Byrnes, May 23, 1946, 860F.00/5-2346, RG 59, NA.

man invasion. During the summer, U.S. representatives in Rumania and Bulgaria reported increasing political violence and repression of the opposition parties. But Secretary of State Byrnes imposed no sanctions on those countries and did nothing to promote free elections other than to put our protests on the record with their governments. Although Byrnes, as a "practical politician," was certainly responsive to domestic political pressures, in this case, his acceptance of the division of the world into two blocs was self-instigated. In September 1946, only 8 percent of the American public felt that we should "give up trying to work with Russia altogether."[113]

The controversy surrounding the firing of Henry Wallace helped define the Truman administration's policy toward the Soviet Union. In early September, Truman was still perplexed and troubled by Soviet policies. He told Clifford he was anxious for the report on Russia. On September 10, he confided to Joseph Davies that he had authorized Byrnes to offer the Soviets a twenty-five-year treaty of joint defense against Germany. "It was calling their bluff," Truman explained. But he feared it would be of no use. "If not," Truman said, *"there was nothing left to do*. Britain and the United States would have to go along without them." Truman added that the treaty was more than fair and would have appealed to Stalin. Molotov was not that kind. Truman still thought that "if he and Stalin could sit down, they could get together on a fair basis that would support Peace, at least for a trial." But it was impossible to do business with Molotov—he was not a "big man" like Stalin.[114]

On September 12, Secretary of Commerce Wallace entered Truman's office for a scheduled fifteen-minute meeting. They discussed Wallace's trip to Mexico, the president's trip to Bermuda, the forthcoming elections. Then Wallace pulled out of his pocket a speech on foreign policy that he was scheduled to deliver that night in Madison Square Garden at a political rally sponsored by leftist organizations.

Ordinarily, the secretary of commerce would not be allowed to make speeches on foreign policy. But Wallace was a special case. He was a former vice president. Wallace also had close ties with left-liberal groups in the Democratic party, whose support would be crucial in the November congressional elections. The Democratic left wing had been threatening to start a third party if their leading spokesman, Henry Wallace, left the cabinet. To avoid widening the already bitter

[113] Daily TS Staff Summary, July 8, August 14, September 5, 8, 1946, RG 59, NA; Clayton to Byrnes, September 10, 1946, SECDEL #857, RG 43, NA.

[114] Davies diary, September 10, 1946, LC, emphasis added.

ideological split in the Democrats' ranks, Truman allowed Wallace unusual latitude in expressing his views. In addition, Truman felt obligated to execute FDR's policies, since the American people had not been given an opportunity to ratify a change in course. Wallace was the last holdover from FDR's cabinet and the symbol of the New Deal. Consequently, that year Truman had allowed Wallace to make several speeches implicitly critical of the administration's foreign policy.[115]

The object of all the controversy was an odd figure in American politics. As a plant geneticist, he had developed a strain of hybrid corn. FDR had brought the shy, humble man with a cowlick to Washington as his secretary of agriculture. A believer in scientific farming, Wallace was fascinated with oriental mysticism. Filled with love for mankind, he found it difficult to relate to individual human beings. A curtain of thought separated him from his listeners. In an administration noted for playing poker and swapping stories over bourbon and branch water, Wallace neither smoke nor drank. He was prone to get carried away by enthusiasm for righteous causes, as when he stated in 1942 that "the object of this war is to make sure that everybody in the world has the privilege of drinking a quart of milk a day." Cynical Washington never understood Wallace. A man of principle, he took advantage of Truman's preoccupation with strikes and domestic politics to embroil the president in a dispute over foreign policy.[116]

Wallace had decided to clear his speech with Truman because he had been warned that it would never get past the State Department. Involved in settling a nationwide shipping strike and pressed for time, Truman skimmed through the speech rapidly, commenting frequently, "that's right" or "that's what I believe." One statement that particularly appealed to Truman was to the effect that we held no special friendship for Russia, Britain, or any other country. He remarked enthusiastically, "By God, Henry, that is our foreign policy!" Wallace then got Truman's permission to quote him. Truman later recorded in his diary that "there were one or two things in the paper which I thought were a little wild but I didn't interpret them as contrary to the general policy." Although there was a passage in the speech attacking a "get tough with Russia" policy, Truman probably did not perceive it as a reference to his administration's foreign policy. Truman and Byrnes believed that they were following a course of "patience but firmness"

[115] Arthur Krock, *New York Times*, September 15, 1946; Hamby, *Beyond the New Deal*, pp. 123-24; Wallace diary, March 15, 22, April 5, 1946, *Price of Vision*, ed. Blum, pp. 563, 567, 570.

[116] "This Great Endeavor," *Time*, September 30, 1946, p. 23; Coffin, *Missouri Compromise*, pp. 283-84; Donovan, *Conflict and Crisis*, pp. 219-20.

toward Russia, a stance somewhere between FDR's "kid glove" policy and a "tough" posture.[117]

But he didn't read the speech carefully. Despite their political differences, Truman liked Wallace personally. They were both Midwestern farm boys, and Wallace frequently appealed to their common background. Truman trusted Henry to "play square" and not try to "put anything over" on him. Wallace was surprised that Truman saw no inconsistency between his speech and the policy Byrnes was following. But he said nothing. Wallace later told his assistant that the president had read his speech but did not understand the full implications of what he was going to say.[118]

Then Truman's propensity for speaking off the top of his head got him into even worse political trouble. Wallace tipped off a favored columnist that Truman had approved his speech. Wallace's aides handed out copies of the address to reporters. At his scheduled press conference that afternoon, a reporter called Truman's attention to this sentence: "I am neither anti-British, nor pro-British—neither anti-Russian nor pro-Russian. And just two days ago when President Truman read these words, he said they represented the policy of his Administration." The question was, "Does that apply just to that paragraph or to the whole speech?"

Truman replied without thinking, "I approved the whole speech."

"Mr. President, do you regard Wallace's speech a departure from Byrnes's policy—"

Without even waiting for the end of the question, Truman snapped out, "I do not."

"—toward Russia?"

"They are exactly in line," Truman replied.[119]

The rally held at Madison Square Garden that night was filled with attacks on Truman for abandoning FDR's policy, supporting British imperialism and adopting a "tough" policy. In such an atmosphere,

[117] Blum, *Price of Vision*, pp. 621, 624; Curry, *Byrnes*, pp. 257-58.

[118] Until recently, the only record of this meeting between Truman and Wallace was the Wallace diary entry for September 12, 1946. In the Truman diary that was recently opened to scholars there are two entries for September 16 and 18 giving Truman's version of the meeting, which support previous surmises that Truman only skimmed the speech. In his *Memoirs*, Truman claims that he had no time to read the speech, even in part (p. 557). Truman diary, September 16, 18, 1946, HSTL; Wallace diary, September 12, 1946, *Price of Vision*, ed. Blum, pp. 612-13; "Conversations with Wallace," September 12, 1946, Bernard L. Gladieux Papers, HSTL; Hamby, *Beyond the New Deal*, pp. 127-28; Donovan, *Conflict and Crisis*, p. 223.

[119] Donovan, *Conflict and Crisis*, p. 224.

the importance of Wallace's remarks—and Truman's endorsement—was greatly magnified.

"We are reckoning with a force which cannot be handled successfully by a 'Get tough with Russia' policy," Wallace declared. "Getting tough never brought anything real and lasting," he contended, "whether for schoolyard bullies or businessmen or world powers. The tougher we get, the tougher the Russians will get." Wallace went on to say publicly what administration officials would admit only in private. "We should recognize that we have no more business in the *political* affairs of Eastern Europe than Russia has in the *political* affairs of Latin America, Western Europe, and the United States. . . ."

"Whether we like it or not the Russians will try to socialize their sphere of influence just as we try to democratize our sphere of influence."

Because of Truman's supposed endorsement, the "Speech" was a bombshell. "Did I catch hell," Truman commented.[120]

From Paris, *New York Times* correspondent Harold Callender reported that Wallace's speech had "cut the ground from under the foreign policy that Mr. Byrnes had labored for a year and a half to develop." Not understanding the American cabinet system, Europeans believed that Truman had repudiated Byrnes. Wallace's speech revived doubts that the United States had a consistent foreign policy and was not retreating into isolationism. According to James Reston, immediately after Truman said he had approved the speech, foreign correspondents cabled abroad that United States policy was switching to a "softer" policy toward the Soviet Union. Moscow responded to the apparent division in the American government with renewed truculence. Within twenty-four hours after the speech became known, Molotov delivered what was viewed as the most bitter and uncompromising speech he had made in Paris, attacking American policy and using many of Wallace's themes. When Molotov had returned from Moscow just ten days previously from what was probably a policy reevaluation at the Kremlin, he had been in a mellow, compromising mood. Real progress had been made on the peace treaties, and it seemed as though the clear and firm policy laid down by Byrnes was beginning to have some results. Now all was endangered by the apparent disunity within the administration's ranks.[121]

On September 14, Truman tried to undo the damage with a clumsy

[120] "The Way to Peace," September 12, 1946, reprinted in Blum, *Price of Vision*, pp. 661-68; Truman diary, September 17, 1946.

[121] Harold Callender, *New York Times*, September 14, 1946; James Reston, ibid., September 13, 1946; editorial, "The Need for Unity," ibid., September 16, 1946.

lie. He claimed that he had not approved Wallace's speech but only his right to deliver it. There would be no change in his administration's foreign policy. Truman tried to persuade Wallace to restrict his speeches during the congressional campaign to social issues, but to no avail; the secretary of commerce was determined to speak out on what he believed in. Byrnes threatened to resign unless Wallace was silenced. On September 20, Truman asked for Wallace's resignation.[122]

Most liberals were outraged by the firing of Henry Wallace. They viewed Wallace's dismissal as evidence that the Truman administration had discarded their beloved FDR's foreign policy along with the New Deal. Shortly after, a large and representative group of liberals met in Chicago and adopted a platform praising Wallace and calling for a return to Roosevelt's policy of "great power unity."[123]

But the Wallace affair did not represent any major shift in American foreign policy. Truman continued to hope that the United States could work out a modus vivendi with Russia, if we were firm and consistent. A day after Wallace's dismissal, Truman wrote former Vice-President John Garner:

> There is too much loose talk about the Russian situation. We are not going to have any shooting trouble with them but they are tough bargainers and always ask for the whole earth, expecting maybe to get an acre. The situation, I think, is cleared up since yesterday and from now on we will have smoother sailing.[124]

Moreover, the president knew that he did not have the public support and military capabilities required to back up a tough, belligerent posture toward the Soviets, even if he had wanted to pursue a hard-line policy. Wallace's views had great appeal to labor organizations, church groups, and other liberal organizations. On the day of Wallace's dismissal, Elbridge Durbrow feared that "the President has just made an historic decision which is certain to bring down on him the wrath of many liberal and leftist groups, and which may cost the

---

[122] Donovan, *Conflict and Crisis*, pp. 227-28; Curry, *Byrnes*, pp. 271-72; Wallace diary, September 18, 1946, *Price of Vision*, ed. Blum, pp. 617-26. In *Mr. President* (p. 128) there appears a controversial Truman diary entry, dated September 19, 1946, in which the president supposedly accuses Wallace, referred to as "Mr. X," of being a pacifist, dangerous dreamer, and part of a "sabotage front for Uncle Joe Stalin." This memorandum was probably written later and predated for Hillman's book. It was not included in the rest of Truman's diary that was recently opened to scholars, and is inconsistent with the tone of the entries for September 16 and 18.

[123] Hamby, *Beyond the New Deal*, pp. 134, 144-45.

[124] Truman to Garner, September 21, 1946, Truman Papers, PSF: Subject File, "Russia, 1945-48," HSTL.

administration control of the Congress in the November elections."[125] Truman told Henry Wallace that we couldn't be tough with Russia because we didn't have the military equipment with which to be tough. With demobilization and reconversion of industry, he said, the United States had only one fully equipped division.[126]

The main difference between the Truman administration and Wallace lay in the realm of methods, not basic objectives of policy toward the Soviet Union. According to James Reston, Truman's repudiation of Wallace "did not do justice to his sincere desire to reach a just settlement with Moscow." *New York Times* columnist Anne O'Hare McCormick wrote that "the most unfortunate aspect of the speech from a foreign policy viewpoint is that it disseminates a false impression . . . that the policy Wallace advocates differs essentially from that pursued by Secretary Byrnes." No one who had followed developments in the international conferences from San Francisco to Paris could doubt that "getting along with Russia" was the cardinal aim of our peace policy. Though Byrnes was "tougher" now than in the beginning, his aim and the American aim had not changed. "The difference is a difference of method," she contended, "an attempt to see if firmness will achieve what concession after concession failed to achieve."[127] A *New York Times* editorial pointed out that Byrnes and Wallace were in agreement on several important points. Wallace insisted that the United States should adopt an independent foreign policy, tying itself neither to the British nor the Russians. Byrnes agreed. The two cabinet members also agreed on the necessity for internationalizing the manufacture and control of the atomic bomb, on Russia's right to special security safeguards in neighboring states, and on the Soviet Union's right to a fair share in the world's oil reserves.[128]

The Wallace episode provoked a public debate that did much to clarify and define Truman's evolving policy toward the Russians. In a series of columns based on discussions with responsible officials, James Reston pointed out the tactical differences between Wallace and Byrnes. The basic assumption of the Wallace approach was that the Soviet Union was a peaceful nation following belligerent policies out of fear of capitalist encirclement. The danger was that the United States would drive Russia to take desperate measures, because of our

[125] Memorandum by Elbridge Durbrow, September 20, 1946, 711.61/9-2046, RG 59, NA; "The Real Choice," *Time*, September 30, 1946, p. 24.

[126] Wallace diary, September 18, 1946, *Price of Vision*, ed. Blum, p. 625.

[127] James Reston, *New York Times*, September 16, 1946; Anne O'Hare McCormick, ibid., September 18, 1946.

[128] Editorial, ibid., September 15, 1946.

superior power. Consequently, Wallace argued that the United States should demonstrate its good faith and reduce military expenditures, turn over our Pacific bases to the United Nations, stop building long-range bombers, and offer the Russians a generous "no-strings" loan. *Then*, the United States could discuss fundamental questions with the Russians, laying the basis for a lasting peace settlement. The Truman administration had considered this premise that the Soviet Union acted out of insecurity, and was prepared to accept it in time. But it was not prepared to rely on it. The administration was not prepared to make the risky concessions demanded by Wallace, ahead of time, just to create a "friendly atmosphere." Byrnes' strategy was to keep talking on specific questions while bringing American power to bear whenever Soviet expansion endangered world security. The administration hoped that when Moscow realized that the United States was serious about enforcing the peace, they would stand and negotiate. Then and only then would Byrnes discuss such issues as disarmament, a large loan, and so on.[129]

Still, Truman's foreign policy was in a transitional stage. American policy was merely negative, confined to passive opposition to Soviet expansion beyond the boundaries of the tacit spheres of influence in Europe established by the wartime conferences. The Truman administration had not defined our vital security interests, nor provided any positive goals that could catch the world's imagination. As *Newsweek* pointed out, "for the Administration he quit, it meant the removal of an obstacle along the rocky road to a clear-cut foreign policy—a journey, Wallace's absence notwithstanding, fated to be far from tranquil in the months ahead."[130]

In a September 24 cable, Byrnes made a first step toward this end by articulating his thoughts concerning the recent shift in American foreign economic policy, and formulating a more general rationale for his spur-of-the-moment decision to cut off aid to Eastern Europe. The secretary of state summarized the new policy: "In a word we must help our friends in every way and refrain from assisting those who either through helplessness or for other reasons are opposing the principles for which we stand."[131]

On the same day that Byrnes divided the world into friends and enemies, Truman was presented with the raw materials for a redefinition of policy toward Russia. In the late afternoon, Clifford handed

---

[129] James Reston, ibid., September 13, 15, 16, 21, 22, 1946.
[130] "The Wallace Nightmare," *Newsweek*, September 30, 1946, p. 19.
[131] Byrnes to Clayton, September 24, 1946, *FR: 1946*, VII, p. 223.

him a copy of the long-awaited report on Russia. George Elsey had composed the document, largely by pasting together bits of memoranda submitted to the president by foreign policy officials and Kennan's diplomatic cables. Like any committee document, it lacked a certain coherence and clarity. Clifford made some changes in the first draft. George Kennan made more substantive suggestions, commenting, "I think the general tone is excellent and I have no fault to find with it." Kennan stressed that the document should emphasize that high-level discussions with Russian leaders could not change the basic Soviet outlook, which was too deeply rooted in their domestic political system to be altered by a single individual, even one as powerful as Stalin. Although individual Soviet objectives might be altered through negotiations, the primary means of influencing Soviet policy was through action—what the United States did, not what it said. Our best chances of influencing the Soviet government, Kennan argued, consisted in keeping the regime confronted with a set of circumstances which made it clear that action contrary to the United States' conception of a decent world order would be to their disadvantage, whereas friendly and cooperative action would be rewarded. This was the underlying philosophy of containment that Kennan later presented in the famous "X" article in *Foreign Affairs*, July 1947. Clifford incorporated Kennan's suggestion almost verbatim into the report.[132]

The Clifford-Elsey report was consistent with the analysis of American foreign policy given by James Reston in the *Times*. The memorandum also answered many of the arguments raised by Wallace in his attacks on the Truman administration's foreign policy. The document warned that "it is highly dangerous to conclude that hope of international peace lies only in 'accord,' 'mutual understanding,' or 'solidarity' with the Soviet Union." Adoption of such a policy would compel the United States to make concessions for the sake of U.S.-Soviet relations that would only increase Soviet demands, since they viewed compromise and concessions as evidence of weakness.

The memorandum did not exclude the possibility that the Soviets might yet decide to abandon their expansionist policies and cooperate with the Western democracies. Nevertheless, it recognized that the United States might be forced to settle for Two Worlds: "If we find it impossible to enlist Soviet cooperation in the solution of world problems we should be prepared to join with the British and other Western countries in an attempt to build up a world of our own . . .

---

[132] Kennan, "Comments on the Document Entitled 'American Relations with the Soviet Union,'" Elsey Papers, HSTL.

recog[nizing] the Soviet orbit as a distinct entity with which conflict is not predestined but with which we cannot pursue common aims." For strategic military reasons, the United States must prevent Western Europe, the Middle East, China, and Japan from falling into the Soviet sphere. "The main deterrent to Soviet attack on the United States, or to attack on areas of the world which are vital to our security, will be the military power of this country." But the Clifford-Elsey report did not believe that war was inevitable, if the United States maintained military strength sufficient to defeat the Soviets decisively. "The Western powers are still too strong, the USSR is still too weak." Consequently, Soviet officials would be careful not to "provoke, by their policies of expansion and aggression, too strong a reaction by other powers."

Foreshadowing the Truman Doctrine, the report recommended that the United States "support and assist all democratic countries which are in any way menaced or endangered by the USSR." Providing military support in case of attack was a last resort; a more effective barrier to communism was economic assistance. This was not a departure from established policy. In 1946, the United States had granted loans to Britain, Italy, and France, largely to counteract the economic appeal of the communist party in elections.[133] The theme of preventing Soviet aggression primarily through economic assistance and if necessary by military force appeared in several official State Department memoranda, beginning in March.[134]

This was part of the age-old doctrine of maintaining a balance of power. As James Reston pointed out, "the generally conceded fact . . . is that the United States and Britain are following the balance of power doctrine in Europe and elsewhere today because there is no other effective system of security to take its place." Equilibrium in Europe had been destroyed by the defeat of the French army, the destruction of Germany, and the rise of the Soviet Union as the only major military power on the continent. The Western powers were acting on the theory that "if the power of the West is equal to the power of the Soviet Union and its satellites, the latter group will hesitate to insist on policies which might bring it into war with nations of equal strength."[135]

[133] McNeill, *America, Britain, and Russia*, pp. 663-64, 691-92, 733.

[134] Memorandum, March 17, 1946 (Draft of Political Estimate of Soviet Policy), ABC 336 Russia (22 Aug. 43), Sec. 1-C, RG 165, NA; Matthews to SWNCC, "Political Estimate of Soviet Policy," April 1, 1946, 711.61/3-1446, RG 59, NA; State Department, "Policy and Information Statement: USSR," May 15, 1946, Clark M. Clifford Papers, HSTL.

[135] James Reston, *New York Times*, September 19, 1946.

The Clifford-Elsey report concluded with the hope that the Soviets would "change their minds and work out with us a fair and equitable settlement when they realize that we are too strong to be beaten and too determined to be frightened."

If the Hovland approach is correct, then Truman should have accepted the Clifford-Elsey version of containment on the spot. The report presented a convincing interpretation of Soviet expansionist activities that had been troubling Truman and other officials, and it proposed an articulate, coherent policy to prevent the Soviets from expanding into areas vital to the United States. Truman was undecided and ambivalent about Soviet motives, and receptive to new beliefs. In addition, the president was insecure about his lack of expertise in foreign affairs, and should have been easily influenced by the united consensus of his highly credible military and political advisers. But, contrary to most historians, Truman did not immediately decide to adopt the Clifford-Elsey report as the basis of our foreign policy.[136] No attempt was made to halt demobilization. Moreover, there was one particular recommendation with which Truman did *not* agree. The report said that the American people should be fully informed about the difficulty of getting along with the Soviet Union, and that the record of Soviet evasion, misrepresentation, aggression, and militarism should be made public.[137] Truman stayed up most of the night reading the document, and early the next morning he phoned Clark Clifford at his home.

"How many copies of this report do you have?" Truman asked.

"Ten," Clifford said.

"I want the other nine," Truman said. "This has got to be put under lock and key," he explained later, after Clifford put the remaining copies on his desk. "This is so hot, if this should come out now it could have an exceedingly unfortunate impact on our efforts to try to develop some relationship with the Soviet Union."[138]

What was the cause of Truman's renewed hopes for a Soviet-American reconciliation? On the same day that he received the Clifford-Elsey report, Truman read an unusually conciliatory interview given by Stalin to a British newsman, Alexander Werth. Stalin denied that

[136] See, for example, Richard Powers, "Who Fathered Containment?" *International Studies Quarterly* 15 (December 1971): 526-42; Ward, *Threat of Peace*, p. 154; Gaddis, *Origins of Containment*, p. 324; Yergin, *Shattered Peace*, p. 245.

[137] "American Relations with the Soviet Union," reprinted as Appendix A in Arthur Krock, *Memoirs: Sixty Years on the Firing Line* (New York: Funk & Wagnalls, 1968), pp. 430, 476, 477, 479, 482.

[138] M. Truman, *Harry Truman*, p. 347; Freeland, *Truman Doctrine and Origins of McCarthyism*, p. 67.

there was any danger of war, and affirmed his unqualified belief in the possibility of lasting cooperation between the Soviet Union and the Western democracies. Contradicting a dominant theme in the Soviet propaganda line, Stalin asserted that Great Britain and the United States could not create a capitalist encirclement of the Soviet Union even if they wanted to. Coincidentally, in London, Anthony Eden called for a new approach to Big Four relations. He contended that the Soviet Union and Western democracies could "live together in peace" if neither attempted "to back their fancies in every other land."[139]

This time, the reaction in Washington was much more subdued and cautious than in March when Stalin made similar overtures through a press interview. American officials believed that Stalin's move was a tactical maneuver designed to quiet tensions raised to a high pitch by Wallace's speech and the bitter public debates at the Paris Peace Conference. The Moscow embassy agreed that Stalin's statement was a tactical move, not an announcement of change in basic long-term strategy. In contrast, *New York Times* columnist Anne O'Hare McCormick judged that the timing of Stalin's declaration was significant, since it came at a time when the peace conference was floundering on the edge between success and failure.[140]

Truman had been invited to address the opening of the General Assembly in New York City. On September 27, Truman told Under Secretary Clayton that he "had in mind using this occasion to make a new statement on U.S. foreign policy in view of Stalin's newspaper interview and Anthony Eden's statement that he thought we needed a new approach to the Russian problem, etc."[141] Secretary of State Byrnes, on the other hand, told a British official that "he was not going to place undue value on speeches because the whole time at the Conference, the platform had been taken to abuse the United States and Great Britain and other countries and then at the end of it all when these seeds had been sown another interview had been given as though nothing had ever been said." The polemical diatribes delivered by Soviet officials at the Paris Peace Conference had recently convinced Byrnes that it was impossible to negotiate with the Soviets on a reasonable basis; instead, we should reward "friendly" countries with economic assistance while punishing those who opposed us. Byrnes called

[139] *New York Times*, September 24, 1946.

[140] Ibid., September 25, 1946; White House Daily Summary, October 7, 1946, RG 59, NA.

[141] WLC to Acheson, September 28, 1946, Dean Acheson Papers, "Drafts—Articles, Speeches, etc.—speeches written and edited for others by Dean Acheson, 1941-49," HSTL.

attention to the conduct of the Russians at the Paris Peace Conference and the Security Council, where they had attacked the United States without notice or reason. The United States would have to watch very carefully and see whether there was any real change in Russian policy, Byrnes said, for while Stalin's statement was being made, Gromyko was attacking the United States and Britain in the Security Council, and this made him naturally very careful.[142]

In his speech to the opening session of the General Assembly, Truman set forth the American agenda—international control of atomic energy, establishment of an international police force, and further progress in setting up an International Refugee Organization. But *New York Times* correspondent Thomas Hamilton noted that Truman's remarks seemed to be addressed to the Big Four's foreign ministers, who would meet in New York on November 4 to begin drafting a treaty with Germany. Declaring that it would be a disaster to the world if the United Nations were broken into "irreconcilable parts" by different political philosophies, Truman asked the General Assembly to set an example of mutual give and take for the Big Four. As if to dispel Soviet fears arising from Byrnes' speech at Stuttgart that the United States wished to build up Germany as a bulwark against Russia, Truman pledged that the United States would insist on peace terms "which insure that both Germany and Japan remain disarmed, that Nazi influence in Germany be destroyed, and that the power of the war lords in Japan be eliminated forever." In general Truman's speech was much more optimistic than Byrnes' report to the nation on the Paris Peace Conference. Truman admitted that there were differences among the Allies. But he insisted that it was not necessary to exaggerate these disagreements, and that no differences of interest stood in the way of settling their problems. "Above all," he emphasized, "we must not permit differences in economic and social systems to stand in the way of peace, either now or in the future."

According to a *New York Times* editorial, Truman "expressed the firm belief of our Government that despite all the disappointments which have accompanied the business of making peace, this is still One World, compact and indivisible." In sum, Truman had reaffirmed FDR's policy of Soviet-American cooperation. After Truman had finished his speech, stony-faced Molotov ignored diplomatic protocol and rushed up to shake his hand warmly. Through an interpreter, Molotov told the president that it was a "great" speech.[143]

[142] Hankey to Foreign Office, 1 October 1946, FO 371/56886, N12449/5169/38.

[143] Thomas J. Hamilton, *New York Times*, October 24, 1946; editorial, ibid.; Arthur G. Altschul, ibid.

Although Truman believed that there was still a chance for "One World," Averell Harriman privately affirmed that "the Russians have declared psychological warfare on the United States, all over the world. It is a war of ideology and a fight unto the death." Similarly, Secretary of State Byrnes divided the world into two categories of nations—"friends" and "enemies" who opposed the principles for which America stood.[144]

On the same day that Truman addressed the General Assembly, the Soviet Government gave orders for additional troops to be demobilized. Eight days previously, the Soviet Union announced that it was slashing the defense budget by 80,800,000,000 rubles. The Soviets were facing an acute labor shortage, and the returning servicemen were needed for work in factories, plants, and collective farms. *New York Times* correspondent Drew Middleton connected the defense cuts with Stalin's assertion that there was no danger of war; and he speculated that the Soviet Union was now entering a period of "greater tranquillity and internal activity."[145]

Even Henry Wallace admitted that U.S. foreign policy had "changed for the better" in recent weeks. He described President Truman's speech as "constructive in the direction of a peaceful world, definitely in the Roosevelt tradition."[146]

Some might dismiss Truman's U.N. speech as a campaign ploy to portray himself as a man of peace. That may be. If so, it was a gesture fundamentally misconceived. The Republicans made procommunism a major campaign issue. Journalist Tris Coffin commented that "the word 'Communism' was whooped about like an Indian war cry." One Republican campaign leaflet showed a donkey staring into a crystal ball and wearing a turban with a Soviet hammer and sickle on it. Republican party headquarters had stacks of recordings on the "Communist threat" to send out in the field. In traditionally Democratic urban districts, Catholic organizations campaigned vigorously against Communism. Worse, Republicans exacerbated the ideological split in the Democratic party by demanding that their opponents take a stand on Wallace's ideas, especially in urban areas where the former secretary of commerce had a significant following.[147]

The election was a disaster for the Democrats. The American public

[144] William Benton to Acheson, October 18, 1946, Clayton-Thorpe Files, "Memorandum-general, Oct. 1946—July 1947," HSTL.

[145] *New York Times*, October 24, 1946.

[146] Ibid., October 25, 1946.

[147] Coffin, *Missouri Compromise*, p. 297; Donovan, *Conflict and Crisis*, pp. 231, 234; Hamby, *Beyond the New Deal*, pp. 135-36.

took out their frustration with strikes, meat shortages, and price controls on the incumbents. The Republicans won control of both houses of Congress for the first time since 1928.

However, Truman secretly continued his conciliatory efforts even *after* the elections. On November 7, Truman reassured Foreign Minister Molotov that the election results would not affect U.S. policy toward the Soviet Union. He renewed his invitation for Stalin to visit the United States. Molotov replied that this was a wish which they shared.[148]

Truman was afraid that the alternative to Soviet-American collaboration was war. He wrote his mother and sister on November 11 about Molotov's visit:

> Molotov was here a couple of days ago and I smiled at him and had the usual pictures taken. But—I'm sure Mr. Molotov is not so honest! He represents a totalitarian state—a police government. Really there is no difference between the government which Mr. Molotov represents and the one the Czar represented—or the one Hitler spoke for. . . . They are kidnapping Germans, they have Japanese, Lithuanians, Estonians, Latvians, Poles, Finns, they are making to work against their wills. *How can I deal with such terrible conditions? I don't want to go to war with them.* I hope we don't have to go to war again for six hundred years. Maybe we won't have to.[149]

Thus, 1946 ended with Truman's renewed, but wary, commitment to Soviet-American cooperation. At the end of a year of drift and indecision, of waffling between confrontation and collaboration, Truman still had no new policy, nor did he perceive any alternatives to the present policies, except the unacceptable prospect of war.

[148] *FR: 1946*, VI, p. 801.
[149] M. Truman, *Harry Truman*, p. 323, emphasis added.

CHAPTER SEVEN

"This Terrible Decision"

TRUMAN might have continued to waver and hesitate had not the combination of an economic crisis in Western Europe and a budget-slashing Republican Congress forced him to use ideological rhetoric to secure passage of a foreign aid bill.

The structure of the international economic system, so laboriously designed and negotiated by the State Department, immediately came under attack by protectionist forces in the 80th Congress. In April, Under Secretary William Clayton was scheduled to attend a conference at Geneva of representatives from eighteen countries to negotiate a general agreement for reciprocal lowering of trade barriers. The conference would also finish drafting a World Trade Charter and International Trade Organization to help restore liberal, multilateral trade. Yet, when the new Congress convened, members of both houses began making noises about higher tariffs. With the support of the majority leadership, a resolution was introduced into the House that would prevent the Administration from making tariff cuts or attending international trade conferences until the Tariff Commission had weighed the needs of American industry for protection. Clayton and Acheson were able to persuade Congress to defer taking action against the trade agreements program only by agreeing to issue an executive order further restricting the president's authority to cut tariffs.[1]

On February 10, Truman told Clark Clifford that he wanted to make a speech on foreign economic policy at Baylor University in early March. "Economic isolationism leads to political isolationism," Truman declared. "This is the course which this country took after the First World War and constitutes the fundamental cause of the Second World War." Yet, just five months previously, Truman had disagreed with Henry Wallace when he made the same argument. Then, Truman had asserted that the "Harding disarmament conference in 1922 was the chief cause of World War II." Truman believed whatever the situation called for.[2]

---

[1] Freeland, *Truman Doctrine and Origins of McCarthyism*, pp. 79-80; Jones, *Fifteen Weeks*, pp. 93-94, 96.

[2] Memorandum with reference to speech of the President at Baylor University, Feb-

As is usually the case with similar historical landmarks, Truman played little part in drafting the doctrine that bears his name. On February 21, the first secretary of the British embassy handed Loy Henderson two *aides-memoire*. The first said that the Greek economy was on the verge of collapse, because of the country's lack of foreign exchange reserves and low level of industrial activity, the byproduct of political instability. Unless Greece received outside assistance, there would be widespread starvation and political disturbances. But His Majesty's government had already strained their resources to the utmost to help Greece, and found it impossible to grant further financial assistance. The second pointed out that Turkey needed financial assistance for military reorganization and industrial development. Since Britain could not provide any further credits, Turkey would have to look to the United States.[3]

Acheson viewed this blue piece of paper as a symbol of the demise of *Pax Britannica*. Would the people of the United States abandon their aversion to power politics and assume the burdens of world leadership from Britain's feeble shoulders? Acheson had some doubts. On February 24, when journalist Louis Fischer visited the State Department, he noticed that Acheson was extremely agitated. "Louis," he said, "this is very confidential, top secret, I know I can trust you." He told Fischer that the British were pulling out of Greece and Turkey for lack of money, and the United States had to find some means of preventing a collapse. "The thing is not so urgent in Turkey," Acheson stressed, "but in Greece it is a matter of days." He was repeatedly interrupted by calls and seemed very tense. The two men departed for lunch at the Metropolitan Club in Acheson's limousine. Acheson immediately cranked up the window behind the driver, then turned to Fischer. "The British are pulling out of everywhere, and if we don't go in, the Russians will." At the club, Acheson ordered exactly what Fischer did, giving the impression that he didn't much care what he ate. "There are only two powers left," Acheson continued. "The British are finished. They are through. And the trouble is that this hits us too soon before we are ready for it. We are having a lot of trouble getting money out of Congress." Acheson looked very grim and threw up his hands to his head in a gesture of desperation. "If the Near East

---

ruary, 10, 1947, Clark M. Clifford Papers, "Presidential Speech File 1945-April 5, 1947," HSTL; Dean Acheson to Thorpe, February 11, 1947, Acheson Papers, "Drafts—articles, speeches, etc.—speeches written and edited for others by DA, 1941-49," HSTL.
[3] *FR: 1947*, V, pp. 32-37.

and France go communist," he said, "I fear very much for this country and for the world."[4]

Other U.S. officials shared Acheson's assessment that the Greek civil war was but the most immediate manifestation of a general world crisis brought about by Britain's declining power and the resurgence of a dynamic, expanding Soviet Union. Loy Henderson observed that the notes on Greece and Turkey were "in line with recent British moves in getting out of Burma, India, and Palestine. . . . The British Government seemed to feel itself unable to maintain its imperial structure on the same scale as in the past." An ad hoc State Department committee, which included George Kennan, Charles Bohlen, Llewellyn Thompson, and John Jernegan, pointed out that "this may be only part of a much broader problem arising for this country in consequence of Britain's economic and political situation." They recommended that immediate studies be made of the "broad foreign policy implications" for the United States of Britain's declining power, and of the other responsibilities that would have to be undertaken if this country assumed a world leadership role. The secretaries of state, war, and navy agreed that "the Greek and Turkish problems were only part of a critical world situation confronting us today in many democratic countries and that attention must be given to the problem as a whole." In a private memorandum, Under Secretary of State Clayton worried that:

> The reins of world leadership are fast slipping from Britain's competent but now very weak hands.
>
> These reins will be picked up either by the United States or by Russia. If by Russia, there will almost certainly be war in the next decade or so with the odds against us. If by the United States, war can almost certainly be prevented.
>
> The United States must take world leadership and quickly, to avert world disaster.[5]

The implications for action flowed directly out of this definition of the situation. As one participant recalled, "the problem was not what should be done, but how to get authorizing legislation from Congress." The Republicans had won control of Congress by promising to reduce income taxes by 20 percent. Throughout January and February, while Europeans were starving and shivering in the harshest

---

[4] Notes on Interview with Dean Acheson, February 24, 1947, Louis Fischer Papers, Princeton.

[5] *FR: 1947*, V, pp. 45-48, 57; Memorandum, 3/5/47, Clayton Papers, "General File—Marshall Plan Memos 1947," HSTL.

winter of recent history, Republican leaders debated over whether the president's budget should be cut by $6 billion or by only $4.5 billion.[6]

On February 26, Secretary of State Marshall presented Truman with a memorandum representing the consensus of State, War, and Navy that the imminent collapse of Greece threatened U.S. security and that "we should take immediate steps to extend all possible aid to Greece and, on a lesser scale, to Turkey." They recognized that other countries would need massive financial aid from the United States, and these situations were being studied in the departments. But Greece required immediate action. Without question, Truman approved "in principle" their recommendations that legislation be submitted to Congress and the American public educated about the need for action.[7]

He had been kept informed about developments in the Greek civil war in his daily briefing memos. In early February, Ambassador MacVeagh had recommended that the United States give aid to Greece to prevent the government's imminent financial collapse and a nationwide communist revolution. MacVeagh warned that "if Greece falls to Communism, the whole Near East and part of North Africa as well are certain to pass under Soviet influence." A week later, the U.S. representative to the United Nations investigating commission reported that the "Soviets feel Greece is a ripe plum ready to fall into their hands in a few weeks." Other members of the U.N. commission judged that the "Soviets, after having been rebuffed in Azerbaijan and Turkey, are finding Greece surprisingly soft and that the matter has gone beyond the probing state and is now an all-out offensive for the kill."[8]

Still, Truman did nothing until the British dumped the problem in his lap. Lacking a set of geopolitical concepts and generalizations, Truman did not yet see the strategic significance of Greece, or comprehend the implications for the United States of the decline of the British empire. Acheson did. Before the British government notified the United States that they could not continue to prop up the Greek economy, Acheson had sent Secretary of State Marshall a memorandum urging that the State Department advise the Greek government to include members of opposition parties, provide technical assistance in reorganizing the Greek civil service, present a special bill to Congress for an urgent loan, and reconsider our policy of expecting the British to provide the Greeks with military equipment.[9]

[6] *FR: 1947*, V, pp. 55-56, 58-59; Jones, *Fifteen Weeks*, pp. 90-91; 138.

[7] *FR: 1947*, V, pp. 58-59.

[8] White House Daily Summary, February 12, 18, 24, 1947, RG 59, NA.

[9] Henderson to Marshall, "Crisis and Imminent Possibility of Collapse in Greece," February 21, 1947, 868.00/2-2047, RG 59, NA.

Because Acheson had a well-articulated, coherent, and stable system of beliefs, he did not vacillate and change his mind as Truman did. Following the Turkish Straits crisis, Acheson maintained his image of the Soviets as expansionist and influenced only by superior military power. In January 1947, Acheson already perceived the United States as engaged in a cold war with the Soviet Union. "What we must do is not allow ourselves to be set back on our heels by their offensive strategy," Acheson told journalist Louis Fischer off the record. "We are kept busy," he complained. "They throw bricks into the window and we push a newspaper in that hole and try quickly to plug another hole, and so on." Acheson advised his staff to seize the initiative from Russia. "One week must be lend-lease week and we must stress the fact that Russia hasn't settled. . . . Next week we will pick another problem and keep on the offensive about it." On February 10, Acheson bluntly told a congressional committee that Russian foreign policy was "aggressive and expanding."[10]

On February 27, Truman called a meeting with congressional leaders. Truman asked them to the White House not for advice on how to handle the Greek crisis, but for their support in getting the necessary legislation through Congress. Inarticulate on military-strategic issues, the president turned over the floor to Marshall and Acheson, who discussed the danger of Soviet penetration into the Middle East and Western Europe. Secretary Marshall warned that "if Greece should dissolve into civil war it is altogether probable that it would emerge as a communist state under Soviet control." The loss of Greece, in turn, could lead to the collapse of pro-Western governments in Turkey, Hungary, Austria, Italy and France. "It is not alarmist to say that we are faced with the first crisis of a series which might extend Soviet domination to Europe, the Middle East, and Asia," Marshall said.

Yet, even this presentation of the domino theory failed to impress the legislators. Alarmed, Acheson whispered a request to Marshall for permission to speak. "This was my crisis," Acheson recalled. "For a week I had nurtured it." It was Acheson's interpretation of the Greek civil war as part of a global struggle between the forces of freedom and totalitarianism that stirred the legislators. We had arrived at a situation unparalleled since ancient history, Acheson declared. The world was dominated by two great powers, the United States and the Soviet Union. Not since Athens and Sparta, not since Rome and Car-

[10] Notes on interview with Dean Acheson, January 3, 1947, Fischer Papers, Princeton; For the press, February 18, 1947, Acheson Papers, "State Dept.—Russia—1948," HSTL.

thage had there been such a polarization of power. Further, Acheson continued,

> the two great powers were divided by an unbridgeable ideological chasm. For us, democracy and individual liberty were basic; for them dictatorship and absolute conformity. And it was clear that the Soviet Union was aggressive and expanding.

Therefore, Acheson stressed, it was not a question of "pulling British chestnuts out of the fire." For if the communists succeeded in gaining control of two-thirds of the world's surface and three-fourths of its population, freedom in the United States would have poor chances of survival. A long silence followed. Then Senator Vandenberg admitted that he had been greatly impressed, and even shaken, by what he had just heard. Senator Vandenberg warned Truman that the only way he could obtain the support of the American people was through a frank, public announcement that the aid was intended to prevent communist takeovers in Greece and Turkey. Truman promised that he would present the case for aid to Greece and Turkey in bold and broad strokes.[11] As Vandenberg wrote in a letter,

> I am entirely frank in saying that I do not know the answer to the latest Greek challenge because I do not know all the facts. . . . But I sense enough of the facts to realize that the problem in Greece cannot be isolated by itself. On the contrary, it is probably symbolic of the world-wide ideological clash between Eastern Communism and Western Democracy.[12]

The theme of "democracy" vs. "dictatorship" appealed to basic emotions—recollections of 4th of July speeches heard dimly as a child in the warm summer night, reverence for the meaning of the American flag, lessons learned in school about George Washington and the birth of the American nation. In Murray Edelman's terms, the dichotomy of "freedom" vs. "totalitarianism" made use of "condensation" symbols designed to "evoke the emotions associated with the situation." And information that is emotionally interesting is more likely to be remem-

---

[11] *FR: 1945*, pp. 60-62; JMJ Notes on Acheson's Presentation to Dept. Working Group, February 28, 1947, Joseph M. Jones Papers, HSTL; Memorandum for the File, "The Drafting of the President's Message to Congress on the Greek Situation," March 12, 1947, Jones Papers; Leahy diary, February 27, 1947, LC; Jones, *Fifteen Weeks*, pp. 138-42.

[12] Vandenberg to John B. Bennett, March 5, 1947, *Private Papers*, ed. Vandenberg, p. 340.

bered, imagined, and hence influential in shaping judgments and opinions.[13]

Recognizing the persuasiveness of the ideological appeal, Acheson made sure that staff members assigned to draft the president's speech highlighted the theme of a "global struggle between freedom and totalitarianism" as the principal justification for U.S. aid to Greece and Turkey. On February 28, at a meeting of State Department officers, Acheson instructed them that "in the public presentation, the concept of individual liberty is basic, and the protection of democracy everywhere in the world." Aid to Greece and Turkey "is not a matter of vague do-goodism, it is a matter of protecting our whole way of life," he explained. Acheson's presentation thrilled the State Department officials. After the under secretary left the meeting, ideas and symbols were quickly and easily batted forth. Francis Russell wondered if they should couch the president's request in "terms of [a] new policy of this government to go to the assistance of free governments." Llewellyn Thompson agreed that was a good argument—that "we were prepared to back any government that was a democracy." Captain Robert Dennison recommended that they "relate military aid to the principle of supporting democracy; U.S. will support free governments to [the] point where we can enable them to defend selves." General Henry Arnold agreed that the "only thing that can sell public is necessity of holding the line, Communism versus Democracy should be major theme."

The developing consensus within the group was summarized in a working paper recommending that the administration's public campaign should be centered around the following themes:

> A cardinal object of United States foreign policy is a world in which nations shall be able to work out their own way of life free of coercion by other nations. . . .
>
> There is, at the present point in world history, a conflict between two ways of life. One way of life is based upon the will of the majority, free institutions, representative governments, free elections, guarantees of individual liberty, freedom of speech and religion, and freedom from political oppression. The second way of life is based upon the imposition of the will of a minority upon the majority, upon control of the press and other means of information by the minority, upon terror and oppression. . . .

[13] Trout, "Rhetoric Revisited," p. 259; Murray Edelman, *The Symbolic Uses of Politics* (Urbana: University of Illinois Press, 1964), p. 6; Nisbett and Ross, *Human Inference*, pp. 45-46.

It is the policy of the United States to give support to free peoples who are attempting to resist subjugation from armed minorities or from outside forces.

At Acheson's direction, this passage was lifted almost verbatim from the report and became the heart of the Truman Doctrine.[14]

George Kennan approved of aid to Greece and Turkey, but objected to the portrayal of the world as polarized between two opposing ways of life. He suggested to Acheson that the president's statement should be much "terser and compact" and submitted an alternative draft. Contrary to his later recollection, Kennan's version also contained an open-ended promise to aid free peoples against the onslaught of totalitarianism: "We cannot now stand aside and see totalitarian regimes imposed upon free peoples for lack of support from our side for the forces of democracy."[15]

But Acheson understood that the mass public does not respond to "facts" but rather to "symbols." Acheson later wrote that:

In the State Department we used to discuss how much time that mythical "average American citizen" put in each day listening, reading, and arguing about the world outside his own country. Assuming a man or woman with a fair education, a family, and a job in or out of the house, it seemed to us that ten minutes a day would be a high average. If this were anywhere near right, points to be understandable had to be clear. If we made our points clearer than truth, we did not differ from most other educators and could hardly do otherwise.

To legitimize a foreign policy, the president must present and defend an image of the international system that is compatible with the action recommended. The Manichean division of the world into "demo-

[14] JMJ Notes on Acheson's Presentation to Department Working Group, February 28, 1947, Acheson Papers; SWNCC Subcommittee on Foreign Policy Information Meeting, 2/28/47, 868.00/3-1547-3-2947, RG 59, NA; SWNCC Subcommittee on Foreign Policy Information: Meeting 2/28/47, Jones Papers, "Truman Doctrine 'Important Relevant Papers,' " HSTL; *FR: 1947*, V, pp. 76-77, 121-22; Memorandum for the File, "The Drafting of the President's Message to Congress on the Greek Situation," March 12, 1947, Jones Papers; Jones, *Fifteen Weeks*, pp. 153-54.

[15] Kennan to Acheson, March 6, 1946, with attachment, 868.00/3-647, "Revised Draft 3/6/47: The President's Message to Congress on the Greek Situation," RG 59, NA; Jones, *Fifteen Weeks*, pp. 154-55; Kennan, *Memoirs*, pp. 332-37; George F. Kennan, "Comments on the National Security Problem," 27 March 1947, 868.00/3-2747, RG 59, NA.

cratic" versus "totalitarian" states created a reality that legitimized the Cold War.[16]

While Acheson supervised the drafting of the message to Congress, Truman left Washington for a long-planned visit with the president of Mexico. On his way home, Truman stopped off at Baylor University to make a speech on foreign economic policy. He emphasized that international cooperation on economic issues was no less essential to peace than political cooperation through the United Nations. Invoking an episodic script, he reminded his listeners that the economic warfare of the thirties—the Smoot-Hawley tariff, Ottawa imperial preferences, Nazi state trading—was a major cause of the Depression. He made a strong plea for the administration's program for a new liberal international economic regime—the International Trade Organization, World Trade Charter, reciprocal tariff reductions. "If the nations can agree to observe a code of good conduct in international trade, they will cooperate more readily in other international affairs."[17] Ironically, within a week Truman would make a speech that would divide the world into rival political and economic blocs.

Truman was back at his desk on March 7. After Acheson brought him up to date on developments in the Greek-Turkish crisis, Truman concluded that he "had no choice but to go forward with the program." The same day he called a meeting of the cabinet, supposedly to get their advice on whether he should request a loan from Congress, but in reality to obtain their support for the decision. Truman told the assembled cabinet members that he was "faced with a decision more serious than had ever been confronted by any President." He asked Acheson to outline the situation. Acheson announced that the "complete disintegration of Greece is only a matter of weeks." While the United States had been seeking to negotiate peace treaties, the Soviets had been moving to encircle Turkey and Germany through satellite nations. By isolating Turkey, the Soviets hoped to acquire control of the Dardanelles and other Turkish territories. Although the Soviets had received a setback in Iran, they had met with considerable success in Greece, as a result of assistance provided by Yugoslavia, Albania, and Bulgaria to armed guerrilla bands. Greece was a war-ravaged land, and the government was inefficient and incompetent. The border warfare in the north meant that no farming could be carried out, thus increasing the need for economic assistance. Acheson pointed out that

[16] Edelman, *Symbolic Uses of Politics*, p. 172; Acheson, *Present at the Creation*, p. 375; Trout, "Rhetoric Revisited."

[17] *Truman Public Papers, 1947*, pp. 167-72.

the situation should be viewed in a global context. "If Greece fell within the Russian orbit, not only Turkey would be affected but also Italy, France, and the whole of western Europe," Acheson declared.

Truman recognized that the Greek crisis was but a small part of a serious Western economic malaise caused by wartime devastation, decline of morale, weak coalition governments, the breakdown of the economic infrastructure, and a series of natural disasters. "The decision is to ask Congress for 250 million and say this is only the beginning," Truman explained. "It means [the] U.S. going into European politics. It means the greatest selling job ever facing a President." The cabinet gave him their unanimous approval. Secretary of War Patterson emphasized that United States security required that Western Europe not be allowed to fall under Russian domination; in particular, our occupation policy in Germany would be defeated by such a development. According to Admiral Leahy, "all the Cabinet members present, with a full understanding that projection of the United States into the political problems of Europe is a direct and positive change in the traditional policy of the United States, recommended that financial assistance be given immediately to the Greek Government and that the people of America be fully and frankly informed that its purpose is to prevent Soviet domination of Europe."

Truman still feared a repetition of the events of the interwar period, when Americans rejected their world responsibilities. "The job is to get the facts to the country to get the support necessary," Truman said. Peering ahead through the lens of an episodic script, he declared, "We can't afford to revive the isolationists and wreck the United Nations." Truman appointed a cabinet committee headed by John Snyder to meet with financiers, businessmen, and labor leaders to enlist their support for a public information program.[18]

On March 12, Truman went before Congress to request $400 million for Greece and Turkey and authorization for a mission of civilian and military personnel to supervise the use of American aid. He described the awesome destruction left by the marauding Germans, the dire financial crisis facing the Greek government, the obstruction of economic recovery by military communist-led guerrillas. But he portrayed the Greek civil war as a global struggle between two alternative ways of life, one based on the will of the majority, the other on the will of a minority forcibly imposed by terror and oppression. "I be-

---

[18] *FR: 1947*, V, pp. 97-100; Leahy diary, March 7, 1947, LC; Notes on Cabinet Meeting, March 7, 1947, Connelly Papers, HSTL; Forrestal diary, March 7, 1947, *Forrestal Diaries*, ed. Millis, pp. 250-51.

lieve," he said, "that it must be the policy of the United States to support free peoples who are resisting attempted subjugation by armed minorities or by outside pressures." The next day, Truman flew to Key West, Florida, where he wrote his daughter Margaret:

> We had a very pleasant flight from Washington.
>
> Your old Dad slept for 750 or 800 miles—three hours. . . . No one, not even me (your Mother would say I) knew how very tired and worn to a frazzle the Chief Executive had become. This terrible decision I had to make had been over my head for about six weeks.[19]

Still, the Truman administration had not fully formulated a coherent strategy for dealing with the Soviet Union, or a vision of the world order that America was trying to create. According to Senator Vandenberg, "I think the President's message defined what is being done in terms of a *doctrine*, a little more definitely than I interpret the situation. . . . To me it is a *plan*; it is part of a *pattern*, and, as such, is to be distinguished from a policy." Based on his discussions with the American embassy, M. E. Dening of the British Foreign Office concluded that "though the thoughts of the State Department and the War and Navy Departments may have been crystallizing for some time past, our approach over Greece and Turkey caught the Administration somewhat unprepared, with the result that President Truman's speech is something of an improvisation." Typically patronizing, he remarked that "with our better oiled machinery we should probably, in similar circumstances, have produced a better-finished article." Dening wondered whether the Americans expected their forthright challenge to force the Soviets to beat a retreat, or whether they were prepared to carry the struggle to its ultimate conclusion. "I cannot help wondering whether they have thought this all out," he noted perceptively. C.F.A. Warner thought that the State Department and the chiefs of staff and Mr. Byrnes had for some time favored the policy of preventing the imposition of communist-controlled governments wherever they could, but, as so often happened in America, they adopted the general policy originally without thinking out what it meant in practice. The British economic crisis and note on Greece and Turkey, however, shocked them into examining what a policy of resistance to communist regimes would involve, and this realization plus the need to use shock tactics with Congress went into the drafting of President Truman's speech.[20]

---

[19] M. Truman, *Harry Truman*, p. 343.
[20] Jock Balfour to Gladwynn Jebb, April 19, 1947, FO 371/67582, UN 2766; "Ef-

Through his background briefings with journalists and testimony before Congress, Acheson made an invaluable contribution to the lengthy process of refining, elaborating, and articulating the containment policy. In so doing, he also shaped in his own mind a set of consistent propositions about Soviet foreign policy and the most effective means of coping with the threat of Soviet expansion—the Cold War belief system. To be sure, Acheson had already concluded, before the Greek political crisis, that the Soviet Union had unlimited ambitions that the United States must seek to contain. Still, he had not yet formulated in his own mind major elements of the Cold War belief system—the futility of negotiations with the Soviets until we had attained a position of strength, the central role of ideology in shaping Soviet foreign policy, the need to bolster strategic "soft spots" throughout the globe. In his presentations to the cabinet, President Truman, Congress, and the State Department, Acheson justified aiding Greece and Turkey by means of the "domino" theory; however, this simple script would not serve as a guide to the complex, concrete situations that would confront the administration in the chaos of the postwar period. Before the Truman Doctrine was even announced to the American people, Acheson was having difficulty explaining why the new policy would not apply to China or Hungary, which was in the sphere of Soviet military power, yet retained vestiges of democracy.

When confronted by unmistakable evidence of Britain's demise as a world power and the need to reconstitute a world balance of power, Acheson did not hesitate to act before he had formulated the principles underlying the shift in policy. His immediate problem was to place the Greek civil war in a broader context for the American public, to justify abandoning the American tradition of nonentanglement in the internal affairs of Europe. In addition, he had to decide how the world conflict between the United States and the Soviet Union should be portrayed—as a confrontation between the United States and Russia, between free enterprise and socialism, capitalism and communism, or freedom and totalitarianism; this definition would set constraints on future American actions. Later, as he attempted to cut the Truman Doctrine down to size, Acheson developed and elaborated many important tenets of the Cold War belief system as a means of explaining to himself and others the shift in American foreign policy.

Though the president's speech unequivocally declared that totali-

---

fects of President Truman's Statement: Assistance to Greece and Turkey," March 19, 1947, FO 371/67582, UN 2001/1754/78.

tarian regimes imposed upon free peoples endangered international peace and U.S. security, the Truman administration had no intention of trying to police the world against communism. Acheson assured Congress that any future requests for aid would be evaluated on the basis of need, American interests, and the likelihood that our assistance would be effective in meeting the problems of that country. The Truman administration recognized that U.S. capabilities were limited, and that commitments should not exceed the power to fulfill them. The president had not launched an "ideological crusade," Acheson stressed. Truman also did not believe that the United States was committed to setting up democracies throughout the world. "There are differences in definition of the word democracy," he told a group of newsmen. "Our definition doesn't work all the way around the world." He hoped that U.S. aid would make it possible for the Greeks to adopt democratic procedures at some time in the future, but it was not our job to interfere in the internal affairs of other countries. In an off-the-record briefing, Truman explained his conception of the Truman Doctrine: "My idea is the restoration of a peace-time economy in these countries with the hope that they will themselves inaugurate a free government that will be for the benefit of the people." Acheson also insisted that U.S. aid to Greece did not constitute a precedent for intervention in the Chinese civil war. But he had difficulty conceptualizing the relevant differences between the two situations in such a way as to avoid offending the "China lobby." Privately, Acheson agreed with Truman that further assistance to Chiang Kai-shek would be like "pouring sand into a rat hole."[21]

On the other hand, the United States should not refuse economic aid to a country just because it had a communist regime. Acheson did not view the communist bloc as monolithic. By providing small, nonprovocative amounts of assistance to countries within the Soviet sphere of influence, the United States could enhance their independence and exacerbate internal strains within the bloc. For example, Hungary and Poland were among five countries for which the State Department was currently requesting $350 million relief in a bill before the House Foreign Affairs Committee.[22]

[21] Senate Committee on Foreign Relations, *Legislative Origins of the Truman Doctrine*, executive sess., 80th Cong., 1st sess., 1973, pp. 21-22; Jones, *Fifteen Weeks*, p. 190; Notes on Cabinet Meeting, March 7, 1947, Connelly Papers, HSTL; Memorandum of Press and Radio News Conference, March 18, 1947, Jones Papers, HSTL; Ayers diary, May 13, 1947, HSTL.

[22] Memorandum of press and radio news conference, March 18, 1947, Jones Papers, HSTL.

Despite the universalistic rhetoric used in his speech, Truman understood that the principal aim of the policy was to prevent the collapse of strategic areas to maintain a balance of power. Eleanor Roosevelt wrote him objecting to our "taking over Mr. Churchill's policies in the Near East, in the name of Democracy." In a May 7 letter, Truman pointed out that her concern seemed to be that "we should not try to stop Communism by throwing our economic weight in at points which are of strategic importance but deficient in democracy." "I would argue," he replied, "that if the Greek-Turkish land bridge between the continents is one point at which our democratic forces can stop the advance of Communism that has flowed steadily through the Baltic countries, Poland, Yugoslavia, Rumania, Bulgaria, to some extent Hungary, then this is the place to do it, regardless of whether or not the terrain is good."[23]

The principal aim of the containment policy was to block further Soviet expansion and political infiltration. By using our economic and military power to restore political stability and economic well-being in various countries, the United States could "create conditions in which at a later stage renewed negotiations may be expected to be more effective." For it was Soviet policy "to probe wherever there is weakness but to make no trial against strength." After an extended period of time in which the United States demonstrated to the Soviets that we were fully aware of our vital interests and prepared to defend them, negotiated solutions might become possible.

The instruments of the containment policy were economic assistance, propaganda, military power, and diplomacy. Through economic assistance, the United States would bolster the stability of strategic "soft spots" throughout the world. In addition, Acheson believed that a foreign information program designed to counteract the lies of Soviet propaganda would be extremely useful as an adjunct to or even substitute for American economic and financial aid. Military power was useful primarily as a means of deterring forcible Soviet expansion. The United States should "assume the military posture indicating to all who may be inclined to doubt that we are not sinking into a condition again where it may take us three or four years to become effective as a military nation." Beyond that, Acheson admitted, military force was of limited utility in carrying into effect U.S. foreign policy. "We have arrived at the point in the art of scientific and technical warfare where the resort to force will mean the defeat of everybody's foreign policy," Acheson warned. "It will mean universal destruction."

[23] Truman to Eleanor Roosevelt, May 7, 1947, Eleanor Roosevelt Papers, FDRL.

Truman also did not foresee the commitment of U.S. troops to contain communism; our assistance was to be economic.

Negotiations with the Soviet Union Acheson ruled out for the foreseeable future. "We must not believe that the fundamental problem between us and the Soviet Union, which is the inherent expansionism and aggressiveness of communism, is soluble by one or any number of talks between the Big Three or in the United Nations." Even if they wanted to, the Russians could not halt the push of foreign communist parties; "ideological evangelism is the small fig leaf of respectability which covers a brutal dictatorship." "Without communist ideology," Acheson explained, "Stalin is no different from Peter the Great or Ivan the Terrible."[24]

John Lewis Gaddis argues that, contrary to popular belief, the Truman Doctrine did *not* constitute a major reorientation in American foreign policy, because the decision to contain Soviet expansion was consistent with the tradition of preventing Europe from falling under the domination of a single hostile power. He writes that "while it is clear from both contemporary and retrospective sources that the men who participated in this decision felt they were living through a revolution, one gets the impression that this sense of exhilaration stemmed from the *way* in which policy was formulated . . . quickly, efficiently, and decisively." But this was not the view held by U.S. officials at the time. On March 11, Acheson cabled the embassy in Greece that the initiation of a long-term program of substantial aid to maintain Greek independence "of course represents [a] major decision in U.S. policy." "We intend to support free people who are attempting to resist subjugation by armed minorities or by outside pressures," he explained. Clark Clifford viewed the president's speech as "the opening gun in a campaign to bring people up to realization that the war isn't over by any means." In his diary, Assistant Press Secretary Eben Ayers predicted that Truman's speech "may well prove to be the most important speech of his life." "The great importance and significance of this speech," Ayers believed, "lies less in the recommendations than in the break which it marks in U.S. foreign policy and in its attack upon the Communist policy of political infiltration." Admiral Leahy noted in his diary that adoption of the president's program "will effect a

[24] Address made off the record before American Society of Newspaper Editors, Dean Acheson, April 18, 1947, Acheson Papers, HSTL; "Greek-Turkish Aid," March 20, 1947, McNaughton Papers, HSTL; Concluding Section of Mr. Acheson's Talk before the American Society of Newspaper Editors, April 18, 1947, Jones Papers, HSTL; Senate Committee on Foreign Relations, *Legislative Origins of the Truman Doctrine*, p. 95; Ayers diary, May 13, 1947, HSTL.

complete reversal of a traditional American policy to avoid involvement in the political difficulties of European States."[25]

The need to legitimize this reorientation of American foreign policy helps to explain why Acheson chose to couch the Greek civil war as part of a global battle between two opposing ways of life. Since the Truman administration had a clear sense of the limits of U.S. capabilities and interests in containing communism, then why did Acheson envelop the request for aid to Greece and Turkey in universalistic rhetoric? In *The End of Liberalism*, Theodore Lowi argues that the Truman Doctrine, containment, and the Cold War illustrate the propensity for U.S. policymakers to "oversell the threat" to create a sense of crisis that will forge a contrived cohesion among the fragmented and divided policy elite. In the American pluralist system, instead of a foreign ministry there are numerous independent agencies sharing powers, so rational deliberation by a unified elite is replaced by bargaining and logrolling. The president is thus perennially tempted to mobilize the American public to pressure the Congress and the executive branch into giving him the support necessary to carry out any foreign policy forcefully and effectively.[26]

Still, the problem runs deeper. The domestic political requirements of policy legitimation and implementation cannot explain why Acheson and others *accepted* major components of the belief system used to justify containment. If the president and other members of his administration cynically fanned the flames of crisis to win congressional support for foreign aid, then the influence on American foreign policy of universalistic rhetoric would have been relatively short-lived. For the public's attention span to foreign affairs is strictly limited; elections are not decided on foreign policy issues. Once the foreign aid bill had passed or the president had secured a treaty, one would expect the crisis to evaporate, and the public's attention to be diverted elsewhere. The problem is that in exaggerating the threat or the American interests at stake, U.S. officials ultimately come to believe their own rhetoric and rationalizations. Vietnam became a vital interest of the United States because our leaders said that it was. Reading contemporary accounts of the drafting of the Truman Doctrine, one does not have the sense that U.S. officials were disingenuous or cynically manipulating

---

[25] Gaddis, "Was the Truman Doctrine a Real Turning Point?" p. 390; *FR: 1947*, V, pp. 108-109; Handwritten notes by Clark Clifford, March 9, 1947, Elsey Papers, "Truman Doctrine" Speech—3/12/47," HSTL; Ayers diary, March 12, 1947, HSTL; Leahy diary, March 7, 10, 12, 1947, LC.

[26] Theodore J. Lowi, *The End of Liberalism: Ideology, Policy, and the Crisis of Public Authority* (New York: W. W. Norton, 1969), pp. 157-88.

the American people. Instead, time and again one finds references to the need to inform the American public of the "grim facts." As Will Clayton wrote in a private memorandum:

> The United States will not take world leadership effectively unless the people of the United States are shocked into doing so.
>
> To shock them it is only necessary for the President and Secretary of State to tell them the truth and the whole truth.
>
> The truth is to be found in the cables which daily arrive at the State Department from all over the world.
>
> In every country in the Eastern Hemisphere and most of the countries of the Western Hemisphere Russia is boring from within.[27]

When forced by events to act, Truman brought his previously wavering and inconsistent beliefs into line. Truman's opposition to the expansion of communism into Greece was instinctual and almost automatic; he had not developed a set of beliefs supporting the containment policy before making the Truman Doctrine speech. A British Foreign Office official, C.F.A. Warner, commented perceptively that "it also seems quite possible that President Truman has not himself grasped the full implications of everything in his speech." Several months later, Truman believed in the validity of the domino theory, at least for Greece and Turkey. In November, Truman told C. L. Sulzberger that "if Russia gets Greece and Turkey, then they would get Italy and France and the iron curtain would extend all the way to Western Ireland. In that event we would have to come home and prepare for war." Truman no longer had any faith in negotiations as a means of settling our differences with the Soviets. He told a group of newspaper editors that we had to stand for what was right and eventually the Russians would come around and agree to it. Truman said that we had tried going along with them as far as we possibly could, trying to please them. "There is no way to please them," he declared. "They deal from day to day and what's done yesterday has no bearing on what's done today and tomorrow. We have to make up our minds what our policy is." The Soviets were influenced only by superior power. Worst of all, they could not be trusted to keep their agreements. "When I make straight out and out agreements with a government," he said, "in the name of the United States of America, and not a single one of those agreements is carried out, I have got to

[27] Memorandum, 3/5/47, Clayton Papers, "General File—Marshall Plan Memos 1947," HSTL.

use other methods." "They understand one language," he vowed, "and that is the language they are going to get from me from this point."[28]

Still, Truman found it hard to believe that Stalin, who so resembled Pendergast, had deliberately and willfully violated his commitments. "Since Potsdam, Stalin has broken every single one of those agreements," Truman remarked to Sulzberger. "Maybe it's not his fault," he speculated. "After all, he is only secretary of the Politburo and has his troubles with the other thirteen members just the way I have my trouble here with my Cabinet and the Congress."[29]

Truman blamed the breakdown of the Grand Alliance on the Soviets' failure to keep their agreements. As always, the "code of the politician" influenced his judgments of political allies and opponents. "I have every kindly feeling in the world for the people who are causing us all the trouble now," he said, "and we made certain specific agreements, none of which has been carried out by the other party. And that is the cause of the present situation."[30] With his penchant for exaggeration, Truman claimed that the Russians had broken forty-seven treaties since 1922.[31] Was this explanation of the origins of the Cold War valid?

Actually, the Soviets had not violated their interpretation of the Yalta agreements, and they had some justification for viewing American protests about "free elections" in Eastern Europe as going beyond the literal wording and implied meaning of the Yalta Declaration on Liberated Europe, which called merely for consultations among the Big Three when all agreed that it was necessary. Unlike Truman, Acheson and other State Department officials did not relate the containment policy to the Soviets' failure to observe international agreements. Instead, the prevailing consensus within the Truman administration was that Britain's decline as an imperial power required the United States to assume a world leadership role and prevent the Soviets from expanding into vacuums left in the wake of Britain's departure.

Why did Truman change his beliefs about the Soviet Union? Truman experienced no epiphany, no sudden revelation of the true motives behind Soviet foreign policy. Concerning the Truman Doctrine

[28] Sulzberger diary, November 4, 1947, *Long Row of Candles*, pp. 364-65; Ayers diary, April 17, May 13, 1947, HSTL; "Effects of President Truman's Statement: Assistance to Greece and Turkey," March 19, 1947, FO 371/67582, UN 2001/1754/78.

[29] Sulzberger diary, November 4, 1947, *Long Row of Candles*, p. 364.

[30] Notes of press conference by the President, September 30, 1947, Ayers Papers, "General File—Foreign Policy," HSTL. See also Truman to Eleanor Roosevelt, May 31, 1947, Eleanor Roosevelt Papers, FDRL; Ayers diary, April 22, 1949, HSTL.

[31] Sulzberger diary, November 4, 1947, *Long Row of Candles*, p. 363.

speech, he acknowledged to a group of newsmen that there had been much speculation "as to the why and the wherefore and . . . how it came about 'so suddenly.'" "It didn't come about so suddenly," Truman said. "It wasn't a sudden proposition that happened in five minutes. It had been developing ever since the Germans surrendered. And it finally got to the point where we had to state our case to the world."[32] The change in Truman's beliefs was gradual. One by one, Truman abandoned the principal assumptions underlying FDR's "grand design," at first only provisionally. At any point, he was prepared to accept evidence that the Soviets were motivated by fear of an Anglo-American bloc, that the Russians could be trusted to keep their agreements, that a personal meeting with Stalin could resolve all outstanding differences. But over time this appeared less and less likely.

Truman did not change his views as a response to pressure from the American public. In February 1947, a State Department survey showed that a strong majority of the public was opposed to the idea of "getting tough" with Russia, and an equal proportion favored continuation of the administration's "firm" policy. Before Truman delivered his speech, Admiral Leahy predicted that there would be a "very active adverse reaction by the domestic political opposition if not by a majority of the people of the United States." Far from being a gesture to propitiate the public, Leahy judged that the "President's stand in this matter will require courage of a high order." At the March 7 cabinet meeting, the president's advisers were worried that the public would perceive the policy as an attempt to preserve the British imperial lifeline.[33]

The bipolar distribution of power after the war contributed to Truman's changing perception of the Soviet Union, but is not a sufficient explanation. After all, it was clear before the war ended that the Soviet Union and the United States would emerge with unparalleled power. Yet it was not until almost two years later that Truman accepted the division of the world into rival blocs. It is doubtful that Truman would have taken action to fill the power vacuum in Europe when he did, had the Russians shown a more cooperative attitude in Germany or refrained from trying to expand into the Mediterranean.

Of the psychological theories, self-perception theory is most useful in explaining the final shift in Truman's attitudes toward the Soviet

[32] Ayers diary, April 17, 1947, HSTL.

[33] "American Attitudes on U.S. Policy Towards Russia," February 19, 1947, 711.61/2 1947, RG 59, NA; Leahy diary, March 7, 1947, LC; Notes on Cabinet Meeting, March 7, 1947, Connelly Papers, HSTL; Elsey to Clifford, 8 March 1947, Elsey Papers, "Truman Doctrine Speech, 3/12/47," HSTL.

Union following the inauguration of the Truman Doctrine. As self-perception theory predicts, Truman was unconcerned about inconsistencies in his beliefs from one moment to the next. He inferred what he believed at a particular time by recalling the most recent and salient Soviet action, or by drawing the appropriate conclusion from U.S. policies. Since American policy toward the Soviet Union fluctuated drastically in the early postwar period, along with Soviet willingness to cooperate, Truman's beliefs were also highly unstable and erratic. As self-perception theory would predict, he did not adopt a Cold War image of the Soviet Union until a few months *after* he had made the Truman Doctrine speech, when he had been given the chance to think through the implications of the new policy.

Truman was not influenced by a persuasive communication about the Soviets, as in the Hovland attitude change approach. Truman did not change his mind because he was handed a well-developed policy with a cogent explanation of Soviet actions. When he approved the decision to give aid to Greece and Turkey, there was no policy but a situation requiring presidential action. Special appropriations were needed from Congress; the request for legislation had to be phrased in terms that would attract public and congressional support. What became known as the containment policy was subsequently defined and elaborated in response to particular events—the "fall" of China to communism explosion of a Soviet atomic weapon, the Korean War.

Further, the Hovland approach predicts that Truman would be among the first to change his beliefs about the Soviet Union, because he lacked confidence in his knowledge about foreign affairs and should have been receptive to the advice of hardliners such as Grew or Harriman. Yet Truman was among the last to give up on FDR's "grand design" for one world. He rejected the combined advice of the State, War, Navy, and White House staffs contained in the Clifford-Elsey report on Russia. Though Kennan insisted that the Soviet foreign policy outlook could not be changed by discussions with individuals, even a leader as powerful as Stalin, Truman responded to a conciliatory interview given by the Russian leader with a renewed public affirmation of Roosevelt's "grand design" in his October speech to the United Nations General Assembly. A month later, he renewed his invitation to Stalin to visit Washington, which the Russian leader had rejected just six months previously.

Nor did Truman change his beliefs to relieve the cognitive dissonance provoked by the inconsistency between his private convictions that only U.S.-Soviet cooperation could contribute to lasting world peace and the "hard-line" policy he adopted for domestic political motives. Truman was able to tolerate great inconsistency in his attitudes and between his attitudes and overt behavior. Thus, as early as October 1945, Truman concluded that the Soviets understood one language—how many divisions have you? Yet he persisted in trying to work out a settlement with the Russians using every means available—the offer of an alliance against Germany, a personal invitation to Stalin, the pressure of world public opinion—except rearmament and mobilization of U.S. military power.

Consistent with attribution theory, Truman gave disproportionate weight to his personal experience negotiating with Stalin at Potsdam. One reason that he was so reluctant to give up FDR's "grand design" was his belief that Stalin was like Tom Pendergast, a fellow politician with whom he could make deals and expect them to be carried out. But Truman did not change his view of the Soviets because he tried to explain Soviet expansion beyond their security sphere in Eastern Europe, contrary to the predictions of attribution theory. Obviously, we cannot know what went on inside Truman's head. But the best available evidence of what Truman thought is in diaries and letters at the time; these do not indicate that Truman tried to figure out the reasons for Soviet actions. Instead, he usually made inferences off the top of his head, often by using analogies or metaphors from familiar experiences. For example, Truman viewed the Potsdam negotiations as a "poker" game in which the United States would place its cards on the table and receive Soviet concessions.

Truman's firm belief in the "code of the politician" helps to explain many actions that are puzzling according to common sense. Because of his concern for maintaining the reputation for keeping his agreements, President Truman insisted on carrying out Roosevelt's commitments to the Russians, against the advice of Churchill and State Department officials. He ordered the withdrawal of Eisenhower's forces to the previously agreed-on occupation zones, refusing to use American troops as a bargaining chip to secure Soviet compliance with the United States' interpretation of the Yalta accords. Though the atomic bomb removed the need for Soviet entrance into the war against Japan, Truman did not abrogate the territorial concessions the Soviets had demanded as their price for entering the Pacific War. Although he was "talking tough" when he first took office, Truman did not use the leverage available to him to influence Soviet behavior.

At the same time, because it was the public reputation for keeping agreements that mattered, Truman was not bothered by the gap between his own rhetoric and deed, by the disparity between his public promise not to recognize governments imposed by foreign powers and his quick acceptance of a whitewashed Soviet puppet regime in Poland. Nor did he expect Stalin to carry out his pledge to hold "free elections" in Eastern Europe, as he made clear to Hopkins in May 1945.

Yet it was not Stalin's violation of his agreements that finally roused Truman to action in March 1947; Stalin's refusal to withdraw his troops from Iran in March 1946 was a much more blatant and egregious violation of his word than the civil war in Greece. Further, though he knew that the Greek government was on the brink of collapse and the rebel forces growing stronger, Truman did not react until the British government and the State Department forced the issue to his attention.

Because he was influenced by the Pendergast persona, Truman expected Stalin to have enough sense to stage elections in Eastern Europe for the benefit of the American people. But, recalling how he himself had been elected to the Senate by carrying the graveyards, Truman did not expect elections held under Soviet auspices to be genuinely free. Over and over, Truman demonstrated his lack of interest in ensuring that the Eastern European governments conducted genuinely free elections: he recognized the Polish provisional government when Hopkins obtained token representation for popular Polish politicians; at Potsdam, he kept referring the issue of satellite elections to the foreign ministers for discussion; he went along with Byrnes' decision to recognize the Rumanian government when it was "broadened" with the addition of two democratic leaders.

Truman's Cold War beliefs did not begin to gel until he was besieged by his advisers and Great Britain to assume British geopolitical interests in Greece and Turkey. Truman phrased his arguments for aid to Greece and Turkey in language that would overcome the renascent political isolationism of the new Congress—freedom vs. totalitarianism. His rhetoric evoked the memories of totalitarian regimes that appeared in Europe in the 1930s. Having publicly declared that the United States must aid free peoples against the threat of communist subversion or aggression, Truman eventually inferred that he believed in related assumptions about Soviet conduct. From this point, the Cold War consensus began to emerge.

A MULTILEVEL EXPLANATION

THE CONTINUING CYCLE of Cold War historiography has produced a complex and ideologically diverse web of interpretations. The conflict between revisionist and confirmationist works resounds, as new archival sources are declassified and private papers become available. Alternative explanations are often irreconcilable because they are based on incommensurable ideologies, research bases, and contexts of historical scholarship. In addition, and more germane for the purposes of this study, the historical interpretations reflect alternative naive theories about human decisionmaking. Since these intuitive conceptions of human nature and information processing are not based on experimentation or rigorous analysis, in interpreting the historical documents historians have provided an often incomplete and sometimes erroneous explanation of American policymakers' thinking and motives in formulating the containment policy.

Both conservative and liberal revisionists blame what they describe as immoral and self-defeating U.S. policies toward the Soviet Union on the personality traits of American leaders; they underestimate the heavy weight of situational and domestic political pressures on the choices taken by Roosevelt and Truman. Their assumption is that if a policy is misconceived, it must be because of ulterior motives of *Realpolitik* or naiveté. This type of thinking reflects the "fundamental attribution" error identified by attribution theorists. Conservative revisionists accuse Roosevelt of "appeasing" Stalin at Yalta and selling out Eastern Europe. In a mirror image, left-liberal revisionists attribute the Cold War to Truman's belligerence, parochialism, and ignorance that led him to oppose legitimate Soviet security requirements in Eastern Europe and use the atomic monopoly as an implied threat to roll back Russian influence in the area.

Realist historians, on the other hand, recognize the force of both the international distribution of power and the domestic political context of isolationism in shaping the containment policy. According to Realists such as Morgenthau and Kennan, the Truman administration conceived of aid to Greece and Turkey as a means of maintaining a balance of power in the Mediterranean once Britain was no longer able to shoulder its imperial responsibilities; but to win the support of the American people, they deliberately misconstrued the policy as an attempt to preserve freedom against the onslaught of totalitarianism. In other words, American leaders were rational in diagnosing the requirements of the international situation, but were led by situational pressures to act contrary to their true beliefs. But since they did not use archival sources, Realist historians did not realize that Acheson and other influential officials could not have misled the public about how they intended to carry out the containment policy in practice, because *they themselves did not know*. Even Acheson, blessed with an articulate and well-developed set of Realist concepts and generalizations, had not formulated basic principles of the containment policy when he recommended that the United States give aid to Greece and Turkey and supervised the drafting of the Truman Doctrine speech. The Realist dictum to preserve a balance of power was not sufficient to guide U.S. officials in dealing with countries such as Hungary, Czechoslovakia, or Poland, which were on the verge of being absorbed into the Soviet sphere of communist systems but whose independence might be strengthened through American aid. Were these countries instruments of the Kremlin or reluctant pawns? Nor did Realist principles help Acheson and the State Department in deciding whether countries such as Korea or China were vital interests that should receive American economic and military assistance. What Acheson needed was a more specific set of generalizations about the behavior of a particular adversary, the Soviet Union, and decision rules about the best means of handling the threat—an "operational code" or Cold War belief system. This he acquired *after* the shift in policy.

Official and confirmationist historians assume that U.S. officials and the public avoided threatening information about Soviet expansionist ambitions as long as possible through strained and tendentious rationalizations of Soviet actions, until the weight of the evidence could no longer be ignored. In other words, these historians accept the "cognitive consistency" model of man as driven to avoid the stress created by inconsistent beliefs and contradictory information. Up until almost two years after the war ended, the Truman administration engaged in wishful thinking and ignored the obvious implications of Soviet repression in Eastern Europe and the crises in Iran and Turkey because of their reluctance to jettison FDR's "grand design" for Soviet-American cooperation. But careful examination of archival sources over time shows that Truman and other U.S. officials did not distort or ignore Soviet behavior that contradicted their original optimistic beliefs about the Soviet Union. Instead, they updated and adjusted their beliefs in response to the facts, as any good scientist would. Soviet domination of Eastern Europe, although morally repugnant, did not arouse any fears of further expansion because the Soviet government's insistence on having friendly governments could be attributed to situational and geographic pressures—more specifically, Stalin's determination not to be exposed once again to the terror of a German invasion. Soviet pressure on Iran, Greece, and Turkey, on the other hand, could not be explained by legitimate Soviet security needs; consequently, Soviet probes in the Mediterranean power vacuum precipitated the change in American policy.

Open door revisionist historians find too much clarity and consistency in American leaders' reaction to postwar events. Beginning in October 1945, Truman made sporadic and spontaneous judgments about Soviet expansionism and the danger of war; yet, almost in the same breath, he would assert that the two countries had no conflicting interests and that Stalin was sincerely concerned with maintaining world peace. It is difficult to see how the vacillating and shifting positions taken by Truman and Byrnes could reflect the influence of any ideology, capitalist or liberal. In addition, as will be discussed below, the historical record indicates that far more influential and controlling than such abstract and theoretical constructions as ideology are concrete and simple schemas such as historical analogies, metaphors, and personae. Instead of deducing policy from a Weltanschauung, decisionmakers match current events to what is familiar, concrete, and close to home.

Explicit and systematic use of alternative social psychological theories of attitude change provides a means of assessing the validity of these differing naive conceptions of human decision processes that underlie alternative explanations of the containment policy. Still, the origins of American Cold War policies cannot be attributed solely to events in the "minds of men." To assume otherwise is to commit the "fundamental attribution error" of overestimating the role of individual personality traits and beliefs in causing behavior, while overlooking the importance of the logic of the situation and environmental constraints.

To provide a richer, more determinate explanation of the origins of American Cold War policies, this study used a composite, multidimensional strategy. First, theories at different levels of analysis—systemic, domestic political, and individual cognitive processes—were applied to historical case material to explain why American leaders began a long-term policy of containing Soviet expansion in the early postwar period. How much do the different theories explain? What do they explain? How can the theories be combined to fill out and complete the historical explanation? Second, social psychological theories were used to explain variations in policymakers' information processing about the Soviet Union from 1944 to 1947. If U.S. officials reached similar conclusions about Soviet actions, then the logic of the situation or the bipolar distribution of power must have been controlling; but if the information was sufficiently ambiguous and the situational constraints lax enough that different individuals could form diverse interpretations of Soviet motives, then a psychological explanation may be needed. The influence of cognitive variables on foreign policymaking can be readily determined in the period in which the Cold War emerged. Within a relatively short period of time, U.S. policymakers' hopes for Soviet-American cooperation faded, to be replaced by the gradual emergence of doubts and fears about the scope of Soviet ambitions. Was the Cold War belief system the cause, concomitant, or consequence of the adoption of the containment policy?

A multilevel explanation is needed to account for the development of American Cold War policies, including variables on the level of the international system, domestic politics, and individual policymakers' cognitive processes. Truman might have continued to waver and hesitate had he not been faced simultaneously with an economic crisis in Western Europe requiring vast infusions of American capital and a Republican Congress determined to slash governmental expenditures. In February 1947, the Greek government was on the brink of collapse under the combined weight of a financial crisis and communist-led guerrilla warfare. Because of their own critical financial problems, the British could no longer assume their traditional imperial responsibilities and were planning to retrench their economic and military involvement in Greece. Aid to Greece would require special appropriations; but congressional leaders warned Truman that the only way to get the legislation through Congress was to convince the American people that the aid was needed to prevent future communist takeovers. Truman also recognized that additional large-scale economic assistance would have to be given to Western Europe in the very near future. Consequently, in the Truman Doctrine speech, he portrayed the Greek civil war as part of a global struggle between the forces of freedom and totalitarianism. When forced by events to act, Truman brought his previously inconsistent, wavering beliefs into line. He adopted assumptions about the Soviet Union—to be sure, already entertained for some time—that rationalized and legitimized the shift in American policy.

The latent and emerging bipolar distribution of power in the *international system* made some form of U.S.-Soviet conflict inevitable.

American policymakers were destined to view the Soviet Union as a rival and potential enemy, because no other country had the motive and capability to threaten U.S. security. Drawing an important theoretical distinction, the Sprouts have pointed out that policymakers define choices and make decisions with reference to the *psychological environment*, whereas the *operational environment* sets limits to what can be accomplished when the decision is executed. In other words, environmental factors are linked to policy decisions only if they are perceived and taken into consideration by policymakers. But in explaining the outcome of a decision, the analyst must also consider the opportunities and constraints inherent in the environment that affect the operational results of any undertaking, irrespective of whether these factors are perceived by policymakers.[1]

FDR's vision of Soviet-American cooperation was betrayed not by the incompetence or anti-Soviet prejudices of his successor, but by the increasing frictions accompanying the rise of two superpowers in an anarchic international system. The emergence of a power vacuum first in Central Europe and then in the oil-rich and militarily strategic eastern Mediterranean merely exacerbated the potential for conflict inherent in the structure of the international system. The United States had an obvious interest in keeping the Soviet Union out of Central Europe and in blocking Soviet expansion into the Near East.[2] In contrast, Eastern Europe had few raw materials or industries attractive to the United States, as evidenced by the lack of any significant prewar trade ties with the region.

International systems theory predicts U.S.-Soviet conflict, but does not differentiate among alternative forms that the rivalry could have assumed. As discussed previously,[3] within the constraints imposed by the international system, the United States and the Soviet Union could have defined their relationship in a variety of ways:

1. a "gentleman's" agreement dividing the world into "spheres of influence";
2. competition for alliance with a reunified Germany against the other superpower;

[1] Harold and Margaret Sprout, "Environmental Factors in the Study of International Politics," in *International Politics and Foreign Policy*, ed. James N. Rosenau, 2nd ed. (New York: Free Press, 1969), pp. 41-56.
[2] On this point, see the Senate Committee on Foreign Relations, *Legislative Origins of the Truman Doctrine*, pp. 84, 94-95, 130.
[3] See Introduction.

3. U.S. isolation within the Western Hemisphere and the Pacific, Soviet domination over Europe;
4. limited adversary—cooperating on some issues, competing on others;
5. "zero-sum" game;
6. war.

The differences among these alternative historical outcomes are not academic. The selection by historical forces of one alternative rather than another had far-reaching effects and practical implications not only for the people of the United States and the Soviet Union, but also for the inhabitants of geographic regions that are arenas of conflict for the two superpowers. The American domestic political context and the Cold War belief system help to explain why U.S.-Soviet conflict was "zero-sum."

Systemic theory also does not explain the timing of the Cold War, why Truman did not abandon FDR's "grand design" until almost two years after Germany's surrender. Throughout this period, Truman improvised, following no consistent policy toward the Soviet Union. Misled by hindsight, historians have not adequately portrayed the genuine torment of indecision experienced by Truman and his advisers. It was already apparent to the State Department by the end of World War II that FDR's vision of great power unity probably could not be realized, at least in the near future. But Truman had no policy with which to replace Roosevelt's "grand design." Desperately, he tried a number of expedients to salvage the policy of Soviet-American cooperation: offer of a long-term alliance against Germany, rallying world public opinion against Soviet expansion, personal diplomacy. None was well thought-out or part of any consistent strategy. Many historians have imposed a retrospective coherence on American foreign policy that simply did not exist at the time.

As one might expect, domestic politics played an important role in the development of the Cold War consensus. In an ideal world, Truman could have informed the American people frankly that aid to Greece and Turkey was essential to preserve the balance of power in the Near East. Instead, he was obliged to couch his request for aid in the evocative emotional symbols of "freedom" and "totalitarianism" to legitimize the policy. In order to obtain the legitimacy needed for effective, consistent implementation of a policy, the president must construct, present, and defend an image of the international system that is compatible with the specific action advocated. Unfortunately, the likelihood of success in this endeavor is greatly enhanced if the image makes use of emotional symbols and metaphors.[4]

This is not to suggest that the domestic political context *caused* the American shift to Cold War policies.[5] Republican criticism and public pressures for a "tougher" policy did not force Truman to abandon FDR's "grand design." Throughout 1946, American public opinion was highly volatile, responding to each event that seemed to portend Soviet unilateral expansion or cooperation. Further, the public was sharply divided in its attitudes toward the Soviet Union. In general, however, major elements of the democratic coalition—labor, liberals, intellectuals, internationalists—favored continuing the policy of Soviet-American cooperation. In March 1947, to win public support for aid to Greece and Turkey, Truman located the Greek civil war as part of an ongoing struggle between democracy and dictatorship. Domestic political pressures influenced Truman's public presentation of the containment policy, but were not sufficient to cause the United States to enter a Cold War against the Soviet Union. Nor do the domestic political requirements of policy legitimation explain why Truman and other U.S. officials accepted the major premises of the Cold War rhetoric used to obtain public support for the containment policy.

Ideological differences between the two countries had created a barrier of mistrust, and gave a sinister cast to objective conflicts of interest. In addition, ideology prevented the free and easy exchange of diplomats and peoples that could have reinforced the basis of Soviet-American cooperation established by the wartime alliance. But Truman did not believe that the Soviet system of government was "any of our business." Soviet-American cooperation was dictated by the postwar division of power between two powerful nations; rivalry between the two superpowers would lead to another and even more devastating war. To Truman this overrode ideological disputes. Although Truman knew that the Soviets were attempting to propagate their ideology in other countries, this did not concern him because he recognized that the United States was also expansionist in sending missionaries and advisers abroad to "tell other people how to live"; we could not very well criticize the mote in the Soviets' eyes without casting out the beam in our own. Acheson was also unconcerned about the conflict between ideologies because he was a Realist. Since our fundamental national interests did not conflict, Acheson saw no

[4] Trout, "Rhetoric Revisited"; George, "Domestic Constraints on Regime Change in U.S. Foreign Policy."

[5] In *Origins of the Cold War*, Gaddis advances this argument.

reason why the two nations should not be able to collaborate in maintaining peace after Germany's defeat. In November 1945, Acheson pointed out that the United States and the Soviet Union were both continental states, rich in resources and living space, capable of improving their peoples' standard of living through peaceful development and trade, without resorting to international conquest.[6]

Although democratic ideology did not cause U.S. leaders to embark on the Cold War, the more specific, idiosyncratic, and policy-related American Cold War *belief system* did exaggerate the intensity and scope of U.S.-Soviet competition. American officials believed in a version of the domino theory—extension of Soviet influence into Greece would result in the crumbling of democratic governments in the Middle East, Europe, and Asia. This type of thinking elevated each peripheral country into a vital outpost of democracy, and foisted upon successive administrations the never-ending task of bolstering up weak client states. Further, for different reasons, American leaders felt that genuine give-and-take negotiations with the Soviets to devise a postwar settlement for Europe had no chances for success. Truman no longer believed that there was any point in trying to influence Soviet leaders; their conduct was internally directed. Acheson accepted George Kennan's thesis that ideological evangelicism was the "fig leaf" by which Soviet leaders sought to legitimize their brutal, repressive policies; the Soviet regime could not halt the expansionist drive of the communist party without undermining the foundations of their own regime. Delaying negotiations with the Soviets until we had attained a position of strength, U.S. leaders deprived themselves of an important instrument for influencing Soviet policy and avoiding war. By the time the United States felt sufficiently secure to negotiate, positions on both sides had solidified, the division of Europe had hardened, and the possibility of neutralizing and demilitarizing Germany was remote.[7] Finally, American leaders' image of the Soviet Union as bent on world revolution and relentlessly expanding into all vacuums removed the possibility of establishing a "limited adversary" relationship with the Soviets; when all conflicts are reduced to ideology, it is difficult to cooperate even to achieve mutual interests.

Neither systems theory nor the American political context can account for variations in the timing and degree to which Harriman,

[6] Address by Dean Acheson, November 14, 1945, *Department of State Bulletin* 13 (November 18, 1945): 787-89.

[7] For examples of missed opportunities for negotiation during the Cold War, see Adam B. Ulam, *The Rivals* (New York: Viking Press, Penguin Books, 1971), pp. 96-98, 104-105, 121-23, 155-56, 237-38.

Truman, Byrnes, and Acheson adopted the Cold War belief system. They interpreted Soviet behavior differently, made disparate inferences about Soviet foreign policy, and adjusted their beliefs in response to various "critical" historical events. Cognitive social psychological theories are needed to explain differences in information processing that led to variations in the timing and extent to which policymakers accepted the major premises of the Cold War belief system.

Since he had no expertise in Soviet affairs, as ambassador to Moscow, Harriman based his judgments about future Soviet policies largely on the basis of impressions acquired firsthand, through face-to-face dealings with Soviet officials. After becoming ambassador to the Soviet Union in late 1943, Harriman consistently favored a tough quid pro quo approach in dealing with the Soviets. His frustrating experience negotiating with the Russian Foreign Office on proposals for military cooperation reinforced his conviction that the Russians respected firmness and regarded a patient, accommodating attitude as a sign of weakness that should be exploited. Harriman's views on the best means of influencing the Soviets placed him at odds with the Roosevelt administration. One of Roosevelt's principal instruments for allaying Soviet suspicions of the West was generous, unconditional lend-lease aid. Another tactic deliberately chosen by FDR to improve U.S.-Soviet relations was patience and refusal to react to Soviet provocations. Consequently, Roosevelt ignored Harriman's increasingly urgent pleas to place U.S.-Soviet relations on a more even, reciprocal basis and to retaliate when the Soviets refused to cooperate.

Two salient, emotionally resonant episodes in which he tried, and failed, to obtain Soviet cooperation—the attempt to obtain Soviet assistance to the Polish insurgents in the Warsaw uprising and negotiations to carry out the Yalta agreements on Poland—had the greatest impact on his beliefs about the Soviet Union. Ambassador Harriman was distraught and horrified when Stalin coldbloodedly refused the request he submitted on behalf of the State Department that the Soviets furnish arms and ammunition to the Polish underground during the August 1944 Warsaw uprising. Harriman recommended that Roosevelt protest in the strongest language the Soviets' immoral attempt to eliminate the democratic opposition in Poland. Though this shocking experience caused Harriman to revise his optimistic judgment that the Soviets would not try to communize Eastern Europe, he was still unwilling to make any firm predictions about Soviet policies in the region. Harriman recognized and accepted legitimate Soviet security interests in neighboring countries, but he abhorred the institution of the secret police, and hoped that the Soviets would not impose their political system on Eastern Europe. Harriman believed that through taking an active interest and coordinating the use of sanctions and rewards, the United States might succeed in persuading the Soviets to stay out of the internal affairs of the satellite countries.

By September 1944, Harriman had formulated a more coherent and differentiated behavior modification strategy of graduated rewards and punishments to teach the Soviets to observe Western standards of international conduct. In Harriman's "firm but friendly" quid pro quo approach, the United States would register its objections if the Soviets misbehaved on minor issues. Where the Soviets showed blatant disrespect for the United States government or mistreated our people, we should retaliate by giving them "tit for tat." For serious infractions of Western codes of behavior, the United States should threaten to break off relations entirely unless the Soviets accepted our position. But Harriman was confident that the Soviets would bow to our legitimate demands because Stalin needed Western economic assistance and technology to rebuild his country and retain the allegiance of the Soviet people.

Since he based his optimism about the prospects for Soviet-American cooperation on the Soviets' recognition of their own economic self-interests, Harriman made use of carrots as well as sticks in his behavior modification strategy. He recommended that the United States provide the Soviets with credits for postwar reconstruction, but only on a strict quid pro quo basis, in return for their political cooperation with American aims for the postwar world. Any credits given should be of limited duration, initially small but expansible, so that the flow of funds could be turned on or off, depending on whether the Soviets demonstrated respect for American vital interests.

Since they were not subjected to Vyshinsky's rude and specious objections, however, Roosevelt, his political adviser Hopkins, and military officials in Washington viewed the Warsaw uprising from the standpoint of *Realpolitik*. Roosevelt was unwilling to jeopardize our collaborative relationship with Russia to assist an uprising that was ill-considered and adventuristic. Since Hopkins scoffed at the Roman Catholic leaders' threat to transfer their support to Dewey in the forthcoming elections, he was willing to allow events in Warsaw to take their course. The Air Force and the Joint Chiefs of Staff regarded an airlift operation as overly risky and of too little military value to justify the costs to U.S.-Soviet cooperation and sacrifice of American lives. Since they could not very well condemn the Soviets for refusing to undertake a military operation that they themselves regarded as foolhardy, Washington officials' favorable image of the Soviet Union emerged intact from the smoke and blood of the Warsaw uprising. Roosevelt did not accept Harriman's blunt argument that the administration's policy of patience and forbearance in the face of provocation was viewed by the Soviets as a sign of weakness and tacit acquiescence to their policies. Harriman's pleas for adoption of a firm but friendly quid pro quo approach were politely ignored.

It was the March 1945 collapse of the negotiations to carry out the Yalta agreements on Poland that finally convinced Harriman that the Soviet program in Eastern Europe was the establishment of totalitarianism, and that Soviet claims to security interests in the region were a cover for ideological evangelicism. He inferred that Molotov was deliberately stalling to allow the Warsaw Poles to consolidate their power. In drawing important conclusions about future Soviet policies from the breakdown of the Yalta negotiations, Harriman failed to consider whether the Soviets were sincerely trying to carry out their understanding of the Yalta agreement; the text was ambiguous and lacked explicit enforcement machinery and procedures. Washington officials, remote from the trials of negotiating with Molotov, viewed the situation more objectively. Roosevelt admitted that the Soviets were justified in claiming that the Yalta agreement placed more emphasis on the existing Warsaw government. James Byrnes, who took shorthand notes of the proceedings, saw no justification under the spirit or the letter of the agreement for Harriman's insistence that an entirely new and democratic Polish government was to be created. As a result of his mistreatment by Soviet officials in Moscow, Harriman came to accept Cold War beliefs about the Soviet Union far sooner than Acheson, Byrnes, or Truman.

Using what cognitive psychologists refer to as an "episodic script," Harriman compared the expansionist impulse of communism to Nazism. The United States' concern for promoting democracy could not be reconciled with the Soviets' desire to establish communist dictatorships controlled by the Kremlin. Yet, *even then*, Harriman still believed that the United States could draw the Soviets into a more constructive, cooperative relationship through a "carrot and stick" policy. Like Truman and Byrnes, Harriman compartmentalized his conclusions about the Soviet Union, maintaining contradictory beliefs simultaneously with no apparent awareness of any inconsistency.

When Truman was unexpectedly thrust into the presidency, he initially had to rely on Roosevelt's advisers to provide him with basic information on his predecessor's policies. And Ambassador Harriman was most influential in interpreting Roosevelt's difficulties with the Soviets for Truman. Whereas Roosevelt had strong, consistent ideas about appropriate strategy and tactics for dealing with the Soviets, Truman's belief system on these issues was from the start relatively inarticulate, blank on many issues, and very loosely connected; he was, therefore, quite receptive to Harriman's recommendations for a "firm but friendly" quid pro quo approach.

Truman's initial support for Soviet-American cooperation was based largely on episodic scripts: the failure of the League of Nations demonstrated that states would not go to war to keep the peace unless their own security was threatened; if the Great Powers had remained united after World War I, Germany could not have risen to provoke another world conflict; if the United States had not turned to isolationism in the interwar period, World War II would not have occurred. Truman did not collect evidence, consider possible situational constraints on Soviet actions, and weight alternative interpretations to formulate the best possible explanation of Soviet actions. Rather, he made off-the-cuff judgments about the Soviets, using analogies to well-known historical events ("scripts"), metaphors, or stereotypical characters ("personae"). Ill-informed about complex postwar issues, inundated by lengthy briefing memos, Truman quickly grabbed at Harriman's common-sensical suggestions. He tried to carry out Harriman's quid pro quo approach in lend-lease policy, the Soviet loan, and the Polish problem.

President Truman tended to respond impulsively to Soviet actions, using well-rehearsed scripts. When he "got tough" with Molotov in April 1945, he was following a script he had used successfully in the past to assert his authority. But contrary to many historians, Truman's "straight one-two-to-the-jaw" interview with the Soviet foreign minister did not signify his abandonment of FDR's "grand design." Instead, it was a tactical change, brought about by Truman's feeling that the "kid glove" approach used by his predecessor in dealing with the Soviets was no longer necessary or effective. Thanks to Harriman's advice, Truman believed that plain speaking and the threat to withhold economic assistance would be sufficient to make the Soviets retreat on the Polish issue. It had never occurred to him that U.S. insistence on Polish self-determination might preclude Soviet-American cooperation. When it was impressed on Truman that Stalin perceived the Polish issue as a "test" of U.S. acceptance of Soviet security needs, Truman sent Hopkins to Moscow to work out some solution that would not offend American public opinion.

Unlike Harriman, Truman did not expect the Russians to hold genuinely free elections in Eastern Europe. His experience with "ghost votes" under the Pendergast machine in Missouri taught him that Soviet occupation forces would manipulate the election results to suit their purposes. Truman did hope for a cosmetic arrangement in which the Eastern European countries would be allowed the semblance of independence. His perception that Stalin was just another machine politician, like Boss Pendergast, gave him confidence that the Soviet dictator would understand the importance of staging "free elections" for the benefit of the American public. Nor did Truman share Harriman's judgment that the Soviets planned to use Eastern Europe as a springboard for expansion into the West. He thought that the Russians would have their hands full dealing with the problems of Hungary, Poland, and Eastern Europe, and would not try to spill over into the West.

Partly in order to undo the alarming damage to U.S.-Soviet relations caused by his abrupt and inept shift to the quid pro quo approach, Truman appointed James Byrnes as Secretary of State. Before he took office, Byrnes was a firm supporter of continued Soviet-American cooperation. Preserving the unity of the allies after the war was essential to world peace, he believed. Still his commitment to Soviet-American collaboration was on shaky cognitive ground, because Byrnes had a rudimentary, sketchy, incomplete, and largely disconnected system of beliefs about the Soviet Union. He was prone to reduce complex international questions to analogies from the domestic political context in which he had made his mark as a legislative fixer and dealmaker. Not surprisingly, Byrnes' image of the Soviets was largely determined by his most recent personal experience negotiating with the wily Molotov.

When Molotov refused to compromise on the issue of German reparations and armistice arrangements for the Balkans at the Potsdam Conference, Byrnes began to fear that the conflict between ideologies would make impossible any long-term program of Soviet-American cooperation. Further, in view of Stalin's many acts of perfidy, he did not think we could rely on anything in the way of promises from them. In contrast, Truman's perception that Stalin was like his former mentor in Jackson County politics was strengthened by their face-to-face meeting. Because Stalin evoked the Pendergast persona, Truman inferred that the Russian dictator also shared the machine politician's most salient trait—he could be trusted to keep his word.

At the September 1945 London Conference of Foreign Ministers, Byrnes flaunted U.S. atomic power to persuade the Soviets to broaden the Rumanian and Bulgarian governments. At the same time, despite Byrnes' strong opposition to even any mention of international control of atomic energy, Truman discussed with his cabinet the question of whether the United States should share the scientific knowledge with Russia. Under Secretary of State Acheson argued that if we wanted Soviet cooperation, there was no alternative but to give full information to the Russians.

Unlike Truman and Byrnes, Dean Acheson had an extraordinarily rich, consistent, and coherent belief system about Soviet policy and the requirements of world order. Looking to the nineteenth-century *Pax Britannica* as a model, he believed that the U.S. should reconstitute an open international economic system to eliminate the underlying causes of fascism and war. Specifically, he argued that U.S. capital should fund overseas economic development, while American military power prevented future aggressors from disrupting the world system. Cooperation with the Soviet Union was also essential to world peace. If the purposes and policies of the great powers were in conflict, there would be no organized peace, but an armed truce. Although Truman agreed with Acheson that international control would be essential to maintain a lasting peace, he was unwilling to give up a counterweight to Soviet troop strength until the peace settlement was negotiated—even though the longer he delayed approaching the Soviets, the more suspicious and embittered they would become. As is apparent, many of Truman's cognitions were inconsistent, and the situational context largely determined which of his many convictions became apparent to him at that particular moment. Acheson, on the other hand, customarily and deliberately deduced specific policy positions from his general foreign affairs philosophy, whenever useful and relevant inferences could be drawn.

When the London Conference broke up in disarray in October 1945, Byrnes inferred that the Russians were taking an aggressive stand on territorial and political questions, because they no longer needed the United States to defeat Germany. He accused the Soviets of welching on all the agreements reached at Yalta and Potsdam. The combination of Soviet subversion in northern Iran, their war of nerves against Turkey, and the London fiasco convinced Truman that the Russians understood one language—how many divisions have you? Yet, he favored continuing the policy of Soviet-American cooperation. There were no irreconcilable conflicts of interest between our two countries, he believed. Besides, Truman thought he could do business with Stalin. Despite his bitterness and indignation at Molotov's rude and abusive treatment of him, Byrnes was also unwilling to abandon FDR's "grand design" because to do so would be to admit failure as a negotiator and peacemaker. In addition, like Truman, he now believed that Stalin was susceptible to reason and appeals to their mutual interests.

Though he had boasted that the Soviets would eventually make concessions if the United States stood firm, Byrnes himself initiated renewed discussions with the Soviet foreign minister at Moscow. Since his "bomb in his pocket" tactics had not intimidated the Soviets, the secretary of state now planned to offer the Soviets atomic energy information, without any quid pro quo, to obtain their cooperation on the United Nations and other political issues. In addition, he planned to act as an honest broker in mediating between Britain and the Soviet Union at the foreign ministers' conference. The Soviets had made no conciliatory gestures that could explain Byrnes' returning to Rooseveltian accommodation; they continued fomenting unrest in northern Iran and conducting large-scale troop maneuvers along the Turkish frontier.

The Soviets' refusal to withdraw their troops from northern Iran by the treaty deadline of March 2, 1946, caused Truman to wonder whether Stalin could be trusted to keep his word. When instead of leaving, the Soviets marched their troops in the direction of Turkey, Teheran, and Iraq, Byrnes indignantly concluded that the Russians were adding military invasion to political subversion in Iran. Believing that he could not continue talking to the Soviets in defense of American principles without the backing of armed might, Byrnes asked Secretary of War Patterson whether it might be possible to slow down that rate of demobilization. While Byrnes attempted to humiliate the Soviets publicly in the Security Council by refusing to take the issue off the agenda, Truman undercut the policy by sending a secret, cordial invitation to Stalin to visit Washington. Truman was not prepared to give up his belief that Stalin, like Pendergast, could be trusted to keep his promises. Because he was a Realist, Acheson was also not prepared to abandon diplomacy or the attempt to establish a cooperative relationship with the Soviets; the under secretary of state feared a terrifying atomic arms race. Even though Acheson foresaw a long period of tension with the Soviets, punctuated by continuing crises, he firmly believed that the United States must try to negotiate an agreement with the Soviets to control the spread of atomic weapons. Although Byrnes expressed his outrage within the government about the Soviets' use of blackmail and subversion in Iran, once the crisis was resolved, he returned to his usual preference for bargaining and compromise. Byrnes told the press that the United States government would refuse to sign a peace treaty unless the Soviets withdrew their demands for a base on the Dodecanese or Tripolitania; in private, however, he authorized his close aide Ben Cohen to sound out military officials on the idea of giving the Soviets a base in return for a twenty-year cooling-off period. Byrnes still had no fixed beliefs about Soviet aims or the best means of influencing their behavior; if a firm policy did not work, he was prepared to try appeasement in the classical sense of acceding to an opponent's limited demands to stabilize a troubled area.

In August 1946, Acheson's interpretation of Soviet demands for bases on the Turkish Straits led to far-reaching changes in his image of the Soviet Union. According to the State Department and military officials, Soviet military fortifications on the Straits were unnecessary as a defensive measure, because Soviet air power was sufficient to prevent a hostile power from forcing the Dardanelles or closing the waterway to Soviet warships. Having excluded possible legitimate security motivations, Acheson inferred that Soviet demands were part of a grand design to dominate the Mediterranean and the Middle East—even though U.S. control of the Panama Canal was based on similar illogical security claims. Truman announced that we might as well find out now whether the Soviets were bent on world conquest, and that he was prepared to pursue the policy "to the end."

Acheson's management of the Turkish Straits crisis made a lasting impression on his beliefs about the Soviet Union. Although he could understand and accept the Soviets' desire for "friendly" governments in neighboring countries as protection against another destructive German invasion, Acheson could not see how Soviet ambitions in the Dardanelles could have any defensive logic. Since the under secretary was, if nothing else, consistent, his new image of the Soviets stimulated a wave of cognitive activity in peripheral, supporting beliefs. Acheson now believed that the Soviets would not be satiated with a limited sphere of influence in Eastern Europe, but had an unlimited appetite for territory and influence. The international system was "tightly coupled," such that the extension of Soviet domination into one country would inevitably lead to the crumbling of neighboring areas. Only the conviction that the United States would meet their aggression with force of arms would deter the Soviets.

At about the same time, Byrnes finally accepted the inevitability of the division of the world into rival spheres of influence. It was the public tableau of the Paris Peace Conference in July-October 1946—where Eastern European countries obediently recited Soviet propaganda, and voting was along East-West lines—which convinced Byrnes that it was no longer possible to cooperate with the Soviet Union. The sight of two Czech delegates applauding Soviet charges of "dollar diplomacy" incited Byrnes to reorient fundamentally the goals of American foreign economic policy from the attempt to create an open world economic system to the containment of communism. On September 24, 1946, Byrnes directed that all future economic assistance be channeled to our "friends," and that the United States refrain from providing any assistance to countries actively opposing American "principles." But he never formulated a compelling rationale to justify to the American public or himself this ad hoc improvised response to Soviet domination of Eastern Europe, nor was this part of a strategy to undermine the unity of the Soviet sphere of influence. When he left office in January 1947, his belief system about the Soviet Union was still impoverished, unelaborated, and disconnected.

By coincidence, on September 24, as Byrnes was independently redefining American foreign economic policy, Truman was presented with the basis for a new global policy toward the Soviet Union. The Clifford-Elsey report, representing the consensus of State Department and military officials after months of discussion, recommended that the United States prevent further Soviet expansion by providing economic assistance to endangered democracies and furnishing military support if they were attacked by the Soviet Union. Yet Truman chose to shelve the proposed policy because Stalin had recently told a journalist that he still believed in the possibility of lasting cooperation between the Soviet Union and the Western democracies. In his October 23 speech to the United Nations General Assembly, Truman reaffirmed the existence of "One World," despite differences in Soviet and American political and economic systems. In contrast, Byrnes was skeptical about the significance of Stalin's conciliatory interviews with the Western press, after the attacks and abuse he had endured from Vyshinsky and Molotov at the Paris Peace Conference.

By the beginning of 1947, Acheson perceived the United States as engaged in a political war with the Soviets in which we had to take the offensive; he told a congressional committee that Soviet foreign policy was aggressive and expanding. Once Acheson had changed his views on the Soviets he did not waver or vacillate. In February, when cables from U.S. representatives unanimously warned that Greece was on the verge of succumbing to a communist-led guerrilla movement, Acheson recommended that the United States furnish immediate, large-scale economic and military assistance to this strategic country— two days before the British formally notified the United States that they were pulling out of Greece and Turkey.

Through his central role in drafting the president's speech to Congress, Acheson was responsible for identifying the policy with the protection of democracy against the threat of totalitarianism. In discussions with Truman and other cabinet officials, Acheson justified aid to Greece by referring to falling countries; capitulation of Greece to Soviet domination through lack of support by the United States might result in the loss of the whole Near and Middle East and northern Africa, and it would consolidate the position of communist minorities in Italy and France.[8] As he articulated, defined, and elaborated the Truman Doctrine to members of Congress and the press, Acheson formulated in his own mind additional premises of the Cold War belief system. He concluded that the United States should try to bolster strategic "soft spots" throughout the globe, because the Soviets probed wherever there was weakness but made no trial against strength. Until the United States built up a position of strength, negotiations would be of no use in halting Soviet expansionism and aggression. The Soviets could not stop promoting communism through subversion or overt aggression, because exhortations to world revolution were essential to the legitimacy of a brutal police state. Without the ideological "fig leaf" of communism, Stalin would be revealed to the world as just another brutal autocrat, no different from Ivan the Terrible or Peter the Great.

In contrast to Acheson, Truman did not alter his beliefs about the Soviet Union until several months after he made the Truman Doctrine speech. Indeed, he was not involved in drafting the Truman Doctrine speech and probably would have taken no action to rescue Greece had not the British and the State Department forced his hand. Several months after the speech, he accepted the "domino theory" that Soviet domination of Greece and Turkey would inevitably result in the extension of the iron curtain all the way to western Ireland; negotiations with the Soviet Union were a waste of time; and the Russians could not be trusted to keep their agreements. When he could no longer avoid dividing the world into rival blocs, Truman adopted assumptions about Soviet conduct that justified the Cold War.

As the preceding discussion indicates, the change in U.S. policymakers' beliefs was gradual and ragged. There was no neat turning point. One by one, U.S. officials abandoned the principal assumptions underlying FDR's "grand design," at first only provisionally and temporarily. At any point, they were prepared to accept evidence that the Soviets were motivated by fear of capitalist encirclement, that they

---

[8] See, for example, Henderson to Marshall, February 20, 1947, 868.00/2-2047, drafted and initialled by W. O. Baxter with Acheson's handwritten emendations and additions, RG 59, NA.

could be trusted to keep their agreements. As the subjective probabilities U.S. policymakers attached to this happy eventuality decreased over time, they began to prepare themselves psychologically for other contingencies. As Acheson commented to a minor official in November 1946,

> There were two possible approaches: first, we could support the United Nations and continue our efforts patiently to draw the Soviet Union towards an accommodation with us. Second, plan to lick the hell out of them in 10 or 15 years. It was clear that we were committed to the first and should do it and not diminish our efforts, but that as practical men we should realize that our efforts might not succeed and that we must therefore be prepared, should it be necessary, to adopt the latter course.[9]

USES AND LIMITATIONS OF ALTERNATIVE SOCIAL PSYCHOLOGICAL THEORIES

During the period in which American Cold War policies evolved, U.S. policymakers used different types of cognitive processes to interpret information about Soviet behavior. Cognitive psychologists have found that human information processing varies according to the quality of the data, problem format, whether an appropriate "problem-solving" set is elicited, and so on.[10]

No one social psychological theory, then, explains the origins of American leaders' Cold War belief system. Some psychological approaches, however, were more directly applicable than others. To summarize, self-perception, schema, and attribution theories were most useful in explaining policymakers' interpretation of Soviet actions and salient cutting points in the evolution of the Cold War belief system.

Of the major cognitive social psychological theories discussed here, self-perception theory provides the best explanation of the shift in U.S. policymakers' attitudes toward the Soviet Union following the inauguration of the Truman Doctrine. Having embarked on a course of

[9] *FR: 1946*, I, p. 985.

[10] See, for example, Nisbett and Ross, *Human Inference*, p. 9; and Baruch Fischhoff, "Attribution Theory and Judgment under Uncertainty," in *New Directions in Attribution Research*, ed. John H. Harvey, William John Ickes, and Robert F. Kidd (Hillsdale, N.J.: Lawrence Erlbaum Associates, 1976), 1:421-52. Similarly, Stein and Tanter theorize that the type of decision process used by leaders varies according to such factors as group decisionmaking norms, perceptions of threat and time pressure, and strategic doctrine. See *Rational Decision-Making*, p. 63.

action that divided the world into two rival armed blocs and increased the risks of war with the Soviet Union, the Truman administration had to find some compelling explanation of why containment of Soviet expansion into Greece and Turkey was necessary and legitimate. As self-perception theory predicted, Truman had not reached any firm conclusions about Soviet foreign policy before external pressures required him to take a clear-cut policy toward the problem posed by the threat of communist expansion into the Mediterranean. The action context compelled him to reach cognitive closure, to settle on an interpretation of Soviet policy that supported the containment strategy. Similarly, although Acheson had decided before the British notes that the United States had to assume Britain's imperial responsibility for keeping Soviet influence out of the eastern Mediterranean, he had not formulated a set of beliefs about strategy and tactics that would underlie the containment policy until he was thrust into the position of defining and delimiting the Truman Doctrine. Because Truman had to give a speech to Congress, justifying aid to Greece and Turkey, a major policy shift came into being.

How often is American foreign policy formulated in response to the "deadlines" for decision established by the president's need to make a speech, an international meeting, a scheduled press conference, or congressional hearings? In these instances, the president frequently develops a belief or foreign policy position through acting and deciding.[11] During the Cold War, as well, American commitments to various endangered countries and outposts—Korea, Taiwan, Berlin, Quemoy—were forged in the fires of crisis; U.S. foreign policy officials did not perceive the strategic value of maintaining a commitment until they were in the midst of defending it.

Acquiring a foreign affairs philosophy is a difficult intellectual task requiring much study and reflection. Even for those statesmen and advisers who have succeeded in developing a coherent belief system, it is often extremely difficult to deduce specific, concrete actions—such as providing military assistance to a beleagured government or extending foreign aid—from a logical conceptual structure. For practical pol-

[11] Morton Halperin, *Bureaucratic Politics and Foreign Policy* (Washington, D. C.: Brookings Institution, 1974). It is important to note that in his case study of U.S. policymaking on the issue of sharing the control of nuclear weapons among members of the Atlantic Alliance, John Steinbruner found that externally imposed deadlines for decision played a critical role in forcing Presidents Kennedy and Johnson to abandon their "uncommitted thinking" about the multilateral force and take a more extreme position than their lukewarm support of the policy would have warranted. See *Cybernetic Theory of Decision*, pp. 268-69, 291, 318-19.

iticians, in-and-outers, administrators, and political appointees, the easiest and quickest way to arrive at their beliefs on foreign policy issues is to take a position first, and then decide how it should be justified. One need not conclude that foreign policymakers are trying to preserve their self-esteem or avoid cognitive dissonance when they use their positions in policy debates as a basis for retroactively inferring their beliefs. They are only following the prescription: watch what we do, not what we say. Jervis, for example, recently observed that

> we normally think that an actor's perceptions of others—their goals, intentions, and characteristics—precede the development of his policy toward them. Although this logical progression is correct for some cases, there are others in which causation flows in the reverse direction—statesmen first set their policy toward another state and then develop the image of the other that supports and would have led to such a policy. The relationship between beliefs and policy is then one of rationalization rather than rationality.[12]

Psychologists Janis and Mann have developed an alternative, motivational explanation for behavior-driven beliefs and perceptions. They start with the assumption that the choice between alternatives which may impose significant costs and risks is inherently stressful. A decisionmaker experiences psychological conflict when it becomes apparent that there are serious risks attached to continuing present policies but that changing to a new course of action may be even more dangerous. If a decisionmaker torn between the dangers of the known and the risks of the unknown sees no hope of discovering a satisfactory alternative, he or she will exhibit "defensive avoidance." That is to say, the individual will ignore evidence of the risks of maintaining current policies, engage in wishful thinking, or shift the responsibility to someone else. If forced to make a decision, the individual will "bolster" the least unacceptable alternative by exaggerating the prospects for success, minimizing the risks, or denying personal responsibility. Applying Janis and Mann's formulation to the study of crisis decision-making, Richard Ned Lebow concluded that policymakers are often led by domestic political pressures to provoke crises; the stress created by the absence of any attractive alternatives to brinksmanship leads them to "bolster" their chances for successfully carrying out a policy that brings with it a high risk of war.[13]

[12] Robert Jervis, "Political Decision-Making: Recent Contributions," *Political Psychology* 2 (Summer 1980): 90.
[13] Irving L. Janis and Leon Mann, *Decision Making: A Psychological Analysis of Conflict, Choice, and Commitment* (New York: Free Press, 1977), pp. 50-52, 57-59, 73-74,

We will not consider here whether, as Lebow argues, emotional needs are more important sources of misperception than the assimilation of information to preexisting beliefs. It should be pointed out, however, that considerations of theoretical parsimony alone would argue against adding an additional unobservable construct when the behavior can just as plausibly be explained by means of self-perception theory. According to self-perception theory, the propensity to infer attitudes consistent with one's actions is a "cold" cognitive process, reflecting nothing more pressing than an interest in accounting for one's own behavior.

For example, Truman was anxious and upset by his inability to achieve FDR's "grand design," since he believed that a breakdown in Soviet-American cooperation would inevitably bring on a new, catastrophic world war. But Truman and his advisers were not motivated to perceive the Soviets as expansionist and hostile for domestic political reasons; the American public generally supported the policy of Soviet-American cooperation in March 1947. It cannot be argued that Truman administration officials were motivated to rationalize to themselves the decision to assume Britain's role of maintaining a balance of power in the Mediterranean; this was a perfectly logical and morally justified response to the vacuum opened up by Britain's imperial decline and the existence of weak governments in the region. Nor were they driven to adopt Cold War beliefs to relieve the stress and possible damage to self-esteem caused by Truman's use of ideological rhetoric in the Truman Doctrine speech. Truman and Acheson were not terribly concerned by the gap between the universalistic, crusading language of the speech and the more limited aims of the containment policy. In background interviews with journalists and congressional hearings, Acheson was quite frank about the constraints on the United States' ability to defend democracies around the world.

If Janis and Mann's conflict theory is correct, then during the period of "drift and indecision," when Truman saw no acceptable alternatives to FDR's "grand design," he should have engaged in "defensive avoidance" of the problem, by ignoring the evidence of Soviet expansionist ambitions in the Mediterranean or rationalizing Soviet actions to maintain his belief that the Soviets would cooperate. Instead, Truman continued to worry and reflect on the problem, while admitting that he did not know what he would do if the Soviets decided to send

76, 85-87, 91-93; Richard Ned Lebow, *Between Peace and War: The Nature of International Crisis* (Baltimore: Johns Hopkins University Press, 1981), pp. 107-11, 170, 177, 222-28.

troops into Turkey. When the British withdrawal from Greece in March 1947 forced Truman to stop vacillating and adopt a policy, he should have "bolstered" his decision to replace cooperation with confrontation by selectively interpreting information. Still, there is evidence that Truman was aware of at least some of the future risks and costs of the new containment policy: American isolationism might be revived, and Congress might not support large-scale U.S. aid or involvement in the domestic political affairs of Europe.

Consistent with self-perception theory, Truman and Byrnes had no stable, well-defined beliefs about foreign policy or the Soviet Union. Truman blithely maintained inconsistent opinions simultaneously, acting on one belief one minute, the other the next, depending on situational variables. Both men vacillated and wavered in their commitment to Soviet-American cooperation, Byrnes even more so than Truman. Within an eighteen-month period, Byrnes went from Rooseveltian accommodation to "atomic diplomacy" to quid pro quo diplomacy to "patience and firmness." At least Truman's support for FDR's grand design was supported by the lessons he had drawn from the interwar period; Byrnes seems to have adopted FDR's policies without fully understanding the historical experience and logic underlying the "grand design."

As Steinbruner pointed out, presidents and other nonexperts in foreign policy often exhibit "uncommitted thinking." High-level officials who have obtained their jobs through elections or political appointments usually have little firsthand experience in dealing with foreign policy issues. Consequently, their beliefs are not grounded in a network of supporting assumptions and examples. Further, the information that is summarized as it proceeds up the organizational hierarchy is remote from the concrete data gathered by foreign service officers or intelligence operatives, and is abstract and conflicting. The pressing burden of having to make decisions on numerous unrelated issues often does not allow the president to make an independent evaluation of the merits of competing intelligence estimates or policy memoranda. As a result, the president or other high-level official is apt to be influenced by incommensurable and inconsistent beliefs on the same issue at different times. The oscillation and vacillation so often found in American foreign policy reflect this pattern of uncommitted thinking.[14]

The same self-perception process of using actions to infer beliefs

[14] Steinbruner, *Cybernetic Theory of Decision*, pp. 128-31; Halperin, *Bureaucratic Politics*, pp. 24-25.

probably occurred among important elements of the attentive public and the average citizen, as well. Liberal theory assumes that the American public has well-defined attitudes on foreign policy issues, which it conveys to Washington. But the mass public does not form opinions on the basis of informed, detached consideration of the "facts." Social psychological studies have shown that informational campaigns conducted by the mass media are generally ineffective in producing significant attitude change. A large percentage of the population is not exposed to political TV programs or newspaper editorials; the people who do listen to persuasive messages are generally already in agreement; and selective attention cancels out any discrepant information which does happen to reach an individual.[15]

Commenting on the phenomenon from a different perspective, Murray Edelman theorized,

> It is therefore political actions that chiefly shape men's political wants and "knowledge," not the other way around. The common assumption that what democratic government does is somehow always a response to the moral codes, desires, and knowledge embedded inside people is as inverted as it is reassuring.[16]

During the Cold War, the American people received external cues to their beliefs about the Soviet Union from U.S. actions in the world system as interpreted by foreign policy officials. From the perspective of self-perception theory, Cold War policies were not a response to the anticommunist values of the American people. Public opinion studies have found that people's beliefs are volatile and vary from one side of an issue to another; indeed, on many subjects they have no attitudes at all. Instead, popular perceptions of the Soviet Union were shaped by U.S. policy and its legitimation in terms of ideological symbols.[17]

Self-perception theory is also useful in interpreting the relationship between ideology and action. Policymakers rarely decide on a course of action simply because they wish to actualize an ideology. Instead, policy is usually developed in response to perceived threats or opportunities, then justified by means of the ideology. Ideology is a con-

---

[15] Jonathan L. Freedman, David O. Sears, and J. Merrill Carlsmith, *Social Psychology*, 4th ed. (Englewood Cliffs, N.J.: Prentice-Hall, 1981), pp. 439-50.

[16] Edelman, *Symbolic Uses of Politics*, pp. 172-73.

[17] From his analysis of survey data and major foreign policy events, Barry Hughes concluded that public opinion generally follows rather than precedes American foreign policy developments. See *The Domestic Context of American Foreign Policy* (San Francisco: W. Freeman and Co., 1978), pp. 107-108.

stant; situations are the dynamic input into the policymaking process. Moreover, the premises of an ideology are stated in broad, global terms. Although ideology may constrain perceptions, estimates, and responses to situations, it is not easy to make operational the general values of an ideology through concrete, specific actions. Consequently, ideology plays a role chiefly in helping to formulate rationalizations after a policy is chosen in response to actual situations.[18]

If ideology serves more strongly to justify than guide policy, this is not to say that it can be subtracted from the policymaking equation. Policy never emerges from one decision. Once an initial step has been explained and rationalized in ideological terms, the interpretive framework constrains and shapes subsequent actions to achieve original policy aims. Policymakers must legitimize actions to themselves as well as to the American public. Once U.S. leaders came to believe that they were trying to preserve freedom in the world against the threat of communism, they took actions consistent with that conviction, as in Korea. The ambitious attempt by Truman's successors to dam the flow of the communist ideology rather than simply contain the increase of Soviet military power ultimately led to the deformation and globalization of containment.[19]

Further, the definition and application of national interests is often subjective and influenced by ideological considerations. That Greece and Turkey were vital interests of the United States was at least debatable. When the Truman Doctrine was launched, Walter Lippmann argued that the United States should give priority to the economic needs of our Western European allies and to removing the threat of the Red Army from the heart of Europe. "By concentrating our efforts on a diplomatic war in the border lands of the Soviet Union, we have neglected—because we do not have unlimited power, resources, influ-

[18] For a useful discussion of this issue, see Werner Levi, "Ideology, Interests, and Foreign Policy," *International Studies Quarterly* 14 (March 1960): 1-31.

[19] Psychological experiments have provided evidence that once people are convinced that they acted on the basis of particular beliefs, they are more likely to engage in belief-consistent behavior in future situations. Daniel M. Wegner, "The Self in Prosocial Action," in *The Self in Social Psychology*, ed. Daniel M. Wegner and Robin R. Vallacher (New York: Oxford University Press, 1980), pp. 138-39; Jonathan L. Freedman and Scott C. Fraser, "Compliance without Pressure: The Foot-in-the-Door Technique," *Journal of Personality and Social Psychology* 4 (1966): 195-202; Leslie Ann McArthur, Charles A. Kiesler, and Barry P. Cook, "Acting on Attitude as a Function of Self-Percept and Inequity," *Journal of Personality and Social Psychology* 12 (1969): 295-302; Mark Snyder and Michael R. Cunningham, "To Comply or Not Comply: Testing the Self-Perception Explanation of the 'Foot-in-the-Door' Phenomenon," *Journal of Personality and Social Psychology* 31 (1975): 64-67.

ence and diplomatic brain power—the vital interests of our natural allies in Western Europe, notably in reconstructing their economic life and in promoting a German settlement on which they can agree," Lippmann wrote. Vital interests are usually defined as those values for which a nation is willing to go to war. There are no geographic factors or commonly understood objective criteria for determining whether an interest is vital; it is a matter of human judgment. In the postwar period, until the disillusioning experience of Vietnam, the United States adopted an expansive conception of its security requirements to include a world substantially made over in its own image.[20]

Finally, ideology leads to the development of policy doctrines that become institutionalized through the creation of bureaucracies. In particular, the Cold War ideology underlay a vast expansion of the power and resources of the executive branch of the U.S. government. By the early 1960s, spending for defense and foreign policy constituted the greatest proportion of the U.S. budget. Since all issues pertaining to Soviet-American relations were defined as relating to national security, the president was generally able to act without undue interference from Congress in the Cold War.[21]

Attribution theory is compatible with a self-perception interpretation, because both provide a cognitive rather than a motivational explanation for American decisionmakers' perceptions. Both theories attribute errors and biases to cold cognitive processes, not "hot" motivational drives. In addition, both theories view people as "problem solvers"; they attempt to discover the principles of "naive epistemology," the rules and procedures by which people go about obtaining a practical understanding of the world.

U.S. policymakers' judgments about Soviet purposes and policies did exhibit several of the cognitive biases identified by attribution theorists. In interpreting Soviet behavior, U.S. leaders were unduly influenced by their own small corner of personal experience. Harriman based his estimates of the Soviet Union's willingness to cooperate on the helpfulness of lower-level Soviet officials in carrying out various joint military projects. Byrnes cut off economic aid to the Soviet bloc largely out of pique and a desire for revenge, because he caught sight

[20] Walter Lippmann, *The Cold War* (New York: Harper & Bros., 1947), p. 26; Bernard Brodie, *War and Politics* (New York: Macmillan Co., 1973), pp. 343-46; Robert Tucker, *The Radical Left and American Foreign Policy* (Baltimore: Johns Hopkins University Press, 1971), pp. 63-64, 67.

[21] Franz Shurmann, *The Logic of World Power* (New York: Pantheon Random House, Pantheon Books, 1974), pp. 101, 105-106; Yergin, *Shattered Peace*, pp. 193-94, 196-201.

of two Czech delegates applauding Soviet tirades at the Paris Peace Conference.

On the other hand, American leaders neglected information that was neither vivid nor concrete—the "nonevent." In concluding that the Soviets were trying to spread totalitarianism throughout Eastern Europe, Harriman neglected moderate Soviet occupation policies in Hungary, Finland, and Czechoslovakia, where free elections were allowed until after the Truman Doctrine was inaugurated. Acheson failed to draw any conclusions from the Soviets' retreat on the Turkish Straits issue, once the United States made its position known.

In addition, U.S. officials were prone to the "actor-observer" fallacy of inferring that particular Soviet actions reflected the fundamental character of the Soviet Union and its leaders, while attributing similar U.S. actions to situational demands or external constraints. Acheson had no doubts that the Soviet request for bases on the Dardanelles was prima facie evidence of long-range aggressive ambitions. He assumed that U.S. military fortifications on the Panama Canal, on the other hand, reflected legitimate national security requirements.

Schemas play an indispensable role in the categorization and interpretation of incoming information. American officials imposed structure and meaning on the world by matching situations and people to cognitive structures stored in memory. The schemas used by Truman and Byrnes were highly idiosyncratic and derived from personal experience. Truman placed inordinate importance on obtaining at least superficial Soviet compliance with the Yalta and Potsdam agreements because he was influenced by the "code of the politician" script—a man who does not keep his word can never again be trusted. Having assimilated Stalin to the Pendergast "persona," Truman firmly believed that the Russian dictator would indeed live up to his commitments. For Truman, the "code of the politician" served as a substitute for policy until he found something to replace FDR's "grand design."

Although one can find numerous examples of schematic processing, the Munich analogy did not figure in the development of the Cold War belief system. It is said that U.S. policymakers were blinded by the specter of Hitler when they perceived the Soviet Union as a threat to Western security. Yet study of the historical evidence shows that U.S. leaders did *not* invoke the Munich script as a rationale for containing Soviet expansion. They did *not* overestimate the similarity of the current world situation to that recent, all-too-memorable historical episode. The threat posed by Hitler had been military. American foreign policy officials were well aware that the Soviet Union was devastated by the onslaught of Hitler's armies, and they did not believe that Stalin would risk war with the United States for the foreseeable future.[22] They did not perceive the Red Army as poised for an invasion of Western Europe. Nor was it a question of appeasing Stalin's demands; the Russians had made no new demands on Turkey, and the Soviet government scrupulously and cautiously refrained from assisting the communist-led guerrillas in Greece.

The danger feared by Acheson and others was that the Europeans were so dispirited, discouraged, and demoralized by the war's destruction that they might turn to communism out of desperation for a "quick fix" to their economic difficulties. As Assistant Secretary Clayton put it, "In every country in the Eastern Hemisphere and most of the countries of the Western Hemisphere Russia is boring from within. This is a new technique with which we have not yet learned how to cope." From this perspective, Soviet absorption of the strategic countries of Greece and Turkey might set off a "bandwagon" effect in Western Europe, convincing the Europeans that communism was the wave of the future and that they should come to terms with Soviet power. Joseph Jones, the official designated by Acheson to write the Truman Doctrine speech, expressed the Truman administration's fears in a memo to William Benton:

> There are many signs that the world is approaching this year the greatest crisis since the turn in the tide of the war in November 1942.
>
> It is primarily an economic crisis centered in Britain and Empire, France, Greece, and China. But this economic crisis will have the most profound political repercussions imaginable. . . .
>
> If these areas are allowed to spiral downwards into economic anarchy, then at best they will drop out of the U.S. orbit and try an independent nationalistic policy; at worst they will swing into the Russian orbit.

Acheson told the congressional delegation that the Russians had been spurring extensive Communist party activity in Hungary, Italy, France, and Austria. In France, Communist party infiltration had been

[22] See, for example, Forrestal diary, October 15, 1946, *Forrestal Diaries*, ed. Millis, p. 212; Truman to John Garner, September 21, 1946, Truman Papers, PSF: Subject File, "Russia, 1945-48," HSTL; Frank Evans to A. H. Tandy, March 19, 1946, FO 371/56840, N4152/971/38; "Greek-Turkish Aid," March 20, 1947, McNaughton Papers, HSTL; Joint Staff Planners, "Estimates of Probable Developments in the World Political Situation up to 1956," November 8, 1946, ABC 381 (1 Sept. 45), Sec. 1-A, RG 165, NA; Memorandum by the Joint Chiefs of Staff to Patterson and Forrestal, March 13, 1947, *FR: 1947*, V, pp. 111-12.

so successful that the Russians could pull the rug at any time, Acheson related. In Italy, communist influence had increased enormously.[23]

Contrary to the Yale attitude change approach, U.S. policymakers' beliefs were not altered by a persuasive communication presenting new evidence and arguments about the Soviet Union. The Hovland approach suggests that American foreign policymakers learn new foreign policy attitudes through intellectual study and thought. Cold War historians have generally agreed that Kennan's "long telegram" of February 1946 electrified U.S. officials, prodding them to the realization that the Soviet Union was a hostile force dedicated to the destruction of the American way of life and unamenable to traditional diplomacy. But, careful examination of primary sources before and after receipt of the "long telegram" reveals no changes in the beliefs of Truman, Byrnes, or Acheson. Byrnes read the long telegram, thanked Kennan for his "splendid analysis," and continued the policy of Soviet-American cooperation. There is no copy of Kennan's "long telegram" in the President's Secretary Files at the Truman Library, nor is there any memo in the State Department's archives that would suggest that a copy of the cable was transmitted to Truman. Thus, it is extremely doubtful that Truman even read it. American officials were empiricists rather than rationalists: that is, their beliefs changed in response to concrete practice rather than rational argumentation.[24] Although such behavior may seem irrational or anti-intellectual, we should remember that policymakers often *must* act, whether knowledge is plentiful or, as is more usually the case, uncertain, incomplete, and insufficient. The abstract, logical, theoretical, data-based arguments preferred by academics and scientists may have little relevance to action.

From a metatheoretical standpoint, use of the Hovland approach leads to the systematic underestimation of the intellectual contribution made by policymakers to the task of interpreting Soviet policies and fashioning an appropriate response. National leaders do not merely internalize the arguments underlying a policy recommended to them by staff members; they develop their own reasons for supporting a course of action.[25]

[23] George Kennan, "Comments on the National Security Problem," March 27, 1947, lecture before the National War College, 868.00/3-2747, RG 59, NA; Memorandum 3/5/47, Clayton Papers, "General File—Marshall Plan Memos 1947," HSTL; JMJ Notes on Acheson's Presentation to Dept. Working Group, Feb. 28, 1947, Jones Papers, HSTL; Joseph Jones to Mr. Benton, February 26, 1947, Jones Papers.

[24] For this distinction, see Giovanni Sartori, "Politics, Ideology, and Belief Systems," *American Political Science Review* 63 (June 1969): 402-403.

[25] For political-psychological theories that propose hypotheses derived from the Hov-

Like self-perception theory, the cognitive dissonance approach posits that action may promote attitudinal change. However, dissonance effects are hypothesized to occur only when policymakers are induced by situational pressures to act contrary to strongly held, consistent beliefs, without adequate justification, and in spite of their fear of important negative consequences. This hypothesis was not relevant because Truman did not have strongly held, consistent beliefs. As we have seen, he had not settled on an interpretation of Soviet foreign policy before the Greek crisis forced him to take a position. Consequently, self-perception theory provides a better explanation of his acceptance of the Cold War belief system several months after making the Truman Doctrine speech. Similarly, when Acheson subsequently adopted additional beliefs to fill out and operationalize the general rationale for the containment policy that was contained in the Truman Doctrine, he was not trying to rationalize actions that were counter to his convictions, but to elaborate and define a policy consistent with his almost instinctive urge to preserve the balance of power.

Cognitive dissonance theory assumes that people have an innate drive for consistency in their cognitions. But practical politicans such as Truman and Byrnes generally do not possess stable, internally consistent belief systems. Even Acheson and Harriman were able to compartmentalize, or attach different probabilities to alternative assumptions maintained simultaneously.[26]

Cognitive dissonance theory also predicts that U.S. policymakers would attempt to preserve their illusions about the prospects for Soviet-American cooperation by ignoring, discounting, or reinterpreting discrepant information. Instead, U.S. officials were quite receptive to evidence about Soviet intentions that contradicted the benign assumptions of FDR's "grand design." Indeed, their openness to conflicting signals caused them to veer in different directions, producing a certain amount of incoherence in U.S. policy. There was no evidence that

land tradition, see Robert Axelrod, "Schema Theory: An Information-Processing Model of Perception and Cognition," *American Political Science Review* 67 (December 1973): 1248-66; and Jervis, *Perception and Misperception*, pp. 122-24. To my knowledge, the hypotheses derived from the Hovland approach that are presented by Axelrod and Jervis have not been applied to case studies of foreign policymaking.

[26] For the classic discussion of belief system constraint, see Philip E. Converse, "The Nature of Belief Systems in Mass Publics," in *Ideology and Discontent*, ed. David E. Apter (New York: Free Press, 1964), pp. 206-61. Research on the "operational code" has explored the question of the interconnectedness of the beliefs in this construct, and presented evidence that they do constitute a "system." On this point, see George, "The Causal Nexus between 'Operational Code' Beliefs and Decision-Making Behavior" pp. 95-124.

U.S. policymakers tried to maintain internal consistency among their beliefs about the Soviet Union by warding off disconfirming information. Rather, they adjusted their assumptions piecemeal, frequently maintaining contradictory convictions simultaneously.

IMPLICATIONS FOR FUTURE RESEARCH

1. Problem of Inconsistency. In the fifties and sixties, consistency theories dominated the field of social psychology, and have recently made a comeback. Yet, Truman and Byrnes pose major difficulties for cognitive dissonance and other consistency theories. These practical politicians maintained incompatible cognitions without discomfort; they did not have a stable, coherent system of beliefs on foreign policy or the Soviet Union. Analysts have often criticized the lack of coherence in American foreign policy, while casting blame on domestic political constraints, bureaucratic politics, or unrealistic objectives. Systematic investigation of the beliefs of foreign policymakers may reveal that an important cause of inconsistency in American policy is conceptual—the absence of a consistent, hierarchical, strategic vision of America's role in world affairs.

2. Rhetoric and Beliefs. We need more studies showing the influence of political rhetoric on individual beliefs. Realist thinkers have frequently lamented that universalistic statements of American foreign policy aims, originally contrived to obtain public support for limited policies, often boomerang and place U.S. leaders in a straitjacket by creating commitments that exceed American interests and power. But the source of constraint may be internal to the minds of politicians instead of being located in the domestic political context. Do politicians internalize metaphors and phrases crafted by speechwriters and officials, as self-perception theory would predict? What effect does this have on the content and conduct of American foreign policy?

3. Analogical vs. Ideological Thinking. This study suggests that for practical politicians and administrators, analogies drawn from personal experience may be more powerful as a source of policy guidance than more abstract, ideological beliefs. Why then do we often assume that politicians and political appointees are guided by such broad philosophical constructs as Realism or Idealism? If policymakers understand emerging situations by comparing them to past cases, what implications does this have for the substance and quality of American foreign policy?

4. Problem of Explanation. The results of this study are consistent with psychological experiments suggesting that the type of cognitive

process that decisionmakers use varies greatly with the way the task is described, the context, and so on. Nevertheless, self-perception, attribution, and schema theories proved to be most applicable to the archival evidence. Which combination of theories provides the best explanation for other real world foreign policy decisionmaking cases? Are the theories contradictory or complementary? The self-perception thesis that changes in behavior promote attitude change under certain conditions could be tested in such cases as the U.S. image of the People's Republic of China following first the Chinese intervention in the Korean War and later the Sino-American rapprochement in 1972, and Egyptian and Israeli perceptions of the other following Sadat's visit and the Camp David accords.

5. A Multilevel Approach. How can psychological theories be linked to or integrated with other levels of analysis—systemic, domestic political, organizational, small group—in a multilevel approach? Do the more macro levels of analysis exclude possible outcomes without determining the final result of a foreign policy decision? Do psychological theories merely trace in detail the links between stimulus and response? Or, as this study indicates, are social psychological theories in many cases essential to explain why one event occurred rather than another?

6. Use of Case Studies for Theory Testing. Close investigation of detailed historical evidence can be used to confirm or disconfirm the predictions of rival social science theories. Although case studies have been criticized as atheoretical or noncumulative, these deficiencies are not inherent but can be avoided through systematic, self-conscious theory testing.

7. Typologies. For what types of people and situations are the psychological theories likely to be valid? Policymakers can be more closely classified into extroverts vs. introverts, occupational background, and role. How do role and cognition interact? For example, do certain types of roles—administrator, political broker, foreign service officer, political appointee, lawyer, in-and-outer—promote particular types of thinking?

8. Limitations of Structural Realism. If various policymakers interpret events differently, then state behavior cannot be explained solely as a response to geopolitical imperatives, the balance of power, or domestic political constraints. The origins of the Cold War is a case ideally suited for Realist theory; the emergence of a bipolar distribution of global power should have been sufficient to explain why U.S.-Soviet relations assumed the form of a zero-sum game. But it was not. If the Realist theory cannot provide an adequate, specified explanation

in this "must fit"[27] case, for what other cases should it be supplemented with theories from other levels of analysis, particularly social psychology?

The implications of this question extend beyond explaining the origins of the Cold War, for if intense U.S.-Soviet conflict is not structurally ordained by the bipolar distribution of power in the international system, then there is latitude and indeed hope for policymakers to develop a more constructive relationship between the two superpowers.

[27] For a discussion of the use of "crucial cases" for theory testing, see Eckstein, "Case Study and Theory in Political Science," 7:79-138.

SELECTED BIBLIOGRAPHY

MANUSCRIPTS AND ARCHIVES

Clemson University, Clemson, South Carolina
  Byrnes Papers
  W. B.'s Book
Library of Congress, Washington, D.C.
  Henry H. Arnold Papers
  Joseph E. Davies Papers
  Herbert Feis Papers
  Felix Frankfurter Papers
  William D. Leahy Papers
  Robert P. Patterson Papers
  Laurence A. Steinhardt Papers
National Archives, Washington, D.C.
Diplomatic Branch
  RG 59   General Records of the Department of State
    Decimal File
    Lot Files:
      Bohlen File
      Harley Notter File
      Matthews-Hickerson Files
      Miscellaneous Office Files, 1910-1944
      Office of European Affairs File
      Records of the Policy Planning Staff
      Minutes of the Committee of Three
      White House Daily Summary
      Daily Top Secret Staff Summary
      Secretary's Summary
      Verbatim Reports of the Secretary's Press Conferences
  RG 43   Records of World War II Conferences
  RG 353   State-War-Navy Coordinating Committee Records
Modern Military Branch
  RG 48   Leahy Files
  RG 107   Records of the Secretary of the Army (Patterson), Subject
          File (Safe File)
          Records of the Secretary of War (Stimson), Subject File
          Records of the Assistant Secretary of War (McCloy)

RG 165   Records of the War Department General and Special Staffs
RG 218   Records of the Joint Chiefs of Staff
RG 319   Records of the Army Staff
RG 334   Records of the U.S. Military Mission to Moscow

Public Record Office, London
FO 371   Foreign Office General Correspondence after 1906 Political

Princeton University, Princeton, New Jersey
Bernard M. Baruch Papers
John Foster Dulles Papers
Louis Fischer Papers
James V. Forrestal Papers
George F. Kennan Papers
Harry D. White Papers

Franklin Delano Roosevelt Library, Hyde Park, New York
Oscar Cox Papers
Louis Fischer Papers
Harry L. Hopkins Papers
Henry M. Morgenthau, Jr. Papers
President's Soviet Protocol Committee records
Franklin D. Roosevelt Papers:
    President's Personal File
    President's Secretary's File
    Map Room File
Eleanor Roosevelt Papers

Harry S Truman Library, Independence, Missouri
Eben A. Ayers Papers
Dean Acheson Papers
George V. Allen Papers
Thomas C. Blaisdell Papers
William L. Clayton Papers
Clayton-Thorpe Files
Clark M. Clifford Papers
Matthew J. Connelly Papers
Jonathan Daniels Papers
George M. Elsey Papers
Bernard L. Gladieux Papers
Joseph M. Jones Papers
Frank McNaughton Papers
Samuel I. Rosenman Papers
Alfred Schindler Papers

Harold D. Smith Papers
John W. Snyder Papers
Harry S Truman Papers:
  President's Secretary's File
  Senatorial and Vice-Presidential Files
  White House Map Room File
  Naval Aide File
  Confidential File
  Personal File
  Post-Presidential Files
  Memoirs File
University of Virginia Library, Charlottesville, Virginia
  Edward R. Stettinius, Jr. Papers
Washington National Records Center, Suitland, Maryland
  RG 84   Moscow Post Files
Yale University, New Haven, Connecticut
  Henry L. Stimson Diary (microfilm publication, Stanford University Library)

Public Documents

Correspondence Between the Chairman of the Council of Ministers of the U.S.S.R. and the Presidents of the U.S.A. and the Prime Ministers of Great Britain During the Great Patriotic War of 1941-1945. 2 vols. Moscow: Foreign Language Publishing House, 1957.

General Sikorski Historical Institute. *Documents on Soviet-Polish Relations, 1943-1945.* 2 vols. London: Heinemann, 1967.

Public Papers of the Presidents: Harry S Truman, 1945-47. Washington, D.C.: Government Printing Office, 1961-1963.

U.S. Congress. Senate. Committee on Judiciary. *Morgenthau Diary (Germany).* 90th Cong., 1st sess., 1967. Vol. 2.

————. Committee on Foreign Relations. *Legislative Origins of the Truman Doctrine: Hearings Held in Executive Session on S. 938.* 80th Cong., 1st sess., 1947. Historical Series, 1973.

U.S. Department of State. *Department of State Bulletin.* Vols. 12-14 (1945-1947).

————. *Foreign Relations of the United States.* Annual volumes, 1944-1947. Washington, D.C.: Government Printing Office, 1965-1971.

————. *Foreign Relations of the United States: The Conferences at Cairo and Teheran, 1943.* Washington, D.C.: Government Printing Office, 1961.

U.S. Department of State. *Foreign Relations of the United States: The Conference at Quebec, 1944*. Washington, D.C.: Government Printing Office, 1970.

——. *Foreign Relations of the United States: The Conferences at Malta and Yalta, 1945*. Washington, D.C.: Government Printing Office, 1955.

——. *Foreign Relations of the United States: The Conference of Berlin (The Potsdam Conference), 1945*. 2 vols. Washington, D.C.: Government Printing Office, 1960.

NEWSPAPERS AND PERIODICALS

Nation, 1944-1947.
New Republic, 1944-1947.
New York Times, 1944-1947.
Newsweek, 1944-1947.
Time, 1944-1947.
Washington Post, 1945-1946.

BOOKS AND DISSERTATIONS

Abelson, Robert; Aronson, Elliott; McGuire, William J.; Newcomb, Theodore M.; Rosenberg, Milton; and Tannenbaum, Percy, eds. *Theories of Cognitive Consistency: A Sourcebook*. Chicago: Rand McNally, 1968.

Acheson, Dean. *Present at the Creation: My Years in the State Department*. New York: W. W. Norton, 1969.

Axelrod, Robert. *Structure of Decision: The Cognitive Maps of Political Elites*. Princeton: Princeton University Press, 1976.

Berelson, Bernard. *Content Analysis in Communication Research*. Glencoe, Ill.: Free Press, 1952.

Berle, Beatrice Bishop, and Jacobs, Travis Beal, eds. *Navigating the Rapids, 1918-1971: From the Papers of Adolph A. Berle*. New York: Harcourt Brace Jovanovich, 1973.

Bernstein, Barton J., ed. *The Atomic Bomb: The Critical Issues*. Boston: Little, Brown, 1976.

Billig, Michael. *Ideology and Social Psychology: Extremism, Moderation, and Contradiction*. Oxford: Basil Blackwell, 1982.

Bland, Larry I. "W. Averell Harriman: Businessman and Diplomat, 1891-1945." Ph.D. dissertation, University of Wisconsin, 1972.

Blum, John M., ed. *From the Morgenthau Diaries*. Vol. 3, *Years of War, 1941-1945*. Boston: Houghton Mifflin, 1967.

————. *The Price of Vision: The Diary of Henry A. Wallace, 1942-1946.* Boston: Houghton Mifflin, 1973.

Bohlen, Charles E. *Witness to History, 1929-1969.* New York: W. W. Norton, 1973.

Bor-Komorowski, T. *The Secret Army.* London: Gollancz, 1950.

Bruce, George. *The Warsaw Uprising: 1 August-2 October 1944.* London: Rupert Hart-Davis, 1972.

Byrnes, James F. *All in One Lifetime.* New York: Harper & Bros., 1958.

————. *Speaking Frankly.* New York: Harper & Bros., 1947.

Campbell, Thomas M. *Masquerade Peace: America's U.N. Policy, 1944-1945.* Tallahassee: Florida State University Press, 1973.

————, and Herring, George C., eds. *The Diaries of Edward R. Stettinius, 1943-1946.* New York: Franklin Watts, New Viewpoints, 1975.

Churchill, Winston S. *Triumph and Tragedy.* Boston: Houghton Mifflin, 1953.

Ciechanowski, Jan M. *The Warsaw Rising of 1944.* London: Cambridge University Press, 1974.

Clemens, Diane S. *Yalta.* London: Oxford University Press, 1970.

Cochran, Bert. *Harry Truman and the Crisis Presidency.* New York: Funk & Wagnalls, 1973.

Coffin, Tris. *Missouri Compromise.* Boston: Little, Brown, 1947.

Curry, George. *James F. Byrnes.* Vol. 14 of *The American Secretaries of State and Their Diplomacy.* New York: Cooper Square Publishers, 1965.

Dallek, Robert. *Franklin D. Roosevelt and American Foreign Policy, 1932-1945.* New York: Oxford University Press, 1979.

Daniels, Jonathan. *The Man of Independence.* New York: J. B. Lippincott, 1950.

Davis, Lynn E. *The Cold War Begins: Soviet-American Conflict over Eastern Europe.* Princeton: Princeton University Press, 1974.

Deane, John R. *The Strange Alliance: The Story of Our Efforts at Wartime Co-operation with Russia.* New York: Viking Press, 1947.

De Luca, Anthony R. "The Montreaux Conference of 1936: A Diplomatic Study of Anglo-Soviet Rivalry at the Turkish Straits." Ph.D. dissertation, Stanford University, 1974.

DePorte, A. W. *Europe Between the Superpowers: The Enduring Balance.* New Haven: Yale University Press, 1979.

De Santis, Hugh. *The Diplomacy of Silence: The Foreign Service, the Soviet Union, and the Cold War, 1933-1947.* Chicago: Chicago University Press, 1980.

De Sola Pool, Ithiel, ed. *Trends in Content Analysis*. Urbana: University of Illinois Press, 1959.

Divine, Robert A. *Second Chance: The Triumph of Internationalism in America during World War II*. New York: Atheneum, 1971.

Donovan, Robert J. *Conflict and Crisis: The Presidency of Harry S Truman, 1945-1948*. New York: W. W. Norton, 1977.

Eaton, Richard, and Hart, La Valle. *Meet Harry S Truman*. Washington, D.C.: Dumbarton House, 1945.

Edelman, Murray. *The Symbolic Uses of Politics*. Urbana: University of Illinois Press, 1964.

Eden, Anthony. *The Reckoning*. Boston: Houghton Mifflin, 1973.

Feis, Herbert. *Between War and Peace: The Potsdam Conference*. Princeton: Princeton University Press, 1960.

———. *Churchill, Roosevelt, Stalin: The War They Waged and the Peace They Sought*. Princeton: Princeton University Press, 1957.

———. *From Trust to Terror: The Onset of the Cold War, 1945-1950*. New York: W. W. Norton, 1970.

Flavell, John H. *The Developmental Psychology of Jean Piaget*. Foreword by Jean Piaget. Princeton: Van Nostrand, 1963.

Freeland, Richard M. *The Truman Doctrine and the Origins of McCarthyism: Foreign Policy, Domestic Politics, and Internal Security, 1946-1948*. New York: Schocken Books, 1971.

Gaddis, John Lewis. *The United States and the Origins of the Cold War, 1941-1947*. New York: Columbia University Press, 1972.

Gardner, Lloyd C. *Architects of Illusion: Men and Ideas in American Foreign Policy, 1941-1949*. Chicago: Quadrangle Books, 1970.

———; Schlesinger, Arthur M., Jr.; and Morgenthau, Hans J. *The Origins of the Cold War*. Waltham, Mass.: Ginn, 1970.

George, Alexander L. *Propaganda Analysis: A Study of Inferences Made from Nazi Propaganda in World War II*. Westport, Conn.: Greenwood Press, 1959.

Gerbner, George; Holsti, Ole R.; Krippendorff, Klaus; Paisley, William J.; and Stone, Phillip J. *The Analysis of Communication Content*. New York: John Wiley & Sons, 1969.

Grew, Joseph C. *Turbulent Era: A Diplomatic Record of Forty Years, 1904-1945*. 2 vols. Boston: Houghton Mifflin, 1952.

Halle, Louis J. *The Cold War as History*. New York: Harper & Row, 1967; Harper Torchbooks, 1975.

Hamby, Alonzo L. *Beyond the New Deal: Harry S Truman and American Liberalism*. New York: Columbia University Press, 1973.

Harriman, W. Averell, and Abel, Elie. *Special Envoy to Churchill and Stalin, 1941-1946*. New York: Random House, 1975.

Helm, William P. *Harry Truman: A Political Biography*. New York: Duell, Sloan, and Pearce, 1947.

Herken, Gregg. *The Winning Weapon: The Atomic Bomb in the Cold War, 1945-1950*. New York: Alfred A. Knopf, 1980.

Herring, George C. *Aid to Russia, 1941-1946: Strategy, Diplomacy, the Origins of the Cold War*. New York: Columbia University Press, 1973.

Herz, Martin F. *Beginnings of the Cold War*. Bloomington: Indiana University Press. 1966.

Hewlett, Richard G., and Anderson, Oscar E., Jr. *A History of the United States Atomic Energy Commission*. Vol. 2, *The New World, 1939-1946*. University Park: Pennsylvania State University.Press, 1962.

Hillman, William, ed. *Mr. President: The First Publication from the Personal Diaries, Private Letters, Papers, and Revealing Interviews of Harry S Truman, Thirty-second President of the United States of America*. New York: Farrar, Straus and Young, 1952.

Holsti, Ole R. *Content Analysis for the Social Sciences and Humanities*. Reading, Mass.: Addison-Wesley, 1969.

Hovland, Carl H.; Janis, Irving L.; and Kelley, Harold H. *Communication and Persuasion*. New Haven: Yale University Press, 1953.

Insko, Chester A. *Theories of Attitude Change*. New York: Appleton-Century-Crofts, 1967.

Jervis, Robert. *Perception and Misperception in International Politics*. Princeton: Princeton University Press, 1976.

Jones, Joseph M. *The Fifteen Weeks (February 21-June 5, 1947)*. New York: Harcourt, Brace & World, 1955.

Kennan, George F. *Memoirs (1925-1950)*. Boston: Little, Brown, 1967; Bantam Books, 1969.

Kiesler, Charles A.; Collins, Barry E.; and Miller, Norman. *Attitude Change: A Critical Analysis of Theoretical Approaches*. New York: John Wiley & Sons, 1967.

Kolko, Gabriel. *The Politics of War: The World and United States Foreign Policy, 1943-1945*. New York: Random House, 1968.

————, and Kolko, Joyce. *The Limits of Power, 1945-1954*. New York: Harper & Row, 1972.

Kuniholm, Bruce R. *The Origins of the Cold War in the Near East: Great Power Conflict and Diplomacy in Iran, Turkey, and Greece*. Princeton: Princeton University Press, 1980.

LaFeber, Walter. *America, Russia, and the Cold War, 1945-1980*. 4th ed. New York: John Wiley & Sons, 1980.

Lazarsfeld, Paul F., and Rosenberg, Morris, eds. *The Language of Social Research*. Glencoe, Ill.: Free Press, 1955.

Lazarsfeld, Paul F.; Pasanella, Ann K.; Rosenberg, Morris. *Continuities in the Language of Social Research*. New York: Free Press, 1972.

Leahy, William D. *I Was There*. New York: McGraw-Hill, 1950.

Levering, Ralph B. *American Opinion and the Russian Alliance, 1939-1945*. Chapel Hill: University of North Carolina Press, 1976.

Lilienthal, David E. *The Journals of David E. Lilienthal*. 2 vols. New York: Harper & Row, 1964.

Lippmann, Walter. *The Cold War*. New York: Harper & Bros., 1947.

Lukas, Richard. *Strange Allies: The United States and Poland, 1941-1945*. Knoxville: University of Tennessee Press, 1978.

Lundestad, Geir. *The American Non-Policy towards Eastern Europe, 1943-1947: Universalism in an Area Not of Essential Interest to the United States*. Oslo: Universitetsforlaget, 1978.

Lytle, Mark. "American-Iranian Relations 1941-1947 and the Redefinition of National Security." Ph.D. dissertation, Yale University, 1973.

MacDougall, Curtis D. *Gideon's Army*. 2 vols. New York: Marzani and Munsell, 1965.

McLellan, David S. *Dean Acheson: The State Department Years*. New York: Dodd, Mead, 1976.

McNaughton, Frank, and Hehmeyer, Walter. *This Man Truman*. New York: McGraw-Hill, 1945.

McNeill, William H. *America, Britain, and Russia: Their Co-operation and Conflict, 1941-1946*. London: Oxford University Press, 1953; reprint New York: Johnson, 1970.

Martel, Leon C. *Lend-Lease, Loans and the Coming of the Cold War*. Boulder, Colo.: Westview Press, 1979.

Mastny, Vojtech. *Russia's Road to the Cold War: Diplomacy, Warfare, and the Politics of Communism, 1941-1945*. New York: Columbia University Press, 1979.

May, Ernest R. *"Lessons" of the Past: The Use and Misuse of History in American Foreign Policy*. New York: Oxford University Press, 1973.

Messer, Robert Louis. "The Making of a Cold Warrior: James F. Byrnes and American-Soviet Relations, 1945-1946." Ph.D. dissertation, University of California at Berkeley, 1975.

Millis, Walter, ed. *The Forrestal Diaries*. New York: Viking Press, 1951.

Murphy, Robert. *Diplomat among Warriors*. Garden City, N.Y.: Doubleday, 1964.

Nicolson, Harold. *Diaries and Letters*. Edited by Nigel Nicolson. Vol.

2, *The War Years, 1939-1945*; Vol. 3, *The Later Years, 1945-1962.* New York: Atheneum, 1967, 1968.

Nisbett, Richard, and Ross, Lee. *Human Inference: Strategies and Shortcomings of Social Judgment.* Englewood Cliffs, N.J.: Prentice-Hall, 1980.

North, Robert C.; Holsti, Ole R.; Zaninovich, George M.; and Zinnes, Dina A. *Content Analysis: A Handbook with Applications for the Study of International Crisis.* Evanston, Ill.: Northwestern University Press, 1963.

Paterson, Thomas G. *On Every Front: The Making of the Cold War.* New York: W. W. Norton, 1979.

————. *Soviet-American Confrontation: Postwar Reconstruction and the Origins of the Cold War.* Baltimore: Johns Hopkins University Press, 1973.

Pfau, Richard A. "The United States and Iran, 1941-1947: Origins of Partnership." Ph.D. dissertation, University of Virginia, 1975.

Phillips, Cabell. *The Truman Presidency: The History of a Triumphant Succession.* New York: Macmillan, 1966.

Range, Willard. *Franklin Roosevelt's World Order.* Athens: University of Georgia Press, 1949.

Rose, Lisle A. *Dubious Victory: The United States and the End of World War II.* Kent, Ohio: Kent State University Press, 1979.

Rosenman, Samuel I., ed. *The Public Papers and Addresses of Franklin D. Roosevelt.* Vols. 12-13. New York: Harper & Bros., 1950.

Schank, Roger C., and Abelson, Robert. *Scripts, Plans, Goals and Understanding: An Inquiry into Human Knowledge Structures.* Hillsdale, N.J.: Lawrence Erlbaum Associates, 1977.

Schneider, David J.; Hastorf, Albert H.; and Ellsworth, Phoebe. *Person Perception.* 2nd ed. Reading, Mass.: Addison-Wesley, 1979.

Sharp, Samuel L. *Poland: White Eagle on Red Field.* Cambridge: Harvard University Press, 1953.

Sherwin, Martin J. *A World Destroyed: The Atomic Bomb and the Grand Alliance.* New York: Random House, Vintage Books, 1973.

Sherwood, Robert E. *Roosevelt and Hopkins: An Intimate History.* New York: Harper & Bros., 1948.

Smith, Gaddis. *Dean Acheson.* Vol. 16 of *The American Secretaries of State and Their Diplomacy.* New York: Cooper Square Publishers, 1972.

Sprout, Harold, and Sprout, Margaret. *The Ecological Perspective on Human Affairs.* Princeton: Princeton University Press, 1965.

Spykman, Nicholas John. *America's Strategy in World Politics: The*

United States and the Balance of Power. New York: Harcourt, Brace, 1942.

Standley, William H., and Ageton, Arthur. *Admiral Ambassador to Russia*. Chicago: Henry Regnery, 1955.

Stein, Janice, and Tanter, Raymond. *Rational Decision-Making: Israel's Security Choices, 1967*. Columbus: Ohio State University Press, 1976.

Steinberg, Alfred. *The Man from Missouri: The Life and Times of Harry S Truman*. New York: G. P. Putnam's Sons, 1962.

Sternberg, Robert J. *Intelligence, Information Processing and Analogical Reasoning: The Componential Analysis of Human Abilities*. Hillsdale, N.J.: Lawrence Erlbaum Associates, 1977.

Steinbruner, John D. *The Cybernetic Theory of Decision*. Princeton: Princeton University Press, 1974.

Sulzberger, C. L. *A Long Row of Candles: Memoirs and Diaries (1934-1954)*. Toronto: Macmillan, 1969.

Truman, Harry S. *Memoirs*. Vol I, *Year of Decisions*. Garden City: Doubleday, 1955.

Truman, Margaret. *Harry S Truman*. New York: William Morrow, 1973.

Ulam, Adam B. *Expansion and Coexistence: Soviet Foreign Policy, 1917-73*. 2nd ed. New York: Holt, Rinehart & Winston, 1974.

Vandenberg, Arthur H., Jr., ed. *The Private Papers of Senator Vandenberg*. Boston: Houghton Mifflin, 1952.

Ward, Patricia D. *The Threat of Peace: James F. Byrnes and the Council of Foreign Ministers, 1945-1946*. Kent, Ohio: Kent State University Press, 1979.

Weil, Martin. *A Pretty Good Club: The Founding Fathers of the U.S. Foreign Service*. New York: W. W. Norton, 1978.

Welch, William. *American Images of Soviet Foreign Policy: An Inquiry into Recent Appraisals from the Academic Community*. New Haven: Yale University Press, 1970.

Welles, Sumner. *Where Are We Heading?* New York: Harper & Bros., 1946.

Werth, Alexander. *Russia at War*. New York: Avon Books, 1965.

Williams, William Appleman. *The Tragedy of American Diplomacy*. 2nd ed., rev. and enl. New York: Dell Publishing Co., Delta Book, 1972.

Wilmot, Chester. *The Struggle for Europe*. London: Collins, 1952.

Woodward, Llewellyn. *British Foreign Policy in the Second World War*. London: Her Majesty's Stationery Office, 1962.

Wright, C. Ben. "George F. Kennan, Scholar-Diplomat: 1926-1949." Ph.D. dissertation, University of Wisconsin, 1972.

Yergin, Daniel. *Shattered Peace: The Origins of the Cold War and the National Security State*. Boston: Houghton Mifflin, 1977.

Zimbardo, Philip G.; Ebbeson, Ebbe E.; and Maslach, Christina. *Influencing Attitudes and Changing Behavior*. 2nd ed. Reading, Mass.: Addison-Wesley, 1977.

ARTICLES

Abelson, Robert P. "Script Processing in Attitude Formation and Decision Making." In *Cognition and Social Behavior*, edited by John S. Carroll and John W. Payne, pp. 33-45. Hillsdale, N.J.: Lawrence Erlbaum Associates, 1976.

———. "The Structure of Belief Systems." In *Computer Models of Thought and Language*, edited by Roger C. Schank and Kenneth M. Colby, pp. 287-399. San Francisco: W. H. Freeman, 1973.

Alsop, Joseph, and Kintner, Robert, "Sly and Able." *Saturday Evening Post*, July 20, 1940.

Apter, David E. "Introduction: Ideology and Discontent." In *Ideology and Discontent*, edited by David E. Apter, pp. 15-46. New York: Free Press, 1964.

Arkin, Robert M., and Duval, Shelley. "Focus of Attention and Causal Attributions of Actors and Observers." *Journal of Experimental Social Psychology* 11 (1975): 427-38.

Aronson, Elliot. "The Theory of Cognitive Dissonance: A Current Perspective." In *Cognitive Theories in Social Psychology: Papers from Advances in Experimental Social Psychology*, edited by Leonard Berkowitz, pp. 181-211. San Francisco: Academic Press, 1978.

Axelrod, Robert. "Schema Theory: An Information Processing Model of Perception and Cognition." *American Political Science Review* 67 (1973): 1248-66.

Bem, Daryl J. "Self-Perception Theory." In *Advances in Experimental Social Psychology*, edited by Leonard Berkowitz, 6:1-61. New York: Academic Press, 1972.

———. "Self-Perception Theory." In *Cognitive Theories in Social Psychology: Papers from Advances in Experimental Social Psychology*, edited by Leonard Berkowitz, pp. 221-82. San Francisco: Academic Press, 1978.

———, and Allen, Andrea. "On Predicting Some of the People Some of the Time: The Search for Cross-situational Consistencies in Behavior." *Psychoalogical Review* 84 (1974): 506-20.

Bem, Daryl J., and Funder, David C. "Predicting More of the People More of the Time: Assessing the Personality of Situations." *Psychological Review* 85 (November 1978): 485-501.

Bem, Daryl J., and McConnell, H. Keith. "Testing the Self-Perception Explanation of Dissonance Phenomena: On the Salience of Premanipulation Attitudes." *Journal of Personality and Social Psychology* 14 (1970): 23-37.

Bernstein, Barton J. "American Foreign Policy and the Origins of the Cold War." In *Politics and Policies of the Truman Administration*, edited by Barton J. Bernstein, pp. 15-77. Chicago: Quadrangle Books, 1970.

Bobrow, Daniel G., and Norman, Donald A. "Some Principles of Memory Schemata." In *Representation and Understanding: Studies in Cognitive Science*, edited by Daniel Bobrow and Allan Collins, pp. 131-49. New York: Academic Press, 1975.

Bransford, John D., and Franks, Jeffrey J. "The Abstraction of Linguistic Ideas." *Cognitive Psychology* 2 (1971): 331-50.

Bransford, John D.; Barclay, J. Richard; and Franks, Jeffrey J. "Sentence Memory: A Constructive versus Interpretive Approach." *Cognitive Psychology* 3 (1972): 193-209.

Bransford, John D., and Johnson, Marcia K. "Contextual Prerequisites for Understanding: Some Investigations of Comprehension and Recall." *Journal of Verbal Learning and Verbal Behavior* 22 (1972): 717-26.

Cantor, Nancy, and Mischel, Walter. "Traits as Prototypes: Effects on Recognition Memory." *Journal of Personality and Social Psychology* 35 (1977): 38-48.

Cartwright, Dorwin P. "Analysis of Qualitative Material." In *Research Methods in the Behavioral Sciences*, edited by Leon Festinger and Daniel Katz, pp. 421-70. New York: Holt, Rinehart & Winston, 1953.

Converse, Philip E. "The Nature of Belief Systems in Mass Publics." In *Ideology and Discontent*, edited by David Apter, pp. 205-61. New York: Free Press, 1980.

Coombs, Clyde H. "Theory and Methods of Social Measurement." In *Research Methods in the Behavioral Sciences*, edited by Leon Festinger and Daniel Katz, pp. 471-533. New York: Holt, Rinehart & Winston, 1953.

Davis, Forrest. "Roosevelt's World Blueprint." *Saturday Evening Post*, April 10, 1943.

———. "What Really Happened at Teheran, I and II." *Saturday Evening Post*, May 13 and 20, 1944.

Dawes, Robyn M. "Shallow Psychology." In *Cognition and Social Be-

havior, edited by John S. Carroll and John W. Payne, pp. 3-11. Hillsdale, N.J.: Lawrence Erlbaum Associates, 1976.

De Luca, Anthony R. "Soviet-American Politics and the Turkish Straits." *Political Science Quarterly* 92 (Fall 1977): 503-24.

Eagly, Alice H., and Himmelfarb, Samuel. "Attitudes and Opinions." *Annual Review of Psychology* 29 (1978): 517-25.

Eckstein, Harry. "Case Study and Theory in Political Science." In *Handbook of Political Science*. Vol. 7, *Strategies of Inquiry*, edited by Fred I. Greenstein and Nelson W. Polsby. Reading, Mass.: Addison-Wesley Publishing Co., 1975.

Fazio, Russell H.; Zanna, Mark P.; and Cooper, Joel. "Dissonance and Self-Perception: An Integrative View of Each Theory's Proper Domain of Application." *Journal of Experimental Social Psychology* 13 (1979): 464-79.

Fischhoff, Baruch. "Hindsight ≠ Foresight: The Effect of Outcome Knowledge on Judgment under Uncertainty." *Journal of Experimental Psychology: Human Perception and Performance* 1 (1975): 288-99.

———, and Beyth, Ruth. " 'I Knew It Would Happen': Remembered Probabilities of Once-future Things." *Organizational Behavior and Human Performance* 13 (1975): 1-16.

Frederiksen, Carl H. "Effects of Context-Induced Processing Operations on Semantic Information Acquired from Discourse." *Cognitive Psychology* 7 (1975): 139-66.

Gaddis, John Lewis. "Harry S Truman and the Origins of Containment." In *Makers of American Diplomacy: From Benjamin Franklin to Henry Kissinger*, edited by Frank J. Merli and Theodore A. Wilson. New York: Charles Scribner's Sons, 1974.

———. "Was the Truman Doctrine a Real Turning Point?" *Foreign Affairs* 52 (January 1974): 386-402.

Geertz, Clifford. "Ideology as a Cultural System." In *Ideology and Discontent*, edited by David E. Apter, pp. 47-76. New York: Free Press, 1964.

George, Alexander L. "The Causal Nexus Between 'Operational Code' Beliefs and Decision-Making Behavior: Problems of Theory and Methodology." In *Psychological Models and International Politics*, edited by Lawrence Falkowski, pp. 95-124. Boulder, Colo.: Westview Press, 1979.

———. "Comment on 'Opinions, Personality and Political Behavior.' " *American Political Science Review* 52 (1958): 18-26.

———. "Domestic Constraints on Regime Change in U.S. Foreign Policy: The Need for Policy Legitimacy." In *Change in the International System*, edited by Ole R. Holsti, Randolph M. Siverson, and Alexander L. George, pp. 233-59. Boulder, Colo.: Westview Press, 1980.

Huston, Luther. "The Vice President Talks of His New Job." *New York Times Magazine*, January 21, 1945.

Jaccard, James. "Toward Theories of Persuasion and Belief Change." *Journal of Personality and Social Psychology* 40 (1981): 260-69.

Jones, Edward E. "How Do People Perceive the Causes of Behavior?" *American Scientist* 64 (1976): 300-305.

———, and Harris, Victor A. "The Attribution of Attitudes." *Journal of Experimental Social Psychology* 3 (1967): 1-24.

Jones, Edward E., and Nisbett, Richard E. "The Actor and the Observer: Divergent Perceptions of the Causes of Behavior." In *Attribution: Perceiving the Causes of Behavior*, edited by Edward E. Jones, David E. Kanouse, Harold H. Kelley, Richard E. Nisbett, Stuart Valins, and Bernard Weiner, pp. 79-94. Morristown, N.J.: General Learning Press, 1971.

Kahneman, Daniel, and Tversky, Amos. "On the Psychology of Prediction." *Psychological Review* 80 (1973): 237-51.

———. "Subjective Probability: A Judgment of Representativeness." *Cognitive Psychology* 3 (1972): 430-54.

Kelley, Harold H. "Attribution in Social Interaction." In *Attribution: Perceiving the Causes of Behavior*, edited by Edward E. Jones, David E. Kanouse, Harold H. Kelley, Stuart Valins, and Bernard Weiner. Morristown, N.J.: General Learning Press, 1971.

———. "The Process of Causal Attribution." *American Psychologist* 28 (1973): 107-28.

Kiesler, Charles A.; Nisbett, Richard E.; and Zanna, Mark. "On Inferring One's Beliefs from One's Behavior." *Journal of Personality and Social Psychology* 11 (1969): 321-27.

Kimball, Warren F. "The Cold War Warmed Over." *American Historical Review* 79 (1974): 1119-36.

Knight, Jonathan. "American Statecraft and the 1946 Black Sea Straits Controversy." *Political Science Quarterly* 90 (Fall 1975): 451-75.

———. "America's International Guarantees for the Straits: Prelude to the Truman Doctrine." *Middle Eastern Studies* 13 (May 1977): 241-50.

Kulski, W. W. "The Lost Opportunity for Soviet-American Friendship." *Foreign Affairs* 25 (July 1947): 676-77.

Langer, Ellen J. "Rethinking the Role of Thought in Social Interaction." In *New Directions in Attribution Research*, edited by John H. Harvey, William F. Ickes, and Robert F. Kidd, 2:35-58. Hillsdale, N.J.: Lawrence Erlbaum Associates, 1978.

————, and Abelson, Robert P. "The Semantics of Asking a Favor: How to Succeed in Getting Help Without Really Dying." *Journal of Personality and Social Psychology* 24 (1972): 26-32.

Lazarsfeld, Paul F., and Barton, Allen H. "Qualitative Measurement in the Social Sciences: Classification, Typologies and Indices." In *The Policy Sciences: Recent Developments in Scope and Method*, edited by Daniel Lerner and Harold D. Lasswell, pp. 180-88. Stanford: Stanford University Press, 1951.

Lee, R. Alton. "The Army 'Mutiny' of 1946." *Journal of American History* 53 (December 1966): 555-71.

Levi, Werner. "Ideology, Interests, and Foreign Policy." *International Studies Quarterly* 14 (March 1970): 1-31.

McArthur, Leslie Ann. "The How and What of Why: Some Determinants and Consequences of Causal Attribution." *Journal of Personality and Social Psychology* 22 (1972): 171-93.

McGuire, William J. "The Development of Theory in Social Psychology." In *The Development of Social Psychology*, edited by Robin Gilmour and Steve Duck, pp. 53-80. London: Academic Press, 1980.

————. "The Nature of Attitudes and Attitude Change." In *The Handbook of Social Psychology*, edited by Gardner Lindzey. Vol. 3, *The Individual in a Group Context*. 2nd ed. Reading, Mass.: Addison-Wesley, 1969.

Maier, Charles S. "Revisionism and the Interpretation of Cold War Origins." *Perspectives in American History* 4 (1970): 313-47.

Mark, Eduard, ed. " 'Today Has Been a Historical One': Harry S Truman's Diary of the Potsdam Conference." *Diplomatic History* 4 (Summer 1980): 317-26.

Marshall, Margaret. "Portrait of Truman." *The Nation*, April 21, 1945, pp. 438-40.

Minsky, Marvin. "A Framework for Representing Knowledge." In *The Psychology of Computer Vision*, edited by Patrick Winston, pp. 211-77. New York: McGraw-Hill, 1975.

Miscamble, Wilson D. "Anthony Eden and the Truman-Molotov Conversations, April 1945." *Diplomatic History* 2 (Spring 1978): 167-80.

————. "The Evolution of an Internationalist: Harry S Truman and American Foreign Policy." *Australian Journal of Politics and History* 23 (August 1977): 268-83.

Mischel, Walter. "Toward a Cognitive Social Learning Reconceptualization of Personality." *Psychological Review* 80 (1973): 252-83.

Mitchell, Robert E. "The Use of Content Analysis for Explanatory Studies." *Public Opinion Quarterly* 31 (1967): 230-41.

Murphy, Charles J. V. "W. Averell Harriman." *Life*, December 30, 1946.

Nisbett, Richard E., and Borgida, Eugene. "Attribution and the Psychology of Prediction." *Journal of Personality and Social Psychology* 32 (1975): 932-43.

Nisbett, Richard E.; Borgida, Eugene; Crandall, Rick; and Reed, Harvey. "Popular Induction: Information Is Not Always Informative." In *Cognition and Social Behavior*, edited by John S. Carroll and John W. Payne, pp. 113-33. Hillsdale, N.J.: Lawrence Erlbaum Associates, 1976.

Nisbett, Richard E.; Caputo, Craig; Legant, Patricia; and Maracek, Jeanne. "Behavior as Seen by the Actor and as Seen by the Observer." *Journal of Personality and Social Psychology* 27 (1973): 154-64.

Nisbett, Richard E., and Wilson, Timothy DeCamp. "Telling More Than We Can Know: Verbal Reports on Mental Processes." *Psychological Review* 84 (May 1977): 231-59.

Ortony, Andrew. "Why Metaphors Are Necessary and Not Just Nice." *Educational Theory* 25 (1975): 45-53.

————; Reynolds, Ralph E.; and Arter, Judith A. "Metaphor: Theoretical and Empirical Research." *Psychological Bulletin* 85 (September 1978): 919-43.

Peak, Helen. "Problems of Objective Observation." In *Research Methods in the Behavioral Sciences*, edited by Leon Festinger and Daniel Katz, pp. 243-99. New York: Holt, Reinhart, & Winston, 1953.

"President Truman's Task." *New Republic*, April 23, 1945, pp. 539-41.

Pryor, John B., and Kriss, Mitchel. "The Cognitive Dynamics of Salience in the Attribution Process." *Journal of Personality and Social Psychology* 35 (1977): 49-55.

Regan, Dennis T., and Totten, Judith. "Empathy and Attribution: Turning Observers into Actors." *Journal of Personality and Social Psychology* 32 (1975): 850-56.

Richardson, J. L. "Cold-War Revisionism: A Critique." *World Politics* 25 (1972): 579-621.

"Rift in the Big Three." *New Republic*, June 4, 1945, pp. 771-72.

Rosch, Eleanor. "On the Internal Structure of Perceptual and Semantic Categories." In *Cognitive Development and the Acquisition of Language*, edited by Timothy E. Moore, pp. 111-44. New York: Academic Press, 1973.

————; Mervis, Carolyn B.; Gray, Wayne D.; Johnson, David M.;

and Boyes-Braem, Penny. "Basic Objects in Natural Categories." *Cognitive Psychology* 8 (1976): 382-439.

Ross, Lee. "The Intuitive Psychologist and His Shortcomings: Distortions in the Attribution Process." In *Advances in Experimental Social Psychology*, edited by Leonard Berkowitz, 10:173-220. New York: Academic Press, 1977.

————; Lepper, Mark R.; and Hubbard, Michael. "Perseverance in Self-Perception and Social Perception: Biased Attributional Processes in the Debriefing Paradigm." *Journal of Personality and Social Psychology* 32 (1975): 880-92.

Rumelhart, David, and Ortony, Andrew. "The Representation of Knowledge in Memory." In *Schooling and the Acquisition of Knowledge*, edited by Richard C. Anders, Rand J. Spiro, and William E. Montague, pp. 99-135. Hillsdale, N.J.: Lawrence Erlbaum Associates, 1977.

Runyan, William McKinley. "Why Did Van Gogh Cut Off His Ear? The Problem of Alternative Explanations in Psychobiography." *Journal of Personality and Social Psychology* 40 (1981): 1070-77.

Sartori, Giovanni. "Politics, Ideology, and Belief Systems." *American Political Science Review* 63 (June 1969): 398-411.

Schlesinger, Arthur, M., Jr. "Origins of the Cold War." *Foreign Affairs* 46 (1967): 22-52.

"Shall America Help Russia Rebuild?" *Nation*, May 26, 1945, pp. 588-89.

Siracusa, Joseph M., ed. "The Meaning of TOLSTOY: Churchill, Stalin, and the Balkans Moscow, October 1944." *Diplomatic History* 3 (Fall 1979): 443-63.

Stone, I. F. "Anti-Russian Undertow." *Nation*, May 12, 1945, pp. 534-35.

————. "Trieste and San Francisco." *Nation*, May 26, 1945, pp. 589-90.

————. "Truman and the State Department." *Nation*, June 9, 1945, pp. 637-39.

Taylor, Shelley E. "Developing a Cognitive Social Psychology." In *Cognition and Social Behavior*, edited by John S. Carroll and John W. Payne, pp. 69-77. Hillsdale, N.J.: Lawrence Erlbaum Associates, 1976.

————, and Crocker, Jennifer. "Schematic Bases of Social Information Processing." In *Social Cognition: The Ontario Symposium*, edited by E. Tory Higgins, C. Peter Hermann, and Mark P. Zanna, 1:89-134. Hillsdale, N.J.: Lawrence Erlbaum Associates, 1981.

Taylor, Shelley E., and Fiske, Susan T. "Point of View and Perceptions of Causality." *Journal of Personality and Social Psychology* 32 (1975): 439-55.

——. "Salience, Attention, and Attribution: Top of the Head Phenomena." In *Advances in Experimental Social Psychology*, edited by Leonard Berkowitz, 11:249-88. New York: Academic Press, 1978.

Trout, Thomas B. "Rhetoric Revisited: Political Legitimation and the Cold War." *International Studies Quarterly* 19 (September 1975): 251-84.

Tversky, Amos, and Kahneman, Daniel. "Availability: A Heuristic for Judging Frequency and Probability." *Cognitive Psychology* 5 (1973): 207-32.

——. "Belief in the Law of Small Numbers." *Psychological Bulletin* 76 (1971): 105-10.

——. "Judgment under Uncertainty: Heuristics and Biases." *Science* 185 (1974): 1124-31.

Verbrugge, Robert R., and McCarrell, Nancy S. "Metaphoric Comprehension: Studies in Reminding and Resembling." *Cognitive Psychology* 9 (1977): 494-533.

Winograd, Terry. "A Framework for Understanding Discourse." In *Cognitive Processes in Comprehension*, edited by Marcel Adam Just and Patricia A. Carpenter. Hillsdale, N.J.: Lawrence Erlbaum Associates, 1977.

Xydis, Stephen G. "The 1945 Crisis over the Turkish Straits." *Balkan Studies* 1 (1960): 65-90.

INDEX

Abelson, Robert, 33, 54-55
Acheson, Dean, 29, 33, 136, 140, 241, 243, 302; and aid to Greece and Turkey, 303-10, 316; and atomic weapons, 214-21, 270-71, 338; changing perceptions of the Soviet Union, 337, 339-42, 351-52; and containment, 313-16, 319; and "long telegram," 256-57, 352; realist views of, 216-18, 220-21, 325, 330-31; and Soviet treaty violations, 278-79; and Turkish Straits, 280-85
Alsop, Joseph and Stewart, 249
Apter, David E., 20-21
Atlantic Charter, 178, 230, 231
atomic weapons, 6, 188-89, 196, 207-10, 213-16, 223-24, 233-34, 237, 270-71, 338
Attlee, Clement, 202, 233
attribution theory, 34-37; and Acheson, 284; and actor-observer difference, 37-38, 350; and Byrnes, 210, 228; and cognitive dissonance, 40; and Cold War origins, 37-42, 65, 349-50; and Harriman, 70, 123; and Hovland approach, 40; and schema theory, 56; and self-perception theory, 46, 349; and Truman, 145, 322
Austria, 182, 246, 277
Ayers, Eben A., 316

Baldwin, Hanson, 273
Ball, Joseph, 278
Baruch, Bernard M., 248
Bem, Daryl J., 42-43, 45n, 47, 49n
Beneš, Eduard, 93, 170
Benton, William, 256, 351
Berle, Adolph, 268, 269
Bevin, Ernest, 202, 228, 236-37, 258
Blackett, P.M.S., 6
Bohlen, Charles E., 77, 167, 174, 176, 178, 221, 226, 257, 304
Bor-Komorowski, Tadeusz, 94, 95
Brown, Walter, 228
Bulgaria, 107, 108, 159-61, 178, 186-88, 198, 199, 212, 223, 231, 245, 246, 288
Burnham, James, 5
Bush, Vannevar, 270
Byrnes, James F., 13, 252, 255, 258, 265, 273; and atomic weapons, 208, 214, 223, 224, 233, 237, 270; and Bulgaria, 223, 245, 246; changing perceptions of the Soviet Union, 208, 214, 223, 224, 233, 237, 270, 275-78, 287-88, 294, 298-300, 336-41, 346; and demobilization, 226, 269; domestic political experience, 192, 193; and firing of Wallace, 291-94; and Iran, 53, 239, 242, 267, 269-70, 272; and London Conference, 221-23, 244; and "long telegram," 256-57, 352; and Moscow Conference, 236-68; negotiating style, 194-95; and Overseas Press Club Speech, 259-63; and Paris Peace Conference, 285-87; and Poland, 117-18, 222, 334; political style, 33, 49-50, 193-94; and Potsdam Conference, 5, 189, 192, 197-98; relationship with Truman, 192, 243-45, 247-48, 258; and Rumania, 222, 223, 245, 246, 323; and Turkish Straits, 202, 207, 225, 232; view of Molotov, 197, 228-29

Chamberlin, W. H., 5
Chiang Kai-shek, 182, 314
Childs, Marquis, 148
China, 182, 208, 314
Christenson, R. M., 21
Churchill, Winston S., 69, 76, 139, 319; and "iron curtain" speech, 263-66; and Poland, 117, 118, 151, 157; and Potsdam Conference, 196, 202, 204-205, 207-209; and spheres of influence agreement, 107-10, 175; and Teheran Conference, 78-79; and Warsaw uprising, 95, 99-100, 106; and withdrawal of U.S. troops from Germany, 161-63
Ciechanowski, Jan M., 182

Clark-Kerr, Sir Archibald, 115, 202; and Poland, 114, 118; and Warsaw uprising, 96, 98, 99
Clayton, William L., 13, 256, 298, 302, 351; and need for U.S. world leadership, 304, 318; and Soviet lend-lease, 166-67, 169
Clifford, Clark M., 277, 316; and Clifford-Elsey report, 278, 279, 288, 294-97
Coffin, Tris, 300
cognitive dissonance theory, 29-31; and Acheson, 353; and attribution theory, 40; and Byrnes, 194; and Cold War origins, 32-34, 64-65, 353-54; and forced compliance, 30-31; and Harriman, 70, 123; and Hovland approach, 40; and self-perception theory, 46-49; and Truman, 149, 321-22, 353
Cohen, Benjamin, 256, 275
Cold War historiography: confirmationist, 14-16, 325-26; conservative, 5-6, 324; neomarxist, 13; official, 9, 325-26; open door revisionist, 9-13, 16, 326; realist, 7-8, 15, 16, 324-25; reconciliationist, 14-15, 324
Collado, Emilio, 169
Conant, James B., 270
Connally, Tom, 251, 268
Connelly, Matthew J., 277
containment, 119-20, 300, 313-19
Crowley, Leo T., 167
Czechoslovakia, 93, 102, 111, 182, 286, 287

Daniels, Jonathan, 128, 135, 148
Davies, Joseph E., 145, 158, 196, 210, 284; as adviser to Truman, 157, 178, 190, 192, 219, 243, 265, 288; and "get tough" policy, 174-76; and Iran, 240-41
Davis, Forrest, 139
Davis, Lynn E., 15
Dean, Vera Micheles, 174
Deane, John, 97, 118, 155; and military collaboration with Soviet Union, 83-87, 104
Dening, M. E., 312
Deporte, A. W., 15
De Santis, Hugh, 39

Donnelly, J. B., 231, 254-55, 260, 262
Dulles, John Foster, 221, 225, 261-62
Dunn, James, 256
Durbrow, Elbridge, 253, 292-93

Eckstein, Harry, 59
Edelman, Murray, 307-308, 347
Eden, Anthony, 126, 152, 298; and Poland, 80, 153, 154, 165; and spheres of influence agreement, 108, 109
Eisenhower, Dwight D., 263
Elsey, George M., 278, 295-97
Ethridge, Mark, 247
Eulau, Heinz, 23, 205

Fazio, Russell F., 48-49
Feis, Herbert, 9, 195
Festinger, Leon, 29, 30, 31-32
Finland, 120, 186, 287
Fischer, Louis, 303-304, 306
Fleming, D. F., 6-7
Forrestal, James V., 155, 200, 210, 217, 220, 256, 259
Four Freedoms, 230, 231

Gaddis, John Lewis, 14-15, 32, 259-60, 266n, 316
Gardner, Lloyd C., 11
George, Alexander L., 62-63
Germany, 160-63, 173, 182, 189, 200-202, 277, 299
Goethals, George, 44-45
Gottwald, Klement, 287
Graebner, Norman A., 7
Greece, 107-109, 199, 303-12, 323
Grew, Joseph C., 159, 161, 178, 321; admiration for Truman, 146, 148; and Soviet lend-lease, 165, 167-69
Gromyko, Andrei, 150, 269, 271, 284, 299
Groves, Leslie, 270

Halifax, Lord, 193, 261, 263, 266
Halle, Louis J., 7, 19, 250
Hannegan, Robert, 265
Harriman, W. Averell, 13, 42, 162, 228, 253, 275, 300, 321; changing perceptions of the Soviet Union, 102-103, 119-20, 122-25, 159, 332-34; and Czechoslovakia, 93, 102; early dealings

with the Soviet Union, 66-68; early hopes for U.S.-Soviet cooperation, 69-70, 76-78; and "get tough" approach, 176-77; and Iran, 268; and Poland, 78, 81-82, 90, 113-16, 152-53, 155, 165; and quid pro quo approach, 82-86, 88-92, 104-105, 121, 332-34; relationship with Roosevelt, 66, 68, 76; relationship with Truman, 66, 68, 158; role as ambassador, 70-71; and Rumania, 103, 115; and Soviet lend-lease, 84-85, 88-92, 163-66, 333; and spheres of influence agreement, 109-12; view of Stalin, 67-69, 123, 183-84; and Warsaw uprising, 92-94, 96-99, 101-102, 106, 333-34; and Yalta agreements, 112, 117-19

Henderson, Loy, 174, 241, 242, 303, 304

Herring, George C., 14

Hickerson, John, 204, 286

Holsti, Ole R., 61

Hopkins, Harry, 112, 126, 142, 235, 323; and Harriman, 66, 68, 76, 84, 91, 92, 101-105; visit to Soviet Union, 170, 176-78, 180-82; and Warsaw uprising, 98, 100-101, 333

Hovland attitude change approach, 25-28; and attribution theory, 40; and Byrnes, 256-57; and cognitive dissonance theory, 29, 31-32; and Cold War origins, 28-29, 64, 352; and schema theory, 56; and Truman, 144, 297, 321

Hull, Cordell, 73, 80-82, 90, 100

Hungary, 108, 109, 120, 186, 199, 212, 245-46, 287

Iran, 53-54, 221, 231, 234-36, 239-42, 267-69, 272-75, 323, 328

Italy, 186, 196, 199, 275

Jacobson, Eddie, 131

Janis, Irving L., 344

Japan, 165, 196, 208-209, 213, 299

Jernegan, John, 304

Jervis, Robert, 22n, 24n, 29n, 35n, 38n, 39n, 41n, 53n, 111n, 131n, 147n, 149n, 344, 352n

Johnston, Eric, 13

Jones, Joseph M., 9, 351

Kelley, Harold H., 36

Kennan, George F., 68, 97, 166, 174, 246, 267, 321, 331; and aid to Greece and Turkey, 304, 309; and Clifford-Elsey report, 278, 295; and "long telegram," 28, 255-57, 352; realist views of, 7, 8, 324-25

King, MacKenzie, 233

Knapp, Wilfred, 14

Kolko, Gabriel, 13

Korea, 257-58

Krock, Arthur, 247, 264, 266

Lakatos, Imre, 25

Leahy, William D., 7, 152, 195, 204, 235, 247, 275, 311; and Poland, 155, 157, 252; and Truman Doctrine, 316-17, 320

Lebow, Richard Ned, 344-45

lend-lease, 84-86, 88-92, 163-71

"levels of analysis": domestic political context, 20-22, 329-31; individual policymaker, 22, 331-32; international system, 18-20, 22, 327-29

Lilienthal, David E., 270

Lincoln, George, 276; and Soviet lend-lease, 166-69

Lippmann, Walter, 7, 110, 118, 173, 268-69, 348-49

London Conference of Foreign Ministers, 221-23, 227, 229, 244

"long telegram," 28, 255-57, 352

Lowi, Theodore J., 317

MacVeagh, Lincoln, 305

Magdoff, Harry, 13

Mann, Leon, 344, 345

Marshall, Charles Burton, 14

Marshall, George, 155, 231, 305, 306

Matthews, Freeman, 255

May, Ernest R., 17, 40, 57

McCloy, John J., 169, 270

McCormick, Anne O'Hare, 262, 268, 293, 298

McGuire, William J., 23, 25

Merriam, Gordon P., 206, 242

Mikolajczyk, Stanislaus, 95, 96, 99, 115

Mikoyan, Anastas, 88, 89, 168-69

Molotov, Vyacheslav, 77, 85, 88-89, 108, 150, 176, 232, 236, 258, 268, 291, 299, 336; and atomic weapons, 210, 221, 223, 233; and Germany, 182, 277; and Poland, 78, 80-81, 114, 115, 118, 151-58, 160, 165, 334; and Rumania, 115, 222-23; and Turkish Straits, 203, 206; viewed by Byrnes, 197, 229; viewed by Truman, 184, 228; and Warsaw uprising, 96, 98-99

Montreux Convention, 203, 205, 206, 279, 281

Morgenthau, Hans, 7, 8, 38, 324

Morgenthau, Henry M., Jr., 148, 181, 189

Moscow Conference of Foreign Ministers (1943), 77, 84

Moscow conference of Foreign Ministers (1945), 236-38

Nicolson, Harold, 284

Nisbett, Richard E., 17n, 36-37, 38n, 39n, 41, 55, 77, 101n, 178n, 195n, 281n, 324n

Oppenheimer, J. Robert, 270-71

Paris Conference of Foreign Ministers, 276, 277, 285-87

Patterson, Robert P., 256, 311, 338

Pendergast, Thomas, 132-34, 136, 177, 178, 197, 272, 319, 322, 323, 336, 338

Perkins, Dexter, 14

Poland, 78-82, 92-94, 111, 113, 117-18, 150-60, 165, 177, 180-83, 190, 200-202, 323. See also Warsaw uprising

Potsdam Conference, 5, 39, 187-92, 195-212

Qavam, Ahmed, 267, 273

Quebec Conference, 100, 161

Rees, David, 14

Reston, James, 179-80, 260, 283, 295, 296; and firing of Wallace, 291, 293-94

Roosevelt, Eleanor, 315

Roosevelt, Franklin Delano, 69, 121, 134, 142, 146, 163; approach to Soviet contrasted with Truman's, 170-72; and need to maintain Soviet friendship, 83-84; and Poland, 81-82, 113-14, 117, 151, 333; and quid pro quo approach, 86, 123, 333; relationship with Harriman, 66, 68; relationship with Stalin, 75, 76, 171-72, 175; and spheres of influence agreement, 107, 109-12; and Teheran Conference, 39, 74, 78-79; vision of postwar order, 3, 7, 70-76, 139-40, 251, 328; and Warsaw uprising, 97-100; and Yalta Conference, 5, 113-14

Rose, Lisle A., 15

Rosenman, Judge, 235

Ross, Lee, 36-37, 38n, 39n, 41, 55, 101, 120, 178n, 195n, 342n

Rossow, Robert, 267

Rumania, 103, 107-109, 115, 120-21, 159-61, 178, 186, 198, 199, 212, 222-23, 245-47, 288, 323

Russell, Donald, 193

Salancik, Gerald R., 43-44

schema theory, 50-54; and attribution theory, 56; and Byrnes, 194; and Cold War origins, 56-57, 65, 350-52; and Harriman, 71, 124; and Hovland approach, 56; and Truman, 350; and types of schemas, 54-56

self-perception theory, 42-46; and attribution theory, 46, 349; and Byrnes, 193-94, 346; and cognitive dissonance, 46-49; and Cold War origins, 49-50, 65, 342-49; and Harriman, 70-71, 123-24; and Truman, 149, 320-21, 346

Smith, Harold D., 163, 223-24, 243

Smith, Walter Bedell, 269; meeting with Stalin, 272-74

Snow, Edgar, 202

Snyder, John W., 311

Soviet Union: and Bulgaria, 98, 159-60, 231, 245; and Czechoslovakia, 93, 102, 182; and Finland, 120, 287; and Germany, 173, 200-201, 277; and Hungary, 120, 245-46; and Iran, 53-54, 221, 231, 234-35, 239, 241-42, 267-68, 272-73; and Poland, 78-82, 92-94, 113, 152; and Rumania, 103,

115, 120-21, 159; and Turkey, 202-204, 206-207, 231-32, 240-42, 272, 279-81, 283, 310; and Warsaw uprising, 94-95, 98-99, 105
Spaatz, Carl, 240
Spain, 206
Sprout, Harold and Margaret, 328
Stalin, Joseph, 69, 86, 116, 119, 173, 246, 272; and atomic weapons, 208-10; election speech, 252-55; and Hopkins visit, 170, 180-82; impression upon Harriman, 67-69, 123; meeting with Smith, 273-74; and Poland, 80, 113, 150-52, 156, 181-82; and Potsdam Conference, 196-202, 208, 210; relationship with Roosevelt, 76, 171-72, 175; and spheres of influence agreement, 107-10, 175; and Teheran Conference, 39, 74, 78-79; and Turkey, 203, 206, 232, 274; viewed by Truman, 178, 183, 196-97, 225, 272, 288, 319, 323, 336; and Warsaw uprising, 94-96, 98-100, 105, 106; and Werth interview, 297-98; and Yalta Conference, 5, 113, 114-15, 139
Steinbruner, John D., 346
Steinhardt, Laurence A., 287
Stettinius, Edward R., Jr., 112-13, 178, 179-80, 192, 224, 227, 228; and Poland, 150, 153, 154, 157-60, 165, 181; and quid pro quo approach, 121, 123, 124
Stimson, Henry L., 113, 118, 146, 154-55; and atomic weapons, 188, 197, 207, 209, 213-20, 237-38
Stone, I. F., 174, 180
Sulzberger, C. L., 39, 160, 172-73, 195, 240, 246-47, 275, 318, 319

Teheran Conference, 39, 74, 78, 84, 87, 172, 175
Thompson, Llewellyn, 304, 308
Trout, Thomas B., 20, 21
Truman, Harry S, 5, 7, 13, 27, 29, 42, 260, 294; and aid to Greece and Turkey, 8, 305-307, 310-12, 314; as senator, 136-38, 142-45; assumption of presidency, 3, 126, 138-39; and atomic weapons, 6, 188-89, 196, 207-10, 213-17, 219-21, 223-24, 233-34;

changing perceptions of the Soviet Union, 184-85, 227, 301, 319-23, 334-38, 341-42, 346; and Clifford-Elsey report, 277-79, 297-98; and "code of the politician," 132-36, 161, 177-78, 269, 322; and containment, 315-19; early political experience, 131-34; and firing of Wallace, 288-92; General Assembly speech, 299-300; and "get tough" approach, 152-53, 156-57, 160-61, 174, 176, 178-79; and Hopkins visit, 176-78, 181; information processing style, 144-49; invitation to Stalin, 269, 272, 274, 301; and Iran, 53-54, 234-35, 239-41, 268, 269, 272; and "iron curtain" speech, 263-66; knowledge of history, 126-29, 143; and Korea, 257-58; military career, 130-31; Navy Day speech, 229-31; perceptions of Stalin, 56, 178, 183, 196-97, 228-29, 254, 272, 288, 319, 322, 323, 336, 338, 350; and Poland, 150-58, 181-83, 190, 200-201; political style, 33, 49-50, 129; and Potsdam Conference, 5, 39, 187-92, 195-97, 198-202, 204-12, 252; and quid pro quo approach, 124-25; relationship with Byrnes, 192, 238, 243-45, 247-49, 258; and Roosevelt's Soviet policy, 170-72, 179-80, 250-51, 329-30; and Soviet lend-lease, 163, 165-66, 168-69; and Turkish Straits, 203-206, 224-27, 232-33, 283; views on world order, 140-44; and withdrawal of U.S. troops from Germany, 160-63
Truman Doctrine, 3-4, 10, 20, 197, 296, 308-309, 316-23, 351
Turkey, 202-207, 225-26, 231-33, 240-42, 274, 279-85, 303, 307, 310-12

United Nations, 225, 236, 242, 257, 271, 305; and atomic weapons, 218, 233, 238; and Iran, 267-70, 272; San Francisco Conference on, 150-54, 158-59, 165, 171, 172; Security Council veto, 250-52; Truman speech at, 298-300

Vandenberg, Arthur H., 211, 215, 251, 261-62, 307; and Poland, 157-59

Vinogradov, S. A., 232-33
Vinson, Fred, 188, 217
Vishinsky, Andrei, 115, 247, 286; and
    Warsaw uprising, 96-97, 99, 233

Wallace, Henry A., 13, 126, 144, 148,
    173, 228, 264, 300, 302; and atomic
    weapons, 217, 233-34; firing of, 288-
    94; view of Truman, 146, 149, 279
Warsaw uprising, 94-101, 105-106, 333-
    34
Werth, Alexander, 297
Williams, William Appleman, 9-13

Willkie, Wendell, 79
Wilmot, Chester, 5
Wilson, Edwin C., 233
Winant, John, 101, 108

Yalta Conference, 5, 112-15, 152, 200
Yalta Declaration on Liberated Europe,
    114-18, 139-40, 150-53, 155, 159,
    161, 178, 198, 202
Yugoslavia, 107, 108, 109, 246, 310

Zhukov, George, 182

Library of Congress Cataloging in Publication Data

Larson, Deborah Welch, 1951-
Origins of containment.

Bibliography: p.
Includes index.
1. United States—Foreign relations—Soviet Union—Psychological aspects. 2. Soviet Union—Foreign relations—United States—Psychological aspects. 3. United States—Foreign relations—1945-1953—Psychological aspects. I. Title. II. Title: Containment : a psychological explanation.
E183.8.S65L36   1985   327.73047   85-42691
ISBN 0-691-07691-X